Individual churches today have a lively ecumenical consciousness, but they often express anxieties about what will become of
them in a future united Church. Questions are being asked
about the goal of such unity. In this book, G. R. Evans asks what
we mean by 'a church', and how different Christian bodies have
understood the way 'a church' is related to 'the Church'. She
surveys the nature of unity and what the fullness of the
communion being reached for might consist of; the place of
diversity of faith and order in a united Church, or ways in which
there can go on being many churches in one Church and how
they might be related to it; and questions about the common
structures one Church would need, and the way in which it
could come to think and act as a single 'body' of Christ. The
book concludes with a discussion of the concept of 'communion', which now looks to be ecumenically very hopeful as a
guide to the way forward.

THE CHURCH AND THE CHURCHES

THE CHURCH
AND THE CHURCHES

Toward an ecumenical ecclesiology

G. R. EVANS

Lecturer in History
University of Cambridge

CAMBRIDGE
UNIVERSITY PRESS

Published by the Press Syndicate of the University of Cambridge
The Pitt Building, Trumpington Street, Cambridge CB2 1RP
40 West 20th Street, New York, NY 10011–4211, USA
10 Stamford Road, Oakleigh, Melbourne 3166, Australia

First published 1994

Printed in Great Britain at the University Press, Cambridge

A catalogue record for this book is available from the British Library

Library of Congress cataloguing in publication data

Evans, G. R. (Gillian Rosemary)
The Church and the churches: toward an ecumenical ecclesiology / G. R. Evans.
p.   cm.
Includes bibliographical references and index.
ISBN 0 521 46286 X (hardback)
1. Church. I. Title.
BV600.2.E94 1994
262'.001'1–dc20   93–42441 CIP

ISBN 0 521 46286 X hardback

Contents

Preface	*page*	ix
Acknowledgements		xii
List of abbreviations		xiii
Introduction		1
1 Local and universal		18
2 Ecclesial identity		121
3 Diversity		174
4 Restoring to order		212
5 Decision-making		251
6 Communion		291
Conclusion		315
Select bibliography		319
Index		326

Preface

Ecumenical discussion today comes back again and again to the anxieties of the divided churches about their survival as ecclesial entities in a future united Church. These anxieties have a long history, but they have become newly acute in the ecumenical climate of the second half of the twentieth century. The history of these concerns is not always familiar to those engaged in today's debates, and that seems a good reason for writing a book about it.

On the history rides a number of ecclesiological concepts and assumptions; it also has a good deal to teach us about the problems we face in seeking to recognise a common faith or order in a future united Church, and in learning to make decisions together as Christians. Above all, the past, which has on the whole not always thought in terms of 'ecclesial communion', now has to be understood in a present where there is comprehensive exploration of the nature of communion.

It is important to try to understand the historical background because ideas are altered by being taken out of their context and they can persist unhelpfully after the times which partly justified them and created division. That obvious usefulness of history does not in itself resolve a profound methodological difficulty. Although theological principles can be seen at work in events, history is not theology. What I have tried to write here can perhaps best be described as a historical theology of the relation of Church and churches, but that is not quite what it is. The genre remains to some degree experimental, but it seems to me to be one which will be needed in a future united Church and is worth persevering with for that reason.

The main thrust of this book has to do with the tendency for all formal structures to solidify. Churches are not an exception. When they form units they do so with a sense of corporate identity which

ix

becomes precious to them. There is a strong present-day sense of the importance of respecting and protecting this individuality.

That can make it difficult for such communities and those who stand outside them alike to recognise the essential provisionality of their ecclesial being. I have tried to argue that all churches must be provisional. None yet embodies fully all that the Church should be. That must mean that there is room for change and a place for the acceptance of limitations. It does not mean that everything about the churches is in a state of flux. The limits of provisionality have to be established. Within the constraints of the problems posed by the difficulty of genre and the definition of provisionality, it has seemed best to adopt a thematic rather than a chronological treatment. Only in this way can we begin to see the repeating patterns for what they are, and the lessons they give.

Many Christians, especially from traditions in whose thinking the relationship of the individual with Christ has been the first concern, may find all this talk of ecclesiality less compelling than those whose sense of 'Church' is strong. I hope a patient reading of the struggles for clarification in earlier Christian thinking, of what it means to belong to a community of those who belong to Christ, will do something to meet their reservations.

Ecumenical progress is beginning to come up hard against the residual difficulties which have become increasingly apparent during the last decade or so. These are likely to prove its most serious stumbling-blocks, if not the rocks on which the ship could founder. They fall broadly into the three groups of topics with which this book is concerned. The first consists of questions to do with the goal of unity, that is, with the nature of the unity we seek, the fullness of the 'communion' which is being reached for, whether we are serious about wanting to be one Church. Second come questions about the place of diversity of faith and order in a future united Church; in other words, ways in which there can go on being many churches in the one Church and how they might be related to it. Third are questions about the common structures one Church would need, and the way in which it could come to think and act as a single 'body' of Christ. The second and third have to be answered in terms of the first, which is why we must begin and end with it. This thematic treatment has, after a good deal of trial and error, proved the clearest way of setting out the issues and their interconnections.

In a way it is too soon to write this book. Almost all the questions raised in it still lie open, and some are as yet impossible to formulate with the precision a good question needs if it is to be answerable in a useful way. But they are questions which urgently need to be tackled, and the exercise of seeking to pose them, or to understand their relation to one another, has, I hope, some value. I have tried in this book to suggest that in the outlines of these huge, intricate and infinitely rewarding areas of discussion may be seen the shadowy forms of the solutions which must be found if there is one day to be one visible Church of Christ witnessing in the world.

Acknowledgements

It is hard to know where to begin or end in expressing thanks for help with the writing of this book. It is, in its way, a product of the innumerable encounters of the present ecumenical scene, the repeated re-evaluation and re-expression of principles in conversation as understanding grows and the relation of the continuities to what is new becomes plainer to us all. For that is undoubtedly what is happening. There is also, among those who are actively engaged in ecumenical work, a great deal of mutual affection across apparent boundaries, which forms a strong working network of common support. A number of friends to whom I am indebted in particular are likely to know who they are.

Abbreviations

AG	Decree of Second Vatican Council *Ad Gentes*
Apologia for the Augsburg Confession	Melanchthon, *Apologia* for the Augsburg Confession of 1530, translated in Tappert *The Book of Concord* (Philadelphia, 1981)
ARCIC I, *Final Report*	*The Final Report* of the First Anglican–Roman Catholic International Commission (London, 1982)
ARCIC II, *Church as Communion*	*Church as Communion*, an Agreed Statement by the Second Anglican–Roman Catholic International Commission (London, 1991)
Bede, *H.E.*	Bede, *Historia Ecclesiastica*, ed. B. Colgrave and R.A.B. Mynors (Oxford, 1969)
Bowmer, *Pastor and People*	J.C Bowmer, *Pastor And People: A Study of Church and Ministry in Wesleyan Methodism from the Death of John Wesley 1791 to the Death of Jabez Bunting, 1858* (London, 1975)
Bullinger, *Decades*	H. Bullinger, *Decades*, ed. T. Harding, PS (Cambridge, 1849–52), 5 vols.
Bullinger, *Of the Holy Catholic Church*	H. Bullinger, in Zwingli and Bullinger, *Of the Holy Catholic Church*, Library of Christian Classics 24 ed. G.W. Bromily (London, 1953)
Calvin, *Inst. Chr.*	Calvin, *Institutio Christiana*, ed. J.T. McNeill, tr. F.L. Battles (London, 1961), 2 vols.
C.Cath.	*Corpus Catholicorum*
CCSL	*Corpus Christianorum Series Latina*
CCCM	*Corpus Christianorum Continuatio Medievalis*
CD	*Christus Dominus*, Decree of the Second Vatican Council on the Pastoral Office of Bishops

CDF *Communion*	*The Church as Communion*, Letter to the Bishops of the Catholic Church from the Congregation for the Doctrine of the Faith, *Catholic International*, 3 (1992), 761–5
CF	*Concilium Florentinum Acta*
Christian Unity	*Christian Unity*, ed. G. Alberigo (Leuven, 1991)
Cochrane, *Reformed Confessions*	A.C. Cochrane, *Reformed Confessions of the Sixteenth Century* (London, 1966)
Codex Iuris Canonici	*Codex Iuris Canonici* (Rome, 1983)
Conciliorum Oecumenicorum Decreta	*Conciliorum Oecumenicorum Decreta*, , ed. J. Alberigo, J.A. Dossetti Perikle, P. Joannou, P. Prodi, and C. Leonardi (Bologna, 1973)
Congar, *Diversité et communion*	*(Paris, 1982)*
Congar, *Essais oecuméniques*	Y. Congar, *Essais oecuméniques: le mouvement, les hommes, les problèmes* (Paris, 1984)
Congar, *Tradition et traditions*	Y. Congar, *La tradition et les traditions* (Paris, 1963)
CR	*Corpus Reformatorum*
CSEL	*Corpus Scriptorum Ecclesiasticorum Latinorum*
CT	*Concilium Tridentinum Acta*
Christian Unity	*Christian Unity: the Council of Ferrara-Florence, 1438/9–1989*, ed. G. Alberigo (Louvain, 1991)
Dvornik	F. Dvornik, *Byzantium and the Roman Primacy* (New York, 1966)
Ehrenstrom and Muelder	N. Ehrenstrom and W.G. Muelder, *Institutionalism and Church Unity* (London, 1963)
Episcopal Ministry	*Episcopal Ministry: The Report of the Archbishops' Group on the Episcopate (Church of England)* (London, 1990)
Faris	J.D. Faris, *The Communion of Catholic Churches: Terminology and Ecclesiology* (New York, 1985)
Richard Field, *Of the Church*	Richard Field, *Of the Church* (Cambridge, 1847–52), 5 vols.
Florovsky, 'Limits'	G. Florovsky, 'The Limits of the Church', *Church Quarterly Review*, 107 (1933)
Friedberg	E. Friedberg, *Corpus Iuris Canonici* (Leipzig, 1879–81), 2 vols.
Growth	*Growth in Agreement*, ed. H. Meyer and L. Vischev (Geneva, 1984)

Hall, *Works*	Joseph Hall, *Works*, ed. P. Wynter (Oxford, 1963), 10 vols.
Henn	W. Henn, *The Hierarchy of Truths according to Y. Congar* (Rome, 1987)
Knox, *Enthusiasm*	R. Knox, *Enthusiasm* (Oxford, 1950)
Kotsonis	J. Kotsonis, *Problèmes de l'Economie ecclésiastique* (Gembloux, 1971)
Krauth	C.P. Krauth, *The Conservative Reformation and its Theology* (Minneapolis, 1871, reprinted Philadelphia, 1963)
Labbe and C. Concilia	P. Labbe and G. Cossart, *Sacrosancta Concilia*, vols. I–XV (1671–3)
Lambeth Conferences	Cited from the Official Report in each case
LG	*Lumen Gentium*, Dogmatic Constitution on the Church of the Second Vatican Council
LWF VI	*In Christ – A New Community* Lutheran World Fellowship (Dar-es-Salaam, 1977)
McNeill, *Unitive Protestantism*	J.T. McNeill, *Unitive Protestantism* (London, 1964)
Mansi	J. Mansi, *Sacrorum Conciliorum Nova et Amplissima Collectio* (Florence, 1759 – Leipzig, 1902), 34 vols.
Niagara Report	*The Niagara Report*, Report of the Anglican–Lutheran Consultation on Episcope, 1987 (London, 1988)
Piepkorn	A.C. Piepkorn, *Profiles in Belief: The Religious Bodies of the United States and Canada* (New York, 1977–9), 3 vols.
PG	J.P. Minge, *Patrologia Graeca*, 162 vols. (1857–66)
PL	J.P. Migne, *Patrologia Latina*, 218 vols. (1844–55)
PS	Parker Society editions of Anglican divines of the sixteenth century (Cambridge)
Ratzinger	J. Ratzinger, *Church, Ecumenism and Politics* (Slough, 1988), tr. R. Nowell; first published as *Kirche, Ökumene und Politik* (Cinisello Balsamo, 1987)

Rome's *Response* to ARCIC	Official *Response* of the Roman Catholic Church to *The Final Report* of the First Anglican–Roman Catholic International Commission, printed in *The Tablet* (December, 1991)
Salamanca	*Yglesias locales y catolicidad, Actas del Coloquio internacional de Salamanca*, ed. H. Legrand, J. Manzares, A. García y García (Salamanca, 1992)
Stormon	*Towards the Healing of Schism*, ed. and tr., E.J. Stormon (New York, 1987)
Sundkler	B. Sundkler, *The Church of South India: The Movement towards Union* (London, 1954)
Tanner	*Decrees of the Ecumenical Councils* ed. N.P. Tanner (Georgetown, 1990), 2 vols.
Tappert	G. Tappert (ed.), *The Book of Concord* (Philadelphia, 1981)
Tillard, *Eglise d'Eglises*	J.M.R. Tillard, *Eglise d'Eglises: l'ecclésiologie de communion* (Paris, 1987)
Tillard, *The Bishop of Rome*	J.M.R. Tillard, *L'Evêque de Rome* (Paris, 1982), *The Bishop of Rome*, tr. J. de Satgé (London, 1983)
UR	*Unitatis Redintegratio*
Vandervelde	G. Vandervelde, 'BEM and the Hierarchy of Truths', *Journal of Ecumenical Studies*, 25 (1988)
Vatican II	*Vatican Council II: The Conciliar and Post Conciliar Documents*, ed. A. Flannery (Rome, 1988)
Verkamp	B.J. Verkamp, *The Indifferent Mean* (Ohio, 1977)
WA	Luther, *Werke* (Weimar Ausgabe)
WCC	World Council of Churches

Introduction

THE SAME AND THE DIFFERENT

There is a sense in many quarters that the ecumenical movement has become becalmed. A number of promising bilateral rapprochements has not yet resulted in the hoped-for unions. Enthusiasm can flag when great and honest effort is not visibly rewarded. But there must be two lessons in the failures, both of which are important for keeping up the spirits. The first is that mending the divisions of hundreds of years will take a great deal more time than anyone expected, though no one should really have expected anything else. The second is that these delays and setbacks are helping us to see what the problems really are.

The reformers of the sixteenth century believed that the removal of accretions which they saw as corruptions could restore primitive and therefore (they assumed) pure Christianity. But at the same time they themselves brought about a shift of emphasis in theological preoccupations towards a concern with sacramental and anthropological questions of grace and sin which had different emphases from those of the first centuries.[1] A systematic reading-through of the contents of ecumenical journals during the last twenty-five or thirty years shows them reflecting the pervasive shifting of both attitudes and expectations which has taken place in almost all churches since the Second Vatican Council, and the ways in which these expectations may be at variance with the stated agenda.[2] So conscious purpose and partly unconscious assumption can often diverge. The task now is patiently to seek to gain access to what is happening in this undergrowth of ideas so

---

[1] A. Houssiau, 'Réception et rejet d'un consensus conciliaire', *Christian Unity*, p. 518.
[2] For earlier manifestations of similar patterns in ecumenism, see O. Rousseau, 'Le Sens oecuménique des conversations de Malines', *Irénikon*, 44 (1971), 331–48.

that the end towards which we are working can be seen more clearly.

At the Council of Florence (1438–45) a party if not the majority of the Greeks hoped to recover the primitive unity of Christians, so that the Church might be one as it had been in the first age.[3] We have said that the reformers of the sixteenth century believed that if innovations (which they were sure were corruptions) were removed, primitive Christianity could be restored. In the seventeenth century many were confident that Christians could come to agree on 'fundamentals' which could safely be taken to have been the basics of the beginning of the Church too. In the nineteenth century Tractarians still held that unity could be restored on the basis of the faith and order of the undivided Church. At the Faith and Order Conference held at Lausanne in 1927, Orthodox Christians continued to call for a return to a unity 'based on the common faith and doctrine of the ancient, undivided Church of the seven Oecumenical Councils and the first eight centuries'.[4] The same ideal was held up by the Orthodox at successive Faith and Order Conferences in the following decades.

The heart of the Orthodox ideal is surely right. If we cannot be sure that a future united Church will be the same Church as that of the Apostles, body of the same Christ, then ecumenical labour must be in vain. Yet in a practical sense it would certainly be impossible to go back. Language and categories of thought have changed, and no one can now enter completely into the mind of the early Church and live there. Bad memory may perhaps be purged, but it cannot be as though separation had never been.[5] It is argued by other Christians that there not only cannot but should not be a going back, that the goal of Christian unity should be a Church which encapsulates and expresses the enlargement of understanding which has come with the intervening centuries of division; and that the providential purpose of the Church's mixed history has been to make that possible. This is to accept that the divided centuries have had their effect, and that a future united Church cannot be what the

---

[3] J.-P. Arrignon, 'Les Russes au Concile de Ferrara–Florence', *Irénikon*, 47 (1974), 188–208, giving the account of Simeon de Suzdal.

[4] V.T. Istavridis, *Orthodoxy and Anglicanism*, tr. C. Davey (London, 1966), pp. 96–7.

[5] These are the sentiments of the hymn, 'Sinners whose love can ne'er forget / The wormwood and the gall.' See, too, A. Bea and W.A. Visser't Hooft, *Peace among Christians*, tr. J. Moses (New York, 1967), p. 213.

undivided Church once was.[6] But it is also to hold that God can bring out of the division something better than that which was lost. Division becomes a *felix culpa*.

The third possibility is that the right way forward is to seek to bring these ideals together in a future united Church which is both demonstrably still the Church of the first centuries and manifestly the living Church of today's world. That is to see the Church as 'a living being ... developing as every living thing develops, changing itself... and yet in essence always the same, and its core is Christ'.[7] This book is written on the assumption that this attempt to hold both together in seeking the goal of unity is the right – indeed the only – way.

THE PROBLEM OF ECCLESIOLOGY

Ecumenism cannot proceed without an ecclesiology. But it is not easy to settle on ecclesiological principles which will be acceptable to everyone and acceptability to the whole community is ecumenically essential. We might choose to keep to the great Biblical themes and images: sheepfold, flock, field, vine, God's building, holy temple, holy city, betrothed, body of Christ.[8] But the Bible's pictures have not kept the Church visibly together. We might work with the rules of order which developed during the first millennium and a half. We might try to strike a balance between the emphases generated within that order and those of the dissident and reforming communities of the sixteenth-century West which challenged some elements of that ecclesiology in the name of getting back to scriptural basics. We might concentrate on recent theory, some of which has been radical, much of it a restatement of earlier notions in modern frames of reference. All these will have their advocates and detractors, and none except the scriptural models will speak to all Christians' thinking.

None of these can be quite satisfactory if it is exclusive of others. If

---

[6] See J.M.R. Tillard, 'Eglise catholique et dialogues bilatéraux', *Irénikon*, 56 (1983), 5–19, pp. 9–10.

[7] Ratzinger, p. 4.

[8] These 'all have God, Christ or the Spirit as active subjects', points out Duquoc. He suggests that in a hierarchically constituted Church, the bishops with the assistance of priests, become the active subjects. C. Duquoc, *Provisional Churches: An Essay in Ecumenical Ecclesiology*, tr. J. Bawden (London, 1986) (*Des Eglises provisoires; Essai d'ecclésiologie oecuménique*, Paris, 1985), p. 47.

we believe it is the same Church which has survived in the world since Christ founded it, then all the accounts which have been given of it, all its pictures of itself, have a place. That is an ecclesiological position in itself, and it is the one adopted here.

If the ecclesiologies of history have all contained truths, if they describe the same Church, they must cohere. The ecumenical task is to discover their coherence. That is not so difficult before we get to relatively modern times. There was organic growth of models and structures to meet pastoral and practical – and sometimes political – need in the centuries up to the Reformation in the West. Reformers' challenges were shaped by what they saw to have happened to the Church, and their thought-forms and assumptions persisted in succeeding centuries. Modern challenge has been of a different order. It has been made out of a sense that we understand things better now; that we see more clearly; that man advances. I think that can be disputed. But the premiss of the intellectual superiority of modern ecclesiology has to be allowed for in the discussion.

What we are to see as the task and role of the Church will depend on the context we envisage for its operation. The loss of general Christian contact with the cultural milieu in which early Christianity developed, especially in the Third World churches whose heritage is different and which now want to assert the value of that heritage in its own right, creates a strong sense that the Christian foundations have to be restated in terms of new and varied cultures. Yet the old ways of thinking have to be synthesised with the new. Members of the Church through the ages will have to be able to communicate in heaven. They have to recognise one another's faith in their own from age to age.

There has recently been a sense in many quarters that conventional ecclesiology has become diverted into a preoccupation with secondary issues. By this are meant the domestic and internal problems of the Church. Thus, it is suggested, ecclesiology has lost sight of 'the heart of the Gospel' and what is 'distinctive and unique' in the Christian religion.[9] So the thrust of the new ecclesiology is to get back to what really matters, and what really matters is saving the world.

Present types of solution to the problem of finding an ecclesiology

[9] E. Schillebeeckx, *Church: The Human Story of God* (London, 1989), p. xiii. (*Mensen als verhaal van God* (Baarn, 1989).)

for the modern world fall broadly into perhaps four groups of further ideas.

The otherness of God and the question of transcendence

One school of thought argues that the key question is whether God is somehow with us, or so absolutely 'other than us' that we can never really know him. (Christians have been here before, notably in the struggle of the first centuries to 'place' Christianity in relation to Platonism.)

This axis of modern ecclesiological concern, running from an extreme doctrine of God-with-us to an extreme doctrine of divine 'otherness' from us, is not in itself highly sensitive ecumenically. But it shares with others a tendency to make ecumenical concerns seem less urgent and less central, because it does not itself put unity at the heart of the Church's welfare.

Eschatological accounts of the Church

The 'eschatological' axis of modern ecclesiology forces us to think big ('your God is too small').[10] The key theme here is the all-embracing character of the Church, its relation to creation in space and time and eternity. Eschatology has always been central to Orthodox ecclesiology. Until the nineteenth century in the West it had been entirely respectable intellectually and academically to set historical events in a framework extending before history to creation and after present events to eternity, and to assess their operation and the lessons to be drawn from them accordingly. Augustine's two cities work in that way.[11] The Church in history was on this view ultimately inseparable from the Church as heavenly community. So in a sense the modern revival of concern for the eschatological dimension of the Church's life has been a return to an old sense of this necessary complementarity.[12]

Yet there seems to be an inherent danger of losing this balance. It turns out not to be easy to hold the *eschaton* in view. Schillebeeckx

[10] John Young, *Our God is Still Too Small* (London, 1988), contributes to this debate.
[11] In *De Civitate Dei*.
[12] *Basic Questions in Theology*, ed. W. Pannenberg, tr. G.H. Kehm (Philadelphia, 1970), pp. 15–80. C. Morse, *The Logic of Promise in Moltmann's Theology* (Philadelphia, 1979), p. 3. Owen Chadwick, *From Bossuet to Newman* (2nd edn, Cambridge, 1987), covers this transition.

speaks of 'The eschatological fullness and freedom of men and women, which is sought and constantly found in a fragmentary way, only to be constantly threatened again.'[13] Jürgen Moltmann took this further, and offered a secure life-line, by placing an emphasis on the concept of promise. If the life of the Church in history points forward it must do so by fulfilling God's promise.[14] This can be seen not only as reinstating in its proper place the Biblical notion of covenant but also as providing a modern substitute for the notion of providence which Christian philosophy took over from the Greco-Roman philosophical tradition.[15] In both cases it is understood that the divine plan overarches history and acts within it to bring about God's intended outcome. This is a comforting doctrine and at the same time one which enlarges the scale of operations. In recent decades a further strand of the historiographical development has been spun. Karl Rahner has tried to effect a reintegration, by denying the possibility of separation between intellectual or speculative theology and the practical theology which derives from events and applies itself to needs.[16]

Schillebeeckx points to four aspects of the eschatological vision which have become particularly appealing in the current sociological climate. The first is the promise that God will be all in all, so that there will be no more pain or tears, no more master–servant relationships, but equality in brotherly and sisterly love. The second is an interpretation of the resurrection of the body in terms of perfect fulfilment for the individual. The third is the ecologists' paradise of the new heaven and the new earth. The last places the emphasis upon the parousia of Jesus Christ, when the whole world will understand the significance of Jesus and the kingdom of God will be consummated.[17]

But such thinking also has an impact, beyond the broad shape of things, on the detailed texture of the Church's being. The recognition that the Church lives its life beyond time as well as in time has implications for the concept of continuity in the Church's life. On

[13] Schillebeeckx, *Church*, p. 133.

[14] J. Moltmann, *Theologie der Hoffnung* (Munich, 1964), *Theology of Hope*, tr. J.W. Leitch (New York, 1967). Newer eschatologies agree that 'the anthropological solution to the eschatological problem' is not adequate. Morse, *The Logic of Promise*, p. 7.

[15] H. Chadwick, 'Providence and the problem of evil in Augustine', *Augustinianum* (Rome, 1987), 153–62.

[16] On this, see conveniently A. Carr, *The Theological Method of Karl Rahner* (Missoula, Montana, 1977), p. 154.

[17] Schillebeeckx, *Church*, p. 133.

this view, interruptions in sequence and apparent historical breaks stand embedded in the timelessness of eternity. Breaks are thus not necessarily ends; and under providence and with the assurance of promise they need not be ultimately destructive of the ecclesiality of the communities in which they occur. Ecumenically as well as ecclesiologically this is reassuring thinking, especially in connection with some of the problems we shall be meeting in the pages which follow.

Engagement with the world

A further group of explanations pressed by recent theological exploration presents an ecclesiology of responsibility. Here the key theme is that love imposes an obligation to strive energetically to achieve fairness and fulfilment for oneself and one's neighbour. The Church is seen as having a primary duty to make that happen. This, too, comes in several forms. Like the ecclesiology of promise-providence it has both ancient and modern features, and can be seen as partly a translation of classic positions into terms with which modern concerns can engage. The precedent in this case is the anti-clerical and anti-hierarchical dissidence which marked the revolts, well documented from the twelfth century, which eventually led to the divisions of the Reformation period in the West. These had a good deal to do with resentment about the abuse of power claimed by the ecclesiastical hierarchy over the ordinary lay believer.

A post-Vatican-II dichotomy is now with us, especially in the last decade, between those who now see the Church primarily as the whole 'people of God', and those who are still inclined to 'identify the Church with their own hierarchical offices',[18] that is, to consider the Church to be a structure in which the people occupy a necessarily subordinate position, and have somehow a lesser membership. Within the Church itself, this has recently seemed to Schillebeeckx to carry with it the additional danger of encouraging inward-looking disputes, from which it becomes hard resolutely to turn our eyes away to the greater issues; for the infighting becomes engrossing.[19] The potential for the distortion of a proper sense of responsibility here is thus twofold. The people of God within the Church fail

---

[18] R. Modras, *Paul Tillich's Theology of the Church* (Detroit, 1976), pp. 15–16.
[19] He argues that 'in a period of Church polarization' it is a mistake 'to be directly concerned with what are really secondary, domestic church problems', *Church* p. xiii.

to experience the duties as well as the liberties of their union in Christ. And they cannot carry out freely and fully their responsibilities to the world as a whole.

Moltmann comments that there is an opposition between the acceptance of authority in the Church and the individual's duty to take responsibility on his own account. 'The more they make our decisions for us, the more they cheat us of the happiness of our full, independent responsibility.'[20] The 'they' is telling here. Again the Church is being implicitly identified with the hierarchy, over against the people. In his view this means that the 'Church will be superfluous ... once it has achieved its purpose ... when "the days come" [Jer. 31: 31–4] in which God will make the new, final, indestructible covenant with men and women'.[21]

Although he would also answer the query what is 'the world' in question by saying 'my main concern is with the *ecumene* of suffering humankind',[22] Schillebeeckx would consider the battle for a balance of responsibilities within the Church as important, alongside the battle to get the balance right outside it. He sees the need for internal reforms in the Church as designed to protect the 'freedom and values' of the Gospel. 'Sociologically speaking ... in a world church, from the moment when the freedom and values of the gospel are no longer protected and supported by institutional structures, above all the so-called ordinary believers' lose their voice 'and with them a great many pastors and theologians'.[23] He sees a continuing tension between the grassroots growth which has sprung up in the Church as a result of the Second Vatican Council and which is an 'authentic flourishing of the gospel' he believes, and the attempts of the hierarchy to contain or even suppress popular initiative.[24] Schillebeeckx would argue here that there must be 'institutional safeguards' for equality if it is to be realised and maintained.[25]

This strong identification with those under authority as having to learn to take responsibility for themselves, is of a piece with a generalised contemporary preoccupation with the problem of oppression, and the correlative demand for justice which extends far beyond the Christian churches but which they feel touches them most intimately because the Church ought to be a community of

[20] J. Moltmann, *Ohne Macht mächtig* (Munich, 1981), *The Power of the Powerless*, tr. M. Khol (London, 1983), p. 39.
[21] *Ibid.*, p. 38.   [22] Schillebeeckx, *Church*, p. 189.   [23] *Ibid.*, p. xiv.   [24] *Ibid.*
[25] *Ibid.*

salvation.[26] This generates a powerful ecclesiology of encounter and struggle.

Schillebeeckx has challenged the principle that order is a good thing. He dislikes the notion, which would have seemed self-evidently sound in earlier ages, that 'the only meaningful transformation of the world and society is in a restoration of things to their ideal order. Whether one puts this ideal order at the beginning of time, the earthly paradise, or in a distant future at the end of times, a coming golden age, makes little structural difference', he suggests.[27]

The objection is to a search for tidiness which can limit freedom (again an ancient issue), an objection especially to allowing that there can be any constraint on God's actions. The implications of this line of thinking have been seen by other theologians as imposing a requirement of involvement upon the Church. Its responsibility is to the needs of the world. 'There is no department of the world's life into which [Christians] are not commissioned to go', argues John Robinson. 'They find themselves concerned with evangelization and with civilization, because ... the two are the same – the bringing to men and society of the *civitas dei*, that divine commonwealth which must ultimately transform the kingdoms of this world till they become the kingdom of God and of his Christ.'[28] An acceptance of the duty of Christian involvement in and Christian responsibility to and for the world seems to be inseparable from an ecclesiology of the responsible Church (envisaged as a Church of the people), and from the thrust towards the development of an anti-hierarchical structure.

Within the last decade 'the world' has come to be identified more broadly as including not only the human community and society, but the natural world. An ecological ecclesiology has developed as an extension and correlative of the social gospel and the gospel of peace and justice and the removal of oppression; and again with a high theme of responsibility. 'To hurt and damage this world is, from a theological perspective, a sin against the Creator of heaven and earth', comments Schillebeeckx.[29]

---

[26] 'Many believers, above all women, have the impression that they are being asked to believe in a God who injures and belittles people, above all women, through religion.' 'I have to discover how I can live with any decency at all as a member of "the First World" in the face of the Third', comments Moltmann. 'Only a history which brings about human liberation can be experienced as salvation history', says Schillebeeckx. As he sees it, the imperative to get this right means that 'the Church exists in the conflict between the lordship of Christ and the powers and forces of society', *Church*, p. 157.

[27] *Ibid.*, p. 230   [28] J.T. Robinson, *On Being the Church in the World* (London, 1960), p. 19.

[29] Schillebeeckx, *Church*, p. xix.

'Many people already have a spontaneous experience of communities in general.'[30] They bring this to their understanding of 'Church' as community. Ecclesiology must therefore take account of this sort of experience in framing an account of the Church which will make sense both to the Church's members and to those outside it.

If we want to say something like that, we should perhaps take account of the findings of sociology. It is of its nature the study of mass movement and mass mind. It has always seemed to me that the thought of individuals who have expressed it in writing furnishes a more finely tuned (historical and modern) index of positions. To take an example, Schillebeeckx portrays modern sociology as polarising the inward 'I' against the outward 'Society' as though the two were independent entities. 'All emphasis is placed either on personal human inwardness or on society. In both cases one of the two poles is secondary ... on the one hand the enclosed personality and on the other society without a subject, still dominate many forms of both liberal and Marxist sociology of religion.'[31]

Now this is far from being a new tension, or one newly recognised. The 'inward' and 'outward' theme is of course of some antiquity; it is a staple of the thought of Gregory the Great.[32] It recurs from age to age. Kant has a strong idea of the enclosed individual, autonomous and being his or her own person. It cannot therefore be argued that we have a uniquely or distinctively modern problem to deal with. The most that can be claimed is a new angle of view.

So I would suggest that partial illuminations are to be had in this way, but not necessarily an account of things which will stand up to the criticism that it does not recognise the classic and perennial features of modern phenomena. In ecclesiology these are crucial. The 'oneness' of the Church through time is as important as its unity in the present. We need to be able to say very precisely not only what is a new sociological phenomenon, but what is a continuing social feature.

Theologies and ecclesiologies in which 'engagement with the world' and social concerns are dominant have tended to have the effect of distracting concern from ecumenical objectives. This is noticeable in recent meetings of the World Council of Churches. Yet it ought not to be an inevitable consequence. It seems to arise out of

---

[30] *Ibid.*, p. 210.   [31] *Ibid.*, pp 46–7
[32] Carole Straw, *Gregory the Great* (Berkeley, 1988).

a sense of the need to husband limited energies and resources, rather than from any inherent conflict of interest.

What are the implications of these radical diggings in the search for one Church? They all tend to assume the Church to be one, or to need to be one, in order to do its great work in the world. They all find divisive differences an irrelevance to that work, or an impediment to it. So they ought to be ecumenically useful. But by the same token, what is not thought to be important will not be given the time and energy necessary to resolving it.

Which of these emphases should ecumenism find helpful? They are not of course mutually exclusive, nor should they be. The Church can work hard for the world and trust God to get things right; it can believe that here and now matters and look to eternity. Much has to do with balance. Ecumenism is about even-handedness, an eirenic respect for the other's difference, so that it ceases to be divisive. That applies equally to the grand schemes of ecclesiology. The revolutionary is not likely to be helpful if its purpose is to dispose of rivals. But it may be invaluable as a corrective.

Provisionality

One ecclesiological axis emerging from recent work is undoubtedly helpful ecumenically. In a pioneering study of the mid-1980s, C. Duquoc argues a case for the provisionality of the individual churches which exist and have existed in the world. There are two prongs to his argument. The first is the principle that the contingency and particularity of circumstances will always make for provisionality. That is roughly to equate 'historical' with 'provisional'.[33] He takes not only this unavoidably non-fixed character but also the concreteness and empirical character of the churches to be a positive value.[34] Over against it he sets, with a pejorative sense, the 'ideal'. 'It is not far from thinking in ideal terms to imposing norms on concrete reality and from the imposition of norms to repressive measures.'[35] 'To begin from the ideal is to condemn or to absolutize one's church or to judge all churches sinful.'[36]

---

[33] He speaks of 'The historical character of churches and consequently their provisional form', Duquoc, *Provisional Churches*, p. viii.

[34] *Ibid.*, p. viii and p. 91,'Provisional denotes the fact that the churches are historical and therefore mortal; it is not a pejorative judgement, suggesting a lack of value.'

[35] *Ibid.*, p. viii.   [36] *Ibid.*, p. viii.

Here I think we need to be careful. There are at least two partly submerged agendas. The first is the setting in opposition two directions of inference in ecclesiology, moving on the one hand from the ideal to the empirical; and on the other from the empirical to the ideal.[37] Duquoc argues that if we postulate that the Church begins from the ideal, history can only damage it. 'If the Church is originally pure and transparent in essence, time is pernicious for it.'[38] But I should think it unnecessary to suggest that these lines of derivation are opposed rather than complementary, pulling against one another rather than reciprocal.

The second agenda is political rather than philosophical. Duquoc writes as a French Roman Catholic, for whom it has seemed a fact of life 'for about twenty years, particularly in France ... that "institution" is synonymous with "repression"'.[39] He therefore finds it necessary to defend the individuality of the 'specific churches' against their threatened effacement by institutional universalism. It has not been so always and everywhere, and I shall argue in a later chapter that it need not be so if we think in terms of 'order' rather than 'institution'. It can be unhelpful to fall into what is sometimes called the 'victim' mentality, if that breeds the habit of seeing indications of oppression everywhere.

The case I myself would want to argue here is that we may postulate a Church which is an ideal without believing that there must be decay over time, that historical provisionality is somehow destructive of the ideal.[40] The 'ideal' elements, the theoretical constructs and ecclesiological models on which the 'flesh' of the divided churches hangs, can themselves be provisional. Provisionality is embodied in the historical and contingent. But it is also a function of doing theology, and especially ecclesiology, in a divided Church, that no account of the ecclesiology can be complete if it is framed in separation.

---

[37] 'The elaboration of ecclesiology does not consist in deducing a doctrine from the relevant parts of Scripture, but in giving reflective expression to the practices of believers.' *Ibid.*, p. 2.

[38] *Ibid.*, p. 25.   [39] *Ibid.*, p. 34.

[40] And productive of 'particular groups engendering exclusion'. *Ibid.*, pp. 3–4. Karl Rahner refers to the various realisations of Church as 'event'. 'Event may be a continuum allowing for a plurality of realisations.' K. Rahner and J. Ratzinger, *The Episcopate and the Primacy* (New York, 1962), p. 27.

THE ECUMENICAL AIM

This brings us to the question of the aim of the ecumenical enterprise. It is fundamental to Orthodox thinking that union with God supposes union among God's people. That is seen in Orthodox canon law as not only a spiritual mystery, but a necessarily visible reality.[41] At the centre of things lies the question whether and in what way a visible unity may unite not only all individual Christians into one communion, but also all churches and ecclesial bodies which are at present separated.[42] That is a much tougher brief, as we shall see.

Although there has always been a strong body of Christian opinion that the Church cannot be fully itself unless it is united, it is not uncontroversial that we ought to be seeking a visible unity. In the sixteenth century faithfulness to the Gospel seemed to the reformers ultimately more important than unity; many of them were prepared to say that visible unity cannot be achieved in this world, that the division of the Church is God's punishment for our infidelity and that fidelity not unity is the necessary goal.[43] Many Christians (of various traditions) would argue that unity in Christ and in the Spirit need not involve visible structures of unity, and perhaps should not do so. Some would go further, and say that there must be a tension, if not a conflict, between keeping the peace and maintaining purity in a fallen world. That is to say, it is suspected that unity involves in practice some compromising with the truth. 'Is it the will of God that some apartness be maintained in order for the divine economy to function, or is it his will that togetherness be pursued even when it means sacrificing commitments to biblical truth not universally affirmed?' asks one doubter, in language of transparent partiality.[44] So, although the will for unity, the *votum unitatis*,[45] is itself perhaps the decisive factor not only in bringing about unity in communion, but even in the very theology of communion,[46] it is not

---

[41] See J. Meyendorff, *Orthodoxie et catholicité* (Paris, 1965), p. 104.

[42] Cf. E. Yarnold, *In Search of Unity* (Slough, 1989), p. 19.

[43] D. Fischer, 'Ministères et instruments d'unité de l'Eglise dans la pensée de Luther et de Calvin', *Istina*, 30 (1985), 8–46.

[44] *A Contemporary Western Theology*, ed. C.W. Carter (Grand Rapids, Michigan, 1983), vol. I, 30.

[45] Cf. J.M.R. Tillard, *L'Evêque de Rome* (Paris, 1982), tr. J. de Satgé (1983), p. 4 and J.M.R. Tillard, 'Le Votum Eucharistiae, L'Eucharistie dans le recontre dest chrétiens', *Miscellanea Liturgica in onore di Sua Eminenza il Cardinale G. Lercaro*, 2 (Paris, 1967), 143–94.

[46] See chapter 6.

everywhere present, or held everywhere to be central. Or it is held to
in a general way, but sometimes without a serious commitment to
finding a means of achieving it.[47]

The *votum unitatis* might in principle still be strong on many
different understandings of what is meant by unity. It has been
suggested, for example, that the ecumenical task is not to create
unity but to manifest a unity which already exists in the one body of
Christ.[48] Some would think in terms of the presence of elements or
vestiges (*vestigia ecclesiae*) in the existing separated Churches,
elements of the one true Church which, in the mystical sense, they
already comprise. Some would press for a 'dualist' view, that there
should be invisible unity alongside an institutional diversity in
which separation persists. Some would simply say that only God can
know his Church, and that we must think in terms of the Church as
a multiplicity of churches in the form of congregations of believers,
where the pure Gospel is preached, and trust him to know his own.
Some would argue that the one Church exists as a promise for
eternity, that it is eschatological, and not to be looked for now.
Others would take a pragmatic view, that we should concentrate on
practical Christianity, mission and service, on the grounds that talk
of doctrine always divides, but common service can unify.[49]

Over against these theoretical constructs lie the experiences of
recent decades. Once mutual suspicion grows less at a local level,
Christians from different traditions begin to work together readily in
common practical projects.[50] They may hold joint services from
time to time, but these must, in most cases, fall short of the single,
shared celebration of the Lord's Supper which would be the sure
mark of their having become one Church.[51] All this is possible partly
because the pleasures of discovering new friends create a honey-
moon period; and that may last for some time, until conflicts of
attitude and expectation begin to emerge. There is the danger to the

---

[47] 'A sincere intention to seek unity is incompatible with an intention to remain permanently
uncommitted to any particular form of unity', comments Lesslie Newbigin, *All in Each
Place*, ed. J.I. Packer (Abingdon, 1981).

[48] N. Ehrenstrom and W.G. Muelder, *Institutionalism and Church Unity* (London, 1963), p. 30.

[49] Some of these are listed in one form or other in G. Wainwright, 'La Confession et les
confessions: vers l'unité confessionelle et confessante des chrétiens', *Irénikon*, 57 (1984),
5–25.

[50] England's present system under the title of 'Churches together in Unity' is an encouraging
case in point.

[51] The rules about eucharistic sharing are complex and vary from case to case among the
churches.

larger endeavour that the *rapprochement* will lead to the difficulty that initiatives at the local level can 'damage the prospects for eventual reunion which may in the end lead to reconciliation among all Christians',[52] if they go too far in a direction where Christians in other places cannot yet comfortably follow them. The emphasis on the local church can itself encourage a one-sidedness, with the larger vision growing dimmer by comparison. But the other, and highly positive, face of that possibility is the setting of good precedent and bold example. It has been suggested (though there are obvious dangers) that 'fast lanes ... where ecumenical progress takes place at a quicker rate than elsewhere' in 'areas of experimentation ... may possibly have the long-term effect of overcoming prejudice in other parts of the world'.[53]

Where conflicts remain or re-emerge, these in their turn may be resolved to some degree by the second of the modes of coming together which has been conspicuously successful in recent decades. Common agreements, in the form of Reports and Statements, have been framed by various partners in bilateral and multilateral conversations. Again, the results work both ways. Dialogue with one Church can make for difficulties with others by virtue of its very success, if it creates a new 'block' of opinion. Or it may prove to ease the way on other fronts. The better mutual understanding of traditions which is the most promising result where things go well can help locally only if the solutions found by these means to old conflicts are well understood at local level, and begin to enter into a developing common tradition, as the shared possession of all the original partners.

That is a process which is going to require a great deal of time. Experiments in introducing these documents to local communities throw up many difficulties. Fears 'of arbitrary action against individuals or local congregations, of minorities being dominated, of Christian traditions being "homogenized out", of an atmosphere of unfreedom and an authoritarian style' can be justified.[54] There is often initial resistance to being asked to take part in an unfamiliar exercise, or to the language and terminology of what is seen as a 'theologians'' document. Old 'party' lines emerge among those who have some hostility to one or more other churches. That can create a

---

[52] Paul Richardson, 'Ecumenism at rest?', *Living Stones*, 1 (4), (1992) 40.   [53] *Ibid.*
[54] James Corridan, 'Authority and freedom in the coming Ecumenical Church', *Journal of Ecumenical Studies*, 12 (1975), 315–347, p. 316.

sense for those unfamiliar with the themes and subject-matter of the
old controversies that nothing has been achieved at all; or it can
prompt a suspicion that some sleight of hand is being practised, and
that what is being offered is a confidence trick.

In any case, the Reports themselves cannot hope to say the last
word on their themes. It would be surprising if disagreements a
thousand, or even 400 years old, could be mended in the course of a
few meetings of groups of theologians, with a definitiveness which
could immediately compel the assent of all involved in the life of the
Church worldwide, although some of their breakthroughs will
undoubtedly do so in time. The solutions proposed need to be
thought through, tried out in new languages, their implications
realised. They need above all to become the common property of the
faithful, to win the minds and the consent of all. That means that
they must become intelligible to many who had not previously
realised that the Communion to which they have belonged had held
a particular view, or seen itself as differing from others; as well as to
those to whom the differences have been crucial. There is, in short, a
vast educational task to be carried out. So neither living an ecclesial
life together as far as possible, nor talking together, will do on its
own as a way of arriving at a united Church; and even taken
together, they provide only a part of what is needed.

One Church is not made merely by working together, nor even by
reaching agreement in a common faith. The issues on which it is
hardest to make progress are ecclesiological, and (to coin a term),
'ecclesiopractical', because they touch the heart of the separated
churches' being. There is a tendency for ecumenical *rapprochement* to
slow down, and sometimes to halt and go into reverse, when the
decision to unite is really faced in practice. There is not a great deal
of difficulty in stating in general terms of oneness in Christ the way
we envisage the goal of unity, so long as we stop short of seeking to
describe, or still more to prescribe, the actuality of a single visible
Church. We have, as it were, a theology of the oneness of the Church,
without a theology of the structures of such a Church.[55] Even in 1930,
when the Bonn Agreement reconciled Anglicans and Old Catholics,
nothing was settled about the structures which would sustain
communion once it had been established. So the language of such
ecclesiology of unity as we have in common is often eschatological:

[55] See S. Sykes, 'Episcopacy, communion and collegiality', in *Communion and Episcopacy*, ed. J.
Draper (Cuddesdon, 1988), p. 42.

the goal is seen as the Kingdom, the rule of God; as the ultimate transformation of the whole of the created universe into a kingdom of justice, peace and integrity, according to the plan and will of God; as not to be fully realised in this life.[56] Patently there is nothing wrong with the eschatological vision. But it does not get us over the difficulties of uniting here and now (or even in the foreseeable future), because it does not confront the causes of remaining reluctance to become one Church on earth in a visible way. The language of 'sign, instrument and foretaste' which is becoming important in ecumenical dialogue must look to the hope of unity now as well as to the *eschaton*.

---

[56] Fischer, 'Ministères et instruments d'unité' 8–46, p. 9, adds the note that division and the unattainability of unity in this world are part of the suffering the Church must bear as punishment for her unfaithfulness.

CHAPTER I

Local and universal

CHURCH AND CHURCHES

'One of the greatest challenges facing the Church today is that of maintaining a healthy balance between the universal expression of the faith of the Church and the particular expression of that faith in each local Church. When the scale tips too far, the whole Church, inseparably universal and local, suffers.'[1] This warning comes from a Roman Catholic commentator, aware of a danger which arises even within a church which is visibly already a single communion. But it arises, too, and more challengingly, in the case of the relation between Church and churches where all are not in communion, and that is the problem to which this book is chiefly addressed.

In the foregoing introductory remarks we have been asking what the Church is for and where it is going. We now need to ask in what form or forms, and by what manner of life, it is going to be itself and do its work. The World Council of Churches embraces as 'churches' ecclesial entities which St Paul would not have recognised as churches in the same way as he did 'the church of Corinth', 'the church of Rome'.[2] The crucial difference between the usage of St Paul and speaking of, for example, a 'Methodist church' or an 'Anglican church' is that he understood the local churches he knew to be simply the one Church of Christ meeting in that place. To put it in terms more fully thought out later, their local 'being the Church' was inseparable from their catholicity and unity with one another at the deepest level. In the undivided Church of later ages that understanding persisted so far as to make it impossible for many centuries for the Church of Rome to recognise ecclesial bodies out of communion with herself as 'churches' at all; this position was revised

---

[1] Editorial, *Catholic International*, 3 (1992), 803.   [2] Ratzinger, p. 114.

and restated in the documents of the Second Vatican Council, where 'churches' (*ecclesiae*) is sometimes used of such bodies alongside 'separated communities' (*communitates seiunctae*)[3]. That has not quite amounted in practice yet to considering them all as equally or equally fully churches.[4]

This raises the question whether some churches are 'more Church' than others; and whether some are 'less Church' because 'institutionally defective',[5] or 'provisional',[6] or 'lacking',[7] or guilty of 'substantial infidelity to the mind of [the] divine founder'.[8] It remains a central difficulty that 'churches' which are thus not quite sure of the fullness of one another's ecclesiality cannot in any visible sense, and often in their own self-understanding, see themselves as together constituting 'one Church'. Christendom has yet to find its way to 'the transformation of the plural of confessional Churches separated from one another into the plural of local churches that are in their diversity really one Church'.[9]

William Pope, a nineteenth-century Methodist theologian saw a good deal of contradictoriness in the 'qualities' of the Church as they are noted in Scripture;

Unity, Sanctity, Invisibility, Catholicity, Apostolicity, Indefectibility, Glory. But we also find by the side of these [terms] which generally describe the Body in its higher and ideal character, qualities in some measure their counterparts or opposites: such as Diversity, Imperfection, Visibility,

---

[3] *UR*, 3.

[4] H. Fries suggests approaching this problem by way of a theory of 'participation'. He asks 'how was it possible that this participation could free itself from the existing Church and thus represent and realize itself as independent? Is it not because this participation was not visible enough, not realized concretely enough where it should have been realized, within the whole to which participation is related? That it here did not attain its due dignity?' Then 'from a Catholic viewpoint, an integration of the Protestant Churches into the Catholic is ... conceivable as the integration of the participating and distinct into the whole'. See 'The ecclesiological status of the Protestant Churches from a Catholic Viewpoint', *Journal of Ecumenical Studies*, 1 (1964), 208–10 and citing E. Brunner, 'Das Misverständnis der Kirche', p. 7.

[5] G. Baum, 'The Constitution of the Church', *Journal of Ecumenical Studies*, 2 (1965), 1–30, 7.

[6] 'The reformers understood their ecclesial decision as explicitly *provisorium* ... but can such an emergency be perpetuated theologically?' asks Fries, 'The ecclesiological status', 203.

[7] Rome's *Response* to ARCIC, 'a Church outside of communion with the Roman Pontiff lacks more than just the visible manifestations of unity with the Church of Christ which subsists in the Roman Catholic Church'.

[8] G.A. Lindbeck, writing as a Lutheran, suggests that 'the usual Lutheran view' is that 'because his churches are, or have the possibility of being, more faithful to Christ, they have a higher ecclesiological status than does the Roman Church', 'A Protestant view of the ecclesiological status of the Roman Catholic Church', *Journal of Ecumenical Studies*, 1 (1964), 243–79, p. 254.

[9] Ratzinger, p. 120.

Localisation, Confessionalism, Mutability, and Militant Weakness. Hence we gather that the true Church of Christ is a body in which these opposite attributes unite.[10]

This grouping implies that certain attributes are not only the opposites of others but also less desirable. It is instructive that he lines up with (1) 'imperfection' and 'militant weakness' not only (2) 'confessionalism' but also (3) 'visibility' and 'localisation'. I subdivide the list into three in this way because we must today distinguish very carefully between these three respects in which a given community can stand over against what is in Pope's final list of what Church should be.

To some degree imperfection, as a concomitant of the human condition, represents the human face of the Church, which is always redeemed by the divine. It is regrettable but unavoidable and will be there still in a future united Church in this world. Visibility and localisation are certainly not pejorative terms. They are, as we shall see, complementary to invisibility and universality, and have their place in a future united Church.

The same test of having a place in a future united Church is, however, not so easily passed by confessionalism, if by that is meant having a faith which is not the same, in some key and church-defining respect, as that of others who call themselves Christians. William Pope confusedly saw something of the complex of difficulties in this area, which have grown far worse confused in the process of development of ecumenical priorities in the twentieth century.

So the challenge presented by the divided Church has made it necessary to rethink both what is meant by 'a church' and what is meant by '*the* Church', and, above all, to seek to see further into the nature of their relationship. Its complexity is reflected in the typographical difficulty which constantly arises of deciding between a small and a capital C for Church. (In this book the capital is reserved for the one Church except in the case of some generally accepted titles such as 'Roman Catholic Church', 'Church of England'.)

Elements of Church

Certain elements or features of a community help to identify it, first as 'Church' and secondly as 'a church'. That is, it must be at the same time the one Church which is the body of Christ; and a distinct

[10] *A Compendium of Christian Theology* (New York, no date), 3 vols., vol. III pp. 266–7.

ecclesial entity, alongside other churches. And each and all of the churches, and also the one Church, will have certain characteristics which define 'Church'. This paradoxical state of affairs has to be described in terms of concepts unique to Christian ecclesiology.

We should begin with a review of the scriptural and traditional picture. In order to be the one Church (for if it is not the one Church it cannot be *a* church), a community must bear witness that it has Christ in its midst;[11] recognise Christ as Lord and affirm and respond to the presence and gifts of the Holy Spirit. It must claim an apostolic origin.[12] It must show salvation at work[13] and announce and look forward to the Kingdom of God. As an inseparable element of its belonging to Christ, it ought to be filled with the mutual charity of its members. It will confess the apostolic faith.[14] Its life will involve the proclamation of the Word of God in Scripture, both in mission to the world and in the teaching of its own members. It will baptise, and celebrate the Lord's Supper.[15] It will have a pastoral ministry which will provide leadership in the corporate act of celebrating the sacraments. The pastor will be the people's earthly head and will have authority among them; he will also be their servant, having no authority in his own right, but only with and among his people.[16] (As we shall see, each of these elements

---

[11] This principle was stated by the Pope on the arrival of a delegation from the Ecumenical Patriarch on 24 January 1972. He spoke of '*Ecclesia*, that gathering in which we are joined with you ... gathered together in the name of Christ, and as a result having him, Christ, our Lord himself, in our midst' (cf. Matthew 18:20). Stormon, p. 241.

[12] H. Fries says that Protestant Churches 'have a common origin with the Roman Catholic Church, namely: the revelation and salvation completed in and with Jesus Christ; the heritage coming from him, the task given by him and the witness preaching him ... the Protestant Churches are characterized by an assent to this origin, and by a claim ... to possess it in its purity, to have saved and maintained it'. 'The ecclesiological status', p. 198.

[13] The working out of the individual's salvation in the Church of which he becomes a member by faith and by baptism was already a preoccupation of Cyprian (d. 258). On his *nulla salus extra ecclesiam*, see *De Unitate Catholicae Ecclesiae*, PL 4, 493–520, and G. Hartel, ed. *CSEL* (Vienna, 1868–71), vi, 'Nec pervenit ad Christi praemia, qui relinquit Ecclesiam Christi'; xiv, 'Esse martyr non potest qui in *Ecclesia* non est: ad regnum pervenire non poterit qui eam quae regnatura esse derelinquit.'

[14] H. Fries stresses that 'Church is first of all the community and assembly of the faithful', 'The ecclesiological status', p. 197.

[15] Ratzinger, p. 8. This point raises difficulties about such communities as that of the Friends or Quakers, who do not celebrate the sacraments.

[16] ARCIC II, *Church as Communion*, 45, includes 'the confession of the one apostolic faith, revealed in the Scriptures, and set forth in the Creeds ... one baptism ... one celebration of the eucharist [as] its preeminent expression and focus ... shared commitments to the mission entrusted by Christ to his Church ... shared concern for one another in mutual forbearance, submission, gentleness and love ... making room for each other in the body of Christ ... solidarity with the poor and the powerless'.

presents its problems when we try to define it in terms which all those which call themselves churches can recognise.)

So there must also be order. 'Order' in the Church includes a great many aspects of the patterns of life and worship which make it recognisably the community of God's people. These patterns do not have to be identical everywhere for us to be able to speak of a common order. But they have to have elements in common, and most Christians would say these common elements must include means of linking communities to one another, or at least to the one Church. There will normatively be a consciousness of continuity in common life with the Church of the Apostles, whether that is seen as running unbroken through time or standing in some relationship of continuity which can survive a break in the temporal record. It is above all essential if Christians are to meet in one body in one Eucharist that there should be not only a sense of being led there by one Spirit, but a common 'order' within which the celebration takes place. With order there must also be discipline.[17] We shall come back to these immensely complicated issues in chapter 4.

We come next to 'elements', which have made themselves felt in various forms, which have seemed to meet human spiritual and emotional need. Miracle ought to be mentioned briefly, as a strong token in the minds of ancient and mediaeval Christians of the presence of the true Church, though less actively so in more recent centuries. Augustine made the sensible (and important) observation that it is not helpful to use miracles as evidence in that way. 'We believe that miracles happen in the true Church because we believe it to be the true Church. We do not believe it to be the true Church because miracles happen in it.'[18] Although it is still lively in its

---

[17] In the view of some sixteenth-century reformers, without discipline there could be no Church. Martin Bucer makes it a mark of the Church. P. Avis, *The Church in the Theology of the Reformers* (London, 1981), pp. 45ff. Here we come up against what has been, historically, one of the greatest areas of dispute about the 'elements' of the Church. The first three of the 'elements' which make up the four articles of the Anglican–Lambeth Quadrilateral of 1888 are relatively uncontentious. They are concerned with the supreme authority of the Bible; the Creeds; the dominical sacraments of baptism and Eucharist. The fourth article speaks of 'the historic episcopate, locally adapted in the methods of its administration to the varying needs of the nations and peoples called of God into the unity of His Church'. *The Niagara Report* of the Anglican–Lutheran International Commission (1989), (29, p. 18), lists Scripture, Creeds and Sacraments and adds as the fourth 'article' of its own 'quadrilateral', the many forms of 'historical continuity [the] bishops and presbyters [of the Church] have been given'. That is clearly a much more modest basis to propose for the structural means by which local churches keep in touch and are linked than the Lambeth Quadrilateral, but it still stresses the importance of a ministerial link.

[18] See R. Knox, *Enthusiasm* (Oxford, 1950), p. 65.

appeal in the Third World and in many Roman Catholic communities in undeveloped parts of the world, since the eighteenth and nineteenth centuries miracle has lost its traditional evidential place for most Christians in the West. Indeed the claim that a truth rests on a miraculous act or intervention can be taken as evidence against it in scientifically minded societies. Thus it has been in the West in recent controversies about the Virgin Birth and the Resurrection. The supernatural place of miracle has been taken in more recent ecclesiology perhaps by the 'heightening', the extreme of authentic personal experience, and by the power of charismatic worship. The appeal to the extraordinary in all these can call out the same response in men and women as wonder at miracle more easily did in past ages.

There will be in the Church a sense of separateness from the world. The separateness is a matter of the Church's keeping itself 'unspotted from the world' and thus it is inseparably linked with 'purity'.[19] But here we come to a major difficulty about the interaction of these 'elements' which also yields a key principle of this book. Churches cannot be fully ecclesial in isolation, nor if they fail to reach out in mission and concern for humanity. The principle of 'separateness' can get in the way both of mission and of relationships with other Churches, in the case of a community which sees itself as the 'remnant', having to keep itself apart in its purity as the true Church. That happened to the Donatists in North Africa in the fourth and fifth centuries, and it has continued to present problems in the case of a number of ecclesial bodies since the sixteenth century, each of which has regarded itself as the only true church.[20] For example, the Calvinist (though by no means radical)[21] Bullinger (1504–75) speaks not only of the need for the Church to keep itself unspotted from the world, but also insists that 'it flees from and in every way detests all unlawful congregations and profane religions, and all wicked men, and willingly and openly confesses Christ

---

[19] James 1:27. Calvin, *Inst. Chr.*IV.i.12, *CR* 32.579–80 stresses the pure ministry of the Word and the pure administration of the sacraments in conformity with it. See, too, Bullinger, *Of the Holy Catholic Church*, 36. J. Ratzinger, 'The ministerial office and the unity of the Church', *Journal of Ecumenical Studies*, 1 (1964), 42–57, p. 43. Ratzinger goes on to suggest that 'A certain hypostatization of the Word took place at that point; the Word became independent in relation to the Church ... it loomed as the existing critical measure of the Church ... Catholic theology, on the other hand, regards the Office as a criterion of the Word.' See, too, Richard Field, *Of the Church*, Book 1, chapter 6, p. 25.

[20] Piepkorn's three volumes include case after case of which this is true.

[21] See chapter 2 on the views of sixteenth-century radicals.

both in word and in deed, even at the risk of its life'.[22] There can also be a different false relation between mission and Christian separateness, if mission goes so open-handedly into the world that the distinctive Christian life becomes absorbed into the local culture to the point where it ceases to be recognisably Christian.[23] If this is right, then we should have to see a being 'not of the world' as a constitutive ecclesial element if and only if it is paradoxically at the same time in and of the world, and at one with other Christians.

Not every community of Christian people in which the elements we have been listing are found has been regarded as a church. Communities of religious in particular have presented something of an ecclesial anomaly in the West from patristic times; Gregory the Great wanted to ensure that religious houses were under the direct control of the Papacy, and as a result they came to lie less clearly under the jurisdiction of their local bishop. It was usual in the Middle Ages to speak of a monastic house as *ecclesia*, and certainly in such a community one could find the pastor with his people, in the form of the abbot and his monks.[24] But a religious Order has never been a 'church' in the way that a group of local churches with their priests form one church with their bishop.[25] For more examples of bodies which fulfil some of the obvious criteria for being ecclesial bodies and are yet not churches, one might point to missionary societies, hospices, schools. There must, then, it would seem, be what might be called an ecclesial 'intention' in a church's coming together. It must 'mean' to be a church.[26]

It will be clear that some of these elements are not simply repeated from place to place in each local Church, but that they are 'held' or 'done' with other Christians everywhere. Others involve, in order to be truly ecclesial, a sense of a different sort of linkage, or continuity,

---

[22] Bullinger, *Of the Holy Catholic Church*, 36.   [23] See pp. 58–77 below on inculturation.

[24] The abbot's relation to the community is not strictly that of the ordained minister to the people in his *cura*.

[25] Accordingly, it has remained possible in the West for the Bishop of Rome to 'exempt any institution of Christian perfection and its individual members from the jurisdiction of local ordinaries and subject them to himself alone', as it is put today. *LG*, 45. Wyclif, and others after him who were hostile to monastic profession, spoke of the Orders as 'sects'. Wyclif meant by that that they set themselves apart from, and even above, the Church. They were certainly not themselves churches, although they might seem to claim to be. See further pp. 000–00 below.

[26] There is a continuing question whether a Eucharist celebrated in a hospital or prison or on a journey, or by a solitary in silence, would make the participant(s) a local Church? P. Stanley Harekes says yes: 'The local church; an Eastern Orthodox perspective', *Ecumenical Review*, 29 (1977), 143.

or cooperation, in its full sense of a 'working together of distinct entities'. Those which are central to the Church's faith its sacramental life, its mystery, its spiritual being are common not just in the sense of being 'alike' in all churches; they are *one* in all churches.

The constitutive elements of the Church must also be linked in the sense of being interdependent. For example, Scripture is itself the product of tradition. It is preserved by the 'handing on' of tradition from generation to generation; but it also governs tradition by its sovereign authority, and all right tradition must be in conformity with Scripture. The Creeds are part of tradition, and at the same time its products; they confess what the Church always holds to be the Gospel faith.[27] Again, the Creeds, as professions of faith, are inseparable from the rite of baptism and thus form part of the Church's sacramental life. This very interdependence of the elements can itself be seen as a constitutive element, because without it churches may run into the danger of resting their claim to be churches on a single essential. *Sola Scriptura, sola fide,* even 'Christ alone' can be misleading tags, if they are taken to be exclusive of other elements.

These basics have been summarised in different ways, and with different emphases, during the Church's history. The ancient fourfold rule that the Church is 'one,[28] holy, catholic[29] and apostolic'[30] is overlaid, for instance among the Protestant reformers of the sixteenth century, by a stress on the presence of a ministry of Word and

---

[27] Though not entirely in Scripture's words. Some Christian communities have not embraced all the credal formulae. The Non-Chalcedonian or Oriental Orthodox Churches, for example, do not accept the definition of the Council of Chalcedon. Others would not wish to associate themselves with any form of credal statement.

[28] See E. Lanne, 'L'Eglise une', *Irénikon*, 5 (1977), 46–58 on the origin and significance of 'one' in the Niceno-Constantinopolitan Creed. Theodore of Mopsuestia is the best witness of this addition. Before him it is attested by Cyril of Jerusalem and Epiphanius of Salamis. It is a formula from Alexandrian theology and is first witnessed in a profession of faith by Alexander of Alexandria in 324. Though the order of 'catholic' and 'apostolic' varies, 'one, holy' does not. Lanne suggests that the intention is to assert the Church's unicity rather than its unity, that is, the forming of a unity despite or because of diversity (p.48).

[29] Ignatius of Antioch seems to have been the first to add 'catholic' to 'one', 'holy' and 'apostolic' in describing the Church.

[30] In the Whitby debate of 664 in England, between Christians of the Roman party and those converted by Celtic missionaries, the two sides variously placed their emphasis upon the catholicity, apostolicity, holiness and unity of the true Church. For Colman apostolicity and holiness come first. For Wilfred, catholicity, unity and apostolicity. Each is prepared to make some compromise, Colman with unity and catholicity for the sake of the apostolicity and holiness which he is sure he finds in the Celtic practice; Wilfred with the evidence of the holiness of the Celtic saints, for the sake of unity, catholicity and an apostolicity which he places especially in the Petrine tradition. We return to this discussion later.

sacrament as the defining indicator that a community is truly the Church.[31]

Richard Field, writing *Of the Church* in the first decade of the seventeenth century, wants to place the emphasis rather differently.[32] He is concerned not only with the local ministry of Word and sacrament, but with the mode of 'connection' between local Churches. All churches have in common, he points out, the 'same beginning and original cause, which is God that hath called us to the fellowship of his Son, and to the hope of eternal life'; and the 'same last end'; 'the same means of salvation, as are faith, sacraments, holy laws and precepts'; the 'same spirit which doth animate the whole body of the Church'; 'the same head, Christ, and guides appointed by him, who, although they are many, yet are all holden in a sweet coherence and connexion amongst themselves'; 'the connexion which all they of the Church have amongst themselves and with Christ'. He thinks it important that all churches should be 'one with the Church and company of believers which . . . at divers times hath filled the whole world'.[33]

There are hints here of the line of Anglican thought which was to lead to the framing of the Chicago–Lambeth Quadrilateral of 1886/8, made up of Scripture, the Creeds, the sacraments and the 'historic episcopate'.[34] The last proved a controversial notion.[35] But its inclusion reflected a concern with 'connexion' among churches, a conviction that although the Church in each place is fully the Church, a microcosm of the one Church, it is also a part of that whole. So we may argue that along with those elements which make a local community a church, and together with the *intention* to be a church, we should place its being linked in a relationship with other local churches as well as with the one, holy, catholic and apostolic Church.

The classical and mediaeval device of looking for 'form' and 'matter' has been applied, with limited success, to the question of the way the constitutive elements of 'the Church' make a specific or

---

[31] See a convenient treatment in P. Avis, *The Church in the Theology of the Reformers* (London, 1981).

[32] Richard Field, *Of the Church*, Book II, chapter 7, vol. I, pp. 85–6.   [33] *Ibid.*, pp. 86–7.

[34] See *Quadrilateral at One Hundred*, ed. J. Robert Wright (London, 1988), for a series of essays on the implications of this text.

[35] It cannot be the case that the episcopate is an essential of the Church, for that would unchurch a great many communities. See *The Study of Anglicanism*, ed. Stephen Sykes and John Booty (London, 1988), p. 306.

local church.[36] It has been argued that if we see the elements which make 'Church' as imposing 'form' on the 'matter' which is the local human and cultural situation, that diminishes the role and the value of the human and particular, making it passive and receptive and denying it the possibility of an active partnership with God.[37] A perhaps more satisfactory understanding sees the constitutive elements as acting rather to transform from within the lives and culture of a group of people as it is already being lived.[38]

In any case, not all the 'elements' can necessarily be seen as 'generative', as 'making' the Church in this way. (For example, the ordained ministry does not make the local church a church; it merely serves it.) Nor can they necessarily be thought of without some provisos even as 'carriers' or 'bearers' of 'Church'. The advantage of the idea that the constitutive elements 'sustain' the Church is that it lays stress on the continuity of the Church in every age with the apostolic community itself. That would also make each local church tomorrow the same local church in continuity with the one which exists today and was here yesterday. But at the same time, there is an implication that it is the unvarying elements which are constitutive and that that which is various and diverse in the Church is not constitutive for its ecclesiality. Not everyone would want to say that, especially in communities where there is a strong emphasis on the priority of the local 'gathered' congregation, or upon the value of diversity.

An approach which has seemed to have something to commend it ecumenically has been to look to a minimum list of constitutive elements of the Church, so as not to set unnecessary barriers in the way by expecting agreement at too many points. The argument that it is simplest to leave the *filioque* out of the Niceno-Constantinopolitan Creed, so that Orthodox and Western Christians may say it together, is a case in point. The Anglican Lambeth Quadrilateral

---

[36] P. Komonchak, 'The local Church and the Church Catholic. The contemporary theological problematic', Salamanca, pp. 559–91. G. Colombo, 'La teologia della Chiesa locale', in *La Chiesa Locale* (Bologna, 1969), pp. 17–38, especially 32–8.

[37] D. Valentini, *Il nuovo Popoli di Dio in cammino: punti nodali per una ecclesiologia attuale* (Rome, 1984), p. 56.

[38] International Theological Commission, 'Select themes in ecclesiology (1969–85)', vol., III p. 4, *Texts and Documents* (San Francisco, 1989), pp. 271–8. There remain difficulties with this which we shall look at later in this chapter (see pp. 58–77).

was devised with this principle of finding a minimum in mind. It
could also be the case that such an approach would avoid 'unchurching' another community in which some elements (such as ministry
recognised by all as apostolic) might be lacking. But it has the
disadvantage that it has about it an air of making emergency
concessions. It cannot in itself resolve long-standing differences
which might open up cracks again in the future. It certainly cannot
be seen as a solution which reflects unanimity in one Church on
matters of faith and order because it avoids confrontation with the
lack of unanimity.

We need not press this discussion further here. These themes will
recur. But it is important to set them out among these main issues as
a starting-point.

'PARTLY THE CHURCH' OR 'NOT THE CHURCH'?

We must also ask whether any flaw in, or absence of, an element can
make a community which intends to be 'the Church in that place',
not the Church. The Church not only 'has', it also 'is' those things
which are constitutive for its being. It cannot be any *more* the
Church in virtue of possessing more than essentials defined in that
way, for they are what make it the Church, although its life may be
enriched by possessing them in abundance.

But the converse may be the case. A church can become damaged
through the loss of one or more of them, and such a loss may go so far
as to take away its very 'being' as a church. Error (which is a breach
of unity of faith) can do that. It can invalidate a church's sacraments
where the unworthiness of a minister cannot. If truth is held but on
the wrong assumptions (on the wrong foundation), it will not of
course cease to be the truth, but it may cease to be constitutive for
the Church. (As one might say, 'Christ is Lord', while holding an
ecclesiology so unorthodox as to make it impossible that Christ is
present in his Church where that is what the Church is thought to
be.)

Certainly, not all the elements can be held to be 'essential ingredients' in the same way. Still unresolved is a set of questions disputed
in the sixteenth century about which are 'divine' and which
'human' elements, which are of the *esse* or essence of the Church, and
which can be thought of as indifferent in the sense that the Church's
being does not depend on them. These questions would have to be

settled before it would be possible to talk satisfactorily in terms of 'ingredients'.[39]

There are of course some elements self-evidently classifiable as divine or human in terms which make sense in any century. The mysterious union between the body and the Head who is Christ and the working of the Holy Spirit by grace is fundamental, and without them there can certainly be no question of a community's 'being the Church'. The 'human' elements might seem on the face of it more likely to be negotiable. Among the 'human' elements the mutual charity of the members of the community (for example) has often been conspicuously deficient. St Paul did not think the Church at Corinth had ceased to be the Church because its members quarrelled (1 Corinthians 1: 10ff.). Calvin says that although there were defects in the Corinthians' administration of the Supper, and discipline and moral tone had greatly declined, and they were broken up into various parties through the ambition of their ministers, nevertheless, because they held onto the fundamental teaching and worshipped the one God and rested their confidence of salvation on Christ, the Church still continued to exist among them.[40] So it has been hard to say in any definitive way what could be 'left out' in such a way as to unchurch a community in the 'human' dimensions of its life. Perhaps the lesson to be drawn is precisely that it is in its divine character that the Church is reliably itself and that human inadequacy will always make the 'human' elements chancy and changeable without necessarily unchurching communities by their variability.

Nevertheless, communities did arise in the early centuries of the Church which were deemed by other communities to have put themselves outside the Church on an essential point of faith, or which had broken away in schism. There was also the problem raised by individuals who had belonged to such a group, or lapsed from the faith altogether, and later wanted to return to the catholic Church. In one case 'Church' had been lost; in the other a person had been lost to the Church. The solution accepted throughout most of the early Church to the problem presented by individuals 'baptised' outside the Church (though not one reached without lengthy dispute) was to admit them to membership as already baptised,

[39] The problem about doing it today is that the sixteenth-century terms of reference can now seem archaic.
[40] Commentary on Galatians 10, and see Avis, *The Church*, p. 41.

provided that they had been baptised with water in the name of the Trinity.[41] For Western tradition Augustine of Hippo's[42] clinching argument had been that since God is the ultimate minister of baptism, baptisms by human ministers not in communion with the catholic Church were, for that reason, not necessarily invalid. Both validity and efficaciousness were at God's disposal. Those who had been baptised but had lapsed were still baptised, but penance was needed to restore them effectively to their baptism as purifier of sin.

In the case of the mutually estranged churches of today matters have always been more difficult. Their baptisms are seen as true baptism despite their separation. There are ecclesiological implications here, as Augustine saw within the framework of the controversies of his own time, and they cannot be dealt with tidily. Baptism does not involve only the individual and God. It is also an admission to membership of the community of Christ's body. That cannot take place in a community which is in no way or sense 'Church'. It must follow that some at least of the communities in which such 'heretical' or 'schismatic' baptisms occurred remained in some manner churches even if only partly or imperfectly 'Church'. Augustine held that the sacraments could not normally be fruitful or efficacious except in unity, for love is an essential element and the breach of unity is the betrayal of love.[43] The Holy Spirit makes the sacraments not only the acts of Christ in the Church, but also of the living Church in the Spirit. That can happen only within the bonds of mutual Christian love.[44] But Augustine's position remains that even in separation communities may act as channels for the work of grace, and the ordinary ecclesial means of grace can operate within them in an extraordinary way, if God so wishes. The device of assuming divine grace to operate directly to tidy up anomalies remains, however, an ecclesiological 'emergency measure'. It cannot be thought a satisfactory solution unless we postulate so fluid an ecclesiology that nothing is secure in the definition of the Church but the work of the Holy Spirit in it.

The need to make 'emergency concessions' for the sake of the faithful arises again and again in Christian history, as theology is tested against human fallibility. The concept of a community's being 'partly the Church' must perhaps fall into that category.

---

[41] See H. Chadwick, *Augustine* (Oxford, 1986), p. 79.   [42] 354–430.
[43] Perhaps there is some departure from the Pauline principle of 1 Corinthians 1:10ff. in this.
[44] Congar, *Essais Oecuméniques*, p. 207.

But that makes it necessary to take a position on 'emergency action'. The notion of 'emergency' carries with it connotations of the extraordinary and dangerous, even the regrettable. The extraordinary and exceptional have proved in the history of the Church to be the Holy Spirit's stock-in-trade. The regrettable is another matter.

We can see how the regrettable has to be accommodated in Augustine's attempts at solutions. The great central difficulty for Augustine was to reconcile a doctrine of the unity of the catholic Church with the principle that baptism carried out outside it could, in duly defined circumstances, be valid (if not efficacious) and was therefore really baptism and not to be repeated. He also found himself obliged to oppose to the Donatists' attractive and Biblically founded assertion that 'purity' was essential to the Church,[45] an ecclesiology which asserted the Church to be a mixed community in which only God can know who are really his. In other words, he had to split down the middle the notion of a sacrament's operation, and separate the idea of its being really a sacrament from the idea of its doing its job. And he had to deny the necessity of a principle (of 'purity') which would seem on the face of it to be self-evidently right.

Both these main thrusts of his anti-Donatist thinking have a number of implications for the problems about communion which face ecumenists today. It remains a stumbling-block to union that the sacraments and order of one ecclesial body cannot be recognised by all others as performing their due functions because they are held by some to lie outside the true Church. It can also be a difficulty that the visible Church is identified by some communions as consisting in those who are 'pure' in God's eyes, whose salvation is sure, and who are known by their faith to be justified in the sight of God; and by others as a mixed community, wheat and tares growing together until harvest.[46]

Augustine became convinced that it would be presumption to try to separate the wheat from the tares in the Church before God's own time came for doing so, for it is not given to man to know who is saved; and that therefore the Church must be understood not as a pure, but as a mixed body.[47] This line of thought necessitates the

---

[45] James 1:27.   [46] See chapter 6 on Communion.

[47] Augustine, *Contra Epistulam Parmeniani*, I.vii.12 and I.ix.15, *CSEL*, 51, pp. 31–5, ed. M. Petschenig (1908). See too G. Bonner, 'The Church and the Eucharist in the theology of St. Augustine', *Sobornost*, 7 (1978), 448–61.

embracing of a further paradox: if the visible Church is thus a mixed body of saints and sinners, that cannot be understood to be the case with the mystical and invisible body of those God alone knows to be his own. So we have both a 'true Church' which is 'impure' and a 'true Church' which is 'pure' and holy, existing one within the other in some ultimately perhaps indefinable relation.[48] So this is an ecclesiological position with two important implications. It does not compromise in any way the belief that God's people are the pure and holy. But it allows that in the bonding of human and divine in the Church God can make space for human failings in ways which do not destroy 'Church'.

Augustine went a significant step further here because he had to deal with the scandal of division. He was able to envisage a communion in parts, an interpenetration of the true Church with that which is not the Church truly or fully. He argued in his book on baptism against the Donatists that the Donatists are in communion with the catholic[49] Church at all points where they are in agreement with it; they are in schism at the points where they disagree. The presumption here is that the catholic Church is the Church universal, even though it does not at present fully include the Donatists. Augustine did not go so far as to envisage a universal Church in which the Donatist churches and the churches of his own Catholic communion were all simply member-churches.

He thinks that individual Christians may be partly in schism (that is, in those points at which they differ from the Catholic consensus), and partly in unity with the Catholic Church (*Contra Epistulam Parmeniani* I.i.2). That means that the Donatists are not wholly out of communion with the Catholics, and for this reason too their baptism need not therefore be regarded as invalid. 'In virtue of that which belongs to the true Church in each of them', they may administer and participate in the true sacraments (I.x.14). This is a very important concession in favour of the notion of communion (currently being developed among Anglicans in an emergency situation) as something which may persist even when it is imperfect, and still be in some sense true communion.

Augustine's desire to acknowledge the remaining 'partial' com-

---

[48] P. Batiffol, *Le Catholicisme de s. Augustin* (2nd edn, Paris, 1920), 2 vols., vol. I, p. 266.

[49] We must vary the typographical convention of a capital C here because Augustine is speaking of what is in effect his own communion, although he also believes it to be the universal Church.

munion or 'degree of communion' has a startlingly modern ring. It helps us over the difficulty set out by Cardinal Ratzinger, in answer to the question (posed to him at an interview) as to whether one can use the Pauline formula of 'the Church of Corinth', 'the Church of Rome' in a similar way to describe 'the Church of Wittenberg', when that means the Lutheran church. 'The answer is quite plainly no', he said. '"The Church of Wittenberg" as such does not exist at all.'[50] 'Churches' whose identity is not local but denominational are not churches in the sense Paul meant. They cannot be in communion with one another in exactly the way in which the Pauline churches were. But it does not follow that they are not for that reason unable to be in communion with one another at all. We must come back to all this in a final chapter on 'communion', but it is important to signal its Augustinian context here.

Augustine also had a good deal to say about the ways in which the Church may be both one and many, and about the manner of the communion of the many churches in the one. Here he was much less inclined to accommodate notions of degrees of communion or being partly the Church.

It had from the first been accepted that the one Church might be fully the Church in each place.[51] The many local churches remained one Church in this way, and no breach of communion was implied in their plurality. Nevertheless, there could be complicating factors of nationalism or tribalism or some other form of claim to regional identity and autonomy. There seems to be some such compounding sense in the case of the Donatists[52] and Augustine saw its dangers to communion. He argues instead for a view of plurality in communion which resolves the whole into, as it were, conceptual parts or elements, some of which may be maintained in communion even where others are not. This, as we have seen, enables him to say that a Christian is in unity and communion with the Catholic Church at some points even if not at others.[53] On the other hand, he would not consider such a Donatist or other heretic or schismatic to be 'in' the

---

[50] Ratzinger, pp. 114–15.
[51] That paradox of being fully one in many exemplifications was to be developed strongly in the West in the Middle Ages in connection with the doctrine of transubstantiation. A number of authors of the eleventh and twelfth centuries stress the fact that the same body of Christ *unum et idem numero* is present in every local Eucharist. See *The Works of Gilbert Crispin*, ed. A.S. Abulafia and G.R. Evans (Oxford, 1986), Index.
[52] Discussed by A.H.M. Jones, 'Were ancient heresies national or social movements in disguise?' *Journal of Theological Studies*, 10 (1959), 280–98.
[53] *De Baptismo contra Donatistas*, I.i.2–ii.3, *CSEL* 51, pp. 146 ff.

Church. A church's claim to an autonomy which makes it somehow self-sufficient for salvation is, paradoxically for Augustine, precisely an indication that salvation is not to be found there.

He explains what he means with some care in a letter he wrote about the Donatist sect for his people, seeking to meet a pastoral need for a clear account of the difference between the Donatist position and their own.[54] The catholic Church is the whole Church (*secundum totum*). Members of Christ are joined to one another by the love of unity (*per unitatis caritatem*) and they are united because they belong to the same Head who is Christ Jesus. No one who is not a member of Christ in this way can have Christ's salvation.[55] Those who dissent from the Head are not in the Church. Those who hold everything Scripture says, but who do not communicate with the unity of the Church, are not in the Church. Those who are in some error of faith dissent in such a way that their communion is not with the whole Church everywhere, but with some separated part. It is clear that these are not in the catholic Church.[56] It is thus possible not to be in the Church, and so not to obtain salvation, by a breach of faith or of communion, and also by loyalty to a 'part' of the Church (*pars separata*) which identifies itself as a distinct ecclesial entity over against the universal Church. The weight of 'over against' is crucial here, for the ecclesial distinctness of churches not so identifying themselves is at war with their being in union with the universal Church. Augustine develops the point in the *Contra Epistulam Parmeniani*. He stresses that the Christians in the local Church of Africa must see themselves as joined in unity with the Church spread throughout the world (*toto orbe diffusa*) 'by communion' (*per communionem*).[57] The Donatist position is ecclesially untenable, because it cannot sustain that principle.

The test of universality is thus crucial for Augustine. How can the Donatists be right when they stand against 'so many Churches throughout the world?' he asks.[58] In a correspondence on the question of catholicity with Honoratus, a local Donatist bishop in 398, he argues that while the Catholics can clearly claim to be in communion with the universal Church, the Donatists must hold to the unlikely view that Christ allowed his whole Church on earth to

---

[54] *Epistola ad Catholicos de Secta Donatistarum* ii.2, *CSEL* 52, p. 232.   [55] *Ibid.*
[56] *Ibid.*, iv.7, pp. 238–9.
[57] I.i.1, *CSEL*, 51, pp. 19–20.   [58] *Ibid.*, I.ii.2, pp. 20–1.

disappear, preserving it only in Donatism.[59] The Donatists also have
to say that the prophecy of the universal Church has been fulfilled
and no longer applies.[60] There must be extraordinary special pleading to sustain the Donatist case.

So we find Augustine on the one hand making a case for partial
communion or degrees of communion, and, on the other, maintaining that only in full communion within the one and universal
Church can salvation be found. Augustine argues that real baptism
or real faith or real worship become efficacious for salvation only
when they are within the one catholic Church. Those who join the
Donatists, clearly understanding that they are becoming members of
a sect which distinguishes itself from the catholic Church, do so in
awareness that there must be some uncertainty about what they are
doing, because they know that the Donatist position is a minority
position. They therefore cannot join in full confidence of salvation.[61]
But their faith, worship and sacraments are not entirely outside
communion if it remains true that by returning to the Catholic fold
the Donatists can obtain salvation without otherwise changing their
position or actions.

It is unclear here exactly what Augustine deemed a Church-
dividing issue other than the fact of the will to separate. He recognises the difficulty that views other than his own about baptism and
communion have been held within the Catholic Church, 'in the
unity of the Church itself', by those whose membership of the Body
of Christ is not to be doubted.[62] This was manifest in Cyprian's time,
when 'greater importance and praise were attached to unity' than to
uniformity of opinion.[63] Difference of view on the question of rebaptism was not allowed to divide the Church then, and, as Augustine
sees it, it is highly praiseworthy that Cyprian and his episcopal
colleagues loved unity so deeply that they continued in unity and
communion even with those they believed to be betraying the truth.
And, significantly, they did not deem themselves polluted by them.[64]
Here, again, there would seem to be a not wholly successful attempt
to hold together a doctrine of degrees of communion or partial
communion, with a strong assertion of the view that only within the
single communion of the one Church can salvation be found.

---

[59] See Batiffol, *Catholicisme*, vol. I, p. 145 and *Contra Epistulam Parmeniani*, I.ii.3, p. 22.
[60] *Ibid.*   [61] *De Baptismo contra Donatistas*, I.iv.5 ff., *CSEL* 51, p. 150.
[62] *Ibid.*, VII.i.1, *CSEL* 51, pp. 341 ff.
[63] *Ibid.* V.vii.8, *CSEL* 51, pp. 268–9.   [64] *Ibid.* VII.iii.2, *CSEL* 51, pp. 343 ff.

Augustine certainly saw the force of the notion that some things may be permissible in an emergency situation which would otherwise be disorderly acts or provisions; he also clearly held that division in the Church constitutes the supreme emergency. In his book on the correction of the Donatists, he tells the story of two men together in a house which is falling down. The great need is to save the house. The opposition in his mind lies between those who 'create schism' and 'set altar against altar' and those who seek peace and unity,[65] as he himself tried in practice to do. For those with the *votum unitatis* some embracing of paradoxes will be necessary.

Communion is a relationship. It 'connects'.[66] Augustine's case is that it may connect more or less strongly or fully, by one thread or many. It may exist between Christians outside the Church and Christ, but it cannot make such a connection between them that they are saved unless it also binds them to all other Christians, for it cannot be full communion with Christ himself without also constituting full communion with the whole Body of Christ. In its capacity to connect in differing degrees communion contrasts with unity. There cannot be partial or incomplete unity. That is not unity at all. So unity is not the same thing as communion. Nor, by the same token, can there be partial catholicity or universality. Augustine was clear on that. But he seems to have thought that holiness might be somehow a mixed element in the Church, and in that sense partial. He had no serious quarrel with the Donatists' claims to apostolicity either, so we must infer that he saw apostolicity as possible outside unity and universality, at least to some degree. So the test of the 'partial' or 'incomplete' reads differently in connection with each of three traditional notes of the Church, and as a result the whole concept of 'communion' sits rather oddly with them if Augustine is right that there may be degrees of communion.

He had in mind of course a particular emergency situation, in which an ecclesial body, the Donatists, differed from the Catholics only in their contention that they, not the catholic Church, were the true Church. The breach consisted almost exclusively in the fracturing of communion, between two bodies which were, in faith and sacraments, otherwise at one. What was lacking was the will for unity which Augustine sees as indispensable for full communion.

---

[65] *Psalmus contra Partem Donati*, CSEL 51, pp. 3, 14–17; *Contra Litteras Petiliani*. II.lxviii,153 ff., CSEL 52, p. 99 and cf. Batiffol, *Catholicisme*, vol.I, pp. 137–8.

[66] *Contra Epistulam Parmeniani*, CSEL, 51, p. 19. I.i.1, pp. 19–20.

Other factors enter in in more recent discussions of the nature of communion, made pertinent by 1,500 years of various and often more complex division after Augustine's time. The conception of a separated community as 'partly the Church' continued to have some place during the Middle Ages in the West, in connection with the schism between Latins and Greeks. East and West regarded one another as heretical. It was at issue for William of Tyre in the twelfth century (writing about the crusader presence in the Holy Land) whether the Greeks there were in fact a church, or indeed Christians.[67] Nevertheless, it was customary for Rome at least to refer to the Eastern Churches as 'Church'. The issue Augustine had been addressing was not now urgent, because individuals were not asking in some numbers to be admitted to one community from the other. Aquinas could say in the thirteenth century that heretics who administer the sacraments according to the 'form' of the Church are in the Church as regards that form of the Church which they preserve ('sunt in ea [Ecclesia] quantum ad formam Ecclesiae quam servant').[68] Post-mediaeval Roman Catholics might prefer to say that separated communions can have the notes of the Church except for *Romanitas*.[69] But the possibility of the existence of some imperfect or incomplete, but partly 'true', Church seems to have persisted.

The notion of a community's being 'partly the Church' was urgently needed again in the sixteenth and seventeenth centuries, when the parallels with the Donatist situation were clear to many. There was a general familiarity with the problem of the distinction between the 'mixed' and 'visible pure' Church. Martin Bucer included a historical survey of the Church in his *De Regno Christi*.[70] He acknowledges that, even in its happiest ages, the Church has always contained sinners and 'the churches never lack [God's] chastising and proving by heretics or false brethren or worldly men, nor will they ever, while they are on pilgrimage and away from the Lord' (cf. 2 Corinthians 5: 6). Even at the worst times, when the

---

[67] *Historia rerum in partibus transmarinis gestarum*, ed. R.B.C. Huygens, *CCCM* 63, 63A (Turnholt, 1986), 2 vols., (I.5) and *PL* 201.218.

[68] Aquinas *In IV Sent.* d.25.q.1.a.2 ad 4.

[69] Congar, *Essais oecuméniques*, p. 208. Cf. a recent comment of G. Wainwright in response to the text of the Congregation for the Doctrine of the Faith on Communion, *Catholic International*, 3 (1992), 770, 'For Cardinal Ratzinger a local church is not "wholly Church" unless there is "present in it, as a proper element", the supreme authority of the Church: the episcopal college "together with their head, the Supreme Pontiff, and never apart from him".'

[70] See H. Bornkamm, *Martins Bucers Bedeutung* (Gutersloh, 1952).

Church falls under 'the service of Antichrist', God preserves 'in these churches some echo of his Gospel and Holy Baptism with the invocation of his name'. So some reformers who thought Rome had separated itself from the true apostolic Church by its doctrine and practices, could say that Rome is still a church, because 'there remain in it baptism, the sacraments, the voice and text of the gospel, the sacred scriptures, the ministries, the name of Christ and the name of God'.[71] On this view, being 'partly the Church' seems to consist in the maintenance of some true ministry of the Word and sacraments, but also of the presence of particular individuals, the 'remnant' of 'citizens of the Kingdom' who remain, even where 'these [ministries] are involved in very many grave errors and labour under a weakness of faith'.

This notion of the 'remnant', as the human 'part' of the Church which in its true ecclesiality is preserved now, became newly important. Heinrich Bullinger sees the pattern already in the New Testament churches, in the cases of the Corinthians and Galatians. They 'erred greatly, in doctrine, in faith and in manners: but who doubts that among them there were many who were most sincere followers of the pure doctrine preached by St Paul? Certain remnants (by the grace of God) are reserved, by whom the truth can flourish again and be spread abroad again in every place.'[72] Perhaps the most important notion here is that even a few members who are truly Christ's can make a community ecclesial. That is of course the rationale of Augustine's mixed community. But this stress on human 'carriers' had not been his emphasis.

A slightly different 'patchwork' image of an imperfect Church is proposed by the Anglican Richard Field (1561–1616). He again, like Augustine, holds that the wicked are 'in' but not 'of' the Church, while its true members 'are in the House of God in such a way that they themselves are the House of God'.[73] On this basis it is possible to say that a faction in a given Church is corrupt, while a proportion of its members remain the true Church. 'The Church . . . is not to be charged with the errors and faults of all that in the midst of her did amiss.'[74] Indeed, the Church 'as it comprehendeth the whole number of believers that are and have been since Christ

---

71 Luther on Galatians (1535), *Luther's Works*, ed. J. Pelikan (St Louis, 1963), vol. XXVI 26, 24; Avis, *The Church*, p. 38.

72 Bullinger, *Decades* V.i,27 and 29.   73 Richard Field, *Of the Church*, I.ix, vol. I, p. 30.

74 *Ibid.*, III.viii, vol. I, pp. 171–2.

appeared in the flesh', is absolutely free from all error and ignorance of divine things that are to be 'known by revelation', and even though those 'believers that are and have been since the apostles' time [may] be ignorant in sundry things, which, though they be contained within the compass of revealed truth, yet are not, of necessity, to be expressly known by all that will be saved', the whole Church cannot err 'in any thing of this nature'. The visible Church never 'falleth into heresy'.[75] Field thus takes us from 'remnant' ecclesiology some way towards a theology of indefectibility.

Not all sides saw things this way in the debates of the Reformation and after. A third notion which gained prominence in the sixteenth and seventeenth centuries is that of both being and not-being the Church. Many Protestants denied that Rome was the Church at all, and Rome could not countenance the notion that reforming communities, whether Lutheran, Calvinist, Zwinglian, Anabaptist or any other, were churches. Anglicans, however, were often willing to see the means of grace as remaining in the Church of Rome, even if in a corrupt form, so that Rome is 'partly the Church' in the sense that it both is and is not the Church. In his *The Old Religion*, Joseph Hall (1574–1656) defends Rome's claim to be at least *a* 'true visible Church'. Rome can be said to be a Church of God according to some aspects of her nature (*secundum quid*). In his *A Common Apology against the Brownists*, Hall explains to the Separatists of seventeenth-century England that the Church of England holds Rome to be 'even a visible Church; but unsound, sick, dying ... of ... diseases, not more deadly than infectious'.[76]

He makes an important distinction between churches 'faulty and corrupted' which is a fourth emphasis of this phase of the debate. There can be no calling a body a church if it overthrows all the essentials. But it can in some sense be called a church if it does not. 'Some raze the foundation; others, on the true foundation build timber, hay, stubble: from those we must separate, from these we may not.'[77] 'Does God separate from the faithful soul because it hath some corruptions?'[78]

The Church is, at once, one in respect of the common principles of faith; and yet, in respect of consequences, and that rabble of opinions which they have raked together, so opposed, that it cannot, by any glue of concord, as Cyprian speaketh, nor bind of unity, be conjoined. That which Rome holds

---

[75] *Ibid.*, IV.1, vol. II, pp. 391–3. [76] Hall, *Works*, vol. IX.48. [77] *Ibid.*, p. 10.
[78] *Ibid.*

with us makes it a church; that which it obtrudes upon us makes it heretical.[79]

If we move to more recent discussion, we still find theologians wrestling with the conception that a church from which their own is separated may still be in some sense a true church, but only somehow 'partly' the Church. Writing of the Orthodox Churches in terms of 'similarity', the Roman Catholic G. Baum commented in 1965 that 'there has never been any hesitation on the part of the Roman Church, at least in the area of practice and policy, to acknowledge them as churches. Their doctrinal, sacramental and hierarchical similarity to the Catholic Church has always been recognised, even if theologians have refused to let this qualify their understanding of the Catholic Church.'[80] A radical distinction is made in chapter 3 of the Decree on Ecumenism of the Second Vatican Council, between the Eastern Churches, which have in the eyes of the Council preserved the apostolic episcopate and the fullness of sacramental life; and the estranged ecclesial communities of the West which have not. In the discussions surrounding this highly important Decree at the council itself the main lines of thought involved a recognition that 'there are many communities of Christians in the world that proclaim the Gospel of Christ, announce the kingdom of God and celebrate baptism and the other sacraments',[81] through which 'we know that God saves and sancti-fies men'. At the same time there is an awareness of the difficulty of determining 'the relationship between the catholic Church and these Christian communions'.[82]

The model which is most readily adopted at present tends to be one of 'diversity'.[83] There is no question but that such communions may 'represent, produce and foster the life of grace', so 'that we must acknowledge the Holy Spirit present in their midst, making use of them as a means of salvation'. So they are 'in all truth "Churches"' ... even if in an analogous sense and less perfectly than' the Roman Catholic Church itself and perhaps the Orthodox Churches. (Degrees of perfection in the Church are clearly assumed to be a possibility here.) No clear statement resulted which would make it possible to say which of the communities in the West were 'churches'

[79] *Ibid.*, pp. 295–6.
[80] G. Baum, 'The ecclesial reality of the other Churches', *Concilium*, 4 (1965), 34–46, p. 34.
[81] Baum, 'The ecclesial reality', p. 34.   [82] *Ibid.*   [83] See further chapter 2 below.

and which 'ecclesial communities'.[84] A notion of partialness manifestly emerged, with yet another shading. The Church is seen as an *éminence grise*, a great presence, which may be more, or less, 'there' in a given community. As Baum puts it, the Christian Church 'is also present, according to various degrees of institutional imperfections, in other Christian Churches'.[85] These Churches may be seen as 'partial', he argued, in the sense that the 'gifts which make up the Church in their totality' exist in them 'with greater or lesser density'.[86] That would imply a shadowiness or insubstantiality, as though the Church were bodied forth in them only comparatively faintly. An enormously important concession is made. But the Council did not get far enough to be able to say why they are not wholly Church and thus automatically in communion. Again, we must come back to this and the post-Vatican II discussion in chapter 6.

So Augustine's problem is still with us. There are strong reasons in a fallen world for hesitating to 'unchurch' those communities which have not strayed far apart but which have in some measure lost communion with one another. Not the least of these would be the difficulty of agreeing, in the present state of the ecumenical endeavour, who was to do the 'unchurching'. Some doctrine that it is possible to be 'partly the Church' is ecumenically indispensable as an interim solution to the problem of our mutual recognition as churches, although it cannot be the right way forward in the long term. More recent ideas about the provisionality of all exemplifications of the Church are more helpful, because they allow us to stress that all the churches are *in via* and not perfectly the Church while they remain divided. We shall be exploring this point further as we go on.

The ultimate solution must lie in unity in one Church. The value of looking further into the history of concepts of being 'partly the Church' would seem to lie in the way it throws up their very unsatisfactoriness and inherent ecclesiological anomalies, and makes it plain that no solution along these lines will do. We have somehow to come to the shared understanding that Church is Church.

That brings us conveniently to the questions about 'wholeness' or

---

[84] *Ibid.*   [85] *Ibid.*, p. 38.

[86] That is, Scripture, the life of grace, faith, hope, charity, the interior gifts of the Spirit, the visible elements, sacramental and hierarchical. *Ibid.*, p. 40. Some involved in the debates disliked the idea of assessing churches by counting up the number of gifts which they have in common with the Roman Catholic Church. *Ibid.*

'completeness' which must balance these issues about the partial and thus to the notion of 'universality' or 'catholicity'.

Catholicity or universality

When a new church is founded it does not make the Church more universal, more whole, more catholic. There is simply a realisation in that place of what is already the 'whole' Church.[87] Nothing more is realised spiritually at a higher level than is realised in local churches.[88] The Church is 'catholic at Antioch', 'catholic at Corinth', and so on.

The New Testament has a strong sense of this completeness of the accomplishment of God's purposes in a given place, and of its continuity with that same completeness or wholeness of accomplishment elsewhere. It is with that picture of things that 1 Corinthians 1: 2 speaks of the community of saints in the *koinonia* of Christ. But the word 'catholic' itself appears only in the canonical titles to certain Epistles in the New Testament. So no real weight can be placed terminologically on the Scriptural warrant.[89] *Katholikos* does not at first have the sense 'catholic' will have later.[90] Nevertheless, the theme of wholeness and completeness persists in patristic sources. Cyril of Jerusalem has catholicity as 'plenitude' or 'wholeness'.[91] In Augustine we find 'universaliter perfecta et in nullo claudicat',[92] with something of the same notion in Vincent of Lérins.[93] 'Catholic' carries the sense of 'integrity' as well as of 'wholeness' and also of 'fullness',[94]

---

[87] See on early local churches Ekkart Sauser, *Woher kommt Kirche? Ortskirchen der Frühzeit und Kirchenbewusstsein heure* (Frankfurt, 1978).

[88] See H. de Lubac, *Les Eglises particulières dans l'église universelle* (Paris, 1971), Antonio M. Rouco Varela, 'Iglesia Universal-Iglesia Particular', *Ius Canonicum*, 22 (1982), 231–2, W. Aymans, 'Die communio Ecclesiarum als Gestaltgesetz der einen Kirche', *Archiv für Kirchengeschichte*, 39 (1970), 81–2.

[89] Etymologically, 'catholic' and 'universal' are, respectively, the Greek and Latin faces of a single notion. But they have ceased to be quite interchangeable. In Western usage 'universal' has become an equivocal term and 'catholic', although it too can be confusing, as referring to the 'Roman Catholic' or to the 'whole' Church, tends to be preferred. Y. Congar, *L'Eglise une, sainte, catholique et apostolique* (Paris, 1970), especially pp. 149–79. Hans urs von Balthasar, *Katholisch: Aspekte des Mysteriums* (Einsiedeln, 1975). A. Dulles, *The Catholicity of the Church* (Oxford, 1985).

[90] *Ad Smyrnaeans* 8.2.   [91] *Catecheses* 18.23, *PG* 33.1044.

[92] *De Genesi ad Litteram Lib. Imp.* I.4, *PL* 34.221.

[93] *Commonitorium* 2.3, ed. R.S. Moxon (Cambridge, 1915).

[94] W. Beinert, Salamanca, pp. 603–41: 'The work which the fullness of the grace of God has promised to the whole of created reality and that the Church of Jesus Christ, as the sacrament of this event of salvation is the meeting place of grace and the world.'

and of *das ganz heil*, the whole of salvation brought to the whole of the world.[95]

All this implies a soteriology.[96] To belong to the body of Christ is by definition to believe oneself to participate in his saving work, for the Church is the community of salvation.[97] As Bede puts it, the Church is the Mediator of the Word and salvation within history because it is 'one nature' with Christ the Mediator.[98] There remain the complex difficulties touched on elsewhere in this study about the freedom of the Holy Spirit to accomplish God's purposes outside the Church as well as within it, but the substantial principle was secure in Western patristic and mediaeval thinking, that the 'catholicity' of the Church must embrace those purposes in their wholeness.

In a world in time the full accomplishment of God's purposes must involve a process. It must also have a terminus, even if that terminus may lie in the *eschaton*. We must see the line of time as running through catholicity as an integral part of it; and the question of the Church's continuity through time as directly related to that of 'local and universal' in the Church. The coming into being of a new church at a point in time is analogous to its coming into being in a given place.

Two significant difficulties stand in the way of ecumenical progress here. Different traditions tend to cling to different periods as definitive for them. For the Orthodox a particular stretch of the past, the period of the Ecumenical Councils, is of especial importance, and the 'process' of tradition since cannot be weighed equally with it in Orthodox theology. For many Protestant churches the period when they came independently into being, especially the

---

[95] Vatican II's *LG* begins by defining the Church as 'sacrament' not only of 'ultimate union with God', but also of 'the unity of the human race'. Pope Paul VI in the Apostolic Exhortation *Evangelii Nuntiandi* says salvation is 'this great gift of God which is liberation from everything which oppresses man'. 'The Church proclaims ... a universal plan of salvation.' E. de Halleux, Salamanca, pp. 23–41, notes that Syriac has to transliterate *katholikos* into *qatoliqi* or *quatoliqa* so the idea is lacking in the language.

[96] Though Muller stresses, Salamanca, pp. 457–88, that catholicity is not limited to the soteriological aspect inherent in it.

[97] See E. Sullivan, Salamanca, on 'integral salvation', pp. 643–9, and on the union of the human race with God.

[98] *Venerabilis Bedae Opera*, ed. J. Giles (London, 1844), vol. III, p. 249, and E.P. Echlin, 'Bede and the Church', *Irish Theological Quarterly*, 40 (1973), 354. It is on this basis that Bede himself can hold the broadly Augustinian position that those persevering in faith and action in the Church will be saved, while those separated from it in faith or action or both will perish. Bede, *In Principium Genesis*, *CCSL*, CXVIIA.111, and cf. Echlin, 'Bede and the Church', 357.

period of influence of a founder or leader, can seem crucial.[99] There can be difficulties in assessing the providential purpose for the catholicity of the Church of the division involving the Protestant Churches of the Reformation.[100] Protestants have in the past been likely to see it as a good and necessary shaking up of complacencies and correction of abuses; Roman Catholics as a damaging mistake.

However compelling the claims of history in time, the eschatological dimension should never be lost sight of. Bede transmitted the conception of the universal Church which he found in Augustine and Gregory the Great, as including the angels and the just among men who have already passed into the presence of Christ.[101] So if we want to say that the catholicity of the Church consists in the completeness of the accomplishment of God's purposes, we must think in terms somewhat like Augustine's *perfectio currens*. That is to say, we must envisage a catholicity over time which embraces mistakes, and periods of ecclesial imperfection,[102] but which is nevertheless in its tendency and under God, still catholicity, because its full scale stretches into eternity, where these will be resolved into fulfilment and completeness. This view of things is crucial to the notion of provisionality with which I shall be working in this study.

As well as a linear 'completing' of this sort, there is an inter-relationship of churches in the world in a given period, making up a catholicity which consists in their sheer being together as one. Do we wish to argue that the catholicity of the Church consists in something more than, or other than, this *communio ecclesiarum*,[103] or that the *communio ecclesiarum* is an entity somehow greater than the individual churches which make it up? (That is a rather different claim, for 'communion' is itself certainly more than 'sum'.)[104] If we want to say that catholicity is more than a collective property or attribute or quality of the local churches, we may want to say that it is in some sense its 'substance',[105] the very reality of the Church. Thus when Ignatius of Antioch calls the Church 'catholic',[106] he is, arguably,

[99] See p. 146–50. [100] Ratzinger, p. 109.

[101] E.P. Echlin, 'Bede and the Church', 357.

[102] See Lionel Wickham, Salamanca, pp. 193–203, on whether a heritage of 'false history' can nevertheless make a true tie.

[103] W. Colombo, Salamanca, p. 3. [104] See chapter 6, p. 295.

[105] See G. Beinert and W. Colombo, Salamanca, pp. 489–93 and 603–41, on this. The underlying philosophical principle here was explored by Augustine and Boethius in their discussion of the applicability of Aristotle's categories in Christian theology.

[106] Ignatius of Antioch, *Ad Smyrnaeans*, 8.2, *Lettres*, ed. P.T. Camelot, Sources chrétiennes, 10 (Paris, 1958).

saying something about its nature. Similarly 'one', 'holy', 'apostolic' assert not qualities or accidents of the Church but something about its being. Here, too, there is provisionality because the being together as one is patently not yet a visible reality, and cannot be said to be an invisible reality while hearts are mutually hostile.

If unity, holiness, apostolicity, catholicity are in some way substantive in the Church and not mere properties, that strengthens the case for the view that they can have force to hold together, to be the glue in, the Church, and even to draw people into the Church.[107] In an address to the theological College of Halki in April 1965, the Roman Catholic Cardinal Bea stressed the way in which unity may do this. 'It is in fact ... unity (... of all those who know Christ and believe in him ...) which will bring the world to faith, as Christ himself tells us in his sacerdotal prayer when he entreats the Father in the unity of his followers, so that by this "the world may believe that you have sent me" (John 16.21).' 'Unity is the sign by which the world is to know and recognise the divine mission of Christ, to believe in him, and to find its own salvation in him.'[108]

It can be argued that the visibility or mutual recognition of ecclesiality and ministry, and a certain self-consciousness of catholicity in the Churches, have both historically and conceptually assisted the development of the very idea of catholicity.[109] Catholicity has always been related to mutual recognition. Pastors ordain one another in the early church (which implies succession).[110] The college of bishops in the Roman Catholic Church has been seen as helping to 'build up the Church as a living organism which grows in living cells and is a unity'.[111] On this view, and here we turn to the present-day Roman Catholic formulation, 'individual bishops share in the government of the universal Church not by being represented in some central organ but by leading as shepherds their particular churches which together form and carry in themselves the whole Church and in doing so lead the church as a whole'. It is 'in governing the particular Church that the bishops share in governing the universal church and not otherwise ... the nature of the Church ... consists of the working together of the plenary powers of the

---

[107] See W. Colombo, Salamanca, pp. 489–93, pp. 1–2 on *potestas/affectus* in this connection.

[108] Stormon, pp. 99–100. This principle must be intimately dependent on that which holds that there is no salvation outside the unity of the Church.

[109] See Michael A. Fahey, 'Ecclesiae sorores ac fratres: Sibling Communion in the Pre-Nicene Christian Era', *Catholic Theological Society of America, Proceedings*, 36 (1981),15–38.

[110] See H. Chadwick, Salamanca, pp. 679–90.   [111] *LG* 22 ff.

primacy', which expresses the Church's unity in diversity, with the living diversity of the local churches, whose bishop is indeed 'bishop of the catholic Church (*episcopus ecclesiae catholicae*) by virtue of the fact that he heads the Catholic Church in his Church and heads it as something specifically Catholic'.[112]

This theology, well developed in the Roman Catholic Communion and broadly acceptable to Orthodox and Anglicans, has the disadvantage of using language unfamiliar and even uncongenial to churches which have, for example, systems of collegial presbyteral *episcope*; and so it is less ecumenically useful than it might be. But it also signals the danger of conflating two usages of 'catholic': to refer to the Roman Catholic Church and to speak of the universal Church. In a future united Church the adjective 'Roman' would be unnecessary, even if that Church were to acknowledge in some form the primacy of the Bishop of Rome. In the present state of division where the ecclesiality of churches not in communion with Rome can nevertheless be recognised, we have to make a conceptual distinction here. Here, too, there are self-evidently provisional aspects of the state of things.

It can be seen at once if we broach issues of this sort that we shall have to get clear what we mean by 'local churches' and what relationships we understand to exist between the local and the catholic Church. That is the next task.

'LOCAL' CHURCH

The elements which make, or are present in, 'Church' must be seen as generating or present in each individual 'church' too, or it cannot be 'Church'. But there must also be differentiating principles, which make churches in some sense distinct ecclesial entities.[113] Such distinct entities cannot be distinguished by anything essential to their being 'Church', except insofar as diversity itself may be said to be of the *esse* of the Church. In a few pages we shall be considering the case for the ecclesial wholeness, authenticity, integrity, of individual churches. But first it is important to look at the implications of the 'elements' approach for characterising the individual church.

---

[112] *LG* 22 ff.
[113] Valentini, *Il nuovo Popoli*, p. 56, cf. C. Welch, *The Reality of the Church* (New York, 1958), p. 48, on the Church's 'humanly subjective pole', and J. Ratzinger, *The Principles of Catholic Theology* (San Francisco, 1987), p. 312 on *Gemeinde* as 'an anthropological reality'.

There must be limitations to the diversity of local churches, if they are to be truly churches. Diversity cannot be right if it is divisive, for that would break the bond of charity in the body of Christ. Some contemporary viewpoints suggest that the elements which make a church 'local' have to be seen perhaps as contingent, human, changeable, belonging to a 'socio-cultural order', and not to the divine and unchanging in the Church.[114] On this view, although a community will be made up of people who come to it with a language and culture and pattern of life of their own, arguably 'no culture can make the Church; only the Word of God, the Eucharist and charisms can make the Church'.[115] It was in this conviction that Pope John Paul II spoke to the bishops of Zimbabwe in 1992 of their 'desire that all things African should find their true significance in Christ'.[116] Nevertheless, some of the elements found in a local culture must obviously be more than incidental. That would be the case on the negative side if they were to prove wholly incompatible with the Christian faith (for example, polytheism). But for many, especially in the Third World, a sense of corporate cohesion which makes them Church in that place will also make at least some aspects of their local culture integral to their being Christians. In the same address to the bishops of Zimbabwe, the Pope commented,

My visits to Africa have made me aware of the many elements in the social and cultural life of the continent which can be fitting vehicles for the communion of the Gospel and the Church's teaching, just as there are other elements in need of healing through contact with the grace of Christ Jesus ... Inculturation, which is not merely a question of externals, matures when the Good News of Christ's triumph over suffering and death effectively shapes the thinking and everyday life of Christians.

The difficulty thus posed, of determining where there ought to be diversity, and where it becomes destructive of ecclesiality, is ecumenically pressing on several fronts. So the first task is to try to

---

[114] de Lubac, *Les Eglises* pp. 43–5 and the Roman Catholic International Theological Commission, *Select Themes in Ecclesiology*, vol. V. p. 1, *Texts and Documents* (1969–85) (San Francisco, 1989), p. 282.

[115] G. Colombo, 'La teologia della Chiesa locale', in *La Chiesa locale* (Bologna, 1969), pp. 17–38 especially pp. 32–8.

[116] 'Proclaim the Gospel boldly', *Catholic International*, 3 (1992), 80–6.

define in this climate what it is that makes an individual 'church' an ecclesial entity.[117]

The gathered portion of humanity

Harekes' contention that a Eucharist celebrated in a hospital or prison or on a journey or even in solitude would make the participant(s) a local church,[118] raises not only the issue of duration in connection with the 'local' church, but also that of its size. In the seventeenth century, the Anglican Joseph Hall thought that 'the number makes no difference to the essence' to such a degree that he was prepared to ask, 'What is a Christian but an abridgement of the Church, or a Church contracted into one bosom?'[119] But here he went beyond the rule of the 'two or three gathered together' of Matthew 18:20. It has been almost universally accepted, as a foundation principle of ecclesiology, that a church must be a community of people, however small, for it is only in community that the elements we have been considering can be present and operative.

The most ancient idea of such a community was that it was the Church in a place (a city or region), which could be identified geographically. Thus we find 'the Church which is at Corinth' (1 Corinthians 1:2; 2 Corinthians 1:1). *Ecclesia* is also used in the New Testament for the Church in a larger area, such as Judaea, Galilee, Samaria (Acts 9:31). But in the Church of later ages, 'place' has perforce sometimes become a metaphorical expression. Today, it can cover a variety of forms of common bond or common interest.

Because they can point to a single worshipping congregation as the basic unit of church life, the denominations which have retained

---

[117] Terms to denote individual churches are at present in a process of evolution into a technical terminology. (See the discussion in Faris.) 'Local', 'particular', 'specific' and others are therefore impossible to use with consistency. I have kept a good deal to 'individual' for that reason. In choosing the term *particularis*, the *Codex Iuris Canonici* of 1983 uses the language of Vatican II. E.g. *LG* 23. 27, 45 and *CD* 11(3), which develops a dense theology of the *ecclesia particularis* and clearly identifies it with the diocese. It gives to the *ecclesia particularis* and its analogues a position and centrality not given to any other form of community or association in the Church, and it sets the term *particularis* on the way to becoming a technical term of ecclesiology. It is nevertheless still the case that the term 'particular' says nothing about the individuating principles of a specific Church, and that it does not, in itself, insist on territory. See de Lubac, *Les Eglises*. W. Beinert, 'Dogmenhistorische Anmerkungen zum Begriff "Partikularkirche"', *Theologie und Philosophie*, 50 (1975), 66, says the primary usage of *Teilkirchen* is to refer to dioceses with infra- or supra-diocesan groups being the secondary or tertiary meanings.

[118] Harekes, 'The Local Church', 143.

[119] *The Peacemaker*, ed. P. Wynter, *Works* (Oxford, 1863), vol. VI, p. 602.

a strong 'congregational' emphasis can claim to be 'local' in a sense which the episcopally based local churches cannot so straightforwardly do. (Here 'presbyteral' patterns have a somewhat intermediate place.) Nevertheless, the underlying meaning of 'local' in 'local church' must have some connotation of the 'gathering' of the community. In the truly local fellowship, God's people meet for worship in his name. This 'coming together' of the gathered community lies at the heart of the ecclesiology of all shades of Christian opinion, though it may be expressed with differing emphases and coloration. Certain points were stressed, for example in the sixteenth century by the Thirty-Nine Articles of the Church of England: 'The visible Church is a congregation of faithful men, in which the pure Word of God is preached, and the Sacraments be duly ministered according to Christ's ordinance in all those things which are requisite to the same' (XIX). Very similar statements can be found in the Confessions of faith of Lutheran and Reformed Churches from the same period.[120] Preaching and celebrating of sacraments are here seen to depend on 'congregating'. In exactly the same terms, the Second Vatican Council says that the Church of Christ is truly present in all legitimate local congregations of the faithful, where the faithful are gathered together (*congregantur*) in the preaching of the Gospel and in the celebration of the mystery of the Lord's Supper.[121] The notion of 'gathering' is also important in recent Orthodox–Roman Catholic conversations.[122]

Three themes have traditionally dominated in the Christian idea of gathering. The first is broadly sacramental. That is, 'a' church is an ecclesially complete whole in which the means of grace are present and in which the Christian may know himself or herself to be a member of the body of Christ.[123] The second is more specifically eucharistic.

The clearest human reflection of the Church's divine vocation is the Christian community united to celebrate the Eucharist, gathered by its common faith, in all its variety of persons and functions, around a single table, under a single president, ... to hear the Gospel proclaimed and to

[120] See Avis, *The Church*   [121] Cf. *LG* 26.
[122] Statement of 1988, Introduction, 4, in *One in 2000*, ed. P. McPartlan (London, 1993).
[123] Lanne, 'L'Eglise locale' 46–66, discusses the drawbacks to the simple device of using communion with the Bishop of Rome as the test of such a community. The proviso is of course indispensable that the celebration of the Lord's Supper is a unity in which all Christians everywhere are joined. See J.M.R. Tillard, 'L'Eglise de Dieu est une communion', *Irénikon*, 53 (1980), 451–68, 452ff.

share in the sacramental reality of the Lord's flesh and blood, ... and so to manifest those gathered there as 'partakers of the divine nature'.[124]

There is a strong emphasis here on the 'gathering' taking place about the minister, who presides at the Eucharist. A third usage, especially stressed by many of the sixteenth-century reformers in the West and their heirs, emphasises gathering to hear the Word of God preached. A modern balance would bring all three together as constitutive for the gathering which makes Church locally. But it would also be necessary to add some idea of continuity in the gathering. To meet once for a Eucharist is not to be a church, although it is to be the Church.

The 'local' church, with such continuity of life, as it was most characteristically found and understood throughout Christendom from an early stage until the sixteenth century,[125] was the diocese. It began as the sort of local worshipping community which can literally be described as 'gathered', with an identity as a church which depends on its being united, with its pastor, in its sacramental life, and in the ministry of the Word. 'Be careful', says Ignatius (*c*.35–*c*.107), 'to observe a single Eucharist. For there is one flesh of our Lord, Jesus Christ, and one cup of his blood that makes us one ... The Church is the people united ... to its shepherd. From this you should know that the bishop is in the Church and the Church in the bishop.'[126]

In theological and ecclesiological principle the diocese has remained such a community, and is so today. But that is no longer the reality. In practice in due course the territorial spread, or the number of Christians, became in most places too great for it to be possible for all the members of the community to meet regularly as a single congregation. The minister with pastoral oversight (the primary meaning of *episkopos*) began to need to delegate certain pastoral responsibilities to helper-priests. They could have indi-

---

124 *Agreed Statement on Conciliarity and Primacy in the Church*, Orthodox–Roman Catholic Consultation in the United States, *Greek Orthodox Theological Review*, 35 (1990), 217–20, para. 3. This is echoed by talk of the 'bishop of each local sacramental centre' as 'not replacing, or acting as a substitute for, the personal priesthood of Christ in the Church. On the contrary, he is the image of Christ at the particular sacramental centre over which he presides; and an image does not take the place of what is absent, but actually participates in, and makes visible, the invisible and truly present reality of which it is the image', P. Sherrard, *The Greek East and the Latin West* (London, 1959), p. 81, quoted in D.W. Allen and A.M. Allchin, 'Primacy and collegiality: an Anglican View', *Journal of Ecumenical Studies*, 2 (1965), 63–80, p. 64.

125 *Episcopal Ministry*, paras. 41 and 51ff.   126 *To the Philadelphians*, 4 and *Letter* lxvi.8

vidual pastoral charge of a series of smaller local congregations which were of a size which could actually 'gather'. So it was then no longer the case that Ignatius' ideal of the bishop with his people became a visible reality in each act of worship together.

The resulting more complex structure has remained, with variations, fundamental to Roman Catholic, Anglican and Orthodox local churches. The diocese can certainly still be described as 'a portion of humanity',[127] having its unity in its relationship to its Head who is Christ, and as united to its pastor, to whom is entrusted the care of that portion of the people. But in episcopal churches, in the case of the present-day diocese, the approach which sees the ecclesial entity we call a 'local church' in terms of the people who make it up by actually meeting seems to present some difficulties. That makes it necessary to justify its continuance. Its strongest claim is that it has built into it a means of uniting the three planes of the Church's life; the local, the universal now and the continuing.[128]

Partly under the pressure of this development towards a figurative gathering of the diocese, 'gathering' itself comes historically to have an extended or even metaphorical meaning, so that it is no longer necessarily a literal meeting, but as with the term local, rather some form of community of interest and a sense of common identity which is seen as constituting the local church. Here we need to work out, as it were, from the literal to the extended sense of 'territory' to begin to see what has been happening.

Territorial 'place': the diocese and the congregation

The traditional, episcopally led, local diocesan Church remains essentially territorial. A much-cited verse in the ancient Church was Proverbs 22:28: 'Ne transgrediaris terminos antiquos, quos posuerunt patres tui.' The principle it was seen to imply was that the territorial arrangements about the existence of boundaries between local churches were absolute for the existence of those churches and had permanence. Canon 34 of the Canons of the Apostles, which belong at the latest to the fourth century, stresses the same point. Each bishop, it says, must limit his activities as a bishop to his diocese and therefore to territories which are subject to him. In this

---

[127] The present Roman Catholic *Codex Iuris Canonici* uses this expression in defining a diocese, Canon 369, and see a little later for discussion.
[128] See *Episcopal Ministry*, which develops this theme.

form, the rule was transmitted, especially through Gratian in the twelfth century, to join the common stock of assumptions of the West at large, as well as being held securely in the East in Orthodoxy.

The bishop's jurisdiction is understood to run strictly within his territorial diocese. By ancient regulation, a priest coming from another place must bring testimonial letters from his own bishop, and cannot exercise his ministry in the new diocese without licence from the local bishop. A diocesan bishop cannot himself exercise episcopal functions outside his own diocese without the express or at least presumed consent of the local bishop.[129]

Just as it is in Orthodoxy and Anglicanism, in modern Roman Catholic canon law the diocese, thus territorially conceived, is still seen as the basic unit of the Church's life; it is given the label of 'particular church'. The diocese is there defined as a

> portion of the people of God, entrusted for pastoral care to a bishop, with the cooperation of the presbyterate, so that, adhering to its pastor and by him gathered (*congregata*) in the Holy Spirit through Gospel and Eucharist, it constitutes (*constituat*) a particular Church in which the one, holy, catholic and apostolic Church of Christ is truly present and operative (*in qua vere inest et operatur*).[130]

This places the stress upon the human community with its pastor rather than upon the location, but the territoriality of the diocese is insisted upon by implication in the series of parallel or analogical structures listed in adjacent canons. A 'territorial prelature' or a 'territorial abbacy' is once more 'a portion of the people of God', established within certain territorial boundaries, and entrusted to a prelate or abbot, who has the authority of a diocesan bishop within it.[131] The normal rule is that a portion of the people of God which comprises a diocese (or its equivalent) is 'limited to a definite territory' in such a way that it comprises all the faithful in that geographical area.

That is a rule which has, in principle, always been important, even though the actual gatherings to hear the Word and for the Eucharist will tend to take place in parishes and the people's sense of

---

[129] *Codex Iuris Canonici* (1983), Canon 390.   [130] Canon 369.

[131] Canon 370. An apostolic vicariate or an apostolic prefecture is again a 'portion of the people of God', but one which has not, for some reason 'yet' been made into a diocese, and in which an apostolic vicar or prefect acts as in the place of a diocesan bishop, but governing it in the name of the Pope. Sometimes there are 'serious reasons' why a portion of the people of God may not become a diocese, and then such a 'portion' may be governed in the Pope's name by an 'apostolic administrator'. Canons 370–1.

being 'gathered' may actually be stronger there than it is when they are gathered about their bishop.

It is, in other words, an idea much stretched in practice. In the divided Church it is almost universally broken. That is to say, in any given territorial area, especially in the West, Roman Catholics, Orthodox, Anglicans, Methodists, Reformed, Baptists, Pentecostalists and others may have congregations which overlap with or are geographically superimposed on one another, and there is no theoretical or practical superstructure which can effect a single truly local 'gathering'.

In Roman Catholic canon law, there is some provision for the fact that in certain circumstances the same territory may contain another diocesan ('particular') church, of a different rite, alongside the first.[132] This provision is designed to accommodate the case of Eastern rite communities which, for historical reasons, exist geographically and thus literally 'alongside' churches of the Roman rite in parts of eastern Europe.[133] The law does not, however, as framed, intend to make provision for equal recognition of the presence of (for example) Anglican dioceses which overlap territorially with those of the Roman Catholic Church. It does not make a concession which would go against the principle that a territorially defined church cannot have two heads or a diocese two bishops. It says, rather, that territorial place may coexist in emergency situations with a culturally defined or a metaphorical 'place' defined by adherence to a tradition.[134] Neither the Orthodox nor the Anglican system makes even as much provision. For non-episcopal churches it is not an issue because it is for such ecclesial communities not a *geographical*

---

[132] Canon 372.

[133] A parallel and matching definition is given by the Second Vatican Council in its decree on the Catholic Eastern Churches. The Catholic Church is said to be made up of the faithful who are organically united in the Holy Spirit by the same faith, the same sacraments and the same government. They combine into different groups which are held together by their hierarchy, and so form particular Churches or rites. 'Between those Churches there is such a wonderful bond of union that this variety in the Universal Church, so far from diminishing its unity, rather serves to emphasise it.' The pastor's relationship to his flock thus stands in its turn in a relationship to other pastors within the universal Church. Each portion of God's people is gathered in the local pastoral relationship, but all are united in this way, and local diversity does not divide. Warfare in the early 1990s in the former Yugoslavia between Orthodox Serbs and Roman Catholic Croats; and resentments among the Russian Orthodox at what has been seen to be proselytising have made for much unresolved pain in relations between Orthodoxy and Roman Catholicism.

[134] The notion is perhaps analogous with that which allows two apparently contradictory passages of Scripture both to be true, by reading one as a literal statement and the other as figurative.

problem to have several churches out of communion with one another in the same area.

There is in the series of Roman Catholic Canons dealing with the diocese also a provision for continuity over time in the phrase *stabiliter erecta*.[135] In this way, the dimension of time can be seen to be as fundamental as that of place, and indeed to constitute a unity with it. We shall come to time a little further on, but it is worth noting the point here.

A problem arises over the natural human size for a local church. Huge dioceses make many if not most bishops mainly administrators. In practice today, most direct pastoral ministries are carried out by priests in parishes.[136] It is these in which the faithful often feel the most lively sense of belonging to a worshipping community which is a 'portion of humanity'. People most readily feel themselves to belong to something small enough to know in that way. It is uniquely the character of the Church that belonging to the small 'known' community is also belonging to the whole. But realisation of the greater belonging will depend to a large degree on there being a real sense of local belonging.[137] The principle that the bishop remains pastor of all congregations in his diocese saves the concept of the 'local' for episcopal churches, and keeps it territorial. But it is not always easy for Christians in a diocese to feel their primary attachment to the larger ecclesial entity when they know their own parish and its priest much better, and worship in that smaller 'local church' week by week.

But the fact remains that there are, structurally speaking, only two grand options. One is to have a multiplicity of individual churches which deem themselves to be mystically one Church, but do not defer to one another, and agree with one another only piecemeal, with all the probable consequences of dispute and division inherent in that. The other is to have a multiplicity of individual churches which deem themselves to be one Church and allow

---

135 Canon 368.

136 See K. Rahner, 'Pastoral-theological observations on episcopacy in the teaching of Vatican II', *Theological Investigations* VI (Baltimore, 1969), p. 366. See, too, Afanasieff in A. Plank, *Die Eucharistieversammlung als Kirche* (Wurzburg, 1980), p. 110 on the idea that there can really be no such thing as the metalocal. It has also been suggested by Corral that too fixedly local a belonging may lead to endogamy, where the bishop is born and dies in the diocese of which he becomes bishop.

137 See J.M.R. Tillard, *L'Eglise d'Eglises*, p. 149. See, too, L. Bouyer, *L'Eglise de Dieu*, (Paris, 1970), pp. 618–26 and, for another view, Lanne, 'L'Eglise locale', 490–2.

some visible expression of that oneness and have means of acting and living together.

LOCALITY AND CONTINUITY THROUGH TIME

'Tradition refuses to submit to the small and arrogant oligarchy of those who merely happen to be walking about.'[138] Discussions of the relationship of local churches to one another and to the one Church of Christ are necessarily conducted by those who happen to be walking about. Christians of past and future cannot take part. In some communities the views of past members are taken into account as far as possible, by consulting their writings. That is perhaps most notably the case in Orthodoxy. But the sense of the importance of doing so can be strong, too, in Protestant Churches. For example, when Lutherans appeal to their 'Confessional' texts of the sixteenth century (such as the Augsburg Confession), they are assuming that their churches' continuing identity has everything to do with the past of the community. So before we leave the literally and territorially 'local' for the metaphorical, we need to note that it is also important to see continuity of a single church through time as constituting a form and an aspect of the 'gathering' which will make it a single ecclesial entity.[139]

It is now becoming commonplace to speak of an ecclesial pattern of 'event', 'state', 'process'.[140] That is proving especially helpful in connection with baptism, whether it takes place at infancy or in the adult believer,[141] because it makes it possible to understand how the unrepeatable event of baptism may stand in a flexible relation to conversion, to the Christian's state of forgiven-ness and reconciliation with God and membership of the Body of Christ, and also to the process of healing in the sinner's soul. This account of baptism makes time a dimension and means of the sacrament's working. Side by side with that understanding of the act constitutive for the individual's becoming a member of the Church, we may put the

---

[138] G.K. Chesterton, quoted in T. Radcliffe, 'The demands of the Mass', *The Tablet* (1 December 1990), p. 1545.

[139] It is central to the Reformed tradition, which has seen the Church as preserved by God through time 'against the rage of the whole world'. A.C. Cochrane, 'The mystery of the continuity of the Church: a study in Reformed Symbolics', *Journal of Ecumenical Studies*, 2 (1965), 81–96, p. 82.

[140] P. Komonchak, Salamanca, 559–91.

[141] The difference of position on these points is conveniently set out in the Lima text of the World Council of Churches on Baptism, Eucharist and ministry, *Growth*, pp. 472ff.

question of the role of continuity in time as a necessary element in the making of a church.

A church must come from the Church Christ founded, and cannot be invented as something new. But many Protestant communities in whose identity the debates of the sixteenth century have a part would take a different view of the character of the necessary 'continuity' from those churches which claim to trace their history uninterrupted through time from the beginning; they would prefer to point to a 'being true to the Gospel' as the real indicator of continuity, and claim that it is able to operate even where there has been an interruption in the sequence of visible ecclesial life, and in the ordering of ministers. A major difficulty here concerns the meaning of 'apostolic succession'. If that is taken to require a linear succession in which there has been laying on of hands from one generation to another, connecting the Apostles in that way with the pastoral ministers of today, then there are many churches which cannot, or would not see the need to, claim such continuity. If, as the Anglican-Lutheran *The Niagara Report* has recently argued, it primarily means the continuing faithfulness of the whole community in the faith, then the gate stands wider.[142] In a number of Protestant churches it is held both that the church is apostolic (true to the Gospel), and that it preserves insights fought for by the first group of Christians to constitute themselves that particular kind of church (Lutheran, Methodist, for instance). So there is an implicit notion of a catholicity in faith and life, which is especially shared with the first Christians of a particular confessional tradition.

Even where the first kind of continuity can be assumed, and a community deems itself to have gone on in time without visible break from the beginning, distinct traditions can arise. These give an ecclesial community a sense of 'being itself over time' which it may regard as a factor in distinguishing it from other communities. The most common, well-established and (from the beginning) respectable traditional variation which is sustained in a church over time and shapes its temporal 'locality' is liturgical.[143] But a sense of there being a different ancestry of teaching, 'Fathers' of one's own, to be cited in dispute with other Churches, also has precedent. That raises issues of another sort, which we must look at in chapter 2; but

[142] See chapter 4 below on restoring order.
[143] See pp. 199–211 below on diversity of rites.

it is helpful to explore one or two examples here in connection with the notion of continuity as maintaining a church in being.

A case in point is the controversy over the date of Easter in the British Isles in the seventh century, where Augustine of Canterbury's converts believed themselves bound by the traditions of Rome, while those of the Celtic missionaries wished to keep to their own Fathers' rules.[144] Cummianus, Abbot of Iona, sees himself as 'successor to abbot Columba and other saints'.[145] Cummianus adapts Cyprian in order to emphasise the point. Cyprian's words were: 'habere non potest Deum patrem, qui Ecclesiam non habet matrem'. Cummianus adds 'one': 'Those who do not have *one* Mother on earth do not have *one* Father in heaven'.[146] Yet it does not seem to have been envisaged that the two parties might, by discussion, arrive together at a common faith and a practice agreeable to the consciences of both sides. It is assumed that, if traditions differ, the task in hand is to discover which is the more authoritative and therefore the truer, and then for both parties to keep to that tradition.

At the Council of Florence (1438/9), it is hard to say how far the Eastern and Western scholars who contributed to the debates were able to regard one another's heritage of texts as their own. There is a good deal of setting of 'our' authorities over against those of the other side, notably in Mark of Ephesus. Andrew of Escobar, with much the same prejudice in favour of his own tradition, takes a strong line on the need for the Greeks to see the error of their ways, and submit to the authority of the Roman Pontiff.[147] He does not despair of being able so to interpret 'the authorities and sayings of Greek doctors as on the face of it appear contrary to Holy Scripture and the Catholic Faith' that they can be shown to be 'catholic'.[148] To the Greeks, ancient tradition is paramount, to the point where Mark of Ephesus says that even if something newly stated is true, it cannot be received, for we have no authority from the Fathers to add to the Creed.[149]

---

[144] When Bertha, a Frankish princess, came to England to be Queen to Ethelbert of Kent, a bishop called Liudhard was sent with her to help her remain faithful to the local Christian tradition of the home in which she had been reared. Bede, *HE* 1.25, p. 74.

[145] *PL* 87.969.   [146] *PL* 87.974, based on Cyprian, *De Unitate Ecclesiae*.

[147] *CF* IVi, pp. 5ff. and no. 46.

[148] *CF* IV.i, p. 21. John Plousiadenos made an exposition of the Council's definition on papal primacy, in which he used Gratian; and at the Council itself a number of Greeks seem to have made use of *florilegia* of Latin sources. See J.H. Erickson, 'Greek excerpts from the Decretum', *Bulletin of Medieval Canon Law*, 1 (1971), 86–7.

[149] *CF* V.i, p. 57. See, too, C.N. Tsirpanlis, *Mark Eugenicus and the Council of Florence* (Thessalonica, 1974), p. 88.

So local churches developed and desired to hold to their own traditions in certain respects, even in the period before differences of 'confessional identity' began to manifest themselves in the sixteenth century.[150] For that reason it is important to signal here the existence of this sense of 'locality' in the form of continuity in time. In an address to the Lutheran World Federation in the 1970s A. Aarflot argued in exactly this kind of tradition that 'to maintain "substantial agreement" with the Lutheran confessions ... means, ... to endorse gratefully the historic form of this confession, while at the same time using it for responsible witness and confession in the historic context in which God has placed us'.[151]

The notion of 'locality over time' has implications for what we shall want to say about provisionality. To be provisional is also to be 'just for now', on the understanding that there may be going to be development. The essential thing here seems to be to see the lines of time in local traditions as properly convergent, even twined together within the unity of the Church, rather than as parallel strands. Any change ought then to be in the direction of unity and away from separation.

THE POLITICAL, NATIONAL OR ETHNIC 'LOCAL' CHURCH AND THE CONCEPT OF CULTURAL 'LOCALE'

In the nature of things every local Church must be in a place; and a place must lie within, or itself constitute, in a secular context, a political or tribal or racial or social or cultural entity. That may be ethnic (as in the case of the call for Maori bishopric in Anglican New Zealand).[152] It may correspond to or coincide with tribal, national

---

[150] See Cochrane, *Reformed Confessions*, p. 83 on the notion that the Church may continue even when its marks disappear, which is to be found in Bullinger, Second Helvetic Confession, vol. XVII, pp. 14 and 15, although it is not universal among the reformers.

[151] Address on 'The Lutheran Church and the unity of the Church', in *LWF VI* p. 37, para.12.

[152] Allen Brent, 'Ecumenical reconciliation and cultural episcopates', *Anglican Theological Review*, 72 (1990), 255–79, discusses this issue with reference to the text of the 1988 Lambeth Conference, Ecumenical Relations section, 41, 'bishops ... appointed to look after particular cultural, ethnic, or racial groupings, ... work across the boundaries of existing territorial bishops. But these are exceptional cases where population movements have led to people of different races, cultures and languages settling down side by side' (p. 255). It is Brent's view that the 'late medieval, territorial and jurisdictional matrix' is a restrictive idea 'as damaging to our prospects of making peace with non-episcopal churches as it is to the development in missionary or former missionary situations, of cultural episcopates', and for similar reasons; he would want to set this over against the idea of 'a cultural community in process of redemption' (p. 256).

or imperial spheres of government. Or it may have some 'cultural' identity (an example here might be a 'Black Pentecostal' Church in the USA which has few if any white members).

A secular government must, if it does not positively persecute Christians (as happened in the early centuries and more recently under some communist régimes), allow for their presence in some way. That means giving them house-room, tolerating their presence, allowing them fiscal privileges, or in some other manner recognising their corporate identity by its method of taxing them. It may mean making a Christian church an instrument to meet state purposes. Marsilius of Padua advocated something of the sort in his *Defender of the Peace* in 1324; in England since the Reformation the Church of England, as the Established Church, has conducted acts of worship for a number of state occasions.[153] Protestant states after the Reformation commonly operated on a rule of 'cuius regio eius religio', with the state religion normally that of the politically and religiously dominant; at the same time, dissident groups flourished, which put that dominance to the test and prevented the survival of monolithic political or national churches.[154] Although since the rise of the modern nation-state, the organisational strength of the Roman Catholic Church at the national level has been relatively slight,[155] Orthodoxy has tended, almost since the Council of Nicaea in 325, to try to make the local structures of the Church and the political frontiers of provinces or states coincide as far as possible. There has been mutual reinforcement of nationalism and religion in Catalonia, Romania, the Balkans, Ireland, Poland, often with a strong collective myth of religious persecution by a dominant group.[156] True pluralism, with toleration and autonomy of religious minorities has been comparatively rare,[157] but wherever there has been an attempt to impose uniformity of religion in tidy conformity with secular boundaries, there have been cracks in the structure.

Relationships between the 'local church' and what may loosely be called units of 'society' are variform, and can be brought together for purposes of discussion only under the most capacious of

---

[153] For a survey of some of the issues this may raise, see *Church and State: The Report of the Archbishops' Commission on Relations between Church and State* (1935) and the subsequent Report *Church and State* (1970), under the chairmanship of Owen Chadwick.

[154] *Religion, State and Ethnic Groups*, ed. D.A. Kerr (New York, 1992), vol. II, p. 3.

[155] James Corridan, 'Authority and freedom in the coming Ecumenical Church', *Journal of Ecumenical Studies*, 12 (1975), 315–47.

[156] *Religion, State and Ethnic Groups*, ed. Kerr vol. II, p. 19.   [157] *Ibid.*, 12.

umbrellas. Nevertheless, they have certain things in common which
have a place here in the discussion of what makes an ecclesial unit.
We shall need to pursue these questions in chapter 2.

Something we may call 'regionalism' can be determinative of the
sense of identity of a local church even at a date before we can
properly speak of 'nationalism'. In the patristic period, the relationship between national identity and the distinction or separation of
churches was not a single issue with a single solution. For every local
church there was a different set of connections binding it to other
churches. The case of the Syrian churches seems to be different from
that of Armenia or Georgia. The schism between Peter of Callinicus
(Jacobite Patriarch of Antioch) and Damian (Coptic Pope of Alexandria) in the late sixth century must in reality have been caused by
something more than the still burning issue of theological difference
over *hypostasis*. There were other factors such as resentment that one
who was a Syrian by birth, as Damian was, but is now Pope of
Alexandria, is interfering in the affairs of the Syrian church. In the
case of the Armenians, there was a special connection with Jerusalem by the title *catholicos* and a hotchpotch of myth, history,
hagiography and liturgy. That was able to give a sense of identity
which overrode many other factors which would have made for
disjunctions. Recognition of common saints in the diptychs, adapt-
ations of liturgy, interchange of letters and individuals and many
other more elusive elements can be strong binders of church life.
Weighing the other way, there was in some places, continuity in the
very conditions which made for disruption. For example at Antioch,
that was the effect of the troubles over the heretical Christology of
Paul, Bishop of Samosata; of divisions over the course of the Arian
controversy; of quarrels with Alexandria and later with Constantinople; of the loss of areas under its jurisdiction.[158]

We have referred to Bede's *Ecclesiastical History of the English People
(gentis anglorum)*. Again and again in its pages he is concerned with
the welding together of the Christians in the island of Britain into a
single church. This concept of an 'English church' was demonstrably distinct from the notion of provincial structure. There was never
an intention to make of Britain a single province with one metropolitan bishop. On the contrary, Gregory the Great expressly
intended that there should be both a southern metropolitan (origi-

---

[158] See Lionel Wickham, Salamanca, pp. 193–203.

nally to have been the Bishop of London rather than of Canterbury); and a northern one with his see at York. Each was to have his own synod of bishops and to enjoy metropolitan honour. Whichever had been ordained first was to take precedence.[159] We have, then, in this case, an inbuilt tension from the first between a national and a 'provincial' structure (in this instance a dual one). Bede is anxious to emphasise the unity of his English church, stressing that Theodore of Canterbury was obeyed by the whole church of the English (*Anglorum ecclesia*),[160] and describing the bishops who assembled at Hatfield for the Council of 680 as 'bishops of the island of Britain'.[161] Something of this very early sense of an 'English' church proved durable.[162]

An 'ethnic' or tribal or language-group basis for the identity of a local Church may rest on older loyalties than anything which can strictly be called 'national'. Cochlaeus, writing in 1538 about the proposal to hold a Council to settle the difficulties in the Church in Germany, says, 'we are on both sides German (*utrique Germani sumus*)'; 'we are profoundly conjoined by nature and place (*natura et loco invicem coniunctissimi*)';[163] 'it is Luther who has divided us in faith (*fide disiunxit nos Lutherus*)'. Here a nascent German sense of national identity is still heavily overlaid by the tribalism of kin-connection and language ties.

When there was an attempt in 1596 to revive the Union of Greek and Latin traditions achieved briefly at Florence, there were special difficulties at the geographical interface between the two traditions. The Ruthenians had a strong tradition of religious dependence on Constantinople and so found it difficult to switch allegiance to Rome.[164] As Orthodoxy has spread, each new local church, conceived as patriarchal with its subordinate bishoprics, has been in principle self-governing. The Patriarchate of Moscow, whose bishop had been a metropolitan from the fifteenth century, was set up from the sixteenth century as autocephalous, and given fifth place after Constantinople, Alexandria, Antioch and Jerusalem. At the begin-

---

[159] P. Meyvaert, *Bede and Gregory the Great*, Jarrow Lecture (1964), pp. 11–13, and P. Hunter Blair, *The World of Bede* (London, 1970), pp. 61ff.

[160] Bede, *HE*, IV.2, p. 332.   [161] *Ibid.* IV.17, p. 384.

[162] Note the comment in *The Church Times*, 2 February 1990, where it was said of one Churchman, 'he is strongly committed to the Church of England but not to this curious invention the Anglican Communion'.

[163] J. Cochlaeus, *Aequitatis discussio super consilio delectorum Cardinalium* (1538), *C.Cath.* 17 (Munster, 1931), p. 9.

[164] Houssias, *Christian Unity*, pp. 521–2.

ning of the nineteenth century there existed seven autocephalous
churches in the Balkans, four Serbian, two Romanian, one Romano-
Serb; and the strong nationalisms thus represented have persisted in
the divisions of the Orthodox in diaspora in the United States of
America.[165] The autocephalous archbishopric of Sinai is an ancient
vestige of this pattern. But normally a local church is autocephalous
only at the level of a province comprising several dioceses. The
problem of maintaining a 'fit' with political divisions which may
make such politically as well as ecclesially 'local' churches able to
continue as natural units is obvious enough. It has been particularly
striking during the events of the early 1990s in Eastern Europe, not
least in the agony of the wars of Orthodox Serb and Roman Catholic
Croat and Moslem in the former Yugoslavia.

A sense of 'ethnic' locality can work negatively in modern times.
Today's Lutheran churches in South Africa are conscious of difficulties of this sort. There is an emphasis on loyalty to an ethnic
group which has for a long time induced Lutheran Christians to
worship in a Lutheran church according to birth, race or ethnic
affiliation, and maintained separate churches on an ethnically
differentiated basis. Along with this, by way of justification, went
the argument that the unity of the church is spiritual and need not
be manifested visibly,[166] so that there is no real segregation at a
spiritual level.

The Second Vatican Council tried to retain the territorial principle while allowing as far as possible for cultural, ethnic and
national needs to be met.

In determining diocesan boundaries the variety of the composition of the
people of God should be taken into consideration as far as possible, since
this may materially contribute to more effective pastoral care ... an effort
should be made to ensure as far as possible that the demographic grouping
remain united with the civil offices and institutions which constitute their
organic structure. For this reason the territory of each diocese should be
continuous.[167]

Is it possible to answer the question whether 'locality' conceived
of in these ways is right for the churches? It would seem that where
there is a natural homogeneity of language, origin, life, it will be
appropriate for the local church to express that. But there is a

---

[165] See J. Meyendorff, *Orthodoxie et catholicité* (Paris, 1965), pp. 41–5. On the diaspora, see
below.
[166] *LWF VI*, p. 215, appendix to Part XI.   [167] *CD* 23.

danger of exclusiveness and of the long-term development of incommensurability of thought-forms with other such 'local' churches. And it is only too clear that the elements of differentiation culturally or ethnically can come so to dominate local thinking that if the political or economic boundaries break up or alter there can be mutual hatred between Christians. Respect for one another's churches is destroyed with the bond of charity. The sense of being 'all Christians' goes under to other loyalties which are 'local' in this national, ethnic, tribal, cultural sense.

The ecclesial identity of missionary churches

The initial means of making new churches in the mission-field involves 'planting' them in fresh territory. But where a 'local Church' in one part of the world reaches out in mission to another part of the world, there will come a time when the missionary church will become a local church in its own right, and it will be appropriate for it to think of itself as rooted in its own locale.

This is a phenomenon as old as Paul's missionary journeys, where again and again the Church goes out to a new place and settles there and becomes the Church 'in' that place. Even at that stage there were problems about the new ecclesial identity. At Ephesus the worship of Diana was hard to eradicate, and elsewhere too there were difficulties about syncretism and what we should now call 'inculturation'. At Corinth there were parties following such leaders as Apollos who could tend to foster division.

Problems like these have persisted throughout the Church's history. When Boniface (680–754) went from England to mainland Europe as a missionary, he placed himself and his enterprise under the tutelage of Rome, to a degree calculated to stifle local variation.[168] Boniface himself expected to meet tensions between what he was bringing, and existing local wishes, which he would resolve

---

[168] In a letter of [12] May 719, Pope Gregory II praises Boniface because he has laid his desire to be a missionary before the Apostolic See, 'testing your design as a single member of the body submits itself to the sovereignty of the head'. Where Gregory I seems to have allowed Augustine of Canterbury some liberty in the matter of rites to be used in converted lands, this Pope saw his missionary as 'a perfectly articulated member of this body', and urged him to stress to his converts the importance of the fact that they were becoming members of that one body. 'We enjoin upon you that, in admitting within the Church those who have already believed in God, you will insist upon using the sacramental discipline prescribed'; that is what is prescribed by the Apostolic See. Boniface, *Letters*, tr. E. Emerton (New York, 1950), Letter IV [12], p. 32, May 719; cf. Letter X [18], pp. 43–4.

by appeal to Rome. 'If I shall discover any bishops who are opponents of the ancient institutions of the holy Fathers, I will have no
part nor lot with them, but so far as I can will restrain them, or if
that is impossible, will make a true report to my apostolic master.'[169]
He wrote to the Pope for answers to pastorally urgent questions.
Could confirmation ever be repeated? Is baptism valid when it is
administered by an unworthy priest, who has, in addition, failed to
enquire about the candidate's faith?[170] The most pressing problems
relating to locality which he met were problems of disputed jurisdiction. Gerold of Mainz had made no missionary efforts, but he
wanted to claim jurisdiction in areas where Boniface has 'spread the
word of preaching'.[171] In all this, the local ecclesial identity was
being thought out with reference to the mother church.

When the Franciscan 'twelve apostles' arrived in Mexico in 1524,
with the Bull *Exponi Nobis* of Adrian VI (9 May 1522), they converted Indians. For some time the new Christians had no local pastoral
ministry but remained dependent on the evangelists for the fulfilment
of their pastoral and sacramental needs. By 1530 this situation was
coexisting with the beginnings of a local ecclesiastical hierarchy.[172]
The intention was to make temporary provision for emergency need,
but on the understanding that a local diocesan structure was to grow
up and supersede these arrangements.[173]

The sixteenth-century reformers did not always see themselves as
missionaries, although Anabaptists were essentially missioners and
Bucer insisted on the missionary task of the Church. But before the
possibilities of the New World began to become apparent, the
mainstream reformers tended on the whole to take the view that the
main work of wandering evangelism had been completed by their
time. Nevertheless, another fresh pattern of 'new church-making'
arose when reforming churches began to engage in mission in the
New World.[174] Some of its implications became plain there as early
as the post-Reformation period. Protestant Churches were estab-

---

[169] *Ibid.*, Boniface's oath to the Pope (November 722), Letter VIII[16], p. 61.

[170] Letter XVIII, p. 54, for Gregory's replies of 726. In 735, Boniface asks for copies of
questions sent to Gregory I by Augustine of Canterbury, with the answers.

[171] *Ibid.*, Letter XVI [24], p. 51.

[172] This was being set up in connection with the annexation of the territories to the Crown of
Castille. G. Borges, Salamanca, pp. 275–301.

[173] The question when, if mission-churches are not local churches to begin with, they become
so is sharply raised by W. Colombo, Salamanca, pp. 489–93.

[174] See J. Jongeneel, 'The missiology of Gisbertus Voetius', *Calvin Theological Journal*, 26
(1991), 47–79.

lished in Latin America by the late 1700s as a result of settlements by the English, Dutch and French. Moravians, in the same period, were beginning missionary work among West Indian slaves, as were Congregationalists, and Methodist missionary societies.[175] These were usually having the effect of introducing Protestant churches alongside the Roman Catholic Church in a given locality, and sometimes churches of more than one denomination. This missionary movement not only went among those the Christian faith had not yet reached, but also had the purpose of converting people from Roman Catholicism. (There has recently been much greater sensitivity on such points, but it is in response to the fear that this kind of thing can still happen that there were Russian Orthodox protests at what seemed to them Roman Catholic 'proselytising' through the making of bishops for Russian territories in the wake of the changes in Russian society in 1991. Russian Orthodox resentment was sufficient to prevent the sending of a representative observer to the 1991 Synod of European bishops in Rome.)[176]

Much of the most effective work on the Protestant missionary front was done by the distributors of Bibles. American and British Bible Societies were carrying Bibles into Latin America in the early 1800s. They did so against the resistance of the Roman Catholic Church, which feared that they would spread Protestantism among the simple faithful. An individual could do a great deal to seed the Scriptures across a wide area. James Thompson travelled from 1817 along the West coast of South America, Central America, Mexico and the Caribbean. Robert Reid Kaller, a Scottish Presbyterian, and also a physician, distributed 3,000 Bibles in Madeira before he went on to Brazil; and reinforced their influence by making provision for education and medical help.[177] The organisational backing of such work was necessarily mixed, and depended to some degree upon the resources and policies of the missionary organs which instituted it. Not all of them by any means had a clear or consistent ecclesiology. The thrust of the endeavour was to win individual souls, and while good efforts might be made to ensure their pastoral care after conversion and for the provision of regular worship and sacramental life locally (as well as teaching), equally,

[175] W.R. Read, V.M. Monterroso, and H.A. Johnson, *Latin American Church Growth* (Grand Rapids, Michigan, 1969), p. 36.
[176] *The Church Times*, 29 November 1991.   [177] *Latin American Church Growth*, pp. 38–9.

they might not. So one of the effects was sometimes to create an undeveloped or loose ecclesiological understanding in the mission field.

'The world is my parish', Wesley was fond of saying. He, like Whitefield his English contemporary, saw the task of mission as central to the life of the Church to a degree which overrode restrictions of 'locality'. Whitefield crossed the Atlantic thirteen times, and although Wesley's missionary work was in England after his conversion, he too envisaged no local limit to the reach of his work. The 'Methodist Societies' came to lead the way in the worldwide development of a genre of 'missionary societies'. These, though not themselves churches, nevertheless planted churches.

The first Methodist Chapel opened in Bristol in May, 1739; by 1771 there were seventy Methodist meeting houses. By 1784 there were 359. This represents a geometrical progression, and also reflects the importance of establishing a place where the faithful could gather regularly, as local community life came into being. The very multiplication of success is thus attested by the beginnings of repeat patterns of 'local church' growth. This was superimposed, especially in the case of England, upon an existing system of local churches at diocesan and parish level. But ironically, it was the very existence of the underlying ecclesial community which made this approach possible.

Wesley conceived of his Methodist groups as *ecclesiolae*.[178] By this he meant that they were to meet regularly for instruction and to give one another (in every sense of the expression) moral support; but not that they should constitute local churches. 'We act at all times on one plain uniform principle – we will obey the rules and governors of the Church, whenever we can consistently with our duty to God. Whenever we cannot, we will quietly obey God rather than men.'[179] For a long time, even after Wesley's death, Methodism strove to avoid setting up its own sacramental life, and did not hold services at times which might take people away from attendance at their local parish church. The separation in early Methodist understanding between itinerant preachers, not necessarily ordained, and ministers

---

[178] *A Contemporary Wesleyan Theology*, ed. C.W. Carter (Michigan, 1983), 2 vols., vol. II, p. 589.

[179] Wesley, in 'Minutes of the 1747 Conference', cited in R.C. Monk, *John Wesley: His Puritan Heritage* (Nashville, 1966), p. 195, and cf. J. Duane Beals, 'John Wesley's concept of the Church', *Wesleyan Theological Journal*, 9 (1974), 28–35.

of the sacraments, to whom the Church is personally entrusted, is crucial.[180]

It was an uncomfortable and ecclesiologically anomalous situation, and, as it proved, inherently unstable. There was too much of that which 'makes a church' in the Wesleyan enterprise for it to be possible for adherents of the movement to remain in the long term within another church. The groups saw themselves as distinct, covenant-based communities. Within them forms of ministry and leadership were arising, and there was provision for training and the exercise of these ministries. There was a strong sense of the authority of the Holy Spirit and of Scripture in the communities. At first they lacked a full ministry of the sacraments. But it might be argued that they had everything else.

After Wesley's death in 1791 two factions became prominent. One wanted to see Methodism identify itself as a church; the other sought to keep to the 'Old Plan'. These had a vision of Methodism as 'a kind of middle link between all religious parties, uniting them in the interests of experimental religion and scriptural holiness', whose preachers were to be 'evangelists to all denominations.[181] This 'Old Plan' had about it the disadvantage that Wesley himself seemed to have been going in the other direction when he (however reluctantly) consented to ordain ministers for his movement; on the other hand, his *Farther Thoughts on Separating* expressed the fear that unless they remained anchored in the Church of England, Methodists might split into a multitude of parties.[182] Even if they were to be seen as a new denomination, it remained a question what they actually were. Samuel Bradburn wrote in 1792,

We are not Episcopalians, we cannot be. We are not Independents, we will not be. Therefore we must be Presbyterians . . . The Methodists are, in their judgement and affections, on the side of the established Church; in their constitution they are mild Presbyterians; in their practice some go regularly to Church, others occasionally conform, many are simply hearers of their own preachers.[183]

Simple and commanding as Wesley's vision might be, it was, then, ecclesiologically far from straightforward, not only in these points of

---

[180] J.C. Bowmer, *Pastor and People*, (London, 1975) p. 35.

[181] *Ibid.*, p. 21, quoting the Address of the London Trustees in the Methodist Archives, see Bowmer's bibliography.

[182] Bowmer, *Pastor and People*, p. 21.

[183] Samuel Bradburn, *The Question*, 'Are the Methodists Dissenters?' *Fairly Examined* (1792), p. 19.

organisation, structure and adherence, but in the very concept of 'Church' which lay behind it.[184]

The effect of Christian missions since 1800 has been to bring into being a worldwide Christianity. Missionary churches have as a rule settled gradually into the ecclesial patterns and structures of their parent churches and become, in their turn, local churches where they are. But their very wideness of scatter has had the effect of throwing into prominence the awkwardness of the question why Christianity has gone out into the world under, as it were, different brand-names. Local converts would ask why Christian missionaries from different Communions in their area were not at one with one another if all preached the same Christ. It is not a coincidence that the period of ecumenical endeavour began as missionary success increased, and has continued to coincide with it.[185]

Perhaps the most radical challenge has been the series of experiments in forming 'united' churches in the Indian sub-continent. These have no precedent ecclesiologically or ecclesially in earlier centuries. They take the concept of the geographical local church with the utmost seriousness and attempt to overcome the absurdities and anomalies of which converts complain by bringing into being one Church of Christ in one place. As we shall see,[186] this created all sorts of structural difficulties, not least the problem that any resulting united Church might find itself out of communion with churches with which its component churches had previously been in communion.

Mission and proselytism easily become confused. In November 1991 Patriarch Alexy II of Moscow visited the United States. He complained while he was there about the appointment of Roman Catholic bishops for Moscow, Karaganda, Novosibirsk and in Belarus without first notifying the Holy Synod of Moscow. This unease was expressed again by the representative of the Patriarchy of Constantinople at the synod held in Rome in the same month. There was criticism, too, of the attempt to set up an ecumenical

---

[184] It could still be asked by Methodist apologists in 1964, 'Do Methodists have a doctrine of the Church?' and answered in 1983, '"Yes" says too much; "no" says too little.' A. Outler, 'Do Methodists have a doctrine of the Church?' in *The Doctrine of the Church*, ed. D. Kirkpatrick (New York, 1964), p. 11. *A Contemporary Wesleyan Theology*, ed. Carter, vol. II, p. 588.

[185] H.P. Van Dusen, *One Great Ground of Hope: Christian Missions and Christian Unity* (London, 1961), p. 14, asks why the period of ecumenical growth coincides with the period of mission and questions this link.

[186] In chapter 6 on restoring order.

centre on the east Siberian coast. Roman Catholic groups were sending in missionaries and training priests in both the Latin and the Byzantine rites. There were also Protestant fundamentalist missionaries, especially from the United States, who were a bewildering phenomenon to the Orthodox. Sometimes these especially seemed to be acting with little understanding of the ancient and complex world of Christian thought and experience into which they were moving.

Most agonisingly knotted of all perhaps are the difficulties created for modern Orthodox–Roman Catholic relations by the legacy of the mediaeval Crusades and the Synod of Brest of 1596, which resulted in the 'uniate' churches. The Crusades led to the establishment of Latin Patriarchs at Jerusalem, Antioch and Constantinople and created a Western presence in Orthodox places. The Synod of Brest compounded this by bringing into existence Churches of the Byzantine way of life, worship and spirituality which owe allegiance to Rome. Nine of the ten Orthodox bishops of the Ukraine agreed to recognise the primacy of Rome while retaining their own rite. These Catholics of the Byzantine rite, or 'uniates', were heavily persecuted after the Second World War. The Pseudo-Synod of Lvov declared them non-existent in 1946. They lost their places of worship and their clergy were imprisoned. Relations had never been easy, but grounds for lasting grievance were now created. The Ukrainians have been the largest group of uniates. But Eastern Slovakian, Eastern Polish, Belorusan and other uniate churches are up against the same problems of disputed property-rights and the right to the recognition of their ecclesial identity in their relations with the Orthodox. From the Orthodox side the uniates can seem infiltrators in their midst, and look like an unenticing model for ultimate reunion between Rome and Orthodoxy. There is the desperate muddle of old cultural, tribal and political rivalries over which is truly the Church in each place. These are bound to take a very long time indeed even to begin to unravel into the goodwill and mutual acceptance which are the first steps towards rapprochement and union.

In an ecumenical age we must ask frankly what is the role and purpose of evangelising in societies which have a long but partially interrupted Christian history, or an established Christianity in conspicuous need of renewal. The Orthodox Churches of Eastern Europe are themselves intensively engaged in mission to their own people. They are struggling with the problem of bringing up to date a vast backlog of those to whom it has been for generations all but impossible to teach the faith. Crowds are coming eagerly for baptism. But more clergy must be trained and that cannot be rushed. The solid bedrock of custom which holds the faithful secure, still anchors the elderly who remember how it was. That was visible in Russian Orthodoxy in the black-clad women laying flowers in the path of their bishop during the days of the coup in August 1991, when much seemed to hang in the balance again. But the young and middle-aged have to learn about the faith and take hold of tradition so that it may go on in their lives. It is essential to the continuity of the Church in these places that it be the ancient local tradition which the people have owned for generations.

The problem with missionary activity by the non-Orthodox in this situation is that it cannot simply help with the revival of a common Christianity, as might be possible in a united Church. That is to say, it cannot in the present limited stage of ecumenical progress contribute to a common endeavour with the Orthodox. It unavoidably brings a style of Christianity which is unfamiliar in Eastern Europe and may seem to an older generation of the Orthodox hierarchy to be not true Christianity at all; or it may easily carry with it the centuries-long and not yet resolved history of Orthodox fear of domination.

This is the crucial point. Proselytism can only happen in division. It is anti-ecumenical. It is a sign that the sense of sharing a common mind has broken down, and with it Christian friendship among equals. If I think you are already in Christ in his Church where you are, I shall not want to win you for my Church. Indeed I shall regard you as already a member of it. I may see a need to help with renewal, if the Church in your place has been damaged by events or has grown apathetic. That is mission. But its purpose will be to renew the Church in your place as itself, not to turn it into a daughter of the Church in my place.

So the concepts of 'local church' bred within mission are vastly complex and contain many contradictions. It was recognised at the beginning of the modern ecumenical movement that they were in certain key respects anti-ecumenical. It has been less clearly seen how strongly the resulting ecclesial anomalies support the case for regarding all separated forms of church as at best provisional.

Locality in diaspora

A special set of problems about 'locality' concerns churches in diaspora.[187] At the time of the Council of Florence in the early fourteenth century, the Armenians did not have a territory as a church. They lived in colonies in Egypt, and across the Golden Horn from Constantinople, in the Crimea. They thus constituted an early example of a continuing local church or churches in diaspora.[188] They have had a long history in that state. In the Habsburg Empire Armenians remained conscious of their long ancestry, the dreadful sufferings of their forefathers, the brevity of the periods when they had governed themselves, in terms inextricably linked with their sense of having first found themselves as a Christian community. The Armenian saints have been a powerful spiritual inspiration. The Old Armenian of the early literature continues in use in the liturgy, as does the old alphabet. There is pride in the uninterrupted continuity of a culture. At the same time, because the Armenians have lived in diaspora for so long, it is possible to find Orthodox Armenians, Roman Catholic Armenians, Protestant Armenians, in different parts of the world, who have partly assimilated to the local religious culture.[189] This is an extreme example, but Christians who have become exiles for political reasons (as many Orthodox in the New World), and sometimes for specifically religious reasons (such as the Pilgrim Fathers in their journey to America in 1620), will naturally seek to maintain their existing way of life as a 'local church' in their new home in something of this way.

The feeling of belonging to a powerful international group can be a major psychological support for minorities. In nineteenth-century Orthodoxy, both Austrian and Russian pressures were exerted on the Ecumenical Patriarchs in connection with the allegiance of bishops who were to serve in the Ottoman Balkans. Bosnian Serbs in the same period could appeal to the Ecumenical Patriarch when they felt the danger of suppression of their cultural identity at the hands of Austria.[190] Conversely, there is likely to be strain, a sense of loss, feelings of deprivation, rejection, confusion, anxiety in a new environment. 'The experience of a new culture is a sudden, unpleasant feeling that may violate expectations of the new culture

---

[187] Which closely parallels the missionary situation in certain respects.
[188] J. Gill, *Eugenius IV, Pope of Christian Union* (London, 1961), pp. 100ff.
[189] *Religion, State and Ethnic Groups*, ed. Kerr, vol. II, p. 95   [190] *Ibid.* vol.II, pp. 14–15.

and cause one to evaluate one's own culture negatively.'[191] There may be a defensive clinging to that culture or an attempt to 'go native'. There can be separation, where the host culture is ignored and one's own is maintained as far as possible; or marginalisation, where the immigrant loses grip on both cultures; or assimilation, with loss of the immigrant's own culture. Only rarely is true integration of the two cultures achievable without a sense of loss.[192]

There is a danger that continuing loyalty to (and sense of belonging to) a church geographically left behind may bring about a sort of fossilisation. In 1872 there was an official Orthodox condemnation of tribalism and racism as heresy. But several national Orthodox Churches insistently said that the maintenance of pastoral authority over their ecclesial 'children' is the natural and legitimate extension of their ethnic identity and that it was one of their rights as autocephalous churches.[193] Orthodox churches in the United States of America often reflect political and ecclesiastical problems and preoccupations in the areas from which their members come.[194] There, churches deriving originally from Russia, Greece, Bulgaria, have not found it easy simply to merge as 'Orthodox'.[195] The ties of cultural, ethnic and national loyalty which held them spiritually to their mother-lands have proved stronger than the apparent geographical common sense of regrouping them all into a local 'multinational' Orthodox Church in the New World.[196] Indeed there is more than an unwillingness to regroup; there is often a positive hostility to the idea. In 1921 a Synod was held at Sremiski-Karlovtsy in Yugoslavia, where there was a declaration by Russian Orthodox outside Russia that they were the sole representatives of the church of Russia. The tendency began to spread, until the Orthodox in the USA were divided into Syrian, Albanian, Serbian, Greek, Ukrainian and Carpatho-Russian 'jurisdictions', frequently making mutual accusations of non-canonicity.[197] This state of affairs has proved hard to reverse. Even if Moscow recognised a single Orthodox Church in the USA, Constantinople might not.[198]

---

[191] Y.Y. Kim and W.B. Budykunst, *Cross-cultural Adaptation* (California, 1988), pp. 44–5.
[192] *Ibid.*, p. 66.
[193] K. Ware, 'Catholicity and nationalism: a recent debate at Athens', *Eastern Churches Review*, 10 (1978), 10–16.
[194] E. Benz, *The Eastern Orthodox Church. Its Thought and Life* (New York, 1963), p. 84, first published as *Geist und Leben der Ostkirche* (Hamburg, 1957).
[195] *Ibid.*   [196] *Ibid.*, p. 48.   [197] *Ibid.*, p. 51.
[198] *Ibid.*, pp. 52–4. *Religion, State and Ethnic Groups*, ed. Kerr vol. II, p. 8.

The problems of 'locality' in diaspora have been especially acute among the Orthodox because of an ecclesiology which places great stress on the centrality of the grouping of a body of the faithful about their bishop in a given place (within structures involving a group of dioceses under an archbishop, metropolitan or patriarch)[199] as mystically constituting Church in the Church. Good canonical order is satisfied if such a church is 'recognised' by the others, and so received into their communion. Such a new church will also have autonomy (that is, as Orthodox order understands it, the confirming of the nomination of its bishops by the church from which it sprang, with that mother-church retaining some rights); or autocephaly, which is complete sovereignty. But in either case, the church is self-administering. The juridical conditions for 'recognition' by other churches have never been fixed and can often be left to the discretion of the 'mother church'. The problem remains in this system that when a mother church declares one of her parts autocephalous there is no obligation on the part of sister churches to recognise that autocephaly. There are desperate difficulties here which have scarcely been addressed ecumenically as yet, and which are proving, especially in the lands where Orthodoxy is predominant or at a geographical interface with Western Christianity, to be so far politically insoluble too.

We should not leave this topic without raising the notion of 'pilgrimage'. Most of the problems about settlement and integration of churches in diaspora arise out of the requirement for them to stay where they have gone to, and thus to find a way of living in the new society. But a concept of perpetual journeying to God and of never allowing oneself to feel at home on earth is deep in Christian tradition. Sojourners may be groups as well as individuals, and must pose peculiar problems of locality, and also of the mode of their being individual churches.

Special kinds of 'provisionality' would seem to be exemplified in all these situations of diaspora and sojourning. Their common feature is a clinging to something which originated elsewhere and which is in some way perhaps misplaced now. So there is a reaction which denies the provisionality of that which is plainly provisional in its precariousness.

---

[199] See below, pp. 78–86 on the ecclesial status of the supra-diocesan church and the notion that the Church ought to have a 'triadic' structure.

Cultural identity and its challenges

National, ethnic, cultural elements in an ecclesial community's self-awareness are inextricably interconnected. The question of the 'cultural' identity of a local Church is more complex still, because it can, paradoxically, be both deeply persistent and at the same time evanescent in the way it identifies itself. This is important in the context of 'inculturation',[200] that nicely judged process by which the missionary Church must allow the Christianity it brings to come to birth among a people and of those people, in such a way that it meets the needs of the people of a culture hitherto untouched, or barely brushed, by the faith. There are early examples of culturally sensitive (though not always successful) solutions to the problem of bringing Christianity to a new place and meeting local requirements. When Augustine of Hippo needed to find a Punic-speaking bishop for a Punic-speaking community he had, under the pressure of circumstances, to get the Bishop of Numidia to consecrate Antoninus, only in his twenties, who was to prove a disaster. The first Orthodox missions preached to people in their own language and provided a liturgy in the vernacular, on the principle that Pentecost gave warrant for the view that each should worship God in his own language.[201] The liturgy says 'with the tongues of foreign peoples hast thou, O Christ, renewed thy disciples, that they might thereby be heralds of God'.

Nevertheless, the cultural coloration of the missionary church, the style of life it brings with it, unavoidably colours the new churches it founds. Theodoric the Great's kingdom, the first to emerge from the age of the migrations, was visibly shaped by Byzantine influences.[202] In much more modern circumstances, the style which comes with the mission has often been denominational.

Missionaries often tried to steer clear of areas where other churches were working, so as to avoid competition for converts. This laudable policy has sometimes had the unforeseen effect of identifying one region or tribal group with a particular denomination. As a result, Christians from different churches are divided not just by worship and doctrine, but also by language and culture.[203]

200 Other terms have been tried: adaptation, indigenisation, acculturation, Church-planting, but none has seemed quite to fit. Congar, *Diversités et communion*, p. 56.
201 E. Benz, *The Eastern Orthodox Church. Its Thought and Life* (New York, 1963), p. 105.
202 *Ibid.*, pp. 107–9.
203 Paul Richardson, 'Ecumenism at rest?', *Living Stones*, 1(4), (1992), 39.

Missions can create fresh problems of mixed identity in new local churches. At one extreme, in for example the nineteenth-century Western missions, Western economic and political values were often imposed as though they were all of a piece with the faith. The consequences in some places have been terrible, and at the least a continuing resentment has been created about what is currently spoken of as 'imperialism'.[204]

At the other extreme is the danger of a syncretism in which Christianity is so assimilated to the local culture as to cease to be Christianity at all.[205] Examples are the cult of ancestors and initiation practices in some parts of Africa, and marriage practices allowing the taking of another wife if the first bears no sons.[206] Between the two lies for each 'cultural locality' a solution which creates a local church that is fully the Church, and at the same time enables an existing way of life to be valued and preserved.

The desired model on the wider political and social front within which all this must fit has not always been the same. In the late nineteenth and early twentieth centuries it was widely accepted that 'the culture of northern and western Europe was superior to that of southern and eastern Europe'.[207] In that confidence American commentators could speak patronisingly of 'the weak, the broken and the mentally crippled of all races drawn from the lowest stratum of the Mediterranean basin and the Balkans, together with hordes of the wretched, submerged populations of the Polish ghettos',[208] and assert that the best thing for these people was that they should become American.[209] Allowing immigrants to remain themselves, or to choose what to take from American culture, seemed a threat to the host culture. 'If our nation is to be preserved, we must all, native

---

[204] One criticism runs thus: 'inculturation, ... if genuine, necessarily implies both affirming the particularity of the local church and remaining within the communion of the universal Church ... The new evangelizing task must begin with the experience of the local Churches, which will always affect the way in which the Gospel message is expressed and received. That so many native peoples suffered in the past because their cultures were simply not taken into consideration in the evangelisation process, and the severe judgement of so many Latin Americans vis à vis the Church, is a glaring example of the price the Church must pay when the legitimate concern for the universal completely overshadows that for the particular.' Editorial, *Catholic International*, 3 (1992), 803.

[205] Vatican II, *AG* 22a and *Redemptoris Missio* 7 December 1990.

[206] Congar, *Diversités et communion*, pp. 59–60.

[207] N. Hutnik, *Ethnic Minority Identity* (Oxford, 1991), p. 26.

[208] Madison Grant, *The Passing of the Great Race* (New York, 1916), p. 79.

[209] E.P. Gibberly says that the USA should 'assimilate and amalgamate these people as part of our American race', *Changing Conceptions of Education* (Boston, 1929), pp. 15–16.

and foreigner alike, resign ourselves to the inevitable truth that unity can be maintained only through the complete sacrifice of extraneous national traits on the part of our foreign nationals.'[210]

This sort of position has become untenable in the West, though not in every part of the world as yet. From the mid-1960s in America and other parts of the Western world it became important to affirm the value of cultural pluralism. Different ethnic and cultural groups were to enjoy social and political equality under a common government. 'Each culture [was] thought to be able to contribute something positive to the fabric of society. Children, therefore, should be taught to be proud of their cultural heritage.'[211] This was in one way at least more realistic. Many migrants leave their homes so as to avoid losing their cultural heritage and to be free to keep their religious liberty. But it is also an ideal which is bound to come up against the fact of prejudice, discrimination and economic exploitation of minority groups. So although the desired model is founded on respect for the incomer's way of life, that respect is unlikely to be freely given. The effect of finding oneself disapproved of can be dramatic. Immigrants may become aggressively proud of the despised characteristic. The Black Power movement of the 1960s is a case in point, with its slogan 'Black is beautiful'. Thus one or two aspects of national, ethnic or cultural identity may become disproportionately prominent. There are mixed consequences here for the lives of ethnically or culturally 'local' churches in diaspora.

An additional dimension of the problem lies in the different worlds of thought which may be involved. Ecumenists have to understand what is uppermost in the concerns of those they address. Gustavo Gutiérrez and Jon Sobrino have commented in various publications that 'talk of God in developing countries is basically different from talk of God in prosperous countries. The conversation partner of the western theologian is the secularised person ... by contrast the conversation partner of the theologian in the Third World is the one who is poor and oppressed.'[212]

A key principle here would seem to be the one we have already noted, that national, political, ethnic, social and cultural distinctives cannot by themselves make a church.[213] But the ministry of the

---

[210] H.P. Fairchild, *The Melting Pot Mistake* (Boston, 1926), p. 155.

[211] N. Hutnik, *Ethnic Minority Identity* (Oxford, 1991), p. 33.

[212] Schillebeeckx, *Church*, p. 53.

[213] Cf. comments in *The Church Times*, 11 September 1992, 'On the whole, it was an achievement of the European churches to have kept alive nationalism in eastern Europe in

Word and sacraments and the other elements which we have suggested do make the local church a church, may have a 'varying interplay' with these human factors. That interplay itself can be creative of a local distinctiveness.[214] In this way, the gifts of the Spirit make each local church unique. Socially, culturally and historically differentiating elements are, of their nature, temporary, and operate at another level of the Church's life. Nevertheless, they may be important in making it 'local' in these broader metaphorical senses. They are certainly likely to be very important indeed to the members of 'local' churches which have the habit of thinking of themselves in this way, and that is in itself ecclesially significant.

The big questions, then, are two: (i) whether all such 'locally' differentiating factors should be equally respected and valued (in this context 'ethnic' is at present a good word and 'racial' for sound historical reasons a bad one); (ii) whether 'Lutheran', 'Methodist', 'Baptist' (to take three 'denominational' examples) reflect legitimate ecclesial cultures commensurate with, say, 'Russian Orthodox' (to take a geographically local instance). These questions are not going to be easily answered. There is too much heat and too much fear in the memories involved for those who identify themselves with a 'local' or 'particular' church thus metaphorically understood. There is a huge agenda of resentment and guilt for past oppression on both sides. To attempt to answer such questions runs us into problems of ecclesial identity which we must tackle in the next chapter.

THE RELATIONSHIP OF LOCAL CHURCHES TO ONE ANOTHER

The kinds of difficulty about what we mean by a 'local' or individual church which we have met so far are greatly compounded by the fact that we are dealing almost everywhere not with a bipolar structure (local–universal), but with a structure in which there stands, between single congregations and the universal church, a wide range of ecclesial entities which are also known as

the face of enforced nationalism. Its other face, however, is demonic. We are asking all churches to look at their nationalism', John Arnold (Church of England) at the Conference of European Churches earlier that week. Marko Orsolic (Roman Catholic from Croatia) said, 'Ethnic and national characteristics are not the principal components of a human being. We need at present, not a national state but a state of democratic rights. A national state is an idol that devours its offspring.'

[214] See G. Colombo, 'La teologia della Chiesa locale', in *La Chiesa locale* (Bologna, 1969), pp. 17–38.

'churches'.[215] Some of these understand themselves to be provinces of the Church.[216] Some of them understand themselves to be national churches. Some understand themselves to be churches in a denominational or confessional sense. The potential for confusion is apparent in Anglican practice. It is possible to speak of 'the Anglican Church' although Anglicanism is really a communion of autonomous provincially based churches. 'The Church of England' is a national church made up of the two provinces of Canterbury and York. (Anglicans do not speak of 'the Church of Canterbury' or 'the Church of York'.) Scotland's Anglican 'Episcopal Church' with its Primus (archbishop) is not the Church of Scotland (which is Presbyterian).

It is ecumenically essential to take a view of the ecclesiological status of such 'churches' and of their position in the ecclesiological as well as the organisational structure of a future united Church. Two or three points may be made straightforwardly at the outset. The first is that this intermediate level of 'locality' is itself divided into many levels, the larger sometimes containing the smaller. The second is that these bigger 'Churches' tend to deem themselves 'higher' than the individual local congregations, although there would seem to be a much less secure warrant for such a claim in Scripture or tradition. The third is that there is a broad division between churches which see themselves as intermediaries, whose function is to integrate, to make a practical possibility the working interrelationship of the smaller churches with the universal; and those which exist in a way which sets churches over against one another, even divisively (the denominations).

We have to try to answer two sorts of question here: (i) What patterns of relationship between local churches do history and present practice recommend? (ii) Need 'local' always mean 'diverse'? The second question must wait for the next chapter. The first we must look at here.

Churches within churches

The primitive ideal was that all Christians in one place should be united in one local church. That breaks down in various ways in today's churches, as we have already begun to see.

---

215 On the terminology in its present stage of development, see Faris, pp. 85ff.
216 Or in the case of Anglican provinces, to be provinces of a communion, the Anglican Communion, which is not coextensive with the Church.

The first mode of being local church within local church has already been touched on. In the Roman Catholic, Orthodox or Anglican episcopal churches, the diocese with its bishop is historically the local church, and the fundamental unit of Church organisation; all three Communions continue to stress its importance. Nevertheless, a diocese is no longer anywhere likely to be (or remain for long) a single congregation. A parish has its own pastor, and can therefore be seen, just as a diocese is, as a worshipping community gathered about its pastor.[217] On the other hand, in these communions it is the bishop who is, strictly speaking, the pastor of all the people in the parish communities of his diocese, and parish priests are multiple agents of one *episcope*. A parish church is in a limited sense a local church in its own right, but it is not, in an episcopal system, regarded as a complete church, because the parish priest's pastoral function is delegated from his bishop;[218] and also because the priest cannot ensure continuity of ministerial succession because he does not have authority to ordain.

The anomalous situation of two or more bishops working within a single diocese can occur. This arises in one of three ways in today's churches.

(i) There may be suffragan or assistant bishops. But in this case they can be regarded as episcopal 'vicars' and their presence does not interfere with the jurisdiction of the diocesan.[219] He remains the diocese's chief pastor. Nevertheless, they constitute something of a pastoral anomaly unless (as is the case in some Anglican dioceses) they have personal pastoral responsibility for a portion of a diocese. Even then, it can be argued that there are really two dioceses not one, and the question arises of the integrity of such a partitioned diocese.

(ii) Or there may be bishops of different denominations, but in this case there will not necessarily be mutual recognition of their episcopate. For each, there is only one diocese there. Yet for practical purposes in the present divided Church, there are in fact parallel jurisdictions with one local church geographically superimposed on another church of a different denomination in the same locality. This is the situation created by the presence of a variety of non-

[217] That is, it can be defined in the same way as a diocesan 'particular Church' is defined.
[218] Jeremy Taylor, *Episcopacy Asserted*, *Works*, ed. C.P. Eden (London, 1847–54), 10 vols., vol. V, p. 156. 'The cure of the diocese is in the bishop ... this taking of presbyters into part of the regiment and care does not divest him of his own power or any part of it.'
[219] *Episcopal Ministry*, paras. 401–64.

episcopal Protestant churches in territorially overlapping local churches in most of the West and the Third World, and even in some Orthodox areas.

(iii) Or there may be two bishops in one place in the circumstances envisaged under the provisions of Canon 372.2 of the present Roman Catholic Code of canon law. This allows the erection of a 'particular' church (in other words, a diocese) within a diocese, in the form of a church distinct by reason of its rite, or remaining distinct for some similar reason acceptable to the Conference of Bishops. This provision is intended to allow respect for the ecclesial integrity of Churches of the Eastern rite in geographical areas where these have, for historical reasons, persisted alongside those of the Roman Catholic community. All these present some anomalies in the pattern of the relationship of local church within local church.

Yet another mode of being a church within a church is the situation in which the missionary church finds itself during the period while it remains attached to its parent church like a strawberry runner to a strawberry plant. Although it is geographically not 'within' its mother Church, it nevertheless remains there ecclesially speaking for a time.

The diocese of Rome is itself a church within a church, her bishop both Bishop of the See of Rome itself and Primate of the whole Roman Catholic Church. The Archbishop of Canterbury is Canterbury's bishop and Primate of the Province of Canterbury and Primate of all England and also Primate of the Anglican Communion.

It is clear that in some at least of these complex structures there must be an element of provisionality because they cannot all fit into one another without modification.

The diocese and the province

We must say something here in a preliminary way about the territorially 'local' Church conceived of on a larger scale, as 'provincial' or 'national', because there is an important question about the ecclesial status of such higher structures, ecclesially speaking. Humanly speaking, certainly it can, paradoxically, be easier to enter imaginatively into a sense of belonging to the larger territorial unit of the national or provincial church than to the diocese, because such a unit is more likely to coincide with secular or national or tribal loyalties. Canon 34 of the Apostolic Canons and Canon 6 of the Council of Nicaea in 325 indicate that there was a regional grouping of sees from an early date. Each of these had a *protos*, a bishop who held first place among them, by ancient custom or because the city in which his see lay happened to be the leading city of the area. Nicaea finds ancient custom to support the existence of a *protos* at Alexandria, Antioch and Rome.[220] Canon 4 of Nicaea endorses this picture of the early formation of provinces with its reference to the coming together of three bishops of the province at the making of a new bishop; Canon 5 decrees that the bishops of each province shall meet in synod every year in spring and autumn.[221]

So the senior bishop, or the bishop of the most important city, came in the early Church to exercise a certain authority over other bishops in the region. Vatican II uses 'particular' as well as 'local' to describe the Church which is an entity consisting of a group of dioceses. But not all would accept this as anything but an analogical usage. Within the Roman Catholic Church such larger groupings of diocesan local Churches are usually understood to be 'not "Church" in the theological sense but organisational forms of Christian congregations which are empirically useful or even necessary, but which can be swapped for other structures'.[222] It may be argued that Lutheran tradition takes much the same line.[223]

The tradition has been a little different in Anglicanism and Orthodoxy. The claim to ecclesial integrity of such a 'church', provincial or national, was plain to some seventeenth-century Anglican apologists. Joseph Hall (1574–1656), Bishop of Norwich, explains in his *A Common Apology against the Brownists* that the Church of England did not, in its becoming divorced from Rome, set up a parallel church to the Roman Catholic in England, 'but stands actually one with all that part of the world within the kingdom

---

[220] Nicaea set up a parallelism between the political provinces of the Roman Empire, by recognising provinces rather than patriarchates. See J. Meyendorff, *Orthodoxie et catholicité* (Paris, 1965), p. 29.

[221] J.M.R. Tillard, *The Bishop of Rome* (tr. London, 1983), p. 50. Cf. Lanne, *Eglises*, p. 293.

[222] Ratzinger, p. 115. Ratzinger sees grass-roots ecumenism as 'rather an adaptation of the idea of the congregation which regards only the congregation as the Church in the real sense; large-scale Churches are seen as an organisational roof that can be shaped this way or differently. Now of course local congregations are the actual cells of the life of faith in the Church.'

[223] *Ibid.* 'Luther was only able to transfer Church structures to the princedoms because he did not regard the concept of the Church as established in these structures'.

without separation'.[224] It is simply a national 'local church'. The Anglican provinces as they have evolved historically have continued to see themselves as 'churches' of the Anglican Communion, with something of the same pattern of autonomy as obtains among the Orthodox.[225] This is a necessary stress in poly-metropolitan systems. Rome had the structural advantage of having a single primate, and thus of being able to evolve a unitary system of higher church government. Neither the Patriarch of Constantinople among the Orthodox nor the Archbishop of Canterbury among the Anglicans could claim that position.

A useful recent study has examined from a Roman Catholic viewpoint the question of the respective ecclesiological status of diocese and patriarchate or province. This 'is considered by many to exist only in virtue of pastoral or administrative necessity'. J.D. Faris argues that 'such an approach is not only offensive to the Eastern Catholic churches, but is not even consonant with canon law or reality'. He argues that the province or its equivalent meets an ecclesial need which cannot be met by the diocese or, directly, by the universal Church. 'The diocese is too small and the universal church is too vast to provide the necessary support for the flourishing of a variety of expressions of the one faith.'[226] The patriarchate 'is an outflow of the natural needs of the Church, inherent in it from the beginning'.[227] This principle of meeting a human need for the Church to be able to be variously itself in each place would seem important. It is, as Faris points out, 'the intermediate ecclesial communions which would' most naturally 'provide the necessary structure for other non-Catholic communions (such as the Anglican Church), to enter into full communion and still maintain their unique ecclesial identity'.[228]

Karl Rahner sees this need being met in the life of the Church today. 'Where energetic and effective national conferences of bishops exist or are in the process of formation, a "patriarchate" is already materially there.' But he makes the proviso that 'there also corresponds to the national (or continental) unity of such a union of bishops a greater Church which has historically, liturgically (or paraliturgically), theologically, etc., its own proper character which enables it to fulfil within the whole Church a function which is

[224] Hall, *Works*, IX.14.   [225] But also with significant differences. See pp. 163–6 below.
[226] Faris, p. 14. Cf. *LG* 13D.   [227] Faris, p. 16.   [228] Faris, p. 16.

proper to it'.[229] Rahner's requirement is that such a church should be intermediate between the diocesan local church and the universal Church through the brotherhood of its bishops (bringing as it were their dioceses with them).[230] He also insists that it must have, to keep it together as an ecclesial entity, common bonds not only of location but of life. This entity seems to him to have claims to exist *iuris divini* and to do so despite being embodied in actual patriarchates and so on whose shape and location is determined by historical circumstance.[231]

Since Vatican II some devolution of work to the bishops' conferences has taken place, but not uncontroversially. So there is a practical acceptance that the Church has *de facto* a triadic structure. Nevertheless, although *Lumen Gentium* certainly regards intermediate ecclesial entities as more than administrative necessities or historical accidents,[232] the texts of the Second Vatican Council do not develop the notion of intermediate ecclesial entities theologically as far as some authors have wished.[233] From 1966–77 the controversial project on the *lex ecclesiae fundamentalis* began to look as though it would opt for a triadic structure in which patriarchates and major archbishoprics as *regiones ecclesiasticae* might have normative ecclesial status with the diocese and the universal Church.[234] The practical and ecclesiological problem in Roman Catholic canon law as it stands at present is that all individual bishops are in direct subordinate relationship to the Roman pontiff,[235] and

---

229 K. Rahner, 'The Episcopal office', *Theological Investigations*, tr. C. Ernst (Baltimore, 1961 ff.), vol. 6.356.

230 A principle which was a leading theme of the 1988 Lambeth Conference of the Anglican churches.

231 K. Rahner, 'On Bishops' Conferences', *Theological Investigations*, tr. C. Ernst (Baltimore, 1961ff.), vol. 6, pp. 377–9.

232 *LG* 13d, and *LG* 23d makes an explicit link between Western *coetus episcopales* and Eastern patriarchates. See, too, Faris, p. 35, p. 40.

233 Faris gives a useful account of the struggle at the council to get the balance right in framing the texts on the Eastern Churches, pp. 41ff.

234 Faris, pp. 58ff. and for an extended examination of the LEF project, pp. 100–2. Robert Kress sees the triadic structure as endorsed by the analogy it affords with the Trinity. 'This Church is an intermediate stage between the purely local Church as a definite, locatable individual community and the universal Church which is easily and readily graspable. This ... way of being Church', he suggests, 'also reflects the real historical and cultural nature of the human being. The human being surpasses his immediately local condition, but does not thereby evanesce into some sort of ... mere humanity.' Robert Kress, 'The Church as *Communio*: Trinity and Incarnation as the Foundation of Ecclesiology', *The Jurist*, 36 (1976), 155.

235 A pattern not mirrored in the Anglican Primacy of Canterbury.

episcopal authority is treated only in a diocesan context.[236]

Nevertheless, in current Anglican as in Roman Catholic and Orthodox ecclesiology, the diocese is clearly understood to be the basic unit of Church life as the parish or province is not. The parish is accepted as having its ecclesial being within its diocese. There are historical reasons for this view in the case of the province which it may be helpful to set out here. When the first Lambeth Conference was summoned in 1867, it was in response to practical difficulties which had arisen in South Africa. In 1863, the Bishop of Natal, John Colenso, appealed to the British Privy Council because his own archbishop had deposed him for his views.[237] The case raised the issue of provincial autonomy, and the Canadian bishops were sufficiently worried by the implications for other provinces to claim themselves to be 'disturbed by recent declarations in high places in our Motherland, in reference to the Colonial Branches of the Mother Church'.[238] In the debates which led to the calling of the first Lambeth Conference,[239] it was plain to the participants that much was at stake if it was to take the form of a council, and its decisions were to be intended to have binding force upon the communities the participating bishops represented. Indeed, it would in practice be impossible to make them so within all the many different legislative frameworks operating in different provinces. The consensus was for conference not council, and accordingly the Lambeth Conferences have always remained simply meetings for brotherly counsel of Anglican bishops. For both practical and ecclesiological reasons, the provisions made in the Anglican Communion for the enactment of ecclesiastical legislation are limited to the intra-provincial.

The first Lambeth Conference saw a need for some working out of the ecclesiology of the resulting provincial autonomy, although the problem was not yet explicitly posed in those terms. The second day of the meeting was spent in discussing the question of the gradation of diocesan and provincial authority. There was a Resolution that lower synods ought to be subordinate 'to the higher authority of a

---

236 Canon 108.3 and see Faris, pp. 58ff.
237 *Historical Records of the Province of South Africa*, ed. C. Lewis and G.E. Edwards (London, 1934), pp. 310–56.
238 R.T. Davidson, *Origin and History of the Lambeth Conferences, 1867, 1878* (London, 1888), p. 31.
239 G.R. Evans, *Authority in the Church: A Challenge for Anglicans*, pp. 48ff.

synod or synods above them'.[240] A committee was set up to look at the regulation and function of synods.[241] But the Committee's Report is quite clear about the primacy of the diocese as the local church in its assertion that the diocesan synod is the primary as well as the simplest form of synodical organisation.[242] Subsidiarity is potentially a little at war here with the legislative framework, but there was really no alternative in provinces where legislation had to be carried out in some way within local political structures.[243]

We have already touched on the argument that the territorial claims of a supra-diocesan unit to be the 'local' Church are of a different order from the claims of a diocese. The diocese can be seen (as it is by de Lubac, for example) as fundamental in a sense which makes it a divinely ordained ecclesial unit, while larger groupings of dioceses exist to meet the social and human needs which arise naturally in each locale, and which are, by their nature, variable and transitory.[244] Nevertheless, the primary territorial unit of the diocesan local church is not autonomous and in that sense is both a distinct church and not a distinct church. That is to say, it is a complete ecclesial body in which the life of faith can be lived by grace to salvation. But it is not self-contained in being free to continue the episcopate within its boundaries (for a bishop is traditionally consecrated by at least three bishops), or (beyond a very few points) to legislate for its own affairs.

Many of these ecclesial anomalies and special circumstances and higher structures which place churches within churches, arise only within a system where the fundamental unit is conceived of as the diocese with its bishop. They cannot arise in exactly this way within the alternative traditions to which many churches which derive their ecclesial identity from the Reformation period and after belong, and where more congregationally based concepts of 'local church' predominate. There are other problems within the 'presbyterian' structure where *episcope* is characteristically exercised jointly by the leaders of congregations, in a tradition which consciously distances itself from a personal and individual episcopacy.[245] But it is in the episcopal churches that the notion of 'locality' is most stretched and

---

[240] *The Five Lambeth Conferences*, ed. R.T. Davidson (London, 1920), pp. 12, 48.
[241] Davidson, *Lambeth Conferences*, p. 58.
[242] *Ibid.*, p. 58, and see chapter 5 below.
[243] As, for example, in the Church of England decisions of the General Synod are ratified by Parliament.
[244] Cf. de Lubac in *Les Eglises*.   [245] See *Episcopal Ministry*, chapter 5.

tested. A congregation remains what the first local churches were, a body of people in one place meeting for worship with their pastor. That must pose a challenging question about the claim of the developed episcopal ecclesiology which makes a pattern of parishes within dioceses right and for the best for the Church.

The pastoral drawbacks which may result from it have, however, to be set against the different drawbacks of a system in which the specifically linking functions of episcopal oversight can not readily be discharged at a universal level. In the episcopal system (for Orthodox, Roman Catholics and Anglicans and in some places for Methodists and Lutherans[246]), a minister with oversight, the bishop, has overall pastoral charge of a geographically linked group of local congregations and their ministers, so that these are always part of a family group. His is a personal office. He is the point at which three intersecting planes of the Church's life meet: that of the leadership of the local community; that of the collegial brotherhood of bishops with their people, linking together the communities of their time; and that of the plane of 'continuity over time' which makes Christians in every age members of the same community.[247]

Thus bishops are ministers of unity not only within their own dioceses but also because they form a brotherhood in which their local communities are united and a link in the unity which unites communities through time. The ecclesiological tension between locality and universality is thus partly exemplified in the differences between the two broad types of system. We shall come back to all this more fully in chapter 4.

---

[246] On Methodist and Lutheran bishops, see *Episcopal Ministry*, paras. 143ff. and 168ff.

[247] The New Testament evidence is not unequivocal. There was clearly no settled pattern of ministerial oversight in the earliest days of the Church. Acts 14:23 shows that it was felt to be right to appoint leaders for local communities in succession to the Apostles who founded them. The Pastoral Epistles stress in several places the importance of ensuring that succession by the laying on of hands. In the second century, Ignatius of Antioch (c.117) describes an episcopate in which the bishop with his team of presbyters and the deacons, together with the people, form a local church which is 'the Church in each place'. We have little contemporary information about the Church's structural arrangements in the second century, but by the fourth it had certainly become the generally settled pattern for the bishop to be the local leader, as president of the local Eucharistic community, and the earliest writers about the history of the Church were anxious to emphasise that Christian tradition had been seamless and consistent. Cf. Anglican–Orthodox Dialogue, *Dublin Agreed Statement* (1984),13; *Niagara Report*, pp. 43–6. The *Niagara Report* adds a number of points to support the view that the personal succession of bishops was uncertain, and of less importance than a succession in the communities themselves. It suggests that the 'congregational episcopate' of Ignatius of Antioch ought to be seen over against the 'later regional episcopate'.

Mother Church and the sisterhood of churches

A testing point of any 'triadic' system must be the relationship of the higher and larger individual churches to the universal Church. That has in fact a long history within the framework of the development of relations between Rome and the other ancient patriarchates. Although there was discussion of the order of precedence among themselves, the great patriarchates of the East early came to think of themselves as sister churches. In the West the See of Rome became synonymous with 'mother church' (*mater ecclesia*). This was not necessarily the same as asserting the seniority of Rome. The Council of Lyons (1274) speaks of 'the elder Rome' and 'the most holy Pope as first bishop' in terms the Orthodox patriarchs could accept without going so far as to call Rome 'mother'.[248] But it implied that there existed a different kind of relationship to that of sisterhood. But the particular local church in Rome in which primacy was lodged because it had been the See of Peter, became conflated in the minds of its Western leaders and people alike with the one catholic and universal body of Christ, and thus with the Church as it stands in a parental relationship to all individual churches. During the Middle Ages, and within the West, this was natural enough, and on the whole it raised no real ecclesiological difficulties, although it remained perhaps anomalous that the Bishop of Rome was also Bishop of the See of Rome itself. It did matter, however, in relations between East and West in the mediaeval period, for Rome's claim to motherhood could and did stand in the way of union. Patriarch John X Camateros (1198–1206) wrote to Innocent III to point out that nothing in Scripture says that Rome is mother of all other churches precisely because that had become a divisive issue.[249]

This imperfectly recognised conflation of the concept of Church as mother with the identification of one particular church as that mother is still found in the fourteenth century. In the debates of the Council of Florence we have reference to a 'mother Church' which is catholic or universal, and ecclesially one entity, without its being clear from the wording what relation it bears to the *ecclesiae* of East and West which met at Florence. If for the Latins, it was perhaps in

[248] J. Gill, 'The Church Union of the Council of Lyons (1274) portrayed in the Greek Documents', *Orientalia Christiana Periodica*, 9 (Rome, 1974), 19, Document 2 (8), dated between 1273 and 1277.

[249] M. Jugie, *Theologia dogmatica Christian. Oriental. ab Ecclesia Catholica dissid.*, IV (Paris, 1931), pp. 386–7.

general to be identified simply with the Church of Rome; that was certainly not the case for the Greeks, for whom the phrase *mater ecclesia* could not have the redolences of the Fourth Lateran Council (Canon 2).[250] The question whether the future united Church was to be the *ecclesia Romana* as 'mother Church', now containing the Greeks; or the Church universal in its mystical oneness, containing both Greeks and Latins in reconciliation and peace, was of crucial importance ecumenically; and also from the point of view of salvation, for as Eugenius IV had stressed, 'noone outside the catholic Church, not only pagans and Jews, but also heretics and schismatics, can share eternal life'.[251]

Both sides were saying that a 'decision to become one' might be made by the whole Church. But for the Latins, thinking in terms of Rome as mother Church, the bringing together into one flock was inseparable from that flock's acceptance of the Bishop of Rome as its 'one pastor'. That theme appears over and over again on Western lips at the Council.[252] Even when the Roman primacy is seen as representative of the whole Church, it had implications for the Greeks that this was not the union of two parts of the 'whole which is the Church', but an act of submission by the Greek churches to the Latin one. The decision to become one would not then be made with the equal dignity of their own churches preserved. There could scarcely be a clearer illustration of the persistence of the problem created by the fusion of the conception of mystical motherhood in the one Church with the discharge of the functions of motherhood in one specific church seeking to act as mother to the others.

A similar anxiety to stress a sisterly, and therefore an equal and not a subordinate, relationship to Rome appears in some Anglican divines of the seventeenth century. This was in the context both of an acute exacerbation of the problems as a result of the divisions of the sixteenth century in the West, and some Protestant acquaintance with Orthodox thinking about sisterhood.[253] 'The Church of Rome was never our mother's mother [that is, mother of the Church of England]', argues Joseph Hall. 'Britain had a worthy Church before [Augustine of Canterbury was sent from Rome]. It is true that the ancient Roman Church was sister to ours. Here was near kindred, no dependence; and no more consanguinity than, while

---

[250] *Mater est et magistra.*   [251] *CF* I(iii), p. 51.
[252] *CF* IV(i), p. 21 and *CF* VI, p. 1 for example.
[253] See pp. 157–60 on Protestant knowledge of Orthodoxy.

she continue faithful, Christian love.'[254] The thrust of the argument here (setting aside its historical questionableness) is that the Church of Rome and the English Church stand side by side as churches because Rome did not 'bear' the English Church directly as a daughter by mission. That argument would not be relevant in the case of the sisterhood of the ancient patriarchates, where only Jerusalem could claim motherhood on that basis.

Today it is possible for a Roman Catholic to use 'sister' language of Anglicans, but with a crucially different emphasis, for Hall was thinking of a territorially local Church which could claim the integrity of being the Church in that place; when Edward Yarnold speaks of the Anglican church as 'ever-beloved sister' of the Roman, he refers perforce to an Anglican Communion of churches, none of which perhaps is wholly its 'local' church in quite that seventeenth-century sense.[255] So the sisterhood he touches on is perhaps more that of worldwide communions.

Different again is the sort of talk we meet, for example, in the texts of the Lutheran World Federation, where the emphasis is upon equality among diverse communions, and where 'full ecclesial communion as sister churches' can be seen to express the meaning of 'reconciled diversity'.[256] Here mutual respect is central, and mutual humility or deference a lesser consideration or one absent altogether.[257] The basic idea is now of equality of ecclesial standing, rather than of equal origin in a territorial church, based in a place which happened to be of political importance in ancient times.

In the context of an ecumenical theology of the local church for today, in some episcopal churches, 'sisters' are usually conceived of primarily as entities above the diocesan level, as metropolitan or patriarchal areas, each of them a mother church to the dioceses it comprises in the sense of having given birth to them. 'Sister' talk thus belongs in the arena of the 'triadic' structuring of the Church. Vatican II puts it like this:

It has come about through divine providence that, in the course of time, different Churches set up in various places by the apostles and their successors joined together in a multiplicity of organically united groups

---

[254] *Apology against the Brownists, Works*, vol. IX, p. 46.
[255] E. Yarnold, *They are in Earnest* (Slough, 1982), p. 95. Cf. A. Bea and W.A. Visser't Hooft, *Peace among Christians*, tr. J. Moses (New York, 1967), p. 205.
[256] *LWF VI*, p. 201, G. Gassman in report of debates, paras. 155,156.
[257] A. Afanasieff says each local church is not merely equal to the others, but essentially the same as the others. Ironically perhaps it was more easily accepted as in principle a good in

which, while safeguarding the unity of the faith and the unique divine structure of the universal Church, have their own discipline, enjoy their own liturgical usage and inherit a theological and spiritual patrimony. Some of these, notably the ancient patriarchal churches, as mothers in the faith, gave birth to other daughter-Churches, as it were, and down to our own days they are linked with these by bonds of a more intimate charity in what pertains to the sacramental life, and in a mutual respect for rights and obligations.[258]

That will not always be the way in which it may have happened. In Anglican provinces, for example, there can have been a gathering together of existing dioceses in a region to form in due course, a new province.

Vatican II's legacy is in some respects internally contradictory here. *Orientalium Ecclesiarum* and *Unitatis Redintegratio* present different models. The first takes the notion of the uniate Churches as a model (and means) for Eastern churches to come to catholic unity. The second sets out the 'sister churches' principle which respects their existing ecclesial integrity.[259] Equality would seem to depend on the equal weight carried by such great sees in collective decision-making as well as upon the recognition of the equality of the votes of diocesan bishops. Thus one finds in the Anglican Communion the Meeting of Primates at one level (which includes primates only), and the Lambeth Conference at another, including the diocesan bishops of the Communion conferring as equals with the primates in their voting.

Outside the traditional episcopal structure the pattern is more complicated still. Local churches may meet in their representatives, and one of them may be chosen moderator or president for a period. But he or she will not hold a primatial position. Before we can speak of 'sisterhood' between denominational churches and mean an equality which implies equivalence, much more must be agreed ecclesiologically than has been even attempted yet. We must get beyond the sometimes strained insistence on mutual respect, which in its present form almost denies the free and easy character of a

the sixteenth century. Cochlaeus says that 'one can and ought to give way (*concedere*) to another for the sake of peace', *Aequitatis Discussio*, *C.Cath.*, 17 (1931).

258 *LG* 23.

259 E. Lanne, 'Eglises unies ou Eglises soeurs: un choix inéluctable', *Irénikon*, 48 (1975), 322. See further, E. Lanne, 'Eglises-soeurs. Implications ecclésiologiques du *Tomos Agapis*', *Irénikon*, 20 (1975), 47–74. Lanne looks at the scriptural case (p. 52) in 2 John 13, 1 Peter 2:17, and 1 Peter 5:9. Cf. Rome's *Response* to ARCIC which speaks of the 'fraternal spirit' in which the dialogue has been conducted between Rome and the Anglican churches.

natural sisterhood (where there is confidence that there can be quarrels, and that the relationship will continue to hold even if strain is put upon it).

Much, then, is provisional in the areas of 'motherhood' and 'sisterhood'. The greatest test and strain put upon this highly charged and precarious state of things at present is in the area of claims about primacy as a universal ministry of unity.

Primacy and the relation of local and catholic

The most developed experiment in setting up a structurally acceptable relationship of the local, the supra-local and the universal, has been the attempt to establish the office of a universal primate. This universal ministry of unity,[260] a ministry having a higher episcopal or 'oversight' function, has also been the most controversial of relationships, partly because it has inspired fears of dominance by a 'super-church'.[261]

We have seen that history, and arguably ecclesiology, is on the side of the forming of higher-level 'local' churches of the metropolitan or local sort. The question of the origin of a higher *primacy* is harder to settle. The first to use the text of Matthew 16:18–19 to prove that Peter was to be the rock on which the Church would rest appears to have been Tertullian.[262] Rome was the See of Peter; it was also the only See in the West to be able to claim apostolic origin at all, although several in the East could do so. Even here the picture is not perfectly clear. Irenaeus attributes the foundation of the See of Rome to both Peter and Paul.[263] Eusebius does the same at first, although he speaks of Peter alone in his later *Chronicon*.[264] Cyprian calls Rome the chair of Peter and the principal church (*cathedra Petri* and *ecclesia principalis*). Towards the middle of the third century, the Bishop of Rome was claiming a special position because he stood in succession to Peter.[265] By the mid-fourth century Peter was becom-

---

[260] There was some sixteenth-century dislike of calling the Pope *universalis*. See Sturnius' view in Cochlaeus, *Aequitatis discussio super consilio delectorum cardinalium*, ed. P.H. Walter, *C.Cath.*, 17 (1931), p. 17.

[261] An expression used with a slightly different loading of the future united Church by Schillebeeckx, *Church*, p. 197.

[262] *De Praescriptione Haereticorum*, CSEL 70.26, Dvornik, p. 42.

[263] *Adversus haereses*, PG 7.849ff.

[264] *Hist. Eccle.* III.2.15.21, PG 20.216, 249, 256.

[265] Tillard, *The Bishop of Rome*, p. 51. Ignatius speaks in this connection of his 'presidency of love', Irenaeus of a *potentior principalitas*.

ing established as the sole founder of the See at Rome. Optatus, Jerome, Augustine say so, and by 354 the catalogue of Liberius takes the same line. So, historically, it is impossible to treat primacy in distinction from Roman claims to it. Even if in practice Rome became the Church's centre largely for political reasons, theologically her claim has a deeper foundation. But we need to look in some detail at the history to get a picture of the issues raised.

Yet in the third and fourth century Rome was surrounded by a series of 'circles' of which it was not the natural centre.[266] In Africa there was an ecclesial centre at Carthage. In Spain and Gaul organisation was not far developed, and in the East Alexandria and Antioch did not regard themselves as falling under a Roman primacy in more than the most notional sense. There was a developing idea of what a primate's task comprised in the fifth century, but it still tended to be framed in terms of provincial or metropolitan rather than universal primacy.[267]

The right of appeal might sometimes involve intervention in the internal affairs of provinces. Here was a potential source of trouble, for it was necessary to distinguish intervention by a bishop acting as metropolitan from intervention by the same bishop who, as bishop of his own local church, had no right to interfere in the affairs of another diocese.[268] The Council of Constantinople of 381 (Canon 3) expresses the principle that the bishop of Constantinople has primacy of honour (and only of honour), after the Bishop of Rome. In the early Church primacy of honour implied rank and therefore authority.[269] But a series of interventions by the Patriarch of Constantinople in the affairs of Thrace, Asia and Pontus gradually began to make the authority of Constantinople appear juridical. By 451 it was accepted that he confirmed the episcopal elections made by metropolitans in all his territories.[270]

'Honour' easily turned to 'right' in the relations of East and West

---

[266] See H. Chadwick, *The Circle and the Ellipse* (Oxford, 1959).

[267] Canon 9 of the Synod of Antioch (431) says, 'The bishops of each province should remember that the bishop resident in the metropolis should occupy himself with all of the province and should exercise surveillance over the whole. Any person with matters to be taken care of, from anywhere in the province, must go to the capital. For this reason, it is decreed that the bishop (of the capital) should have precedence over all the other bishops, and they shall not undertake any serious matter without consulting him.' Dvornik, p. 32.

[268] J. Meyendorff, *Orthodoxie et catholicité* (Paris, 1965), p. 30.

[269] See B. Daley, 'Position and patronage in the early church', *Journal of Theological Studies*, 44 (1993), 529–53.

[270] Meyendorff, *Orthodoxie*, p. 31, points out that in Egypt there were no subordinate metropolitans and the patriarch confirmed episcopal elections.

too. The Pope refused to ratify Canon 28 of the Council of Chalcedon. In a row over Maximus, who persuaded Ambrose and the Synod of the West at Aquilegia that he was the legitimate bishop and had been expelled unjustly, his complaint to the emperor was that the affairs of Antioch and Constantinople had been conducted without consultation with the West. The East saw this as interference. As a result, rights of self-government were asserted.[271] So from an early stage a tension was coming into being between primacy as a ministry of unity and claims to local autonomy.

The idea of the Pentarchy of patriarchates evolved more fully during the eighth and ninth centuries. Theodore of Stoudion sets out the classic pattern. Among the successors of the Apostles, 'he who occupies the throne of Peter is the first; the one who sits upon the throne of Constantinople is the second; after them, those of Alexandria, Antioch and Jerusalem. That is the Pentarchic authority in the Church. It is to them that all decision belongs in divine dogmas.'[272] The principle does not in itself exclude the idea of primacy; there is allowed to be a 'first'. But it lodges something close to infallibility in the five together, not in one as primate among them.[273]

During the period of the later Ecumenical Councils, it was not thought that the Pope would necessarily do more than receive their decrees, together with the four ecumenical Patriarchs and the bishops of all their provinces. Nevertheless, it seems to have been understood that the Pope had in some sense a more senior role. Gelasius I (492–6) says that a council which is *bene gestum* is one which has been above all approved by the Apostolic See. The Pope must, according to Nicaea II (787), 'cooperate' while the other Patriarchs have only to 'agree'.[274] What was in fact happening was a progressive shift towards assertion of papal supremacy. Rome was beginning to be seen to have a regional primacy, a patriarchal primacy and also a distinctive apostolic responsibility within the communion of the churches, in which its theologically and ecclesiologically higher claims would reside. But at the same time, the

---

[271] Dvornik, pp. 46–7 and see Ambrose, *Epistolae*, 12, 13, 15, *PL* 16.987ff., 993ff., and *Historia Ecclesiastica* of Theodoret, ed. I. Parmentier (Berlin, 1911), pp. 289ff., and *Opera Omnia*, ed. C. Schenkl (Vienna, 1896), *CSEL* vols. 32ff. See too Mansi 3.581–8.

[272] Letter 129 to Leo the Sacellarius, *PG* 99.1417C.   [273] Dvornik, pp. 101–4.

[274] Ep.26.6, *CSEL* XXXV.380. See too V. Peri, 'La synergie entre le Pape et le Concile oecuménique. Note d'histoire sur l'ecclésiologie traditionnelle de l'Eglise indivise', *Irénikon*, 56 (1983), 163–92.

justification of this ministry of unity when it was in fact proving historically to be divisive was a delicate business.[275]

Gregory the Great (who was responsible, despite his refusal to accept the title of *universalis papa*, for substantial moves towards the enlargement of the Bishop of Rome's claims to universal primacy) could still write to the Patriarch of Alexandria: 'In rank you are my brothers, in manner of life my fathers. I have therefore not given orders but have simply done my best to indicate what I think useful.'[276] By the time of Gregory VII, 500 years later, and after the formal breach with the East, the claim is unequivocal. The *Dictatus Papae* (no. 2) says, 'Only the Roman pontiff deserves to be called universal.'[277] Now, in the hierarchy of the five patriarchates, Rome is clear what it must mean to be first.[278]

Yet it was never suggested that a primate, even a universal primate, is more of a bishop than any other. He holds no higher order. He reverts to being simply a bishop if he retires from office.[279] His bishops have the pastoral charge entrusted to them fully and they are not vicars of their primate in the way that their priests are their own vicars. 'They exercise their inherent authority in their own right.'[280] The difference can only be that, while remaining a brother-bishop collegially with other bishops, the primate is set by his office of service to the Church's unity in a different relationship to the community at large.

We have to begin to make a distinction here, between the way this universal primacy looked from Rome from at least the end of the eleventh century,[281] and the way it has appeared in the experience of other communions, in other words, at its divisive as well as its unitary aspects.[282] For those in communion with Rome, Roman

---

275 Tillard, *The Bishop of Rome*, p. 51.
276 *Loco enim mihi fratres estis, moribus patres*, Letter 8.29, *PL* 77.933C, and ed. D. Norberg, *CCSL*, 149A (Turnhout, 1982), pp. 550ff.
277 *PL* 148.407–8 and see Tillard, *The Bishop of Rome*, p. 52.
278 See H. Marot, 'Note sur la Pentarchie', *Irénikon*, 32 (1959), 436–42.
279 *Codex Iuris Canonici* (1983), Canon 332.2.
280 *LG* 27, Flannery, p. 383. Tillard, *The Bishop of Rome*, p. 40.
281 See, for a recent survey, *Papal Primacy and the Universal Church*, ed. P.C. Empie and T. Austin Murphy, Lutherans and Catholics in Dialogue 5 (Minneapolis, 1974), p. 158.
282 Each of the different unions of Eastern Churches has its own history in relation to the Roman Catholic Communion. See E. Lanne, 'La Conception post-Tridentine de la Primauté et l'origine des Eglises unies', *Irénikon*, 52 (1979), 55. It is interesting to note in this connection the comparative lateness of John Henry Newman's acceptance of papal primacy. See P. Misner, *Papacy and Development: Newman and the Primacy of the Pope* (Leiden, 1976).

primacy provides a straightforward touchstone of unity.[283] In the Middle Ages in the West, as earlier, it was natural to turn to Rome for a ruling.[284] Western scholars in the eleventh and twelfth centuries would argue that Rome was alone in not having been shipwrecked by heresy.[285] There was no question in Western minds but that Rome had a primacy of a type unique in its relation to the Church as a whole. The problems have chiefly concerned the way in which that relationship has been understood outside the Roman Catholic Church itself.

Ideas about primacy in other communions: (i) the Orthodox

No communion has gone as far as the Roman Catholic in the development of a theology of primacy. But others have experience, and theory, of the principle that one bishop may be senior to another at a 'metropolitical' or 'patriarchal' level of primacy. In Orthodoxy today the authority of the Ecumenical Patriarch as Orthodox Primate is that of a *primus inter pares*. It is pastoral, not juridical, in conception. He hears appeals from Orthodox Churches and promotes contact and communication between them.[286] This pattern has evolved partly in conscious differentiation from the path the development of primacy has taken in the Roman Catholic Church, under the pressure of the generally unfortunate history of Orthodox perceptions and Orthodox experience of Roman Primacy. Consequently Orthodoxy strongly stresses the concept of a primacy of honour rather than one of jurisdiction.[287]

Constantinople was seen from its foundation as the new Rome, and as having if anything a stronger claim than Rome as an 'apostolic see'. By legend, the See of Byzantium had itself been founded by St Andrew, who was St Peter's brother and a disciple before Peter himself. Photius (*c.* 810–95) may have been creator of this story and also of the belief that Constantinople was descended

[283] Cf. W. Ullmann, *The Mediaeval Papacy, St Thomas and Beyond*, Aquinas Society of London, 35 (London, 1960), p. 2, 'What actually made medieval Christendom one entity, one unit, one body, was the indisputable fact of the papacy acting as the organ of unity', also in *Law and Jurisdiction in the Middle Ages*, ed. G. Garnett (London, 1988), vol. VI, p. 2.

[284] See Anselm of Havelberg, *PL* 188.1216–17 and 1233. The Synod of Sardica invites priests to appeal to Rome 'in order to pay honour to the holy memory of the apostle Peter', Mansi 3.23.

[285] *PL* 188.1216.

[286] K. Ware, 'L'exercice de l'autorité dans l'Eglise orthodoxe, I', *Irénikon*, 54 (1981), 451–71, 'II', *Irénikon*, 55 (1982), 25–34.

[287] J. Meyendorff, *Orthodoxie et catholicité* (Paris, 1965), p. 78.

from the Church at Ephesus, which was founded by John the Evangelist.[288] On that basis a primacy could certainly appropriately be claimed for the Patriarchate of Constantinople. At first the chief concern in making that claim was to diminish the prestige of Alexandria in the West, so that the political centrality of Constantine's city should be consolidated. There was no immediate purpose of setting up a rivalry with Rome for first place.[289] Since Roman primacy had until the fourth century much depended upon the city of Rome's political leadership of the empire,[290] this was no more nor less than a political accommodation to a changed political situation.[291] Indeed until the fourth century it had not been necessary for the bishops of Rome to invoke the Petrine origin of the see to support the claim to a primacy on a basis which could be seen to outweigh those of other claims. In the pontificate of Gelasius I (492–6) there was a significant development of the theory of a papal plenitude of power over against the Greek patriarchates. In a letter to Anastasius the Pope outlined his image of the two swords of temporal and spiritual power and the role of the Bishop of Rome in directing their wielding.[292] In Justinian's legislation Rome is described in 535 as 'mother of laws', and the Church of Rome as the *caput omnium ecclesiarum*.[293]

Roman assertion of a universal primacy involving jurisdiction as well as honour in its relation to the Greeks went on throughout the Middle Ages. In the twelfth century we find Innocent II writing to William Patriarch of Jerusalem to accuse him of ingratitude when the Roman Church has striven so hard to free the Eastern Christians from the Moslem domination of the Holy Land.[294] Aquinas equated the Greek 'error' of denying Roman primacy with that of saying that the Holy Spirit does not proceed from the Son.[295]

At the Council of Lyons the Greeks could say that Rome's bishop is 'first bishop'.[296] The Greek concern was to arrive at an agreed

---

[288] F. Dvornik, pp. 104ff.   [289] *Ibid.*, pp. 46–7.

[290] And Paul had, after all, sent his letters to the capitals of the Roman Provinces.

[291] *Ibid.*, p. 29.   [292] *PL* 59.42–3.

[293] *Novel*.IX of May 535, *Corpus Iuris Civilis*, ed. W. Kroll (Berlin, 1954), 3 vols., vol. III, p. 91 and Codex Justinianus i.i.8 *Corpus Iuris Civilis*, vol. I, p. 11, *PL* 66.15.

[294] *PL* 201.589, William of Tyre and ed. R.B.C. Huygens, *CCCM*.

[295] *Contra Errores Graecorum* (1263–4), written at the request of Urban IV, Second Part, c.32.3–13, *Opera Omnia, iussu Leo XIII*, vol. 40a. See too G. Rocca, 'St.Thomas Aquinas on Papal Authority', *Angelicum*, 62 (1985), 472–84.

[296] J. Gill, 'The Church Union of the Council of Lyons (1274) portrayed in the Greek Documents', *Orientalia Christiana Periodica*, 11 (Rome, 1974), Documents I and II, pp. 15,19.

definition of the canonical position of the Pope in his primacy and to provide strict conditions for appeal against sentence to the Pope.[297] From the Latin side we find the contention that the Greeks err in saying that the Pope does not have power to bind and loose individuals or churches ('de statu fidelium vel ecclesiarum') without the counsel and consent of the four Greek patriarchs.[298]

At the Council of Florence Rome's primacy was to be recognised by the Greeks 'according to what is contained in the acts of Ecumenical Councils and in the sacred canons'. This proposal by the Latins at the beginning of the discussion on primacy 13–16 June 1439 was disingenuous, for they intended much to be read into these texts which was in fact of later development.[299] The Greek patristic texts used to support the two Roman Catholic definitions of 1870 'did not prove convincing to those whom they were meant to convince'.[300]

If we move to more modern attempts at *rapprochement* between Rome and the Orthodox we find some jockeying for position over primacy at the time when Patriarch Athenagoras was invited to send observers to the second session of the Second Vatican Council.[301] A letter of Cardinal Bea reassured that each autocephalous church was invited to send two delegates and that they need not be mere spectators but could affect the course of discussions by explaining their points of view to the Council Fathers, even though they might not speak in the sessions.[302] The Orthodox were sensitive about issues of seniority, autonomy and jurisdiction. The address of Metropolitan Meliton to Pope Paul VI at their meeting in February 1965 cautiously takes Rome to be 'your venerable Church'.[303] By 1973 an address of Patriarch Dimitrios includes the reflection, 'When we speak about "our Churches" what we have in mind is the local Churches, each having its own jurisdiction, and this being held in respect.'[304] In 1975 a Letter of Cardinal Willebrands to Patriarch Dimitrios I on the question of the date of Easter looks to 'the

---

[297] *Ibid.*, p. 42.
[298] B. Roburg, 'Einige Quellenstücke zur Geschichte des II Konzils von Lyon', *Annuarium Historiae Conciliorum*, 21 (1989), 108–9.
[299] E. Lanne, in *Christian Unity*, p. 362 and *CF, Acta graeca*, p. 464.
[300] E. Lanne, 'Jusqu'à quel point une primauté romaine est-elle inacceptable pour les églises orientales?', *Concilium*, 64 (1973), 53, and S. Harkianakis, *ibid.*, pp. 103–8.
[301] On the *Tomos Agapis* and the context of all this, see too pp. 160–1.
[302] Stormon , pp. 49–50.
[303] *Ibid.*, pp. 85–6.   [304] *Ibid.*, p. 239.

practical possibility of reaching a solution which would not amount to the assertion of prior claims by one tradition over another'.[305]

Claims to Roman primacy (and with it conceptions of a universal primacy) have tended, then, to look to the Orthodox like a challenge to the supra-local ecclesial units of their own patriarchates, and thus to function as divisive rather than as a ministry of unity.

Ideas about primacy in other Communions (ii) the Anglican tradition
It has been a consistent contention of Anglican apologists that the existence of metropolitan sees is a result of natural growth; that it is a product of local and historical circumstances.[306] The 'dignity' of a bishopric was seen from the sixteenth century breach with Rome as linked to the (usually political) importance of its *sedes*.[307] Then 'the office of the metropolitan ... was affixed to the place and bishop' of such a see, 'as to Rome, Constantinople, Alexandria, etc.',[308] as Whitgift pointed out, speaking as Archbishop of Canterbury in the late sixteenth century.[309] This emphasis on the locale corresponds (though with differences of style and emphasis) to the emphasis of the Orthodox in forming their patriarchates.

In 1562 John Jewel published his *Apologia Ecclesiae Anglicanae*. Among the points he was anxious to establish was the right of 'local' churches (such as that in England) to legislate for their own affairs. The Roman Catholic Thomas Harding responded with a defence of the rights of Roman primacy to exercise a 'universal power over the whole world'.[310] In the exchange which followed, Jewel examined ancient usage of the term *primatus* and sought to make two distinctions which were to be of continuing importance in Anglican thinking. 'Among the old fathers', he argues, *primatus* is used, not exclusively for a primacy like that of the Bishop of Rome, but 'for any superiority or preferment before others'. It is not, in short, a technical term. Moreover it is applied equally to 'every of the four

[305] *Ibid.*, p. 275, 18 May 1975.
[306] See my article, 'The Anglican Doctrine of Primacy', *Anglican Theological Review*, 72 (1990), 363–78.
[307] Cf. 3 Jewel, PS, p. 313.   [308] 11 Whitgift, PS, p. 271.
[309] The principle that the metropolitan *sedes*, once fixed, should not move, was gently queried by the 1867 Lambeth Conference. 'It seems most in accordance with primitive usage that the metropolitical see should be fixed', but it is not deemed to be 'essential' and provincial synods are regarded as having powers to move it (which was the Canadian view). The Conference of 1897 said, 'we are of opinion that the Archiepiscopal or Primatial title may be taken from a city or from a territory, according to the discretion of the province concerned' (Resolution 8).
[310] 1 Jewel, PS, p. 336.

patriarchs', and not solely to Rome.[311] He thus helped to lay a foundation for the approval early Anglicans show for 'patriarchy' rather than 'primacy'. Such an emphasis is of a piece with the stress on the natural, human, even political importance of certain places as proper *loci* for leadership.

At the same time, Jewel tried to show Harding a difference between a bishop as 'bishop of the universal Church; for that it is his duty to care, not only for his own flock, but also for all others of the whole Church of God', and the acceptance of one bishop in particular as 'universal bishop' with 'infinite and immoderate power'.[312] This second principle is of importance as preserving a key understanding of the bishop as minister with special responsibility for unity and the preservation of the Church's universality, in a climate of thought which could not readily accept a primate as especially entrusted with that task, because it could not at that date be separated from 'power'.

The Anglican concept of primacy defines it so as to distinguish it from that of Rome in certain key respects, for the suspicion was that a primacy lodged in the See of Rome would try to assert an overriding or intrusive authority.[313] John Philpot, who was burned at Smithfield in 1555, took the view which was to become classically Anglican, that there is conciliar warrant for the *multiplicity* of ancient patriarchates. And Rome, he argues, far from being supreme among them, 'was placed the lowest', after Jerusalem, Constantinople and Alexandria, and 'so continued many hundred years, for the time of seven or eight general councils'.[314] The objection here was again to the elevation of Rome above the other patriarchates, rather than to the notion of patriarchs in itself.

In order to justify their own church order as self-governing within a nation-state, Anglican apologists of the first generations needed to show that it was proper for them to retain archbishops of their own, and for there to be patriarchs (in the Eastern Churches at least, and

---

[311] 1 Jewel, p. 366 and citing Crabbe's *Concilia* (Cologne, 1551), vol. I, p. 411. The debate about titles continued, with claims that only 'archbishop', 'patriarch', 'metropolitan' were warranted by early tradition. Parker, PS, p. 115; Rogers, PS, pp. 328–9; 11 Hooper, PS, p. 237; 11 Zurich, PS, p. 228, Letter 94; 11 Whitgift, PS, pp. 90ff. and pp. 141–2, and p. 150.

[312] 1 Jewel, p. 426.

[313] Hooper tries to pin down more exactly in what 'superior preeminence' consists and what its grounds are. It is not, he believes, 'of God's laws', but a human design, 'instituted for a civil policy'. 11 Hooper, PS, p. 237.

[314] Philpot, PS, p. 43. Cf. 1 Jewel, PS, p. 386; Whitgift, PS, p. 220.

perhaps also in the West), but that there were no grounds for accepting a universal primacy. They had to demonstrate the rightness of the dependency (in some respects) of lesser upon greater bishoprics, and at the same time to stop short of identifying a single supreme bishopric which could have authority of a different order in the Church. Hooper attempts it by proposing that there should be accepted for Rome only 'a preeminence, as we here in England say, that all the bishoprics in England are subject to the archbishoprics of Canterbury and York'.[315] In fact Anglicans have always accepted an office structurally higher than that of archbishop or metropolitan, first in their welcoming of the validity of the ancient patriarchates, and secondly, within England itself, in the case of the undisputed primacy which the See of Canterbury has enjoyed over that of York since the twelfth century. White Kennet, writing on ecclesiastical synods in 1701, did not hesitate to call the Archbishop of Canterbury, 'Primate of all England'.[316]

Gradually a situation came into being which was different in kind from that envisaged and discussed by the first Anglican apologists. That is to say, a 'local church' of England which could be seen as resembling early patriarchates in certain key respects,[317] began to develop into a 'Communion' of such local churches, each with its metropolitan; and the structural position of the Canterbury primacy was radically altered. It became necessary to ask whether Anglicans wanted Canterbury to exercise a primacy comparable with that of Rome in these changed circumstances. The answer was No. But some sort of primacy was clearly wanted, and for historical reasons,[318] it has so far been to Canterbury that Anglicans have looked to provide it. The possibility, now from time to time seriously canvassed, that it might be lodged elsewhere would make a break with a tradition linking history to ecclesiology.

The 1908 Lambeth Conference follows earlier conferences in taking the view that 'no supremacy of the See of Canterbury over primatial or metropolitical Sees outside England is either practical or desirable'.[319] It was with that principle in mind that the 1878

---

[315] 'No man', he argues, will say that one of these is 'supreme head to other bishoprics'. 11 Hooper, PS, p. 264.

[316] Kennet, *Ecclesiastical Synods* (London, 1701) thus addresses his book.

[317] See later on Wales, Ireland and Scotland.

[318] Less compelling of course than those which have given Rome the historically natural primacy of the West.

[319] Lambeth Conference, 1908, p. 418.

Conference had recommended that a bishop consecrated for the purpose of exercising episcopal functions outside England should not take an oath of canonical obedience to the Archbishop of Canterbury.[320] Nevertheless, the 1908 Conference wished to 'bear witness to the universal recognition in the Anglican Communion of the ancient precedence of the See of Canterbury'.[321] The 1948 Conference thought it wise of previous Lambeth Conferences to have rejected proposals for a 'formal primacy of Canterbury'.[322] But it still seemed natural in 1968 to speak of the See of Canterbury as 'the focal point of our Communion'.[323] There is, in other words, a conscious tension between a strong sense of the reality of the Canterbury primacy, and an anxiety that it should not, as the Archbishop of Canterbury himself put it in a speech to the Conference of 1978, be 'papal' or 'patriarchal'. The notion that the person of the Archbishop of Canterbury should be a centre or focus is both welcomed and regarded with caution. The heritage of mistrust of the papacy continues to be strong in this kind of anxiety, and still because of a fear of a primacy's seeking to exert a 'power over'.

In connection with the question of function, we find a similar sense that there is a primatial job to be done, and a similar uncertainty about exactly what it consists in. This 'symbolic primacy, not a primacy of jurisdiction';[324] this 'living focus',[325] also has a structural function. The 1897 Conference 'left' the formation of the Central Consultative Body then planned to the Archbishop of Canterbury, 'who already finds himself called upon to do very much of what is proposed to be done by this Council' (Encyclical Letter). Eighty years later, the 1978 Conference requested the Archbishop of Canterbury to convene a meeting of Anglican bishops with bishops of churches in which Anglicans have united with other Christians (p. 42). It saw him as acting as a 'permanent link' between the Lambeth Conference and the Anglican Consultative Council, as president of both (p. 102), and understood him to exercise metropolitical authority over isolated dioceses, which were not yet within provinces, although it acknowledges that there 'is a lack of clarity about what metropolitical authority involves' (p. 103). In 1988 the Archbishop of Canterbury was asked to convene a commission to

---

[320] Letter and Reports, Note B and cf. Resolution 9 of 1897.
[321] Lambeth Conference, 1908, pp. 418ff.
[322] Lambeth Conference, 1948, p. 84. [323] Lambeth Conference, 1968, p. 141.
[324] Lambeth Conference, 1968, p. 137.
[325] Lambeth Conference, 1978, p. 102.

consider the practical implications of Resolution 1 of the Lambeth Conference of that year, which dealt with the results of independent action by provinces which wished to consecrate woman bishops.

We have, then, a history of attitudes to the Canterbury primacy which is not entirely consistent. There has always been 'honour' in the loose sense of respect; and that was warmly evident at the Lambeth Conference of 1988. There has always been some form or element of legal jurisdiction, and certainly an acknowledgement that here is an office with authority, both moral and practical, to do that which has proved necessary for its fulfilment.

After suspicion of Rome began to melt,[326] and the Second Vatican Council had transformed the ecumenical scene, and as the first Anglican–Roman Catholic International Commission began to meet, we see the Lambeth Conferences begin to think seriously about the possibility of some sort of universal primacy.[327] It is recognised that in a future united Church, 'within this larger college of bishops, the primacy would take on a new character which would need to be worked out in consultation with the Churches involved'.

Primacy in a future united Church

The Church is made up of head and body. Christ is its head, as sixteenth-century reformers were anxious to insist, for they thought the Roman primate a usurper of his headship. There is still a Lutheran concern that the papacy may be guilty of a 'usurpation' of the sovereign authority of Christ.[328] So if the possibility of a universal primacy is to be canvassed in the forming of a future united Church, several difficulties have to be got over, not least among them this old suspiciousness in the ecclesial communities which do not have Orthodox and Anglican experience of a primacy which is real, though not, in their own traditions, 'universal'. It has been hoped that 'Lutherans increasingly recognise the need for a ministry serving the unity of the Church universal. They acknowledge that, for the exercise of this ministry, institutions which are rooted in

---

[326] See, for example, the Committee Report on Church Unity of the 1958 Lambeth Conference, 2.48–9.

[327] In 1968, for example, we find: 'Within the college of bishops it is evident that there must be a president. In the Anglican Communion this position is at present held by the occupant of the historic See of Canterbury ... This primacy is found to involve, in a particular way, that care for all the Churches which is shared by all the bishops'. Lambeth Conference, 1968, p. 137.

[328] The Lutheran–Roman Catholic Commission of 1980 on infallibility.

history should be seriously considered.'[329] The remaining anxiety is to ensure that 'papal primacy serve the Gospel and that the exercise of its power not subvert Christian freedom'.[330] Lutherans could be said to have experience of primacy, at least at something comparable with a 'metropolitan' level,[331] without necessarily being willing to accept the term or the concept in any traditional sense. There is good historical Lutheran precedent for the view that councils of the Church have a significant unifying role,[332] but not for the principle that they should be called and presided over by a primate. The problem of the balance of authority between universal and local churches as represented in their primate and their bishops is largely unfamiliar ground to many communions. The possibility of acceptance of primacy, and especially of a universal primacy, has barely been looked at yet in many Protestant communities, and the world of thought involved is deeply unfamiliar to some of their ecclesiologies, beyond a negative gut-feeling arising out of the tradition of regarding the Pope as Antichrist.[333]

The first task seems to be to separate the case for a personal ministry of unity in a future united Church from the history of attitudes to a specifically Roman primacy. Then we need to consider that case on its merits. Only then can it be asked whether such a ministry ought to be 'Petrine' in a sense which would make the Bishop of Rome its natural holder.[334]

The notion of 'limitation of office' has been perhaps the most significant development in recent thinking in this area. *The Final Report* of ARCIC I suggests that jurisdiction can be defined as 'the authority or power (*potestas*) necessary for the fulfilment of an office' (Authority I, Elucidation 6). Thus its writ cannot run, by definition, unless there is a need in the community for it to meet. It follows, too, that the jurisdiction of a bishop, who must, as pastor, teach the faith, provide for the administration of the sacraments in his diocese and maintain the Church in holiness and truth (Authority II.17), is authoritative for the faithful of his diocese, while that of the metropolitan differs not simply in scale but in function. 'It is not merely the exercise of [jurisdiction] in a broader context' but otherwise the same as that of a bishop in his diocese. For one thing, it does not

---

[329] *Ibid.*   [330] *Ibid.*, p. 22.   [331] See the Appendix to the *Niagara Report*.
[332] Empie and Murphy, *Papal Primacy*, p. 11.
[333] See p. 131.
[334] See further Chapter 3 on diversity, pp. 184–90 for discussion on substantial agreement, citing H. Chadwick, *The Tablet*, 8 February 1992.

override, or give the primate power to interfere in, the bishop's local
exercise of his office. For another, it has additional responsibilities in
connection with other bishops, such as 'assisting' (Authority II.16
ff.). That is to say, the primate is a personal focus of unity among
bishops, just as bishops themselves are the persons in whom the three
planes of the church's life intersect. If jurisdiction is defined in such
terms, the attempt to set a primacy of 'honour only' over against one
in which there is also some element of jurisdiction ceases to be
appropriate, because jurisdiction loses the connotations of the auto-
cratic and overriding which Anglicans and Orthodox have feared.

The most testing question about jurisdiction asks whether it can
claim direct divine sanction. Henry VIII of England wanted to
claim both a divine and a human institution for his supreme royal
headship for, he said, the ratio of both human and divine law
required it.[335] So when the First Vatican Council used the language
of divine right of the successors of Peter it was not making an
assertion peculiar to papal monarchy. The ARCIC I statements on
authority say frankly, 'this language [of *ius divinum*] has no clear
interpretation in modern Roman Catholic theology'.[336] ARCIC
suggests that there is really no difficulty if this expression 'is understood as affirming that the universal primacy of the bishop of Rome
is part of God's design for the universal *koinonia*' (*ibid.*). There is no
claim that 'universal primacy as a permanent institution was
directly founded by Jesus during his life on earth', nor that the
universal primate is somehow a 'source of the Church' so that
Christ's salvation had to be channelled through him.[337] 'Rather', it
is suggested, 'he is to be the sign of the visible *koinonia* God wills for
the Church and an instrument through which unity in diversity is
realised. It is to the Universal Primate thus envisaged within the
collegiality of the bishops and the *koinonia* of the whole Church that
the qualification *iure divino* can be applied' (Authority II.11). That
is to say, the divine commission is seen as a gift to the whole Church
in its ministry, which primacy serves, and not of absolute personal
power to an individual. So the divine commission is seen as clear,
providing it is also understood what it is a commission *for* and what
its limits are.

---

[335] See E. Cardwell, *The Reform of the Ecclesiastical Laws* (Oxford, 1850), p. xxviii, Letter of
Henry VIII, and for a recent essay, H. Chadwick, 'Royal ecclesiastical supremacy', in
Humanism, Reform and Reformation: The Career of Bishop John Fisher, ed. B. Bradshaw and E.
Duffy (Cambridge, 1989), pp. 169–202.
[336] ARCIC, A I.24b.   [337] ARCIC, A II.11. See chapter 3, pp. 186ff.

The pastoral authority of a bishop in Orthodox, Roman Catholic and Anglican traditions is entrusted to him so that he may exercise oversight, which means teaching the faith through the proclamation and explanation of Scripture, providing for the administration of the sacraments according to Christ's institution and maintaining in holiness and truth the local church for which he is responsible.[338] It is, in other words, exactly the authority he needs to exercise his office and no more, and it is always at the service of the community. In Lutheran thinking, too, it is seen to be 'an important political principle that authority in any society should use only the amount of power necessary to reach its assigned goal'.[339] 'A canonical distinction between the highest authority and the limited exercise of the corresponding power ... needs to be emphasised.'[340]

If primacy is to be a genuine expression of *episcope* it will foster the *koinonia* by helping the bishops in their task of apostolic leadership both in their local church and in the Church universal. Primacy fulfils its purpose by helping the churches to listen to one another, to grow in love and unity, and to strive together towards the fullness of Christian life and witness; it respects and promotes Christian freedom and spontaneity; it does not seek uniformity where diversity is legitimate, or centralize administration to the detriment of local churches.

A primate exercises his ministry not in isolation but in collegial association with his brother bishops.[341]

There is a striking disjunction of style between the traditional analysis of the issues historically surrounding primacy and the framework and patterns of contemporary thought. Disjunction is not incompatibility, and it is certainly not contradiction. But it may mean not speaking the same language. This blockage against comprehension makes it necessary to ask whether primacy is really the best structural device for a ministry of unity in a future united Church, and if not, whether there is a better alternative to it.

The position of ecclesial structures intermediate between the smaller local units and the universal is crucial here. Much of the anxiety about primacy has arisen out of a sense – and sometimes experience – that it is dangerous for there to be no checks and balances. Allowing the gathered episcopate to act effectively as a counterbalance to primatial authority would be an important

---

[338] Cf. ARCIC A I.5 and II.17.   [339] Empie and Murphy, *Papal Primacy*, p. 21.
[340] *Ibid.*
[341] ARCIC A I.21.

reassurance. It has been an issue in Roman Catholicism since the Second Vatican Council whether this, seen as desirable in the conciliar documents, is going to be possible in practice and become a reality.[342] Making and keeping it a reality would be even more challenging in a future united Church embracing all shades of ecclesiological opinion, where, at present at least, the gathered leadership of individual churches would comprise more than bishops, and among it leaders who understood their relationship to their own community differently.

In an episcopal system, it is understood that the bishop has a role which makes him able to act with and among his people and bring his church with him in decision-making. In many Protestant communities in the sixteenth century any ministry of unity was likely to be collegial strictly at the level of leadership of local worshipping congregations, as in Presbyterianism, or even chiefly administrative. Such constructs as the World Alliances or Federations of Reformed or Lutheran Churches, even the World Council of Churches, have carefully refrained from claiming the *kind* of unitary purpose traditionally envisaged for a personal episcopal primacy.

So we have a long way to go. The best argument would seem to be in favour of the natural place in the Church of a ministerial office whose primary function is to serve its unity.

THE RELATION OF THE LOCAL TO THE CATHOLIC CHURCH

It is when we begin to try to answer the question whether the non-universal (local, particular, even metropolitan) or the universal Church is principally and primarily Church and has some priority over the smaller church that it begins to become clear that this talk of a bipolarity, or even a triadic structure, does not go ecclesiologically deep enough. A recently influential line of thought emphasises that a basic local Christian community is already a realisation of the universal Church.[343]

A number of practical ways of living in a relationship of commu-

---

[342] See extended discussion in Duquoc, *Des Eglises provisoires* (Paris, 1985), *Provisional Churches*, tr. John Bowden (London, 1986).

[343] L. Boff, *Ecclesiogenesis: The Base Communities Reinvent the Church* (Maryknoll, 1986), p. 9. But he thinks that there are degrees of 'expression' of the universal Church, with these communities at the lowest level. Cf. Lanne, 'L'Eglise locale', 62–4.

nion[344] with other local churches were already commonplace in the early Church.[345] Prayers might be said for other communities at the Eucharist and Eucharistic bread could be shared. New bishops were installed by inviting bishops from neighbouring churches to join in consecrating them. Regional synods and councils were convoked. Letters were exchanged and circulated.[346] These seem to be tokens or signs of the existence of a communion upon which the local churches all depend for their very existence as churches. If it can be argued that the existence of the local church depends upon its being in communion with other churches, that a local church cannot in fact be 'Church' in isolation,[347] that might be taken to imply that the (local) churches are the primary ecclesial entities,[348] at least in the sense of being the building-blocks. Any 'higher', 'catholic' or 'universal' Church might then be thought of as conceptual rather than itself a living and fundamental ecclesial reality. If that were to be the case, or if in any sense the one Church is held to be a construct of the many, the relationship of local churches to one another would be of prime importance in the forming of a united Church. Certainly there has been, as a result of the Second Vatican Council, despite the unfinished character of its own work on the principle, a shift towards a 'communion' ecclesiology of this sort, not only in the Roman Catholic Church but also outside it, as others have taken in the Council's implications.[349]

It is uniquely the character of the Church that belonging to the small 'known' community is also in the fullest sense a belonging to the whole. It was clear as early as Bede's day (he is discussing the miracle of the loaves and fishes), that 'the different groups of those eating designate the distinct gatherings of churches throughout the

---

[344] It is sometimes argued that the one Church is simply a communion of (local) churches, a *communio ecclesiarum*. We shall come to that possibility in chapter 6, but we need here at a much earlier stage to look at the question of the patterns of relationship in which local churches may stand to one another.

[345] See Michael A. Fahey, 'Ecclesiae Sorores ac fratres: Sibling Communion in the Pre-Nicene Christian Era', *Catholic Theological Society of America, Proceedings*, 36 (1981), 15–38, and C. Vogel, 'Unité et pluralité des formes historiques d'organisation ecclésiastique du IIIe au Ve siècle', in *L'Episcopat et l'Eglise universelle*, ed. Y. Congar and B.P. Dupuy (Paris, 1962), pp. 591–636.

[346] M. Fahey, Salamanca, p. 106, note 22, for bibliography and G. Borges, *ibid.*, pp. 275–301 on meetings of local churches in early Latin America.

[347] P. Komonchak, Salamanca, pp. 559–91.

[348] Depending on the way in which 'communion' is understood. See chapter 6 on the variety of usage.

[349] See Legrand, 'Nature de l'Eglise particulière', pp. 113–15.

world which make the one *catholica*'.[350] The church in each place is
both a portion and a microcosm of the universal Church. As a part it
is incomplete without the other local portions, and without the
whole which they constitute. As a microcosm it is itself 'Church' in
its fullness. So the local church is a single entity as a microcosm. As a
'portion of the whole' it may be complex in structure, that is, made
up of congregations within dioceses within a province, for example.
Each of these subordinate portions (congregation, diocese,
province) can be at the same time the local 'Church in each place' in
the sense of a microcosm.

If the relationship of the local church to the whole Church is of a
sort to which nothing else in creation affords an exact parallel, there
can be only imperfect structural analogies, and, as we have seen,
some have argued we should not be looking to structures at all, or
not primarily to structures, but to mystery. The problem with
solutions along those lines is that they are inherently not practical.

There is the additional complication that since each local Church
is in some respects uniquely itself, it can be seen to stand in a unique
relation to the Church as a whole.[351] That, too, may require the
seeking of practical structural solutions to protect its uniqueness. At
the same time, since it is also provisional, its relation to the Church
as a whole cannot be static.

Which is prior: local or catholic?

The archetypal idea that the one Church is somehow the 'source' or
'origin' of the many, appears in Cyprian. He uses the familiar
images of the Trinity in a manner appropriately modified to make
them apply to the Church. The sun emits many rays, but it is one
light; a tree has many branches, but one trunk standing on a firm
root; many streams flow from a single spring, where 'numerousness'
appears in the plenitude, but unity is preserved in the source.[352] It
was of the first importance to Cyprian that the Church's unity
should be seen in this way in its relation to and dependence upon the
unity of God. But there remains the substantive difference that
whereas in God the plurality of the Persons does not diminish or
alter or add to the unity of the Godhead, in the Church the model is
that which is found in all creation, of the many multiplying from the

---

[350] *In Marcam*, CCSL, CXX.513.   [351] L. Wickham, Salamanca, pp. 193–203.
[352] Cyprian, *De Unitate Catholicae Ecclesiae*, 5, pp. 213–14.

one. Yet of all creatures the Church is unique in being united with God himself in Christ.

Do we want to say that the one catholic or universal Church is primary? That is, to see as the governing idea the notion that a single apostolic tradition flows out to individual churches, all founded directly or indirectly under apostolic impulse. In that way the catholic Church may be seen as articulated in local churches with their particular variations. (If minority, or separated churches were to be included in the definition, they would present an extreme case of such 'articulation'.) That is the view taken by Irenaeus, Eusebius and those who framed legends about the apostolic origins of their own churches in the early centuries. On this view catholicity or universality is certainly a primary attribute of the Church. The particular exemplifications locally have to be explained in terms of that catholicity.

That is the position of a recent *Letter* from the Congregation for the Doctrine of the Faith to the bishops of the Roman Catholic Church. The universal Church, it argues, 'is not the result of the communion of the Churches, but, in its essential mystery, it is a reality ontologically and temporally prior to every individual particular Church'. Thus local churches are 'particular expressions of the one unique Church of Jesus Christ. Arising within and out of the universal Church, they have their ecclesiality in her and from her.'[353] This presents a difficulty when set beside the phrase of *Lumen Gentium* 23, *ecclesia in et ex ecclesiis*. The Congregation suggests here that this must be seen as inseparable from *ecclesiae in ecclesia*, making them complementary.[354]

Alternatively, we may say that priority belongs to the particular local churches, that the local worshipping community is where 'Church' arises,[355] and that unity and catholicity are simply a historically arrived at (and not necessarily permanent) outcome of their having agreed to conform with one another in faith and order. On the face of it, it would be surprising that so much conformity should have been achieved, and for so long, if that is true. On the other hand, history affords strong evidence of the frequency with

---

[353] CDF *Communion*, para. 9.

[354] John Paul II, Address to the Roman Curia, 20 December 1990, no. 9, *Acta Apostolicae Sedis*, 83 (1981), 745–7.

[355] C. Hill suggests that the debate about priority is really in a modern guise the dispute between Congregationalists and others in the sixteenth century. See his Response to CDF *Communion*, p. 774.

which a founder of a church gives it his own stamp and only afterwards does it seek to make contacts with other communities and build up with them an agreed structure of ecclesial organisation.[356]

Things look even less tidy if we raise the question of the sense 'priority' is going to carry. Does it refer to ontological priority, as the CDF *Communion* text suggests? Does it imply 'first in time'? In that case, clearly Christ founded the universal not the local churches directly; yet a catholicity consciously arrived at through the mutual acceptance of local churches could only come into being (and historically did come into being) with the founding of a plurality of local churches. Does 'priority' imply 'first in order'? First in importance? Are we speaking of the visible or the invisible Church? These questions are hard to settle. The CDF *Communion* text has stimulated some useful responses, some of which have a place in what follows.

One way of answering the question of temporal priority or priority of order is to ask whether baptism introduces the individual first into the universal or the local church, and whether ordination first and foremost introduces a new bishop into the College of Bishops or makes him pastoral head of his local church.[357] Through baptism, argues the CDF *Letter on Communion*, the Christian 'is inserted into the one, holy, catholic and apostolic Church. He does not belong to the universal Church in a mediate way, through belonging to a particular church, but in an immediate way, even though entry into and life within the universal Church are necessarily brought about within a particular church' (para. 10). As to the episcopate: the primary pastoral function of the bishop in his own diocese is seen in the documents of Vatican II as constitutive for that diocese's very being as a local church. In this way, each bishop leads the one Church *in* the particular church. All the particular churches are in communion in the one Church. As *Lumen Gentium* puts it (23), 'It is an established fact of experience that, in ruling well their own Churches as portions of the universal Church', the bishops 'contribute efficaciously to the welfare of the whole Mystical body, which, from another point of view, is a corporate body of Churches'. So it can be argued that the very absurdity of posing the question is

---

[356] For the framework and some of the expression of this distinction, I am indebted to the paper given by Lionel Wickham at the Colloquium at Salamanca in April, 1991, Salamanca, pp. 193–203.

[357] E. Lanne, 'L'Eglise locale', 497–506.

informative, and again we are led to conclude that local and universal are complementary and correlative.

It may be useful to list the reasons for asserting the priority of the universal or catholic, or of the local, in any or several of these senses. On the side of the priority of universal to local may be said:

Christ founded only the universal Church.[358]

The universal Church has an absolute ontological priority.[359]

Only the universal Church is comprehensive and includes the Church in heaven.[360] (What might be called the argument from definition.)

The universal Church is prior, because it is the Church-from-above, the very mystery of salvation, which exists in all the local churches.[361] (The argument from salvific function.)

Only the universal Church can be the universal sacrament of salvation.[362]

The universal Church is the cause, exemplary, efficient and final, of the local church.[363] (The argument from causation.)

Only the universal Church is assured of being indefectible and infallible.[364]

Only the universal Church is assured of being holy.[365]

Only the universal Church precedes all local churches in time.[366]

No local church is promised indefectibility, holiness and so on, except the one original mother church of Jerusalem.[367]

The universal Church is prior to the local as a body is to its organs: 'As in a body the unity of the organism precedes and sustains the individual organs, because the organs would not exist if the body did not, so also the unity of the Catholic Church precedes the plurality of particular churches which

---

[358] W. Bertrams, 'L'"ufficio dell'unità" della Chiesa e la moltitudine delle Chiese', *Vita e pensiero*, 54 (1971), 83. See, too, C. Colombo, 'La teologia della chiesa locale', *Vita e pensiero*, 54 (1971), 261–5, A. d'Ors, 'Iglesia universel et iglesia particular', *Ius Canonicum*, 28 (1988), 295–303, and A. Bandera, 'Yglesia particular y Iglesia universal', *Ciencia Tomista*, 105 (1978), 80–7. See also, H. Legrand, 'Nature de l'Église particulière', *Unam Sanctam*, 71 (Paris, 1969), 113–15. The question was also raised during the redaction of Christus Dominus. Veuillot said 'certum sit Christum condidisse Ecclesiam suam, i.e. universalem, in qua postea tantum constitutae sunt particulares Ecclesiae seu dioeceses', *Acta Synodalia, III/IV* (Vatican, 1975), pp. 117–18.

[359] *Ibid.*   [360] B. Mondin, *La chiesa primizia del Regno* (Bologna, 1986).

[361] Boff, *Ecclesiogenesis*.

[362] Bertrams, 'L'"ufficio dell'unità"', Bandera, 'Yglesia particular'.

[363] Bertrams, 'L'"ufficio dell'unità"'.

[364] Bandera, 'Yglesia particular', Colombo, 'La teologia'.   [365] Colombo, *ibid.*

[366] Ratzinger, p. 75. Except the mother church at Jerusalem.

[367] Colombo, 'La teologia', p. 261.

are born from this unity and receive their ecclesial character
from it.'[368]

The local Church depends on the universal.[369]

The whole Church cannot be said to result from the addition or
sum of all the local churches. The generative principles
(Word, Spirit, Eucharist, apostolic ministry) generate a local
church as the Catholic Church, the communion constitutive
of any local church generating also the other local churches
and the communion among them that is the one catholic
Church.[370]

On the side of the priority of local over universal may be said:

Once the mother church at Jerusalem was the one local church,
and then it realised the universal Church.[371] (An argument
from history.)[372]

The principle of subsidiarity says that 'it is ... unjust and a
gravely harmful disturbance of right order to turn over to a
greater society of higher rank functions and services which
can be performed by lesser bodies on a lower plane'.[373] (An
argument from order.)

The Church which is born in the Eucharist is *prioritamente* the local
church. Christopher Hill, from an Anglican standpoint, cites
the Orthodox Zizioulas on the importance of not *contrasting*
locality and universality. 'All structures aiming at facilitating
the universality of the Church create a network or communion of Churches, not a new form of Church.'[374] Nevertheless, 'each eucharist community fully manifests the one, holy,

---

368 Ratzinger at a meeting of the College of Cardinals, 1985.
369 *Ibid.* See, too, comment of C. Hill on CDF *Communion*, p. 774, that particular churches
     cannot be self-sufficient ecclesiological subjects.
370 See Aymans, 'Die communio Ecclesiaru.' 'The real point of comparison is not between the
     universal Church and any individual local Church but between the universal Church and
     the communion of all the local Churches. The universal Church does not transcend
     communion of local churches; it is that communion. Otherwise the universal Church
     would be a universale ante rem.' P. Komonchak, Salamanca, pp. 559–91.
371 Cf. J.M.R. Tillard, 'L'Universel et le Local: Réflexion sur Eglise universelle et Eglises
     locales', *Irénikon*, 60 (1988), 30.
372 C. Hill comments that Ratzinger sees the Pentecost multitude of languages as indicating
     the universal Church, CDF *Communion*, p. 774.
373 Pius XI in *Quadragesimo Anno* and John XXIII in *Mater et Magistra, Acta Apostolicae Sedis* 23
     (1931), p. 203 and 56 (1961), p. 414, cited by P. Shannon, *The Code of Canon Law*
     (1918–67), pp. 26–30.
374 J.D. Zizioulas, *Being as Communion* (St Vladimir's Press, 1985), p. 258 and C. Hill, CDF
     Communion, p. 775.

catholic and apostolic Church, not in itself in isolation, but to the extent of its communion with all the others'.[375]

'There is no truly ecclesial act which is not by origin an act of a local church.'[376]

The communication and reception of the faith is particular and is the first principle of the Church from which all that is universal in the Church derives.[377]

Both the local and regional (particular) churches enjoy a certain priority in regard to the universal Church for they are the ecclesiological correspondents to certain priorities in the nature and culture of humanity.[378]

A new local Church has its genesis from below, from the poor, although this remains a concrete realisation of the universal.[379]

Canon 368 of the Code of Canon Law (1983) and *Lumen Gentium* 23a speak of particular churches as those 'in quibus et ex quibus una et unica Ecclesia catholica existit'.[380]

If the arguments on both sides are so strong and so numerous, we must at least canvass the possibility that we shall find in the end that local and universal are so profoundly complementary and interdependent that it can no more be settled which is 'prior' in any sense than it would be proper to ask whether unity or Trinity is 'prior' in the Godhead. Olivier Clément, from an Orthodox vantage-point, maintains that the universal Church and the local churches as eucharistic communities exist together, with no precedence of either over the other.[381] Geoffrey Wainwright, writing as a Methodist, suggests that Ratzinger is wrong in giving the universal Church the ontological and mystical priority he does. In his view, 'the local and the universal Church are [both] historical interpretations of the Una Sancta, even though they should not be purely and simply identified with it. They have their unity in the Una Sancta. There is only one Church of God, whether it is expressed locally or univer-

[375] Olivier Clément, reply to CDF *Communion*, p. 769.

[376] B. Forte, *La chiesa icona della Trinità: Breve ecclesiologia* (Brescia, 1984), pp. 48–54.

[377] S. Dianach, *La chiesa misterio di communione* (Turin, 1977), pp. 132–5.

[378] Robert Kress, 'The Church as *Communio*: Trinity and Incarnation as the Foundation of Ecclesiology', *The Jurist*, 36 (1976), 156.

[379] Boff, *Ecclesiogenesis*. Cf. the German term *Gemeindeprinzip*. See P. Komonchak, Salamanca, pp. 559–91.

[380] K. Mörsddorf, 'Die Autonomie der Ortskirche', in *Schriften zum Kononischen Rechts*, ed. A. Aymans (Paderborn, 1989), pp. 287–9.

[381] CDF *Communion*, p. 768.

sally.' He too cannot therefore accept that there is any way to 'assign a priority exclusively to either the local or the universal Church'.[382]

Models of the relationship of local and catholic

In attempts to express the character of the relationship of local to catholic or universal in the Church, a number of models and analogies have been suggested, which we may briefly review here.

(a) Image, analogy, macrocosm and microcosm

The first takes the local church to be an image of the greater Church,[383] with the local church a microcosm of the catholic. This is, in essence, the Orthodox model,[384] and it is one wholly congenial in the Roman Catholic and Anglican systems of thought. But it is unfamiliar in churches which have traditionally seen the local gathered community as the visible Church in a rather different way.

(b) Parts of a whole

The second sees local churches as parts of a geographical whole.[385] At the Council of Florence, Isidore of Kiev spoke in his *Sermo de modo procedendi in Concilio* of the 'parts and wholes' which were a favourite theme of contemporary Western scholasticism.[386] 'It is obvious', he says, 'that if the bringing together of parts makes a whole, neither part on its own (that is the Eastern or Western Church) can be called a "whole".' Nor will he hold with paradoxical talk of the part being what the whole is, or the whole the part. He sees Greek and Latin Churches as halves making up a single whole when they are brought together.[387] They are two *ecclesiae* which must be mystically and spiritually made one.[388] Modern Roman Catholic usage prefers 'portions' because it carries a less decided sense of 'separate pieces'

---

[382] CDF *Communion*, p. 770.

[383] 'The particular Churches are in the image of the universal Church and not vice-versa' (see *LG* 23a) 'Draft Statement on Episcopal Conferences', *Origins*, 17 (1987–8), 735.

[384] The whole Christ is present in each Eucharist *unum et idem numero*; there are not a lot of Christs. See *LG* 23.1 and P. Komonchak, Salamanca, pp. 559–91, note 28. The Church in each place may be seen as both a part and a microcosm of the universal Church. See J. Erickson, Salamanca, pp. 653–77, on whether this is primarily Eucharistic or baptismal.

[385] Not parts but portions, J. Erickson, Salamanca, pp. 653–77.

[386] See too M. Spinka, *John Hus at the Council of Constance* (New York/London, 1965), pp. 4, 9, on the idea of Ockham that the *universitas fidelium* is the genus and the *Romana ecclesia* the species. The forthcoming study of mediaeval mereology by D.P. Henry will make an important contribution here. The ultimate source of this *topos* in the mediaeval West is probably Cicero's *Topics*.

[387] *CF* Xi, p. 6.   [388] *CF* Xi, p. 77.

and a stronger implication than the word 'parts' that the local portions belong together and together make one.[389] A version with good Biblical backing sees the local churches as cells in the body of the Church. But both 'parts' and 'cells' fail to carry the sense of the completeness of each local church which 'microcosm' does.

(c) Mutuality

A third line of thought is that the local and particular, on the one hand, and the universal, on the other, are complementary and mutually dependent manifestations or expressions of the body of Christ.[390] That is to say that when the local church in one place (say, South America) is concentrating on the poor and in another (say Asia) is involved in inter-faith dialogue, the whole Church is doing those things. 'Among the individual particular churches there is an ontological relationship of mutual inclusion; every particular church, as a realisation of the one church of Christ, is in some way present in all the particular Churches "in which and out of which" the one and unique Catholic Church has its existence.'[391]

On any definition of the character of the 'communion of local churches', mutual charity must be fundamental, and with it, such concomitants as mutual courtesy, mutual recognition, mutual communication and cooperation. But it is hard to say exactly what each of these ought to amount to. Mutual charity should presumably certainly involve a will for unity, the *votum unitatis*. Mutual charity perhaps even (and further) implies mutual inclusion.

It might on this model be thought to be the case that the communion of the many local churches is in fact the mutual inclusion which exists among them. The various churches can be seen as bringing to one another not only their 'natural' cultural 'gifts', but also their special Christian experiences generated by the encounter between Gospel and culture. The achievement of catholicity would then require the 'symphonic harmony of all the special, local,

---

[389] 'The catholic tradition, as it has been restated by the Second Vatican Council, is not characterised by the idea that all existing "Churchdoms" are mere fragments of a true Church which does not exist anywhere but which one must now try to form by putting all these fragments together; this kind of idea would turn the Church into purely the work of man.' Ratzinger, p. 120. *LG* 13(a); *UR* 4(k)(i). See too Kilian Mc Donnell, 'Vatican II (1962–4), pueblo (1979), Synod (1985): Koinonia/Communio as an integral ecclesiology', *Journal of Ecumenical Studies*, 25 (1988), 399–427.

[390] J. Erickson, Salamanca, pp. 653–77.

[391] Pope John Paul II in an address to the Roman Curia commenting on *Lumen Gentium* on *in quibus et ex quibus* 13 on 21 December 1984.

ecclesial experiences'.[392] This would make 'inculturation' and mutual 'reception' central notions in ecclesiology, so that 'The local – with all it entails of the cultural, the "contextual", the geographical, the religious, the historical – belongs to the material in which the *ekklesia tou theou* is truly incarnated.'[393]

Pope John Paul II commented that 'among the individual and particular Churches there is an ontological relationship of mutual inclusion ... every particular Church, as a realisation of the one Church of Christ, is in some way present in all particular Churches, ... in which and out of which the one and unique catholic Church has its existence.'[394] Local churches put at one another's disposal the ecclesial richness which is proper to each. 'In accordance with what is involved in the mutual relations of members we have one Lord and Saviour, whose grace we share together in the sacraments.'[395] If this is the model, then we are dealing with a mystery which defies description in any mechanical terms, for it must be at least as much a matter of relationship as of structure. So perhaps we should be thinking, when we do think structurally, in terms of the network of relationships and functions found at an early date among local churches.[396]

In mutual communication, the New Testament suggests that the norm and purpose ought to be to achieve and live in unanimity of heart and life (1 Corinthians 12:25; 2 Corinthians 13:11). There are difficulties about that which we shall come to later. Growth of cooperation is easier to measure and has in some degree been achieved from time to time in the church's life. Mutual courtesy between local churches must be the fruit of the relationship of mutual charity. It certainly includes and implies mutual respect.[397] There can be no mutual charity between local churches without

---

[392] P. Komonchak, Salamanca, pp. 559–41.

[393] Tillard, 'Eglise d'Eglises', p. 30, but see earlier on the idea that the cultural is not constitutive for the Church. Here again we touch on the vexed question whether or how far the culturally variable is able to be constitutive of 'Church'.

[394] Commentary on *LG* 13, addressed to the Roman Curia, December 21 (1984), *Acta Apostolicae Sedis*, 77 (1985), 503–14.

[395] Stormon, pp. 53–4, 22 November 1963, Letter of Patriarch Athenagoras to Paul VI.

[396] See for example T.J. Harrington, 'The Local Church at Rome in the second century: a common cemetery emerges amid developments in this "Laboratory of Christian Policy"', *Studia Canonica*, 23 (1989), 167–88, and J.F. Baldovin, 'The urban character of Christian worship: the origins, development and meaning of stational liturgy', *Orientalia Christiana Analecta*, 228 (Rome, 1987).

[397] That respect for others has to be seen as inseparable from concern for the maintenance of the truth, Stormon, p. 151.

mutual recognition. The recognition that other local churches stand in the same relationship to the universal as one's own is both a mark and a prerequisite of the maturing of the idea of catholicity.

Mutual hostility between local churches at every level is historically as least as typical as mutual charity. Yet division is itself a relationship between local churches, albeit a bad and broken relationship (a 'scandal for the world and an obstacle to mission', as the Second Vatican Council puts it).[398] Despite its negative character, the relationship of division has had some positive results. The development of theological insights has from the beginning depended a great deal upon controversy in the church. But the mutual hostility, or even mutual suspicion, which precedes it and lingers after it, are incompatible with the charity which is universally recognised (in principle if not in practice) as ecclesially essential.

Mutual courtesy and mutual respect imply, though they do not define, mutual ecclesial recognition. They also tend to remove the fear of being swallowed up which is founded on mistrust, and the reluctance to accept 'submission' to one's partner in dialogue as a condition of reunion, for these can have no place between ecclesial equals. Other lessons are not so obvious. Ecclesial equality is hard to define where the partners in dialogue are working with different conceptions of what a church is. The recognition of 'Church' in the other is not necessarily the same thing as the recognition that the other is equally or fully Church. So the mutuality model, though helpful, does not appear to offer a complete solution.

Prepositional relationships

A series of accounts of the relationship of universal to individual churches leans on a prepositional articulation of the tension between them.

'One from'

A possibility here is to see the catholic Church as 'one from' the Churches which make it up. This notion is expressed by Bede.[399] The Church is called the most beautiful of women for while the beauty of the many churches throughout the world is very great, like

---

[398] *UR* 1.
[399] *In Cant., Venerabilis Bedae Opera*, ed. J. Giles (London, 1844), vol. III, p. 217.

women ripe in spiritual splendour, how much greater is the beauty
of the whole Catholic Church which is 'one from' all those Churches
as its members? This is one way of construing the important phrase
of the Second Vatican Council, *in quibus et ex quibus*,[400] which sees the
Church as both subsisting in and having her being from the local
churches.

'One with'

Again we can take the relation of local to universal as Richard Field
does. He argues that a single local Church would be universal 'if it
could clearly demonstrate itself to be one with the Church and
company of believers; which . . . at divers times hath filled the whole
world'.[401]

Embodied in

The nineteenth of the Church of England's Thirty-Nine Articles
says that 'The visible Church of Christ is a congregation of faithful
men.' That could be read as implying that the universal Church is 'a
federation of these [local] units'. John Robinson, commenting on
this says no, 'but while the Church is always the great Church, it can
nevertheless, and must, be embodied in units which can still be
described as "the Church" – the Church as it finds expression "at
Corinth", "in your house"'. 'These units', he says, 'are not simply
bits of the Church; they are the body of Christ in its totality, as it
exists in this or that of its cells.'[402]

Becoming and happening

We might say that catholicity is realised in the local church by that
church's witness and mission, so that the catholic Church 'happens'
in each local church. It is an idea fundamental to the texts of the

---

[400] *LG* 23, also found in the first draft *De ecclesia* presented to the Council in 1962, referring to
        particular churches (dioceses), 'prout in illis et ex illis, ad imaginem Ecclesiae universalis
        formatis, una et unica ecclesia Catholica existit'. Cf. R. Greenacre, 'Causa Nostra Agitur:
        an Anglican response', *The Jurist*, 48 (1988), 394. It has never been the Anglican view that
        the Church of Christ 'subsistit in ecclesia Anglicana'.
[401] Richard Field, *Of the Church*, Book II.viii (Cambridge, 1847–52), vol. I.86–7: 'This it
        cannot demonstrate, but by making it appear that it hath neither brought in any new and
        strange doctrine in matter of faith, nor schismatically rent itself from the rest of the
        Christian world.'
[402] John Robinson, *On Being the Church in the World* (London, 1960), p. 83. Cf. Faris, p. 54, on
        the notion that the local has a kind of human priority.

Second Vatican Council and to all Orthodox ecclesiology that the Church as a whole 'happens' in each place in the Eucharist.[403] This is to suggest that the local church is an expression, or concrete realisation, of the catholic,[404] and that the catholic Church realises itself in the portions of the people of God in local churches. An important rider here is that the Church locally is not limited to a 'partial' realisation of 'Church'.[405]

Representation

Or perhaps the relation of local to catholic is one of representation.

The Church of . . . Christ truly exists in the local Church . . . In each of them the mystery of the Lord's supper is celebrated, something so great that the whole universal Church can perform nothing greater . . . the whole Christ is present through the one Spirit by whom all are filled with life and united among themselves . . . Each local church is a true representative of the total and universal Church, which itself carries on its life in these local Churches.[406]

Quality

It might also be suggested that each local Church is qualitatively the Church, so that its relationship to the one Church is that it is 'of the same kind'.[407]

Each and all

Finally it could be argued that what is in each is found in all, and it is in this way that together they are the one.[408]

On the face of it none of these models can be said wholly to misrepresent the relation of local to catholic, although none of them is wholly adequate. But we have a long way to go before the whole

---

[403] B. Baum, 'The ecclesial reality of the other Churches', *Concilium*, 1 (1965), 34–46, pp. 43–4.

[404] The Second Vatican Council was able to recognise that although other ecclesial bodies may be institutionally imperfect, they may 'concretely and actually' realise the Church of Christ better. Baum, 'The ecclesial reality', p. 42.

[405] Muller, Salamanca, pp. 251–89, suggests that the Church 'realises' itself first in different particular churches which are not just parts, but of which each represents the totality of the reality which is the Church.

[406] Baum, 'The ecclesial reality', p. 42, cites a speech by Eduard Schick, Auxiliary Bishop of Fulda, Germany.

[407] *LG* 26a.   [408] On 'each and all', see further pp. 262–5 on decision-making.

set of them can find its place in a developed ecclesiology, beyond the obvious inference that they make it plain that the relation of local to catholic is complex and multifaceted.

It is hard to be conclusive about all this. The inherent anomalies in usage of the highly equivocal term 'church' are evident. But it is not easy to distinguish its senses tidily. Worshipping community can be house, church, parish, diocese, national or ethnic or patriarchal or metropolitan church, denominational church, all overlapping and at points incommensurable. These 'churches' in their multiplicity somehow fit within or perhaps simply are the one Church; yet each of them is itself the one Church; but some of them seem to unchurch themselves by unchurching others and thus lack the bond of charity with other Christians which Augustine thought essential to being Church. It is all very untidy and at present clearly ecclesiologically provisional, as well as provisional in its practical working out.

If we are going to get any further we have to turn to the notion of ecclesial identity, the 'locality' or 'individuality' of churches seeking to be themselves differently, and often in separation from other churches. That is the theme of the next chapter.

CHAPTER 2

Ecclesial identity

'NEW' CHURCHES

'New' individual churches come into being. They understand their inception or their continuance (for many of them believe themselves to be not new but continuing)[1] in ways which can differ radically, and are sometimes inherently incompatible. Within the churches of the centuries before the Reformation in the West, a new local Church typically began through mission to hitherto unchristianised territories.[2] Or it might prove necessary, as a local church grew, to divide its membership into multiple congregations; these remained under the pastoral care of the bishop, but were served by priests to whom he delegated the care of portions of his flock. In neither case was it necessary to justify what was done by rethinking the underlying ecclesiology. The new church was simply the Church in a new place. Since the Reformation the picture has become much more complicated. Churches have come into being which have not thought of themselves in that way, or which have not been thus regarded by other churches. Paradoxically, they have often seen themselves not as 'new' but as the original apostolic Church,[3] in a way that it seemed to them previously existing churches were not.

---

[1] This was a phenomenon much to be seen in the Church of England in the period immediately following the decision of the General Synod in November 1992 to ordain women as priests, when some of those who could not accept the decision deemed themselves to be 'continuing' the Church.

[2] Though not necessarily wholly so. For example, Augustine of Canterbury came in the 590s to a British Isles already partly converted in Roman times.

[3] In the nineteenth century, the American Lutheran C.P. Krauth insisted that it was in keeping with Lutheran ecclesiology to hold that 'there are to be no absolutely fresh starts. If the foundation were removed, the true course would not be to make a new one, but to find the old one and lay it again. But the foundation never was wholly lost, nor was there, in the worst time ... an utter ceasing of the building of gold, silver, and precious stones upon it', Krauth, p. viii.

But what begins as, in intention, a reform of something existing, frequently comes to be seen as 'constitutive of something new'.[4]

There is also a fundamental difference of ecclesiology in the very notion that a church can be self-generating under God and not an offspring of an existing local church by mission or multiplication of converts locally. In the discussions of the 'radical' Reformation in the sixteenth century we often find the assertion that the remnant of the true Church is now so scattered that God must bring it together afresh by a direct call: 'The church is dispersed among the heathen [so] no persons on earth can without a special call from God gather up the same and bring again its sacraments into use.'[5] This makes the assumption that the initiation of an ecclesial entity may involve something quite different from bringing a new diocese or parish into being within an existing structure,[6] or even geographically extending the existing Church by means of an ecclesial strawberry-runner (as in 'Church-planting').[7] It claims that it can involve (a) going back to God for direct authority and (b) justifying doing so on the grounds that no 'body' at present claiming to be the Church is any longer the Church at all.

An action of that sort is a challenge to existing ecclesiology. It opens up the possibility of a group's believing it is itself the sole recipient of the Holy Spirit.[8] Moreover the appeal to such direct and special justifications for claiming to be 'Church', has tended to arise from and to perpetuate various sorts of special pleading about what a church is or ought to be.

The question we have to try to answer here is whether such modes of 'ecclesiogenesis' are valid, so that a 'denomination' of its member-churches may create a 'local church' in an ecclesiologically acceptable way.

---

[4] H. Fries, 'The ecclesiological status of the Protestant Churches from a Catholic viewpoint', *Journal of Ecumenical Studies*, 1 (1964), 203, 'a conception of church without the structure it had had up to that time, and which, it was believed, could perform its service of word and sacrament without that structure ... brought the [ministerial] offices themselves so much into question that people thought it might be possible to abandon them or to substitute something else for them'.

[5] Letter of Sebastian Franck to John Campanus, 1531, translated in *Spiritual and Anabaptist Writers*, ed. G.H. Williams (London, 1957), p. 152.

[6] J. Erickson, Salamanca, pp. 653–77.

[7] See W.R. Read, V.M. Monterroso, H.A. Johnson, *Latin American Church Growth* (Grand Rapids, Michigan, 1969), on 'church-planting'.

[8] Ratzinger, p. 10. See, too, C. Hay, 'The ecclesiological significance of the Decree on Ecumenism', *Journal of Ecumenical Studies*, 3 (1964), 343–53, p. 344 stresses 'the Council's

A crucial factor would seem to be the relationship in which a 'new' church deems itself to stand to other churches and the Church. Characteristically, the 'denominational' pattern is to hold one's community to be Church and to regard other like churches as also Church, but to remain in some doubt about the ecclesiality of churches outside that ambit. A significant variation is to hold 'being Church' as of incomparably less importance than being an effective instrument of the Spirit in the salvation of individuals. That uncertainty can be overcome only by alteration of some sort (in attitude or actual practice), on the part of some or all churches. But I think it can be taken as an ecumenical axiom that it is not possible to regard churches which stand off from one another as standing at the same time in a right relationship to the Church.

The undertow of ecclesial identities

Joseph Hall, Anglican Bishop of Norwich (1574–1656), gives a shrewd list of some of the less edifying motives, the 'inward grounds of contention', which seem to him to underlie the divisions in the Church. His first is pride: 'I am holier than thou.' The second is 'self-love': 'I think ... that I have the Spirit of God' (cf. 1 Corinthians 7: 40). 'This it is that turns every man's goose into a swan, and causes the hermit to set more value upon his cat than Gregory upon the world.' The third is envy and malice: 'My ... rival, my enemy is advanced: I lie still neglected: am I so tame as to suffer it?' His last is covetousness, which expresses itself as criticism of those who 'have turned hucksters of the word of God, to the corrupting thereof, to their own advantage.'[9] These four reduce broadly to two: a conviction of the purity and spiritual superiority of vision of one's own church, and of God's special (or exclusive) approval of it; and hostile feelings towards other communities of Christians, which appear to outward judgement to be triumphing in the world (with the suspicion that that has been achieved by corrupt practices and deliberate deception of the faithful).

Hall puts bluntly what cannot be said with quite such frankness in the ecumenically more diplomatic climate of the late twentieth century. Barriers are still often erected inwardly in some such terms

---

implicit acknowledgement that Christ's Church cannot be "appropriated" by any particular denomination'.
[9] *The Peacemaker, Works*, vol. VI, pp. 614–18.

as these in Christian minds because old unconscious justifications for separation have not been brought out and looked at honestly. Many still believe that they are 'separated for the sake of truth'.[10] Hall sketches 'ways of peace' designed to get over these hurdles.[11] The first must be to labour to remove these obstinate inward grounds of contention. Then there needs to be a cultivation of a different habit of mind, a 'meek and humble temper'. That has to be coupled with 'charitable affection to our brethren', suppressing even the beginnings of quarrels, 'a yieldableness upon sight of clearer truths', 'avoiding the multiplication of unnecessary questions', 'to labour and pray for further illumination in all requisite truths', and – in a startling foreshadowing of the Lund principle – 'to comply with our brethren so far as we safely may'. Apart from avoiding asking a great many questions,[12] which may not always be right, these are unexceptionable principles on which ecumenical endeavour in any age would have to proceed if it were to make progress. The difference between the barrier-creating 'inward grounds of contention' and these remedies lies in the will for unity, which seeks *rapprochement* rather than looking for reasons to stay apart.

When the tide seems to be flowing most vigorously toward union between Churches, an 'undertow' is often perceptible, tugging the other way. It takes the form of a deep sense of 'self' in the still-divided churches, an anxiety to hold to an ecclesial 'identity' even at the cost of unity. This needs to be distinguished from the indisputably legitimate and proper sense of 'belonging' to a 'local' church which would be present in an undivided Church (and which exists in some measure within each communion at present); there local churches would regard themselves as at one with the Church and with each other. Each is complete as 'the Church in each place', but only because of the relationship in which it stands to the one Church. It also needs to be distinguished from the desire to preserve distinctiveness in the form of a non-divisive diversity.[13] A church which defines itself, for example, by adherence to a 'confessional' position which has historically set it over against certain other churches cannot stand in that relationship to those other churches, and therefore not (certainly on the visible level) to the one Church.

---

[10] 'Dogmatic belief creates the denominations, and because of their fixed creeds the separated churches cannot be united.' T. Sartory, 'Reunion of Christians despite Catholic dogmas', *Journal of Ecumenical Studies*, 1 (1964), 82–98, p. 82.

[11] *Ibid.*, pp. 613 ff.   [12] See pp. 184–90 on the hierarchy of truths.

[13] See Chapter 3.

It also makes it difficult for such a church to understand itself as provisional.

So we need to clarify what can be meant by 'ecclesial identity', or 'confessional identity', or any sense of corporate identity as a church which is not united or in communion with other Christian churches. Here – to change the metaphor – we move onto eggshells. The sense of 'identity' which Christians feel in their own church is a matter of great sensitivity. It may amount to no more than a collective preference for a certain familiar pattern of liturgy, or a 'flavour' or 'colour' in worship in which almost undefinable elements taken together make up a beloved whole, in which the worshippers feel at home. Singing, clapping, personal testimony, free prayer, open invitation to repentance,[14] make an obvious contrast with the solemnity of a fixed liturgical sequence followed with high ceremonial in an ancient cathedral. Each commands loyalty both from those to whom it makes a natural appeal because of differences of temperament and from those for whom one style of worship or the other makes a theological statement. For some protestants 'ritual' smacks of abuses rejected at the Reformation. The use or avoidance of acts such as crossing oneself or kneeling speaks of old disputes and can carry an ecclesiology embedded within itself.

Concatenations or groupings of elements of behaviour, style, attitude and assumption have come in the long term to characterise the resulting separated ecclesial bodies. There are also examples of groupings of sets of ideas. Certain patterns of thought seem to cluster. As John Henry Newman puts it, in connection with his theory of the development of doctrine, but in terms which are pertinent here: 'Doctrines are members of one family, and suggestive, or correlative, confirmatory, or illustrative of each other. One furnishes evidence to another, and all to each of them; if this is proved, that becomes probable, but for different reasons, each adds to the other its own probability.'[15] Changes in such patterns can seem to pose a threat at the profoundest level to what is both dear because familiar, and held to for ideological reasons. Even to make comparisons can be to try to compare the incommensurable.

There are systems in which the sense of identity of a Church is

---

[14] Piepkorn, vol. III, p. 76. [15] *The Development of Doctrine*, pp. 93–4.

impossible to articulate in words at all, so deeply interfused in it are ancient subtleties of style and attitude.[16] In Orthodox tradition the vision of the most beloved Orthodox saints and Fathers is still alive. The simplicity and asceticism of the life of the desert, with its emphasis on soberness and self-denial and discretion and trusting prayer and practical wisdom, on those things which make men fools for Christ's sake, are still attractive; the appeal of martyrdom is still strong as athletes for Christ fight ordinary but hard-to-control human desires; a Neoplatonist-inspired spirituality lives on, with its implicit dualism of matter and spirit. At the same time there is a love of elaborate ritual in worship.[17] The central consciously held principle is classically summed up in Greek documents of the Council of Lyons of 1274. 'Our holy Church should remain without change in all the dogmas and customs transmitted to it from of old, neither neglecting nor altering any point of them, but standing firm for all time on what was till this present day practised and honoured.'[18]

Sometimes by contrast a call for simplicity and accessibility sends details of doctrine and liturgy below the surface of a Church's conscious style. In the Salvation Army the declaration of faith takes the form of 'Articles of War', which is signed by converts who want to become soldiers, and the converts are enrolled during a corps meeting (that is, an act of worship). The essence of the matter is seen as simply salvation 'by the power of the Holy Spirit combined with the influence of human ingenuity and love.'[19]

So it is at the risk of caricature and of trying to compare the incommensurable that we must try to sketch some of the commoner aspects of the self-images of separated ecclesial bodies which may discourage them from taking decisive steps towards union when it comes to it, or even being very interested in trying. We need, too, to

---

[16] D. Attwater, *The Christian Churches of the East* (Milwaukee, 1935–7), 2 vols., vol. I, pp. 159–65, characterises Orthodoxy as mystical, contemplative, largely unsystematic and theologically patristic, and comments that 'what really separates [the Orthodox] from Rome is not so much theological dogma as the events of history and a fundamental difference of mind and temperament'. See, too, Chadwick, Salamanca, pp. 679–90.

[17] *Orthodox Spirituality* (London, 1945), by an unnamed Orthodox monk, evokes this quality of Orthodox life well. On the Lambeth Quadrilateral, see pp. 26, 27. All this colours and flavours patterns of life and worship in which Scripture, Creeds, sacraments and historic episcopate are as plainly central as they were to the Anglican Lambeth Conference of 1888, but with a significantly different atmosphere and emphasis.

[18] J. Gill, 'The Church Union of the Council of Lyons (1274) portrayed in the Greek documents', *Orientalia Christiana Periodica*, 11 (Rome, 1974), 15.

[19] Piepkorn, vol. III, pp. 73–4.

bear in mind what Hans Küng has called 'paradigm' change,[20] the shifting of that 'constellation of beliefs, values, techniques',[21] which characterises the theology of an era, and which is in part a reflection of its general cultural pattern. Küng draws a useful parallel with the movement in physics from Ptolemaic to Copernican, Newtonian and Einsteinian models.[22] One may move into another by a gradual process, so that it is only in the middle of a period that it is most characteristically itself.[23] For Küng's 'paradigms' we might substitute in Christian polemic the emphasis upon certain leading ideas in a given period, or at least chief preoccupations: the Christological and Trinitarian debates of the early centuries, for example; or the anxieties of the sixteenth-century reformers about 'justification'.

A special difficulty we must confront in this chapter concerns the paradoxical persistence of certain patterns of ecclesial self-consciousness of 'confessional identity' beyond the period in which they were natural and timely. Baptists, for example have justified their continuance as Baptists on different grounds in different periods.[24] The question is, if the good reasons there were for beginning do not necessarily persist, whether a given ecclesial body is justified in continuing to proclaim its distinct identity for the reasons it originally did so, and in basing its claim to be a certain kind of church upon them. If it alters its basis, can it be the same church as it was? Is there a way of acknowledging provisionality which will allow it to move towards other churches and still somehow be itself?

From dissidents to reformers

Before a plurality of ecclesiologies became current, the only ecclesiologically serious test-case was the dissident, heretical or schismatic community. The Donatists in North Africa from the fourth century did not see themselves as a new church. Their quarrel with the Catholics was over a point of order. They argued that the local catholic church had allowed a break in the ministerial succession, by accepting as Bishop of Carthage in 311 a candidate consecrated by a *traditor*, one who had given up the Scriptures during the persecution under the Emperor Diocletian. From their own point of view, the

---

[20] H. Küng, *Theology for the New Millennium*, tr. P. Heinegg (NewYork/London 1988).
[21] *Ibid.*, p. 132, quoting Thomas Kuhn.
[22] *Ibid.*, p. 134.   [23] Cf. *ibid.*, p. 213 on 'epochal thresholds'.
[24] A shift discussed by P.M. Harrison, *Authority and Power in the Free Church Tradition. A Social Case Study of the American Baptist Tradition* (Princeton, 1959).

Donatists were doing the reverse of initiating schism, or seeking to make the Church afresh. They were the guardians of its continuity.

Catholic apologists were forced to think hard ecclesiologically to accommodate the difficulty they posed. We have seen how Augustine of Hippo framed the principle which allows for the possibility that a separated community in which some of the essential elements of the Church persist may be somehow partly the Church,[25] and its sacraments, though inefficacious, may be valid; all that is needed then for reconciliation is the return to the unity of the Church. Not all early examples could be so easily resolved, and a variety of opinions is found in the early Christian centuries as to the mode of reconciliation, or indeed whether reconciliation can be possible at all.[26]

From the late eleventh century a number of new dissident and heretical groups began to appear in the West. They were broadly of two sorts: dualists, spiritual heirs of the Gnostics and of Augustine's Manichees;[27] and anticlerical or anti-establishment groups, such as the Waldensians, who preached a return to apostolic poverty and simplicity of life, but who held no views radically irreconcilable with orthodoxy on matters of faith except (in some cases) on sacraments and ministry. These are all seen by the Roman Church's apologists at the time as having taken themselves out of the Church. The standard formula in the mid-thirteenth century for expressing the principle on which they might be deemed to belong to it again, speaks of returning 'to the unity of the Church'. The sentences enacted against heretics in Toulouse in 1246 by the Inquisitors Bernard Gui and Jean de Saint-Pierre on behalf of the Church, for example, include relaxations of excommunications where the heretics have repented and declared their wish to return not 'to the Church' but 'to the unity of the Church'. Conversely, the proper procedure for dealing with unrepentant heretics is to make their separation from the Church quite explicit. Beguins, whose imitation of apostolic poverty and connections with the radical 'spiritual' Franciscans had them condemned by the Church in 1311, are stated by Bernard Gui to 'hold errors and erroneous opinions and to dogmatize against the true faith and the *status* of the Holy Roman

---

[25] See earlier on being 'partly the Church'.   [26] L. Saltet, *Les Réordinations* (Paris, 1907).
[27] See S. Runciman, *The Mediaeval Manichee* (Cambridge, 1947), on whether they were their actual heirs.

and universal Church and against apostolic power'. Such a group is pejoratively spoken of as a *secta*.[28]

Bernard Gui uses *secta* of all his classes of heretic, the latter-day Manichees; the Waldensians; the Beguins and converted Jews who have 'returned to the vomit' of their former persuasion. The term seems to have some connotation of locality. The Beguins or *fratres pauperes* have recently arisen, he explains, in Provence and Narbonne and in some areas of Toulouse.[29] But its chief sense is of a self-contained and separatist group which has arrogantly deemed itself better than the Church in some way.[30]

Even if the *secta* is essentially a splinter-group and not a church, it has some claim to be thought of ecclesially, nevertheless. Among the sentences of Bernard de Caux and Jean de Saint-Pierre against those found guilty of heresy are descriptions designed to help inquisitors identify heretics of various sorts. Belonging to such a *secta* is seen as not only a matter of believing what its members believe, but also of associating with them, and especially perhaps of eating with them bread which they have blessed.[31] Thus we have a shared faith, the gathering of the worshipping community, and the common 'Eucharist' and so, arguably, the defining marks, or at least some of the key marks, of the presence of the Church. The answer to our questions in the case of a 'sect', then, is that in many instances its members have a conviction which is challenged by the mainstream Church. At that stage all that is needed for unity is for its members to acknowledge that they have made a mistake and return to the fold. If that does not happen, because the issue is not an error but a difference of emphasis or a correction of balance in the life of the community, the germs of a real church may be apparent, and then the principal anomaly in the situation becomes the state of separation between them.

Perhaps the most important single change of the Reformation

---

[28] By which is meant against the authority of St Peter lodged in the Bishop of Rome. Bernard Gui, *Manuel de l'Inquisiteur*, IV.9, ed. G. Mollat (Paris, 1926), vol. I, p. 184.

[29] *Ibid.*, vol. IV.1, p. 108.

[30] The meaning of the term seems to have undergone some evolution by Wyclif's day at the end of the century. He uses it, perhaps metaphorically, though equally pejoratively, of the *sectae* of the monastic orders, the friars and so on. Calvin also thought rival monastic orders and fraternities could be seen as 'destroying the communion of the Church', *Inst. Chr.*, IV.xiii. 14–16, *CR* 30.935–7, and see McNeill, *Unitive Protestantism*, p. 258. Nevertheless, the sect remains 'something contradictory and unnatural, a paradox and an enigma'. G. Florovsky, 'The limits of the Church', *Church Quarterly Review*, 117 (1933–4), 117–31, p. 117. Cf. Krauth, p. 189 on 'sectarian orthodoxy' and 'Christian orthodoxy'.

[31] *Documents*, ed. Douais, pp. 23ff.

period in the West concerned the image dissident groups came to have of themselves. They began, reluctantly in many cases, to see themselves as 'churches'. There seems to be no exact equivalent of this among the mediaeval *sectae*. To some extent this radical shift was masked by the fact that, in the congregationally based 'gathered church' ecclesiology of many reforming schools of thought, the churches to which they belonged were in a recognisable sense simply local churches which had withdrawn from communion with a catholic Church which they believed to have become corrupt. That could also be claimed, and was, on behalf of a larger, for example, a national church; it happened in the case of the Church of England. Thus Peter Heylyn says in the preface to his *A Briefe Answer to Henry Burton* (London, 1637), referring to the Church of England, that 'in the reformation of this Church, we introduced no novelties into the same, but onely laboured to reduce her to that estate and quality, wherein she was in her originall beauty, and the Primitive times'. Despite the widespread conviction among the sixteenth-century reformers that there was no making of new churches in their process of reform, but only a return to the apostolic Church, a new situation was in fact created. Two or more ecclesial communities, out of communion with each other and both claiming to be the original and continuing Church, came into parallel existence in a single area. The question not then fully addressed, but now ecumenically urgent, is whether they could both be the local church there, and how they were to continue to live in relation to one another.

NOT NEW BUT CONTINUING

Justifications

Perhaps no division in the history of the Church has been brought about by purely religious causes. Differences of theology have tended to contribute to the justification of division rather than prompting it in the first place. The group of justifications which follow next have in common the overriding assumption that there has been no making of a new church but faithfulness in continuity with the old. Here the first essential is to be able in conscience to hold that the existing Church or churches are either not any longer truly 'Church', or that they are imperfect or inadequate vehicles of a grace which is now acting more fully and vigorously in the new community. The Reformed tradition, for example, has stressed 'the perennial nature of the Church' and the continuity of Reformed with primitive Christianity. It claims in support of this position that the uniqueness and eternal validity of Christ's work guarantees the oneness of his Church through the ages. His Kingship never fails. God will not let his Church perish.[32]

The Church has fallen into error, or into the hands of Satan, and is therefore no longer the Church

A decisive step was taken in the West at the end of the twelfth century with the first murmurs that the Church was now under the control of Antichrist. This became a strong and consistent line of attack from the thirteenth to the sixteenth century and beyond. Similar sentiments persist even much later.[33]

It began to be argued that Antichrist now sat in the chair of St Peter. If that were true, the behaviour of the Roman Church could be seen – and was seen – as involving a positive conspiracy against the truth and a diabolical design to carry off the souls of the people of God to Hell. Wyclif and later dissidents had willing listeners when they said that.[34]

But it could not be thought that God would not have foreseen this happening, or that he could be outwitted by Satan. 'Since the holy and omniscient Spirit anticipated that all these outward ceremonies would go under because of Antichrist and would degenerate through misuse, he gladly yielded these tokens to Satan and fed, gave to drink, baptised and gathered the faithful with the Spirit and the truth in such a way that nothing would be lost to truth, although all outer transactions might pass away', suggested Sebastian Franck in a letter to the lapsed Lutheran John Campanus.[35]

---

[32] Thus the Roman Catholic Church of the sixteenth century is the Church 'suspended'. J.J. Von Allmen, 'The continuity of the Church according to Reformed teaching', *Journal of Ecumenical Studies*, 1 (1964), 424–44.

[33] In 1839 in the *Historical Part of the Testimony of the Reformed Presbyterian Church in Scotland* (Glasgow, 1839), pp. 32ff., we still find the Pope linked with Babylon, and it is asked why God allowed this 'determined opposition to the Gospel scheme of redemption' to go on for 1,260 years. Rome is accused of suppressing evidence.

[34] R. Bauckham, *Tudor Apocalypse* (Abingdon, 1978).

[35] *Spiritual and Anabaptist Writers*, ed. G.H. Williams (London, 1957), p. 150.

It was a corollary to such claims that it must be the duty of true Christians to resist the usurper.[36]

But a church whose identity rests on such a conviction of the absolute otherness, the total alienation from Christ, of another church, cannot logically become united with that church without altering a good deal of its reason for existing, unless it is satisfied either that it was wrong (psychologically difficult to admit) or sees alteration in the other church (liable to be mistrusted).

We have always been the Church; it is you who are the innovators[37] and the schismatics

When challenged that they are dividing Christ's Body by their separation, communities frequently answer that it is not they but their opponents who are causing the schism. Both sides consider themselves to be faithful to Christ. Often both sides claim to want peace. But either the intransigence of the other side, or the wiles of Satan, prevent it. As peace comes closer, warns Jean Gerson (1363–1429) (only too accurately),' the enemy of peace rages more wildly ... If he can, he will introduce division among those who are about to bring about union, by means of pride, lust or envy, so as to continue the schism.'[38] The 'schism' to which he refers took place in the context of the conciliarist debate, and was not strictly of the sort which is now the object of ecumenical concern. It involved Pope and anti-Pope, and a party anxious to replace a monarchical papal government with a conciliar government by bishops acting together.[39] But, *mutatis mutandis*, similar comments can be found in a variety of ecumenical contexts in other ages. It is a perennially

---

[36] It was another that those who were seen to fail to meet standards of Christian faithfulness should be subjected to extremely severe personal discipline. A case in point was the brutal process of 'excommunication' among seventeenth-century Quakers in the New World, of those somehow not fitting in. In one case at least, a woman bearing a malformed child was held to have been punished by God and held up by him as an example to be shunned. See J. Minsser, 'Mary Dyer and the "Monster" story', *Quaker History*, 79 (1990), 20–34, pp. 20ff. George Eliot's Silas Marner is driven out of his worshipping community when he is suspected of theft. George Eliot, *Silas Marner* (London, 1861), Part I, chapter 1. He was 'solemnly suspended from church-membership ... only on confession as the sign of repentance, could he be received once more within the fold of the Church'.

[37] 'In the early stages of any schism, its promoters ... seldom fail to reproach the Catholic Church with a spirit of innovation.' Knox, *Enthusiasm*, p. 60.

[38] Jean Gerson, tractate on the *Unity of the Church*, 1409, ed. E. du Pin, *Gersoni Opera Omnia* (Antwerp, 1706), vol. II, pp. 113–18.

[39] See for an up-to-date account, P.E. Sigmund's introduction to his translation of Nicholas of Cusa, *The Catholic Concordance* (Cambridge, 1991).

recurring reaction. Anglican divines of the seventeenth century often take the line that it is Rome not the Church of England which is schismatic. In a discussion of the role of the Augsburg Confession published in 1977 one contributor remarks on the danger that if Roman Catholics come to accept the Augsburg Confession, some Lutherans will feel obliged to say that the Confession itself is not in accordance with Luther's mature thought; or that Melanchthon framed it in such a way as to avoid certain issues (such as the Papacy, purgatory, the sacrifice of the Mass),[40] and it is therefore not definitive on matters which still stand between Rome and the Lutheran community. This attitude has better possibility of being brought round to a unitive stance because all that is required is a concession that there may have been fault on both sides, or that at any rate the ecclesial identity of neither side depends on the maintenance of separation. Nevertheless, it would still take a high degree of acceptance of provisional character of both churches hitherto, to make it possible to attempt it.

We have returned to the apostolic life

If a number of religious Orders in the later Middle Ages believed themselves to be returning to the simplicity and poverty of the lives lived by the Apostles, and thus to be following as directly as possible the example set by Christ,[41] the driving force was always in part revulsion against the wealth and corruption which was seen to exist in the Church. Twelfth-century diatribes are already full of such accusations.[42] But there was also a positive inspiration, a vision of a Christian life lived in simple trust in the Lord.

These Orders were not churches. Nevertheless, from the twelfth century, many of the new and more extreme religious Orders began to seem to the authorities in the Church to constitute a threat, and to be placing themselves in some ways outside the Church.[43] Persecution sometimes made them see themselves as having become outcast because they were 'elect'. They therefore served to some degree to raise the same anxieties as would-be ecclesial communities wishing to separate themselves from Rome were to do in the sixteenth century, though for different reasons. Their existence forced the

---

[40] H. Schmüte, *The Role of the Augsburg Confession* (Philadelphia, 1977), p. 51
[41] See in general G. Leff, *Heresy in the Later Middle Ages* (Manchester, 1967), 2 vols.
[42] E.g. Peter the Chanter, *Verbum Abbreviatum, PL* 205.   [43] Leff, *Heresy*, vol.I, p. 7.

Church to condemn what they stood for, in order to defend itself and
to make it clear that they were an undesirable phenomenon. So we
have the apparent absurdity of the Church's attempts from the
thirteenth century to demonstrate that far from advocating poverty,
Christ had condemned it,[44] at least in some of the forms it was taking
in the fringe groups.

The threat these groups posed was partly political, and especially
to the property-structures of society. A few were overtly revolutionary. Cola di Rienzo set up a (brief) revolutionary commune in
Rome in 1347, with the dual vision of reviving the old glory of Rome
and bringing in a new era of purity and poverty.[45] The first Christian Emperor Constantine (d. 337) was held to have given an
endowment to the Church in his Donation[46] which Sylvester, the
Pope of the day, ought not to have accepted.[47] The Church could be
said to have gone astray since then; for corruption had crept into it
as a result of its wealth.[48] The essence of this dissident mediaeval
concept of 'being apostolic' did not consist primarily in its continuity
with the time of the Apostles or with their persons. There was no
insistence that a linear succession was necessary, such as that which
could be seen in the laying on of hands in the ministry of the Church.
To be 'apostolic' was simply to imitate the Apostles who imitated
Christ. Wyclif, writing *De Officio Pastorali* at the end of the fourteenth century, says exactly that. 'Each person ought to follow
Christ ... The apostles and other priests of the Lord after them
imitated Christ in his evangelical poverty.'[49]

The same straightforward approach to defining 'apostolicity' is
evident in the sixteenth century, although there is now an awareness
of the importance of an idea of succession. Conrad Grebel's Letter to
Thomas Münzer of September 1525 says: 'Christ in the old and
especially in the New Testament bids his messengers simply proclaim the Word.'[50] The Swiss Reformer Johannes Bullinger
(1504–75) cites Tertullian as one who 'greatly esteems (and rightly)

---

[44] *Ibid.*, and especially pp. 51ff.
[45] See P. Puir, *Cola di Rienzo* (Vienna, 1931), also *Briefwechsel des Cola di Rienzo in Vom Mittelalter zur Reformation* vol. II, (Berlin, 1912–29).
[46] The Donation of Constantine was in fact a forgery, as began to be recognised in the fifteenth century.
[47] Leff, *Heresy*, I.9.   [48] Gui, *Manuel*, vol. II.i, p. 35.
[49] Wyclif, *De Officio Pastorali*, I.ii, ed. G.V. Lechlin (Leipzig, 1863).
[50] Letter from Conrad Grebel to Thomas Münzer, 5 September 1525, ed. C.A. Cornelius, *Geschichte der Münsterischen Aufruhrs*, vol. II (Leipzig, 1860), pp. 240–7 and tr. W. Rauschen-busch in *The American Journal of Theology*, 9 (1905), 91–9, and Bullinger, *Decades* V.i (1551).

the continual succession of pastors in the Church, yet he requires it to be approved by the sincerity of the apostolic doctrine, indeed he accepts as apostolic churches those churches which are instructed in pure doctrine and yet cannot make any reckoning of a succession of bishops'.[51]

Carried within the emphasis on poverty was an implication that institutional structures were corrupting and unnecessary; and within its stress on simplicity and directness the notion that preaching the Gospel was the one thing needful. That is not to say that all dissidents set a lower value on the ministry of the sacraments. But the seed was there. Those prejudices would have to be eased for it to be possible for the heirs of these groups to enter into communion with certain types of Church structure in a future united Church. Experience shows that they still lie very close to the surface in surprising places.[52]

The distinction between the two conceptions of 'apostolic' is important. If to be apostolic is to imitate Christ, there need be no ecumenical blockage here. But if it involves proven succession of some sort from the Apostles there are real difficulties.[53]

We are the (persecuted) remnant clinging to the truth

For Arnold of Villanova at the end of the thirteenth century, as for many in the contemporary 'poverty' movement, the supreme test was Christlikeness attested by poverty of life. It was endorsed by the evidence of the persecution of these 'apostles of poverty' by a corrupt Church.[54] At the same time, there needed to be a deliberate evacuation of the power and authority of the Church of Rome, so as to make it plain that it was God's will to entrust the perpetuation of his Church to the poor and faithful remnant. That view is widely found, among different sorts of late mediaeval dissident.[55] The Pseudo-Apostles begun by Segarelli of Parma in 1260 are, says Bernard Gui, of the opinion that the entire authority given to Rome by Christ is 'omnino evacuata et eam cessavit propter malitiam prelato-

---

[51] Bullinger, *Decades*, VI.i (1551), para. 23.
[52] See *Proceedings* of the General Synod of the Church of England for November 1985, debate on *The Priesthood of the Ordained Ministry*.
[53] See chapter 4.
[54] Arnold of Villanova (d.1311), *De Tempore Antichristi* (before 1297), ed. H. Finke in *Aus den Tagen Bonifaz VIII* (Münster, 1902), and see Leff, *Heresy*, pp. 177ff., especially p. 182.
[55] Gui, *Manuel* vol. I.i, p. 10, and cf. Leff, *Heresy*, vol.I, pp. 195ff.

rum.'[56] it is of significance here that the issue is not whether the Lord gave special authority to Peter over and above the other Apostles. It is accepted that Peter was entrusted with it; but he has lost it, or rather his successors have lost it, through their own fault.

There are different views as to what has to be done to restore the Church to Christ. The Spiritual Franciscans, with their Joachimist traits,[57] were inclined to see the progressive unfolding of the Gospel as accounting for and taking place in the alterations from one generation to the next, and not to look on the corrupted Church as no longer the Church at all.[58] It is a Church divided into spiritual and carnal, but still one Church. The *ecclesia carnalis* has fallen into the hands of Antichrist, but it has not thereby ceased to be the Church. The Spirituals' duty is to wrest it from the usurpers' hands and give it back to Christ. The spiritual remnant is to bear personal witness and to suffer, and that will bring about the renewal of the Church and its reform; it will not bring a new Church into being, for that is not what is needed; nor will it bring the existing Church under a new Gospel. The eternal Evangel which Joachim of Fiore had spoken of is not a new Gospel, but a full and spiritual understanding of the present Gospel.

This conviction that there is one Church and it has never been wholly lost to Satan (indeed is indefectible), is of crucial importance. It is worth raising here the possibility that the failure of the Council of Florence proved to be a determinant in this respect. Greek and Latin Christians became two Churches in a way they had not acknowledged themselves to be before, and thus the pattern was set for a new sort of plural ecclesiology.[59]

Many of the mediaeval themes continue unaltered in the new sixteenth-century context. Among the radicals, Thomas Münzer preached a sermon before the Princes on Daniel 2, on 13 July 1525, in which he told his audience of 'poor, ailing, disintegrating Christendom', and spoke of the work of the 'servants of God' to counsel and aid her. But even these real friends of God must be wary, so that they are not misled by Satan and his servants. But at

[56] Gui, *Manuel*, vol. III, pp. 1–3, pp. 85–6.
[57] Joachim of Fiore (*c.*1132–1202), controversial though he was (and condemned by the Fourth Lateran Council), succeeded in putting into circulation through his prophecy the view that all world history was the working out of God's purposes in successive Ages of Father, Son and Holy Spirit, and that the end was in sight. See M. Reeves, *The Influence of Prophecy in the Later Middle Ages* (Oxford, 1969).
[58] Leff, *Heresy*, vol. I, pp. 76 and 176.   [59] See G.R. Evans, in *Christian Unity*.

the same time there was a new willingness to start afresh and to make the Church anew in a small congregation or gathering of the faithful. 'There must be … sent into the churches of the realm evangelists', says Martin Bucer, 'from whose whole life and manner of devotion it is obvious that they are … seeking … those things which pertain to the glory of Christ and the repair of the churches.'[60]

In all these grounds for challenging the Church or actually breaking away from it, there is an element of enmity towards other Christians who are in some way falling short, or even working against Christ who ought to be their Lord. It is this hostility which is the ultimately irreconcilable element in the ecclesial identities of such churches or proto-churches, ecumenically speaking. To abandon it would, in many instances, mean abandoning a *raison d'être*. It has to be argued that legitimate provisionality cannot extend to include hostility.

THE FREEDOM OF THE SPIRIT

We are led directly by the Spirit

Much of what we have considered so far in this chapter has involved a challenge to order in the Church on the grounds that it has become corrupt. But order can be challenged more radically. Tertullian (*c.* 160–*c.* 220), while still a Catholic, credited Montanists (whom he later joined) with the belief that while the Holy Spirit fell upon the Apostles at Pentecost, the full gift of the Paraclete was reserved for a later age.[61] The belief that the Holy Spirit may be given spontaneously and powerfully, not only within but perhaps quite independently of the Church's structures, has created a series of ecclesial patterns.

The perennial and natural (and the New Testament suggests divinely ordained) tension in the church between 'charism' and 'order', between the freedom to follow where the Spirit leads, and the maintenance of a settled order in the Church, has been vastly stimulating. But it always generates pressures. At some periods they have been divisive. That may happen because of a dislike of certain

---

[60] Martin Bucer, *De Regno Christi*, Book II, chapter IV, paras. 384–6.
[61] *De praescriptione haereticorum*, 52, ed. E. Dekkers, J.G.P. Borleffs, R. Willems, *CCSL* 1, 2 (Turnhout, 1954). See too Knox, *Enthusiasm*, p. 34.

aspects of contemporary 'order' as much as out of a belief that 'charism' ought to be supreme.

Anticlericalism underlies much of the dissidence of the later Middle Ages, and constitutes its chief challenge to an existing order seen as exemplified in the ordained ministry. Then, as we have noted, the emphasis was upon the corruption and wealth of many of the clerical class. For Wyclif it consisted partly in a resentment of clergy behaving as though they were secular 'lords'.[62] But gradually the objection shifted. In the Reformation period, a series of more theologically complex objections was framed. 'Priests' were seen as usurping the unique High Priesthood of Christ, as seeking to add to his sacrifice on the Cross by teaching a doctrine of the sacrifice of the Mass which was held to imply that his sacrifice had been insufficient for the sins of the whole world and needed to be repeated. They were described as imposing burdens on the faithful (in the penitential system in particular), which were unnecessary, and certainly not indispensable for salvation.[63] One consequence was a shift of emphasis in some quarters to the concept of an equal 'priesthood' of all believers. Robert Browne, the founder of the Brownists in England, began a community in Norwich about 1581, in which he stressed that all the people were 'king, prophet and priest' under Christ.[64] But there was a tendency to confuse here the notion of believers as individually priests, with the Scripturally explicit principle of a collective priesthood of all believers in Christ, and by virtue of their union with Christ. One result of all this was a tendency in some reforming quarters to emphasise the duty to preserve the freedom promised to Christians in Scripture, even if that had to be done at the expense of the maintenance of order.

The balance between charism and order will never be easy to maintain. Too much order rigidifies and creates oppression. Too much spontaneity can produce chaos. The most that can be hoped for in the mending of divisions is an acceptance by extremist positions that there ought to be a balance, and that they have got it wrong. But to ask charismatics to submit to regulation, or a highly ordered ecclesial society to open itself freely to the action of the Spirit, is to ask it to risk ceasing to be itself as it understands itself.

---

[62] Wyclif, *Tractatus de Officio Pastorali*, ed. G.V. Lechler (Leipzig, 1863), vol. I, p. iv.

[63] See my *Problems of Authority in the Reformation Debates* (Cambridge, 1992).

[64] W.C. Braithwaite, *The Beginnings of Quakerism* (London, 1912), 2nd edn revised J. Cadbury (Cambridge, 1955), p. 5.

When Protestant Pentecostals and Roman Catholics met in dialogue and produced a Final Report in 1976 the text was careful to make it clear that the discussion had not set out 'to concern itself with the problems of imminent structural union'.[65] Nor did it prove possible to issue a joint statement in the form of an agreement. The text simply 'represents the content of the discussion'.[66] It is instructive that it proved necessary to avoid direct consideration of 'the relationship of the charismatic movement among Catholics to the Catholic Church', although it was hoped that it might prove illuminating there.[67]

Baptists and individualists

Out of the 'radical' Reformation, which took lines of thought about the freedom of the Spirit to extremes, came a number of more moderate churches in the 'Free Church' tradition. The Baptists began, not perhaps directly as a result of Anabaptist movements of the Reformation, but more probably because of left-wing Calvinist activity in Holland and in England in the early seventeenth century. There was also some reaction against the mainstream Protestant churches, with what were seen as their centralising and increasingly hierarchical tendencies. Baptists see a radical disjunction between 'the competence of the individual to discern the mind of Christ within a community of worship and discipline' which is itself free 'to govern its own affairs apart from the direction of Church Councils or associations of churches'; and any system within which 'officers' have authority to interfere with those freedoms.[68]

Ecclesiologically speaking, the chief difficulty with this has been that this primary emphasis upon the freedom of the individual has a tendency to contradict the concept of the autonomous gathered church.[69] Individuals may in fact take a stand on a variety of 'Baptist distinctives' so that it is difficult for Baptists to settle on a

---

[65] 4, *Growth*, p. 422.   [66] 46, *Growth*, p. 430.   [67] 9, *Growth*, p. 423.

[68] P.M. Harrison, *Authority and Power in the Free Church Tradition. A Social Case Study of the American Baptist Tradition* (Princeton, 1959), pp. vii-viii. One author comments, 'Let it be understood that the basic doctrine of Baptists is the dignity, sanctity and competency of the individual believer. I do not mean to say that we put this doctrine ahead of our belief in the sovereignty of God ... or justification by faith ... or of the necessity of religious experience ... but it is this belief in the dignity, sanctity and competency of the individual which Baptists through the ages have felt compelled to emphasise.' E.H. Pruden, *Interpreters Needed* (Philadelphia, 1951), p. 54.

[69] Harrison, *Authority and Power*, p. 26.

single clear polity; indeed, within the boundaries established by the post-Calvinist Free Church movements, the Baptists have considered every mode of 'church-order'.[70] There has also been a shift over time. The emphasis upon the free movement of the Holy Spirit in the Churches, and upon Gospel freedom, tended by the early nineteenth century to have become overlaid in Baptist thinking by an almost exclusive stress 'upon the sovereignty of man and the freedom of the local congregations from any form of ecclesiastical control'.[71]

Some commentators would argue that drawbacks have emerged. The first is that 'in the Baptist situation the desire to curtail the influence of ecclesiastical personnel was so emphasised that other needs of the church organisation were sacrificed'.[72] Something of an improvised, *ad hoc* Church order has tended to result.[73] A second drawback has been a tendency for individuals to achieve great power informally, and thus in ways which are difficult to control. This has had the result that the great aim of avoiding any kind of ecclesiastical 'caste-system' proves in practice hard to achieve.[74]

One lesson of all this is that continuity over time (in this case in 'Baptist' principles) may coexist with very great discontinuities without apparently destroying the conviction of Baptists that there is a 'Baptist' identity. This is a useful illustration of the kind of provisionality which can coexist with a continuing sense of identity in what is in fact considerable diversity. But it is open to question whether the Baptists themselves would see theirs as an 'ecclesial' identity, and not rather a set of attitudes characteristic of individual Baptist Christians. We have to postulate that there may be a type of distinctive Christian identity which is not ecclesial in its own self-image.

Pentecostalists

Something similar applies in Pentecostalism. Modern Pentecostalism again springs from the desire to be responsive to direct action and inspiration by the Holy Spirit. Here perhaps are to be found the

---

[70] *Ibid.*, p. 33.   [71] *Ibid.*, pp. 11–12.   [72] *Ibid.*, p. 7.

[73] Winthrop S. Hudson, 'Are Baptists so peculiar?', *Christian Century*, 70 (2) (18 November, 1953), 1234 and 'Stumbling into disorder', *Foundations*, 1, 2 (April, 1958), 45. See, too, William R. McNutt, *Polity and Practice in the Baptist Churches* (Philadelphia, 1935), pp. 21–2.

[74] Harrison, *Authority and Power*, p. 7 and p. 217, p. 219 and cf. D. Martin, *Tongues of Fire: The Explosion of Protestantism in Latin America* (Oxford, 1990).

true heirs of the sixteenth-century radicals. The position of the Pentecostalist churches is therefore ecclesiologically peculiar. They do not function within a 'new order'. Bodies – or individuals – see themselves as largely independent of most formal order. Common (generally speaking) to the multiplicity of the forms Pentecostalism takes is an emphasis upon baptism by the Spirit. This must take place after conversion. It is seen as prophesied in Scripture and as the event of Pentecost, but also as repeated since Pentecost in each new generation of God's people. Its sign or token is speaking with tongues.[75]

There is in principle no reason why a member of another church should not remain so after his baptism by the Spirit.[76] There are Roman Catholic and Anglican charismatics as well as Orthodox for whom the life of the Spirit is central. But Pentecostal manifestations often have been mistrusted and even feared in the more mainstream churches and Pentecostals often discouraged from continuing their membership. Earlier this century a Los Angeles Presbyterian church meeting declared,

From this time onward, no man or woman will be allowed to hold membership in this Church who is sympathetic with, has part in, or attempts to bring this teaching among our people, or attempts to send members or attendants of this Church to places where this so-called Pentecostal movement holds sway ... Our Confession of faith gives no room for holding, teaching, or expressing sympathy for, participating in, or attending so-called Pentecostal or tongues meetings.[77]

Those who 'go over' to Pentecostal churches have often brought into them the prejudices of their church of origin. 'Many who formerly were Lutherans, Methodists, Baptists, Quakers, and so on, still retain their old views regarding various important questions.'[78] Consequently there have been internal squabbles. Groups have tended to be loyal to particular leaders who started Pentecostalism

---

[75] See J.T. Nichol, *Pentecostalism* (New York, 1966), pp. 7–11. It is of importance that there has been a shift from the original Pentecostal principle of Acts 2 that speaking in tongues is comprehensible, to the modern expectation that it will not be understood by the hearer.

[76] The Evangelical movement has fared rather differently ecclesiologically. It is possible to be an Evangelical and remain an Anglican, or a member of some other church. This must be put down partly to the powerful emphasis upon the personal salvation of the individual which has always made ecclesiological considerations somewhat secondary for Evangelicals.

[77] 'Persecution of Pentecostals' in *Pentecostal Testimony* (May 1938), p. 11.

[78] T.B. Barratt, 'An urgent plea for charity and unity', *Word and Work*, 39 (April 1911), 105ff.

in an area, and even to fight other groups and their leaders.[79] So the development of the inchoate ecclesiology of such churches has frequently been further complicated by fissiparous tendencies within them, and once more it seems that the individual's 'Pentecostal identity' is the key factor rather than a corporate sense of *ecclesial* identity.

The integration of such attitudes in a single great communion presents first of all the difficulty that those who hold them resist such integration. Radical prejudices against other churches come piecemeal, and often out of ignorance, and with a simplified sense of what was historically at stake.

THE CALL TO PERFECTION: GOD TELLS US THAT WE MUST SEPARATE OURSELVES FROM YOU

We come now to a group of starting-points for 'new' churches which have proved historically to be intimately interrelated. These also have connections with the doctrine that the Holy Spirit acts directly and independently of established order when he chooses, and must be obeyed when he calls. Exclusiveness is always associated with the belief that one's community sets strictly Christian standards and has a higher call. Tertullian helped to establish the 'rigorist' tradition in the third century.[80] The Circumcellions in Augustine's North Africa engaged in dramatic acts of self-immolation, and even went so far as to make violent attacks on catholics in which they demanded their own martyrdom on pain of the other's death.[81] This is an ecclesially oriented asceticism, and thus quite different in its tendency from that which informs monastic and eremitical life. It insists that something special is required of those God especially loves. They do not belong in the world. They are to be perfectly pure and that may mean being utterly exclusive.

The belief that God demands withdrawal not only from the world, but also from others calling themselves Christians but variously failing to be the true Church, takes a number of forms through the centuries. The call to withdrawal may rest on the grounds that separatists themselves are preserving continuity of order. (As the Donatists in late antique North Africa regarded the ordaining bishop as an apostate, and due order as having been

[79] Nichol, *Pentecostalism*, pp. 81ff.
[80] Knox, *Enthusiasm*, p. 37, for a useful brief setting the context.   [81] *Ibid.*, pp. 58–61.

broken.)[82] But more commonly, a perceived breach of faith or error about priorities on the part of others is the reason.

The leaders of separatist groups frequently argue that it is God's will that his people should keep themselves pure by separation. Joseph Hall outlines the views of the Separatists of early seventeenth-century England on this point. The 'Brownists' to whom he is addressing himself claim that separation was 'first founded in the enmity which God himself put between the seed of the women and the seed of the serpent'.[83] So it has scriptural warrant.

Even within otherwise non-separatist movements with perhaps 'enthusiasm' rather than 'excess', calls for 'purity' linked with 'apartness' from other Christians may arise. In early nineteenth-century Methodism those who met in Classes often looked with suspicion on those who just came to worship at the Chapels and gave to the Connexional Funds, but did not properly belong. There was fear that they would create impurity in the movement.[84]

By definition, an ecclesiology of separateness is irreconcilable with unity with other Christians. The only way forward here would seem to be to come to understand purity in its association with holiness within the Church as something which must be lived *within* a fallen human community. But that is to sacrifice what has for many seemed the essence of the matter.

Holiness

It is important here that the Holy Spirit is seen, in Orthodox and in radical Protestant ecclesiology, as acting in significantly different ways. To the Orthodox he is above all the informing presence of holiness. It is he who makes the sacraments vehicles of grace, and who teaches and guides the Church. He is not in Orthodoxy ever a Spirit of separatism. To Protestant radicals he is perhaps primarily the Spirit of freedom, who can and does act independently of the ecclesial structures and who refuses to be bound by rules of human devising. It is in this light that 'separatism' and an exclusivist 'purity' tend to have been regarded in certain Western ecclesial communities as belonging with the 'holiness' which results from the

---

[82] See chapter 4 on restoring order.
[83] Genesis 3:15. Joseph Hall, *A Common Apology against the Brownists, Works*, IX.11.
[84] Bowmer, *Pastor and People*, p. 85. Jonathan Crowther, *The Methodist Manual* (Halifax, 1810), p. 130.

indwelling of the Holy Spirit. In 1948, Pentecostals of the Pentecostal fellowship of North America added to the 1943 Statement of Faith of the National Association of Evangelicals in the USA, 'We believe that the full Gospel includes holiness of heart and life, healing for the body and baptism in the Holy Spirit, with the initial evidence of speaking in other tongues as the Spirit gives utterance.'[85]

The 'Holiness' movement in the USA seems to have arisen partly from within Methodism. Important elements in the movement's teaching were the idea we have met in Pentecostalism, that there is a blessing for the Christian to seek and receive, which comes after, and is distinct from, conversion;[86] that it involves conscious endeavour to be led by the Spirit in all things; that believers ought to be looking always for the imminent return of Christ;[87] and that the believer must shun the world and all worldliness, and all that is not truly and purely the Church.[88]

Thus the drive for holiness is a drive for getting priorities right, and for reform, and it need not be incompatible with communion with the whole body of Christians. Ecumenically, the difficulties lie in the accretions and associations with which the idea of 'holiness' is sometimes hedged about.

The enthusiast

That brings us to the enthusiast. He is 'so sure of being in the right, that he would hold it an infidelity to countenance the scruples of those who disagree with him'.[89] This approach has certain ecclesiological implications in practice. 'The enthusiast always begins by trying to form a church within the Church, always ends by finding himself committed to sectarian opposition',[90] comments Knox in a classic study of *Enthusiasm* which I shall not try to extend here. Knox points to a type of ecclesiological problem we have not yet con-

---

85 Nichol, *Pentecostalism*, p. 4.
86 Cf. K. McKendrick, *The Promise Fulfilled: A History of the Modern Pentecostal Movement* (Springfield, Missouri, 1961), p. 47, quoting Reuben A. Torrey, 'The baptism with the Holy Spirit is an operation of the Holy Spirit distinct from and subsequent to his regenerating work ... an impartation of power, and the one who receives it is fitted for service ... [this is] not merely for the Apostles, nor merely for those of the apostolic age, but ... for every believer in every age of the Church's history.'
87 Cf. Nichol, *Pentecostalism*, pp. 26–8.
88 *Ibid.*, pp. 5–7. But in the early years of the Pentecostal movement in the British Isles, converts were not encouraged to form separate assemblies, but to remain in their churches. See D. Gee, *The Pentecostal Movement* (London, 1949), p. 88.
89 Knox, *Enthusiasm*, p. 18. 90 *Ibid.*, p. 109.

sidered, the inadvertent formation of a body of ecclesial claims as a result of resistance within an existing community to a particular plan of reform. He describes such a body as a sect, and thus throws up again sharply the question of the definition of a sect.[91] At the heart of that definition must lie the principle of deliberate segregation. I should like to suggest that that is incompatible with being a church and that the lesson of all these movements which consider themselves to have 'special' blessing is that they do not acknowledge that it is impossible to be the only church (with a small c).

The eclectic church

A final category of 'new church' which can conveniently be mentioned here is the eclectic mix of elements brought together by some driving social need. Rastafarians in the Caribbean have become the main rivals to Pentecostalism and to conservative Evangelicals there. Like some other marginal radical groups the Rastafarians look to a true Zion somewhere else – in this case in Ethiopia. There is a tendency for such groups to alternate between withdrawal from the world and coming explosively back into it in acts of physical militancy (a pattern found among the fourth-century Donatists, too). The Rastafarians have, like other groups of this sort, a mixed spiritual heritage. There is a spirituality derived from Methodism and the 'Holiness' churches of America which Methodism fathered, mingled with a 'black' spirituality stamped with the mood of the slave cultures of the early United States. 'It is the same kind of potent amalgam we find in the union of hymns and spirituals and protest songs which gave rise to the blues and to jazz. It crosses the most ancient layers of the "spirit" with the most modern manifestations of spirituality.'[92] Such ecclesially 'mixed' bodies are held together by bonds of particular common interest which may well be cultural or political. They can dissolve as quickly. They pose the issue of the stability of ecclesial bodies which seek to unite. The making of careful arrangements and agreements is appropriate only between bodies of settled opinions and established order. If all is provisional that may not be what is needed.

[91] I have not attempted in this book to tackle the question of the 'sects' such as the Moonies which exist outside or on the remote fringes of the Christian tradition.

[92] David Martin, *Tongues of Fire: The Explosion of Protestantism in Latin America* (Oxford, 1990) pp. 119, 164.

It will be evident as we go on that these elements uppermost in the ecclesiologies of churches which have become divided, especially in the West, do not tidily separate one from another. There is considerable overlap in the groupings of ideas definitive (in their members' eyes) of given churches. The kinds of difficulty about uniting which they present in their various combinations are very numerous indeed. We have to ask whether creating all these 'interfaces' (which is undoubtedly necessary) is going to be enough. These defining convictions are archetypal. They recur again and again in different periods and patterns, and they will do so in a future united Church. The task is to ensure that they do so without creating fissures in it, and breaking once more the bond of charity which is being so painstakingly mended.

THE CHURCH WHICH FOLLOWS A GREAT LEADER

Usually revelation grasps an individual, and through an individual it grasps a group; this group can then become a medium of revelation for other groups.'[93] A new ecclesial entity may come into being through the influence of one man with an idea (or a grievance).[94] It should be said that such a strong leader is very likely to be saying something which is true, or criticising something which needs to be criticised. But when that necessary message has been received and acted upon, he may continue to be revered in a way not necessarily always helpful to his followers' sense of belonging to the one Church. A number of today's churches still identify themselves at least in part by the name or following of a single figure. Lutherans, Calvinists, Methodists, for example, hold a great leader centrally within their traditions. The effects of a church's beginning in this way will, manifestly, vary with the character of the leader and with other factors in its history. But certain tendencies commonly emerge.

There will often be a strong, apparently simple, leading idea, to which people have been able to attach themselves in the early days of the movement. Luther's 'justification by faith' is far from being theologically uncomplicated;[95] but it can be grasped as a message of hope and comfort with an appealing and liberating directness. A similar sense of immediate release from sin and personal certainty of

---

[93] R. Modras, *Paul Tillich's Theology of the Church* (Detroit, 1976), p. 24.
[94] Cf. Apollos in 1 Corinthians 1:12.
[95] See A. McGrath, *Iustitia Dei* (Cambridge, 1986), 2 vols.

salvation came to Wesley when his 'heart' was 'strangely warmed' on 24 May 1783. 'I felt I did trust in Christ, Christ alone for salvation; and an assurance was given me that He had taken away *my* sins, even *mine*, and saved *me* from the law of sin and death.' 'By this faith', he reflected, 'we are saved from all uneasiness of mind, from the anguish of a wounded spirit, from discontent, from fear and sorrow of heart.'[96] At the age of twenty-two, George Fox, founder of the Society of Friends, heard a voice which said, 'there is one, even Christ Jesus, that can speak to thy condition', and when he 'heard it', he says, 'my heart did leap for joy ... My desires after the Lord grew stronger, and zeal in the pure knowledge of God and of Christ alone, without the help of any man, book or writing.'[97] Those who have known this joy and peace and certainty want to share it.

Simplicity and directness can be seen as virtue.[98] Seventeenth-century Quakers rejected what they saw as the contemporary playing of games with doctrine, and (with them) religion as a thing of doctrinal profession.[99] That such an experience could come to men of little education in theology and make them powerful witnesses, as it had in the beginning of the Church, is clear enough from the Wesleys' experience. Wesley relates in his Journal how 'God sent Mr. Bray to me, a poor, ignorant mechanic, who knows nothing but Christ; yet, by knowing Him, knows and discerns all things.' This was on 11 May 1738. Wesley went on wretchedly reaching out for faith for many days. On Whitsunday, 21 May, he was able to say, 'I believe, I believe'; but still he did not feel sure. He sent for Mr Bray. 'I ... asked him whether I believed. He answered, I ought not to doubt of it; it was Christ spoke to me.' Wesley was looking for a felt certainty, from one whom he believed to have it himself.

The appeal of the simple and immediate solution to spiritual difficulties could indeed lie in its very independence of the intellectual struggle with what comes to be seen as a mistaken or inadequate or misleading 'academic theology'. George Fox tried

[96] Wesley's *Journal, Works*, ed. F. Baker (Oxford, 1975), vol. I, pp. 23–4.

[97] George Fox, *Journal (1647)*, ed. J.L. Nickalls (Cambridge, 1952), vol. I, p. 11.

[98] A case of an individual who came to certainty without a systematic study of theology is the American Indian Papunhank, among the Quakers, who had been for many years 'unsettled', until he 'received an assurance that Love was good and that he needed no further inquiry upon it'. G.S. Brookes, *Friend Anthony Benezet* (Philadelphia, 1937), pp. 482–3 and 488.

[99] W.C. Braithwaite, *The Beginnings of Quakerism* (London, 1912), 2nd edn revised J. Cadbury (Cambridge, 1955), p. 17. See, too, D.W. Maxey, 'New light on Hannah Bernard, a Quaker "heretic"', *Quaker History*, 78 (1989), 61–86.

enquiring of various priests in his own search for a faith that would satisfy him, but he found them ignorant, weak or corrupt, and he came to the conclusion that 'being bred at Oxford or Cambridge was not enough to fit and qualify men to be ministers of Christ'. The idea was reinforced when he found that the Dissenting ministers were incapable of helping him either. He 'was as a stranger to all, relying wholly upon the Lord Jesus Christ'.[100] Such rejection of existing theologies, especially where they appear to fail to get at the root of the faith, can strengthen the independent conviction that a special revelation is being made to one individual.

That may be partly the result of ignorance, that is, of simply not knowing that what seems a new theological insight is far from being without precedent. Fox remarks on his own realisation that 'all Christians are believers, both Protestants and Papists; and the Lord opened to me that, if all were believers, then they were all born of God and passed from death to life, and that none were true believers but such; and though others said they were believers, yet they were not'.[101] In Fox's case his conviction that he was to learn only from within reinforced this tendency. 'I would get into the orchard or the fields with my Bible by myself', he says. 'Did not the apostle say to believers that they needed no man to teach them, but as the anointing teacheth them?'[102] Wesley looked to a similar direct teaching, by the method of the *sortilegium*, when, on 11 May 1738, he 'rose and looked into the Scripture. The words that first presented were, "And now, Lord, what is my hope" ... I now found myself at peace with God and rejoiced in the hope of loving Christ.'

To become the founder of a church or churches, a leader must spread his ideas. When George Fox turned to that task, he did so by travelling about England and holding Meetings. These had the attraction of the simplicity of what he had to say, and of his own powerful conviction; and sometimes of excitement. He tells of one occasion when a group of local rowdies, one of them a known murderer, came to disrupt the Meeting. The Friends showed them no violence. Local Friends told him later that this gang 'used to come and break stools and make fearful work'. But on this day, 'the Lord's power had bound them'.[103] Fox notes that 'several strange and sudden judgements came upon many of these conspirators

---

[100] George Fox, *Journal*, p. 7.   [101] *Ibid.*, p. 7.   [102] *Ibid.*, p. 7.
[103] *Ibid.*, pp. 179–80.

against me'.[104] That is in itself a revealing comment. He felt himself led to his work and guided in it to the point where he saw the hand of God in every event connected with it. He was reckoning miracles as proofs.

A sense of loyalty to the teachings of a great leader and founder may remain strong for many generations, and become indefinitely a distinctive feature of the community's sense of identity. This can be a negative as well as a positive factor, both pastorally and ecumenically speaking. Pastorally there is the danger of authoritarianism, or hero worship.[105] On the doctrinal side, the leader's thought can bulk too large. A draft of 1920 on the way to the Methodist Union of 1932 in England contained the following: 'the evangelical doctrines for which Methodism has stood from the beginning, as held by the three Conferences, and generally contained in John Wesley's *Notes* on the New Testament and the first four volumes of his Sermons, *subject to the authority of divine revelation recorded in the Holy Scriptures*, shall be the doctrinal standard of the Methodist Church'. The words in italics were added only at the revision stage. In the debate of the last two or three decades of our own day about the acceptance of the Augsburg Confession by the Roman Catholic Church, Lutherans can be found anxiously arguing that if that can be done, the Augsburg Confession itself must be looked on with suspicion as not maintaining the position of Luther's mature thought and therefore not committing Lutherans.[106]

A great danger in cults of a single memorable leader with an attractive and apparently simple vision is that these attributes may all be present in the personality and teachings of the mad and the fanatical and the eccentric. An example has been the foundation of the Renovated Church of Jesus Christ by Michel Collin, a Roman Catholic priest, born in France in 1905. He claimed that in 1935, two years after he was made priest, Christ himself consecrated him to the episcopate. In 1950, God the Father gave him the papal crown and consecrated him to be the future successor to Pope John XXIII. He believed that in 1963 he had succeeded Pope John as Clement XV.[107]

For a church which has gathered about a great leader or a

---

[104] *Ibid.*, pp. 179–80.
[105] Murl Owen Dirksen, 'Pentecostal Healing', Ph.D. thesis, University of Tennessee, Knoxville (1984), cited by Martin, *Tongues of Fire*, p. 168.
[106] *The Role of the Augsburg Confession*, ed. J.A. Burgess (Philadelphia, 1977), p. 51.
[107] Piepkorn, vol. I, pp. 311ff.

visionary, and which has continued to focus on him for generations after his death, it may not be at all easy to envisage union with other churches who do not share this reverence.

THE CHURCH WITH 'CONFESSIONAL IDENTITY'

Not unrelated to the ecclesial focus on a great leader can be loyalty to a particular doctrine, or set of doctrines, and the concomitant rejection of others. In the sixteenth century a number of reforming ecclesial communities published formal statements of their faith. The Lutheran Augsburg Confession and the Church of England's Thirty-Nine Articles are important examples of this kind of 'confessional' assertion. The model was the *theses* or *conclusiones* or *articuli* or *loci communes* (commonplaces) of formal *disputatio* in the academic schoolrooms of the Middle Ages.[108] They belong in this way to the same family as Luther's Ninety-Five Theses. They have an adversarial and combative aspect because they assert the truth of propositions which are known to be contentious. The usual pattern is to append to the assertion some quoted authority by way of support or syllogism by way of proof, just as was done in the university disputation. A convenient illustration is Article XVIII of the Church of England's Thirty-Nine Articles:

They also are to be had accursed that presume to say, That every man shall be saved by the Law or Sect which he professeth, so that he be diligent to frame his life according to that Law, and the light of nature. For Holy Scripture doth set out unto us only the Name of Jesus Christ, whereby men must be saved.

These lists of points deemed to be definitive of a community's identity as a church have retained a central position in some churches and can present difficulties when it comes to agreeing in the faith with other churches. This raises issues about diversity to which we come in the next chapter. Loyalty to such confessional documents can be dogged. Loyalty and nostalgia mingle. A distinction has to be made here between confessional articles which simply make assertions, and therefore have a capacity to be used in reconciliation; and those which contain some explicitly hostile reference to other Christian bodies. It requires some climbing down for a

---

[108] I discuss these at some length in *Problems of Authority in the Reformation Debates* (Cambridge University Press, 1992).

communion to repent of these, and a good deal of security and trust for it to be able to do so without a fear that it is risking its own dissolution.

THE ECCLESIAL IDENTITY OF THE ANGLICAN CHURCHES

Anglicanism falls into an ecclesial category of its own because the Church of England of the sixteenth century came to see itself as both 'catholic' and 'reformed'.[109] Henry VIII's breach with Rome took place over the personal matter of his wish for a divorce which the Pope of the day refused him. The most urgent need was therefore to claim independence of jurisdiction for the English Church so that the issue could be dealt with internally. But Henry had been influenced by ideas making their way into England from Lutheran and other reformers on the Continent. In Thomas Cranmer (1489– 1556) he had an Archbishop of Canterbury who himself had reforming ideas. Gradually, and a little uncertainly at first, the Church of England framed a series of Thirty-Nine Articles[110] which could stand as their 'confessional' statement alongside such documents as the Lutheran Augsburg Confession. Calvinist notions found their way into the tradition as the century went on. At the same time the Church of England never abandoned the threefold ministry, kept the apostolic succession of the episcopate in continuity with the mediaeval sequence,[111] and in many other respects preserved continuity of order as well as of faith with the mediaeval Church.[112]

The Church of England's ecclesial identity was strongly bound up at first with its conception of itself as a 'national church'. That could not last as it expanded. The extension of the Anglican Communion beyond the British Isles[113] took place as a result of the colonisation of the North American continent from the sixteenth century, and of missionary endeavour elsewhere in succeeding centuries. At first the

---

[109] Its independent history as a Church separated from Rome since the sixteenth century has in many respects been a chapter of accidents. See the excellent article by Kenneth W. Stevenson, 'Anglican identity: a chapter of accidents' in his *The identity of Anglican Worship* (London, 1991), pp. 184–96.

[110] See E.C.S. Gibson, *The Thirty-Nine Articles* (London, 1896–7), 2 vols.

[111] This was disputed within the Roman Catholic community, culminating in the text of 1896 which declared Anglican orders null and void.

[112] That succession has of course been disputed by the Roman Catholic Church. On the issues, see G. Dix's classic, *The Question of Anglican Orders* (London, 1944).

[113] With the proviso mentioned earlier. On Wales, Ireland, Scotland see *The Anglican Tradition*, ed. G.R. Evans and J. Robert Wright (London, 1991).

American colonists remained under the jurisdiction of the Bishop of London. That became inappropriate as well as impractical. In 1784 three Scottish bishops consecrated the first native American bishop. The pattern since has been for each province to be self-regulating with Canterbury having no jurisdiction but only a primacy of honour outside England. The proliferating Anglican Provinces were held together at first by a sense of identity to which the common liturgy of the Book of Common Prayer was profoundly important; and by their possession of a ministry recognised everywhere in the Communion. But that sense of ecclesial 'identity' has now become difficult to pinpoint as fresh liturgies are developed and mutual recognition of ministry is no longer possible everywhere in the Anglican Provinces, where some have ordained women as priests and bishops while others have not. There remains the test of being in communion with the See of Canterbury, and a concept of 'degrees of communion' developed by the Eames Commission set up as a result of the first Resolution of the Lambeth Conference of 1988. But it is now extremely difficult to characterise an 'Anglican identity' or for Anglicans to move ecumenically as one ecclesial body.

These are the bones of the matter historically. Despite its possession of the Thirty-Nine Articles, Anglicanism has less reason to think of itself 'confessionally' than other churches which separated from Rome in the sixteenth century because there was and has remained so much historical accident in its composition. It falls into none of the rough categories we have been looking at. Recently the debate about Anglican identity has been opened up, notably by Stephen Sykes and Paul Avis.[114] William Temple had argued that 'there is not ... a system of distinctively Anglican theology'.[115] Sykes responds with the contention that

No Roman Catholic would regard his theology as less catholic because it is Roman, or Greek Orthodox his theology less orthodox because it is characteristic of the Greek church, or Lutheran or Calvinist less wholly true because it is protestant. The designations 'Roman', 'Greek' and 'Protestant' are verbal conventions useful for identifying the differing features of various accounts of Christian faith, not alternatives to the term 'catholic'.

---

[114] Paul Avis, *Anglicanism and the Christian Church* (Edinburgh, 1989), p. xvii.
[115] Introduction to *Report on Doctrine in the Church of England*, p. 25.

He wants to speak of 'Anglican' theology in a similar way.[116] H.R. McAdoo has taken much the same line as Temple and suggested that Anglicanism simply has no system of theology of its own.[117] Here Sykes argues that while it may be true that it lacks a specifically Anglican corpus of doctrine, that does not mean that it lacks a corpus of doctrine of its own.[118] His point is that Anglicanism consists of a set of characteristics, not peculiar to Anglicanism, but together constituting something ecclesially distinctive, at least 'a distinctive standpoint and a distinctive way of communicating that standpoint'.[119] This seems to me a truism if we are talking of the 'style' or 'feel' of a church; both wrong and dangerous if it were to become a reason for taking a stand on a distinctiveness which ultimately denies provisionality and the possibility of coming closer to other churches. Anglicanism has become a living example of provisionality in practice.

ECCLESIAL IDENTITY IN THE ORTHODOX AND ROMAN CATHOLIC CHURCHES

In continuing to think of herself as the true and sole 'mother church', abandoned by all these dissidents and reformers who had regarded themselves as churches without her, Rome had, until the Second Vatican Council, seen little need to change her ecclesiological position *vis à vis* other churches.[120] Yet Roman Catholic and Orthodox Churches have needed to think out a position on their own claims to ecclesial identity at several stages, in the face of the

---

[116] Stephen Sykes, *The Integrity of Anglicanism* (London, 1978), p. 59.

[117] H.R. McAdoo, *The Spirit of Anglicanism* (London, 1965), p. 1 and *Being an Anglican* (Dublin and London, 1977).

[118] Sykes, *Integrity*, p. 67.   [119] *Ibid.*, pp. 67, 73.

[120] The sequence of development of the thinking of Vatican II on the crucial question whether the true Church is to be identified exclusively with the Roman Catholic Church has been traced by a number of observers and critics. Schillebeeckx provides a convenient outline in *Church: The Human Story of God* (Baarn, 1989). He identifies a shift from an emphasis in the first draft on the principle that the mystery of the Church is the Roman Catholic Church, with a stress on social, juridical and corporate aspects; the second outline, he argues, placed at the heart of things the notion of believers as the body of Christ through their personal union with Christ, with the idea that the visible community and the mystical body are not two things but one reality, with a human and a divine element. The third draft stressed the Lordship of Jesus; it placed the kerygma of the Kingdom of kingly rule of God between express confession of the Trinity and affirmative proclamation of the mystery of the Church. The divine kingdom thus becomes visible in the words, acts and miracles of Jesus, and finally in his whole Person. He sends his Spirit and gives his Church the task of proclaiming the kingdom of God. This Church exists in (*subsistit in*) the Roman Catholic Church.

challenges posed first by their mutual estrangement in the Middle Ages, then by the further questions raised by the Reformation, and now in the climate of the ecumenical movement.

In this last context one Orthodox scholar who was an experienced and committed ecumenist wrote at the time when Vatican II's *Constitution on the Church* and *Decree on Ecumenism* were new, on the limitations of Roman Catholic ecclesiology in at least one pair of Orthodox eyes. 'In the East', he comments, 'theology did not attempt to delve into the question of the nature of the Church, not only because there was no similar Reformation there, but also because in the Church the mystery of the revelation of God in Christ is apprehended and known through the direct communion and participation of the individual in the community of the Holy Spirit.'[121] 'The Orthodox are reluctant to formulate a system of ecclesiology ... The Church is her own life.'[122] This is, of course, itself a profound ecclesiological statement.

So, as a result of different historical pressures and different intellectual and spiritual emphases, ecclesiological explorations by Roman Catholics and the Orthodox have run along different lines from one another and also from those of the 'new' and 'dissident' and other churches we have been reviewing, many of which have thought a great deal about their ecclesial identity as they have framed their constitutions.

Both Roman Catholics and Orthodox can point unequivocally to continuity of tradition from the beginning. Neither Communion has needed to make the case that it is 'Church'; indeed, both can and do take the view that they have no separate ecclesial identity. Each would say that it is simply the Church.[123] So the only way in which we can usefully explore the development of their respective senses of ecclesial identity is to look at their attempts to understand themselves over against others. The longest history of failed attempts to achieve union has been between churches descended from the Greek-speaking Eastern half of the late Roman Empire and those descended from its Latin Western part. It is an instructive story in more hopeful times, because it illustrates again and again how real is the danger that a scheme for union of which much is expected will

[121] N.A. Nissiotis, 'The main ecclesiological problem of the Second Vatican Council and the position of the non-Roman Churches facing it', *Journal of Ecumenical Studies*, 2 (1965), 32. See, too, Ion Bria, *The Sense of Ecumenical Tradition: The Ecumenical Witness and Vision of the Orthodox*, World Council of Churches (Geneva, 1991) on Nissiotis.
[122] Nissiotis, 'Ecclesiological problem', p. 38.   [123] Useful here is Bria, *Sense*.

be deeply destructive of mutual goodwill if it fails. Such failures can set back progress by many generations. It is also a story which underlines the need for great patience.

I have already suggested that the formal separation of East and West in 1054 had much earlier roots, in the cultural divergences of the Latin and Greek territories from the end of the ancient world. This was partly a matter of the loss of one another's languages. That has had continuing consequences and results in a number of fresh difficulties even today. 'Justification', a term of great importance in mending the divisions in the Western Church is not directly translatable into the language or even the world of thought of Orthodox theology. For 'sanctification' there is 'theosis', but that is not an exact match. The Orthodox 'synergy' does not carry the Western Pelagian connotations of acquiring merit before God, but is seen rather as a free, willing cooperation of the new man with God, in the power of the Spirit. These latter-day divergences reflect the difference of emphasis in philosophical and theological culture which was already apparent in the fifth century. Even at that stage Greek thinkers were tending to go the mystical and Platonist way, Western ones the way of reasoning faith. One ecclesiological consequence was the development of a contrast between Roman emphasis on visible order and hierarchical structure, and Orthodox stress on the presence of the Holy Spirit in the mystical Church.[124]

In addition, there was the grumbling appendix of Roman claims to a primacy which the Eastern patriarchates were unable to accept, at least in the terms in which Rome itself saw it. It is a great irony of the story that the elaboration of the theology of the papacy which proved so separative from Rome took place from the eleventh century while, and partly because, East and West were divided and the Orthodox no longer posed a check to papal monarchy.[125] The gulf which opened up as a result of the Anathemas of 1054 did so over a long period. It reached the point of full estrangement during the Crusades, when, in 1204, Constantinople was sacked by the Latins. After that a Latin clerical hierarchy came into existence in the East in parallel with the existing Greek one.[126]

There was also the addition in the West of the *Filioque* clause to

[124] Nissiotis 'Ecclesiological problem', pp. 32–3.
[125] J. Meyendorff, *Orthodoxie et catholicité* (Paris, 1965), pp. 77–8, and see V. Grumel, 'La question romaine avant 1054', *Revue des études Byzantines*, 10 (1952), 5–23.
[126] J. Ratzinger, 'Schisme anathématique. Les consequences ecclésiologiques de la levée des anathèmes', *Istina*, 20 (1975), 87–99.

the Nicene Creed. That gave grounds for the Greeks to argue both
that the Western Church was heretical (in holding a wrong doctrine) and that it had broken faith with tradition (in making an
innovation): both attacks on her ecclesiality.[127]

The problems of mutual incomprehension and different ecclesiological agendas are well exemplified in the debates on the *Filioque*
during the Middle Ages. When Anselm of Canterbury addressed
himself to the question at the request of Pope Urban II at the
Council of Bari in 1096, he made no attempt to discover Greek
reasons for the Greek position. He simply set out a rational basis for
the Latin case.[128] Anselm of Havelberg a generation later went to a
great deal of trouble to talk to the Greeks themselves, on their own
ground, and he had with him interpreters who could speak Greek as
well as Latin.[129] Nevertheless, Anselm's own account of the talks in
his *Dialogue* is resolutely that of a Western mind with Western
preoccupations about such issues as that of the *duo principia*, framed
in Western terms of reference. It is true that he writes to win a
Western readership. But it is hard to believe that if he had achieved
any deeper insight into the subtleties of the differences of Greek
perceptions, it would not have been to some degree at least reflected
in what he writes.

The same accusation of fundamental incomprehension of the
approach of the other side can equally be levelled against the
Greeks. The 'Union' of the Council of Lyons in 1274 did not endure,
but it gave the Greeks a chance to discover something of the Latin
doctrine of the Holy Spirit, and it is significant that Augustine and
Aquinas were soon translated into Greek. An intra-Greek debate
went on. Gregory of Cyprus, who became Patriarch of Constantinople from 1283, called a Council in 1285 to reply to the dogma
promulgated at Lyons on the Holy Spirit. Gregory pursued the
theme further in a treatise of his own of 1288, in an attempt to
establish an intermediate position between the two extreme parties
in Byzantine thinking.[130] These terms of reference, and especially

---

[127] On the earlier part of the story, see V. Grumel, 'Photius et l'addition du filioque au
symbole du Nice-Constantinople', *Revue des études Byzantines*, 6 (1947), 218–34.
[128] See G.R. Evans, *Anselm* (London, 1989), pp. 60–6.
[129] M.J. de Guillou, 'Dialogue entre Anselme de Havelberg et Néchites de Nicomédie sur la
procession du Saint Esprit', *Istina*, 3/4 (1972), 375–442. G.R. Evans, 'Unity and diversity:
Anselm of Havelberg as ecumenist', *Analecta Praemonstratensia*, 57 (1991), 42–52.
[130] O. Clément, 'Grégoire de Chypre "De l'ekporèse du Saint Ésprit"', *Istina*, 3/4 (1972),
442–56.

the refinements of their implications, would have been hard for any Latin-educated theologian to follow, even if he had some Greek, and they could take little or nothing from the Latin tradition or terminology. It was partly on the problem of mutual incomprehension, with all its baggage of incompatibility and incommensurability of terminology, the hidden agendas of different worlds of thought and above all the fundamental differences in ecclesiology which emerged again and again, that the Council of Florence foundered.[131]

Orthodoxy and Protestantism against Rome

The scene shifted in the sixteenth century to attempts by Protestant reformers to make common cause with the Orthodox against Rome.[132] Here again we meet mutual incomprehension. To the reformers of the West the problem of Roman domination and Roman corruption, as they saw it, stood so high above the horizon that a common dislike of 'Papacy' could seem a ground on which at least some sort of compact, if not union with the Orthodox, could be built. Encouraged by their new mastery of classical and New Testament Greek, a number of Protestant scholars made serious attempts to learn something of Byzantine ways.[133] In scholarship in this area reformers hoped to find the demonstration that what they were doing was not prolonging or worsening schism in the Church but returning to apostolic and original doctrine and structure. A test of this restored authenticity must be the relationship in which such a reformed Western Church would stand to the Orthodox Churches which claimed to have maintained authentic apostolicity in unbroken continuity.[134]

Because of the pressure it was under from the Turks, Orthodoxy

---

[131] H. Chadwick and G.R. Evans, *Christian Unity*, both touch on this point.

[132] It has even been possible to see 'the Reformation' as ... 'the consequence – and also the victim – of the great and fundamental divide between the Christian East and the Christian West'. WCC, Faith and Order Paper 76, *The Orthodox Churches and the Churches of the Reformation* (Geneva, 1975), p. 63.

[133] Melanchthon's pupil, Hieronymous Wolf (1516–80) became interested in Byzantine history. He published some Byzantine chronicles and thought of printing a *Corpus Byzantinae Historiae*. See E. Benz, *Wittenberg und Byzanz* (Munich, 1971) (reprint of Marburg, 1949 edition), also G. Ostrogorsky, *History of the Byzantine State* (New Jersey, 1957), p. 3

[134] See L.N. Parijski, *Tradition und Glaubensgerechtigkeit* (Wittenberg, 1961), p. 76, E. Benz, *Die Ostkirche in Lichte der Protestantischen Geschichtsschreibung von der Reformation bis zum Gegenwart* (Frieburg/Munich, 1952), and *The Orthodox Church and the Churches of the Reformation* in WCC Faith and Order Paper, 76 (Geneva, 1975).

was also interested in what was happening in the West. Patriarch Joseph II of Constantinople sent the Thessalonikan Deacon Dimitrios Musos to Wittenberg in 1559 to discover what he could about Protestant opinions. This led to Melanchthon's presenting the *Augsburg Confession* to the Ecumenical Patriarch, and subsequently to correspondence between Jeremias II, Patriarch 1572–9, and a number of Tübingen theologians.[135] Maximus Margounios worked at Padua and became an enthusiastic humanist. He studied Aristotle and Aquinas and translated Gregory of Nyssa, Maximus the Confessor and John Climacticus into Latin. He read Augustine. He corresponded over a period of years with Lutheran theologians at Tübingen (especially Martin Crusius and David Hoeschl). His study of the *Acta* of the Council of Florence disturbed him; he became much concerned over the problems of achieving unity and published a *Handbook* in 1587 on the *ekporesis* of the Holy Spirit and an elucidation in 1588 on Augustine's *De Trinitate*. It was his conclusion that at base Greek and Latin doctrine is the same.[136]

Often the goodwill was there. But of course each side framed its comments in its own terms. When the Lutherans sent the *Confessio Augustana* to Greek theologians, they expected the Orthodox to perceive at once that this was a return to the apostolic Church. On that, unity would surely follow. The Patriarch of Constantinople was to write in some approval of the Augsburg Confession, with assertions of a desire for union.[137] It is possible for the Orthodox to speak of a *coniunctio utriusque ecclesiae*, and thus to imply that the Lutherans too are a church. But the restraining factors preventing union have to do with faithfulness to the tradition.[138]

Similarly, the Lutherans reach out in goodwill, but again on their own terms. Martin Crusius translated the *Compendium Theologiae* of Jacobus Heerbrand of Tübingen into Greek, without any sense of the polemical character of its preoccupations and the fact that they were peculiarly topical to the contemporary West. The Church is defined as a 'gathering' (*coetus*) of the people of God, which he

---

[135] John Karmiris, 'Orthodoxy and Protestantism' in WCC Faith and Order Paper, 76, p. 45.

[136] J.-M. Garrigues, 'Maxime Margounios et son commentaire du De Trinitate de saint Augustin (1588)', *Istina*, 3/4 (1972), 465–8.

[137] Benz, *Die Ostkirche*, especially pp. 94ff. *Acta et Scripta Theologorum Wirtembergensium et Patriarchae Constantinopolitani D. Hieremiae, 1576–81* (Wittenberg, 1584), p. 141, 143.

[138] *Ibid.*, p. 77.

recognises as his people on earth.[139] There is talk of two Churches, God's and Satan's,[140] of the visible and invisible Church,[141] of the Headship of Christ (and not the Pope) in the Church,[142] all special preoccupations of the current Western debates.[143]

Nevertheless, the attempts at both ecclesial and cultural *rapprochement* continued in the seventeenth century. There was particular warmth in the intercourse between Orthodox and Anglicans in this period. Leaders of the Eastern Church corresponded with a series of Archbishops of Canterbury. In 1615 the Metropolitan of Philadelphia asked the Archbishop of Canterbury to pray 'for the unity of Christ's Church'. The Patriarch of Alexandria, Cyril Lucar (1601–20), corresponded with Canterbury and was invited to send young Greeks to be educated in England. Metrophanes Kritoupolos was despatched, and stayed until 1624, making many friends in Oxford.[144] But no real progress was made towards a further ecclesiological meeting of minds.

What can be said now? Some of the autocephalous Orthodox churches are in dialogue with churches of the Reformation locally, for example the Evangelical Church in the Federal Republic of Germany with the Russian Orthodox.[145] But ecclesiologically and structurally there is no way in which such local bilateral dialogues can bring all Protestantism and all Orthodoxy together. And the old difficulties remain difficulties. It can be agreed, as it was in 1959 at Arnoldsheim, that Scripture is fundamental and tradition must not contradict it. For 'its concordance with Scripture is the essential criterion of its authenticity'.[146] But it is much harder to agree on the scope and authenticity of apostolic tradition after the New Testament Canon was settled, and how the continuity of the pure apostolic tradition in the Church is to be understood and weighed.[147] At Zagorsk in 1963 classic differences over the status of councils were still apparent.

The Orthodox theologians hold the conviction that the ecumenical councils are organs of the Church, which in like measure reflect as well the consciousness of the Church as the will of God manifested by the Holy

---

[139] Martin Crusius, tr. of *Compendium Theologiae* of Jacobus Heerbrandus (Wittenberg, 1582), p. 755.
[140] *Ibid.*, p. 760.   [141] *Ibid.*, pp. 761–2.   [142] *Ibid.*, pp. 765–6.
[143] Cf. Constantine Patelos in WCC Faith and Order Paper, 76, p. 63.
[144] V.T. Istavridis, *Orthodoxy and Anglicanism*, tr. C. Davey (London, 1966), pp. 2ff.
[145] WCC Faith and Order Paper 76, p. iii.
[146] *Declaration*, p. 10 and WCC Faith and Order Paper 76, p. 8.   [147] *Ibid.*

Spirit. The Evangelical theologians believe that the activity of these synods is not grounded in the manner in which they were convened, but in the fact that the ecumenical Church hears through them the voice of the Holy Spirit.[148]

There is still much mutual incomprehension.[149]

Yet something has begun to come out of all this in terms of a rethinking on all sides of what is meant by ecclesial identity. Orthodoxy can make 'a qualified recognition of the saving presence of Christ beyond its own canonical boundaries', at least in the case of individual believers. 'There exists, moreover, a growing body of Orthodox thought which would go considerably further in acknowledging the Christian identity and value of certain other communities, on the ground that the one apostolic faith can, and does, express itself in a diversity of historical forms.' Thus 'each would contribute to the enrichment of all'.[150]

Orthodoxy and Rome: the modern story

In 1698 Dositheus Notaras published the *Tomos Agapis*, a collection of polemical Byzantine texts on the heresies of the Latin Church. In 1971 the same title was given to a collection of documents relating to the lifting of the 1054 Anathemas in 1965, and the concomitant meeting of the Pope and the Ecumenical Patriarch at Jerusalem.[151] The choice of a title which would echo and at the same time purge something of the bad memory of the relationship between Greek East and Latin West and their heirs was deliberate.[152]

The *Tomos Agapis* experiment was also an attempt to come to terms with the question of sisterhood and motherhood in the

---

[148] Zagorsk document, p. 29, WCC Faith and Order Paper, 76, p. 8.

[149] N.A. Nissiotis, 'Orthodox reflections on the Decree on Ecumenism', *Journal of Ecumenical Studies*, 3 (1966), 329–42, p. 334. WCC Faith and Order Paper, 76, p. 19.

[150] *The Orthodox and the Unity of the Church, Consultation of Eastern and Oriental Orthodox Theologians* (Crete, 1975) in Orthodox Contributions to Nairobi, p. 38 and WCC Faith and Order Paper, 76, p. 30.

[151] J. Meyendorff, 'Eglises-soeurs. Implications ecclésiologiques du *Tomos Agapis*', *Istina*, 20 (1975), 35–46, p. 35.

[152] The lifting of the anathemas of 1054 was in itself largely a rectification of an absurdity. The list of condemnations in Humbert's Western catalogue of Greek errors is hopelessly inaccurate as a description of Greek faith and practice. What was condemned was not in fact so. V.J. Phidas, 'Anathèmes et schism. Consequences ecclésiologiques de la levée des anathèmes', *Istina*, 20 (1975), 87–99. Moreover, the excommunication of 1054 was directed personally against the Legates and Patriarch. It did not condemn all Christians of the East. Meyendorff, 'Eglises-soeurs', p. 36.

relationship of the Roman Catholic and the Orthodox Churches. In *Anno ineunte* (1967), the Pope refers to himself as 'Bishop of Rome and head of the Catholic Church' and calls the patriarch the 'Orthodox Archbishop of Constantinople and Ecumenical Patriarch'.[153] But the *Tomos Agapis* strongly stresses sisterhood.[154] Orthodox ecclesiology, for its part, cannot allow a universal jurisdiction to a local church (Rome). But it can allow that there may be a centre where the conciliarity of the Church can manifest itself.[155]

SELF-DETERMINATION AND UNIVERSAL INTENTION

'Why do you allege different jurisdictions, different regions of the heavens, in order to have intercourse with him whom you have decided is a criminal, when others have no communication with him?' asks Gerbert of Aurillac, in 986. 'There is one Catholic Church, spread over the whole earth.'[156] It has always been accepted that, in certain matters, of strictly internal concern, a local church may decide for itself. The difficulty lies in defining which these are, and in agreeing what is to be done about matters which also affect certain other local churches, or which are the concern of the whole Church. Internal sovereignty has not guaranteed spiritual health in churches. It can be divisive.

The notion of non-interference existed from an early date. 1 Corinthians 1:2, 10:32, 11:22 and 2 Corinthians 1:1 show that the Church of Corinth, for example, for all its faults, does not lack what is needed to make it the Church in this part of the *oikoumene*. In 1 Corinthians 1:2 it is bracketed with all people everywhere who worship Christ as Lord. In 1 Corinthians 10:32, the Corinthians are asked to act with concern for the whole Church of God, and in 11:22 they are warned that they are not doing so, in a rather different context from that in which it arises most pressingly now.

[153] E. Lanne, 'Eglises soeurs. Implications ecclésiologiques du *Tomos Agapis*', *Irénikon*, 20 (1975), 47–74, pp. 48–9.
[154] E. Lanne, 'Le premier Colloque ecclésiologique de Vienne entre Orthodoxes et Catholiques: un événement qui pourrait faire date', *Irénikon*, 47 (1974), 219–23, but Lanne hints that although Vatican II advances the Roman position on sisterhood, it cannot be taken for granted that all other ecclesial communities have moved an equal distance along the same road, or that thinking within the Roman Catholic Church itself has gone the same way.
[155] Meyendorff, 'Eglises-soeurs', p. 46.
[156] Letter 93 (no. 87 in Havet), to Abbot Mayeul in the name of Archbishop Adalbero, *The Letters of Gerbert*, ed. H. Pratt Lattin (Colombia, 1956).

In the *Ecclesiastical History*, Eusebius quotes Dionysius' letter, where he refers to Deuteronomy 19:14 in the Septuagint version. 'Thou shalt not remove thy neighbour's landmarks, which thy fathers placed.' He is discussing the practice of not requiring a second baptism of those who came from another Church. This, Eusebius says, was of long precedent. 'Long before, in the days of the bishops that were before us, in the most populous churches and the synods of the brethren, in Iconium and Synnada and in many places, this course was adopted. And I do not dare to overturn their decisions and involve them in strife and contention.'[157] The rule of acting 'with the intention to do what the Church does (*intentio faciendi quod facit ecclesia*)' can already be found in the thirteenth century in the West, and that of acting 'for the purpose for which the Church acts' at the end of the twelfth.[158] But the issue in the discussions of this earlier debate was whether a celebrant separated from the Church can offer the Eucharist *in persona ecclesiae*; the possibility of a local Church itself acting without universal intention in the making of ministers (that is, without reference to their acceptability to other communities) had arisen as yet only in the case of heretical groups of the Waldensian type, which were not strictly claiming to be churches at all.

The principle that when in doubt about what to do a local Church should always act with 'universal intention' would seem unexceptionable. But it has frequently not been adhered to, as when a given local community simply does not see the implications for the wider Church of what it is about to do; or when some other reason for action seems to override concern for catholicity it may be a case of deeming some other 'intention' more compelling. A recent test-case has been the question of the ordination of women to the priesthood and especially to the episcopate in some provinces of the Anglican Communion. At the Lambeth Conference of 1988 Resolution 1 accepted it as a matter of constitutional fact that, legislatively speaking, each province was free to make its own decision on the matter. The Resolution sought to maintain the highest possible degree of communion at least in terms of mutual charity and acceptance if some provinces moved ahead of others. Some

---

[157] Ed. K. Lake (London, 1926–32), 2 vols., VII.7.5.
[158] See Y. Congar, 'Propos en vue d'une théologie de l'Economie dans la tradition latine', *Irénikon* 45 (1972), 200, traces the principle back to Prevostinus early in the thirteenth century.

provinces have indeed felt that pastoral need or what is seen in their own societies as a matter of justice is the overriding consideration, and have consecrated women bishops. As a result mutual recognition of ministry is no longer possible throughout the Anglican Communion. Women priests ordained in one province will not necessarily be allowed to exercise their ministry in another; male priests ordained by a woman bishop cannot be recognised everywhere as priests.

So between the twin poles of the responsibility to act with universal intention, and the right to live without external interference, hangs a string of difficulties, as the local church finds itself responsible for the conduct of its own life in matters of discipline and liturgical usage.[159] Liturgy is also theology and no church can regard itself as free to devise forms of service which give the lie to the apostolic faith. It is also true that discipline overlaps with the larger dimension of order in the Church, and that there must therefore be some restriction on the local church's authority to 'legislate' for its own affairs, if it is to remain at one with the catholic church. A local church may rightfully have its 'own theological and spiritual patrimony'.[160] But there can be no 'local dogma'; the faith is common.[161]

Autocephaly and autonomy

In the episcopally ordered churches there exists a special technical form of ecclesial distinctness and self-government. In Orthodoxy, an autocephalous Church can choose its own president and bishops without any church elsewhere having right of confirmation or right of veto. It has no jurisdiction over sister-churches. Local (in this sense) sacramental life is thus complete and, up to a point, self-contained. It has its own order, which is believed to derive as a branch of the family tree from the apostles.

The autocephalous church is not, however, allowed for that reason to believe what it wishes. It has a duty to guard the common Orthodox faith without alteration. These recognised limits preventing diversity of faith and interference in one another's order or discipline preserve the communion of all these local churches. The autocephaly such sister churches have cannot be conferred except by a mother church. The mother church of a daughter must inform

---

[159] *LG* 23d.   [160] *Ibid.*   [161] See further, pp. 183ff.

all her own sister churches of the elevation of that daughter to the level of sister.[162]

Formally speaking, the Orthodox have had much more practice in dealing with the concept of autocephaly than any other Communion. Canon I of the Council of Union (879–80)[163] and a proclamation during the fourth session of the Council insist that each Church should preserve its own customs and maintain its own rights. 'Each see has a number of ancient traditional practices ... it is proper that the Roman Church should hold to its practices, but the Church of Constantinople should also preserve the customs that it has inherited from the past.'[164] Within this pattern of autocephaly of the local Church thus defined, differences of practice grew up between East and West. The Byzantines worked on the basis of the 'apostolic canons' and decisions of ecumenical Councils and certain local synods and some imperial ordinances. In the West, from the beginning of the sixth century they began to add the decretals of the Pope to the conciliar canons and to take no systematic note of Imperial legislation.[165]

The autocephalous Church is often specifically identified with the 'local' church of the 'intermediate' sort we have been discussing,[166] between individual congregation and universal Church, and is seen as being something like an ecclesial nation-state. This can create a focus upon the Patriarch, the Holy Synod,[167] the Council and governmental structures, to the detriment of the otherwise characteristically Orthodox emphasis on the true consensus of all the people. It can also cause to work less effectively structures which are designed to make wider communion possible.[168] In the late nineteenth century fuller Orthodox development of the concept of autocephaly was encouraged by reaction against Vatican I and the idea that Rome had abandoned respect for autocephaly in favour of monarchy. That has gone with a tendency for autocephaly to find its

---

[162] These points have been sharply clarified by the demands of the mission situation, where such new creations can arise. A. Joos, 'L'Autocéphalie et l'autonomie ecclésiales d'après de récents documents du patriarchat de Moscou', *Irénikon*, 44 (1971), 23–38.

[163] Mansi 17.479, Dvornik, p. 124.   [164] Mansi 17.489.   [165] Dvornik, p. 124.

[166] See pp. 8off.

[167] Episcopal conferences do not easily converge structurally with a pattern of autocephaly. See C.J. Dumont, 'Conférences episcopales et autocéphalie des Eglises', *Istina*, 30 (1985), 131–5. See, too, P. Meyendorff, 'Régionalisme ecclésiastique: structure de communion ou couverture de sparatisme?, in *Les Églises après Vatican II*, ed. G. Alberigo (Paris, 1981), 131–5.

[168] See *Eglise locale et Eglise universelle*, Editions du Centre Orthodoxe du Patriarcat oecuménique (Chambésy/Geneva, 1981), *passim*.

communion with other autocephalous churches in the past, and looking to the *eschaton*, but not perhaps so actively or urgently to world-wide communion as something to be worked for now.[169]

Anglican provincial *autonomy* is rather differently conceived.

Anglicanism is a communion of autonomous Churches. This means that each national or regional Church is juridically independent ... The mother-Church of the Communion is the Church of England, consisting of the two Provinces of Canterbury and York. The Anglican Communion defines itself by the fact of being in 'full communion' with the See of Canterbury – although there are now other non-Anglican Churches which are also in full communion with Canterbury such as, for example, the Old catholic Churches of the Union of Utrecht.[170]

Autonomy, then, is primarily governmental, and there is no defining sense of the sacramental completeness of each provincial church in the Communion, although that is assumed in the fact that each province can make its own ministers and its own rules about who may be ordained. In Anglicanism, independent provincial government has been seen as building up common life. It 'offers opportunities for mutual consultation ... on any questions of faith, order or discipline which cannot satisfactorily be dealt with by a single bishop of diocese'; at the other end of the scale, it 'facilitates common action in regard to other provinces' and ensures that dioceses 'realise' their 'proper relationship to the whole Church'.[171] The 1948 Lambeth Conference was sanguine about these reflections of the conference of 1930. That conference was seen as having set out a satisfactory basis for the development of autonomous provincial organisation. But the notion of 'interdependence' was already beginning to seem more important than it had done, and it was necessary to pose the question of the essential 'coherence' of the Anglican 'form of authority' and to ask whether it might 'conceal internal divisions which may cause its disruption'.[172] These have

---

[169] The notion that it is the Orthodox, not Rome, who can truly claim to have preserved the Catholic Church as the pure Bride of Christ is repeated many times in the Response of the Orthodox Patriarchs to Pius IX's 'Letter to the Eastern Churches' (1848), para.16.

[170] R. Greenacre, '*Causa nostra agitur*? An Anglican Response', *The Jurist*, 48 (1988), 384–96, notes that a province is not necessarily coterminous with a national Church, although this misuse of the term 'province' has crept into Anglican usage. See Colin Podmore, review of J.M.R. Tillard and R. Greenacre, *Lost in the Fog? The Lesson for Ecumenism* (1988), in *Mission and Unity Digest*, 42 (1990), 8.

[171] Lambeth Conference, 1930, *Committee Report* on the Anglican Communion, III.2.

[172] Lambeth Conference, 1949, *Committee Report* on the Anglican Communion, pp. 84–6.

most notably begun to appear in areas where 'universal intention' seems to conflict with rights of 'self-determination'.

THE FUTURE OF ECCLESIAL IDENTITIES

In the history of division in the Church it has often been the case that a church knows itself by contrast with what it believes it is not. In the already cited address on 'the Lutheran church and the unity of the Church' which he gave to the Lutheran World Federation's sixth meeting, A. Aarflot spoke of the 'specific features distinctive of the life and work of Lutheran churches', as they appear in catechisms, liturgies, hymn books, in the form taken by the ministry and in the character of Lutheran spiritual life. 'But', he comments, 'they emerge with particular clarity in the common and committed formulation of the Christian convictions of the Lutheran churches in face of specific challenges.'[173] In other words, the Lutheran churches have best known what they were when confronted with difficult questions about it. In a way less doctrinally based but similar in the sense of an identity which can be defined in part by difference from others, some Pentecostals see themselves as opposed to the 'complacent, prosperity-ridden, coldly formalistic Church and its members' which lack tokens of Spirit-led holiness.[174]

So, when they have addressed themselves to union, churches have been obliged to think hard about their own 'identities', and, paradoxically, it may be ecumenism which sharpens the sense of that which distinguishes a separated church from others with which it has not been in communion. The process of uniting, then, involves coming to terms with highly sensitive points in the uniting churches' self-images.

Lutherans and Reformed were responsible for mutual condemnations in the sixteenth century. The result was a separation between them which can still form one of the profoundest gulfs within the Protestant community. In 1973 the Concord of Leuenberg was agreed between these European churches issuing from the Reformation.[175] To produce it they had to clarify ecclesial identity on both sides. They concluded that they believed they were able to 'declare' and 'realise' ecclesial communion on the basis of a 'common understanding of the Gospel'. They made a list of elements

---

[173] See *LWF VI*, p. 37, para.12.   [174] J.T. Nichols, *Pentecostalism*, p. 26.
[175] Given in *Istina*, 29 (1984), 169ff.

common to their two traditions: a 'new experience of the Gospel as vehicle of freedom and certitude'; pure and original witness of the Gospel in Scripture seen as the norm of life and doctrine; the free and unconditional grace of God, shown in the life, death and resurrection of Christ and offered to all who put their faith in this promise; the belief that only the mission entrusted to the Church to proclaim this witness to the world ought to determine the actions of the Church and its ecclesial structures, with the Word of God remaining sovereign in relation to any of the human structures of the Christian community; the receiving and confessing 'afresh, in concert with all Christianity' of 'the faith expressed in the ancient creeds of the church'.[176] These common grounds are drawn out by making a distinction 'between the fundamental witness of the confessions of the sixteenth century [what they can be taken now to have meant at the deepest level] and their historic form'.[177] Two processes can be seen at work in this area: the second is the subject of the next chapter. The first is relevant here. This is the addition of words such as 'new', 'pure and original', 'only', 'human' to the list of elements just quoted. These are added to a list which would be common to most Christian traditions, with the implication that only these traditions have them really, or in their fullness.

There seemed in the first half of the twentieth century no barriers to the unity of the Baptists (mainly the American Northern Baptists) and the Disciples of Christ at the organisational level, because both had much the same system of church-government, but when they moved towards *rapprochement* there proved to be 'differences of orientation to religious life and experience',[178] such as the Baptists' suspicion that 'the Disciples are sacramentarian with respect to baptism' in believing 'in baptism for the remission of sins'.[179] Something similar by way of the discovery of difference where it had not been so clearly noticed before appears to have happened in the forming of the United Church of Canada in 1925. At a preliminary meeting in 1902, the Congregationalists identified themselves as democratic, liberal, individualistic and as standing for concern for lay opinion. The Presbyterians saw themselves as defending a history of resistance to bishops and officialdom; and as holding a faith enshrined and institutionalised in the Westminster Confess-

---

[176] *Ibid.*, p. 170.   [177] *Ibid.*, p. 171.   [178] Ehrenstrom and Muelder, p. 311.
[179] *Ibid.*, p. 269.

ion.[180] Yet there was felt to be a supportive common Protestant 'ethos'.[181] The Methodists emphasised their concern for the world's salvation and for the need to be practical and flexible so as to meet the needs of the missionary situation. The strongest 'restraining' force in the Methodist system seemed to them to be, not tradition or history, nor a theological formula, but the idea of obedience of the congregation to the district superintendent. The result of such sharpening of the sense of ecclesial distinctness may be a series of discussions in which a great deal of time is given to such points of importance to the ecclesial identities of the churches involved.[182] But where common interest in the outcome of unity is strong and no deeply vested interest stands in the way, things may turn out very differently. An example is the forming of the Methodist Union in England in 1932, out of the Wesleyan, Primitive and United Methodists. In 1878 lay representatives became part of the Wesleyan Conference, which was the governing body of the Old Connexion. There was a shift away from the principle that the ministry has 'oversight' of the Connexion to a new emphasis on the 'representative' character of pastoral office, with the ministry having no authority which the laity did not possess and acting as the laity's representatives. The other Methodist churches had already moved in this direction, and the Wesleyan Methodists now conformed with their pattern. The union therefore involved no major structural change, and it seems to have been wanted by a laity impatient with – or ignorant of – the fine differences of ecclesiological understanding which had been keeping Methodists segregated. It required no radical reorganisation at local level, and it may have been supported as readily as it was because it was not seen as costing a great deal in terms of change of life and attitude of those voting for it.[183] These may be important factors, practically speaking, in welding together existing church orders into one.

---

[180] Ehrenstrom and Muelder, p. 178.   [181] *Ibid.*, p. 182.

[182] Even in 1924, the Methodist scheme for union had not expressed a position on the Methodist Church in the Church of Christ as a whole, or taken a view of the historic creeds, or framed a coherent doctrinal policy on lay administration of the Eucharist, with all that that implied for ministry and ecclesiology. Ehrenstrom and Muelder, p. 210 and p. 213. Indeed, the theology of ministry itself remained cautious to the point of vagueness. 'The office of a Christian minister depends upon the call of God ... Those whom the Church recognises as called by God and therefore receives into its ministry, shall be ordained by the imposition of hands as expressive of the Church's recognition of the minister's personal call.' *Ibid.*, p. 209.

[183] *Ibid.*, pp. 203–5.

Despite all these difficulties about identity, there is certainly progress. For example, it can now be said with some confidence that Lutherans would no longer think that Roman Catholic teaching puts the uniqueness of Christ's work in doubt. Both sides in the Lutheran–Roman Catholic discussion can agree that apostolic succession is essentially fidelity and continuity in the message and teaching of the Apostles.[184] There is mutual enrichment; for instance, Orthodoxy's sense of the mystery of the Church and Protestant emphasis on the ministry of the Word have both made a difference to Roman Catholic thinking.[185] Within Protestantism there has been some peaceful growing together, 'each sharing with the rest what was once its own peculiarity. This process has gone so far as greatly to reduce the psychological uniqueness of every group.'[186]

Pulling against that is a sense that much has been invested. Heroes of the faith have died for certain principles, which it would be treason for their successors to abandon. The nineteenth-century Lutheran Krauth could be seen as rescuing Lutheranism 'at a time when the Lutheran Church in the United States was in grave danger of losing sight of its heritage'.[187] Krauth himself said that 'the life of a Church may be largely read in controversies ... the glory or shame of a Church [may] be determined when we know what it fought for and what it fought against ... how much it did, and how much it suffered to maintain that truth, and what was the issue of its struggles and sacrifices'.[188] There may be a complex of fears, resentments, suspicions, even residual hatred of an enemy. These are extremes. They exist in a few societies where political factors have tended to sustain old rivalries and to distort the picture which two Christian communities have of one another. But everywhere separated communities 'gradually develop a distinct ethos and express their faith in different terms'.[189]

Then there is the problem of 'closed traditions'.[190] There can be no real *rapprochement* unless a community which is closed to change

---

[184] H. Meyer, 'Réflexions méthodologiques sur la constitution du dialogue luthéro-catholique', *Istina*, 29 (1984), 356–75, especially 360–1.

[185] See E. Lanne, 'La "Réception"', *Irénikon*, 55 (1982), 199–213, especially p. 208.

[186] J.T. McNeill, *Unitive Protestantism* (London, 1964), p. 11; this author sees that 'general consolidation of Protestantism' as 'a stage in the complete unification of Christianity', p. 12.

[187] Krauth, Preface.   [188] *Ibid.*, p. 141.

[189] H. Chadwick, *The Tablet*, 1 February 1992, p. 36.

[190] See J.M.R. Tillard, 'Eglise catholique et dialogues bilatéraux', *Irénikon*, 56 (1983), 7.

can come to see itself differently in its relation to other churches. Related to, and depending upon this is a third factor, a form of 'pride' in the ecclesial reality of one's community.[191]

There is something deeper here, perhaps. It is noticeable in the formal official conversations themselves that members of commissions often begin to find themselves arguing on the 'other' side at key points. There appear to be theological temperaments of at least two broad types,[192] which, although they have coincided broadly with the styles or 'typologies' of separated Churches, do not do so tidily; and which may cross ecclesial boundaries or coexist within the same Church. An Evangelical, for example, may say that he 'ordinarily finds more genuine Christian fellowship with Evangelicals outside his own church body than with non-Evangelicals within it'.[193]

Various attempts have been made to identify the defining characteristics of such persistent polarities. The church which stresses sacrament is set against the church which rests all on the ministry of the Word.[194] A tendency to see salvation as proceeding solely from the action of God, without human cooperation, is set against the view that grace invites the soul's participation in its own remaking.[195] The view that Scripture interprets itself to the solitary reader is set against the view that there exists in the Church a divinely appointed *magisterium* which is to guide Christians in the interpretation of Scripture.[196] But perhaps closer to the kind of difference commonly met with is the following appeal (to emotion as much as to reason): 'Even the most unsophisticated evangelical is *at least intuitively aware* [my italics] of the gulf that historically separates him from Roman Catholicism and the Eastern Churches in respect to the other major elements of evangelical belief: *sola scriptura*, *sola gratia* and *sola fide*, personal commitment and personal witness (in opposition to the *opus operatum* in all its forms) and a moment-by-moment eschatological orientation.'[197] This speaks of a rationalisation of what is perhaps really being held at the level of gut-reaction.

---

[191] This may show itself, for example, in a refusal to enter into any form of 'reunion' scheme where conditional reordination might be involved.

[192] E. Marty, 'Patterns of Protestant Thought', in *Steps to Christian Unity*, ed. J.A. O'Brien (London, 1965), pp. 201–14.

[193] J.W. Montgomery, *Ecumenicity, Evangelicals and Rome* (Michigan, 1969), p. 18.

[194] G. Ebeling, *Dogmatik des christlichen Glaubens* (Tübingen, 1979), pp. 307–14.

[195] Y. Congar, 'Regards et réflexions sur la christologie de Luther', in *Das Konzil von Chalkedon*, ed. A. Grillmeier and H. Bacht (Würzburg, 1954), vol. III, pp. 457–86.

[196] A. Brandenburg, *Die Zukunft des Martin Luther* (Münster, 1977).

[197] Montgomery, *Ecumenicity*, p. 15.

Another, and much more recently conceived, type of claim to ecclesial identity, stresses the importance of preserving cultural (which are not necessarily theological) differences between churches in order that the life of each church may faithfully mirror the society in which it finds itself. The intention here is to emphasise the equality of all cultural traditions and to avoid imputing privileged status to any, especially to the white culture of the wealthy West.[198] We have already touched on some of the difficulties about this.[199]

Perhaps most dangerous of all is the confusion of cultural differences of this sort with differences of 'ecclesiastical culture' between churches which have fallen out of communion with one another. In this second case we are dealing with the notion of 'churchmanship': the style and set of attitudes which amounts more or less to a 'culture' and which often arises out of, or is defined in the circumstances of, division. The great risk of seeking to preserve such 'cultural' differences as these is that they are likely to prove not only inherently divisive, but also continuers of division. The *genie propre* of a church may well contain entirely legitimate elements, but these will need to be distinguished from the points at which that church defines itself ecclesially by its controversies with others and its difference of 'confession' or practice from those others.[200]

Some attempts have been made to express that distinction, and at the same time to characterise the forms of churchmanship which persist in separated churches and sometimes within a single church.[201] E. Lanne calls such forms 'typologies'. They are not, he stresses, structures, although each type will tend to generate certain structural patterns.[202] Lanne's own inclination is to link the 'typologies' closely to the processes of growth in the cultural context of each province or nation from the time of its conversion. There is, he suggests, an early forming in each place of a 'typologie commune', made up of the forms of ecclesial life, confession of faith, liturgical celebration and the character of the theological schools of the region. His particular concern is with the differences of this sort which mark Orthodox and Roman Catholics, and with the question whether these need be a barrier to communion today. In united

---

[198] A. Bea and W.A. Visser't Hooft, *Peace among Christians*, tr. J. Moses (New York, 1967), p. 205. And see earlier pp. 58ff.

[199] See pp. 58ff.   [200] Tillard, 'Eglise catholique', *Irénikon*, 56 (1983), 8.

[201] For example in the Church of England, where the General Synod has 'Catholic', 'Evangelical' and 'Liberal' 'parties'.

[202] But Evangelicals can be found in both episcopal and non-episcopal structures.

churches, quite substantial differences of liturgy and discipline are accommodated.[203]

Here we need to set out two paradoxes. The first, already touched on, I shall call the 'Meyer paradox', because it is economically framed by H. Meyer in an article of 1984. He suggests that each of the 'ecclesial families' of Christendom lives by convictions it deems necessary to the whole Church of Christ, but which in fact serve to identify it itself as a distinct ecclesial community. The problem here is that different confessions insist on different elements as essential while at the same time making it one of the essentials that their list should constitute the defining marks or notes of the Church.[204]

The second paradox is O. Cullman's. He argues that unity presupposes diversity; it cannot by definition be mere uniformity. Thus diversity may be seen as a necessary structure of unity.[205] Cullman would go further and point to a polarity of unity and diversity within that structure as itself a necessary element. He regards this as something discoverable in the New Testament's talk of the diversity of charisms in the one Church, and indeed as involving the gift of a distinct mission to each of the diverse churches.

Cullman's argument that diversity of spiritual gifts makes each church a means of meeting the needs of different spiritual temperaments has the disadvantage that it does not make it easy to see how the needs of such as now belong to churches which became separated at the Reformation were met before the sixteenth century. The Waldensians of the twelfth century; Wyclif and the Lollards; the Hussites, all set in place a number of planks of the platform upon which the sixteenth-century reformers stood.[206] They have not since been accorded the status of ecclesial bodies even by those who followed in their footsteps. Nevertheless, they were arguably receiving and responding to the particular gifts of the Spirit which were later to result in the forming of the churches of the Reformation: for

---

[203] E. Lanne, 'Pluralisme et Unité: possibilité d'une diversité de typologies dans une même adhésion ecclésiale', *Istina*, 14 (1969), 171–90. See Marty, 'Patterns'. See Tillard, 'Église catholique'. *Irénikon*, 56 (1983), 7. H. Meyer, 'Différence fondamentale, consensus fondamentale', *Irénikon*, 58 (1985) 163–5; L. Lambinet, *Das Wesen des Katholisch-protestantischen Gegensatzes* (Einsiedeln/Cologne, 1946); W. Beinert, 'Konfessionelle Grunddifferenz', *Catholica*, 34 (1980), 36–61; Meyendorff, *Orthodoxie et catholicité*, p. 109 on the significance of 'reform' in the history of Christianity.

[204] H. Meyer, 'La notion d'unité dans la diversité réconciliée', *Irénikon*, 57 (1984), 32–7.

[205] O. Cullman, *Einheit durch Vielfalt* (Tübingen, 1986).

[206] See A. Hudson, *The Premature Reformation* (Oxford, 1988).

example, the calls to trust to Scripture alone, to every-member ministry, to openness to the leading of the Spirit.

Both Meyer and Cullman are thus concerned to defend and justify a diversity which is of a fundamentally different sort from that which arose liturgically among the local churches of the first Christian centuries. Let us try to put the problem squarely. Grotius (1583–1645) argued that no reason for discord can be so important that it would not be outweighed by the corresponding reason for concord. ('The Lord acknowledges as his disciples only those who are peacemakers ...'[207]) Perhaps the most testing question, then, about the justification of diversity, concerns the degree to which it may or must breed discord, or at the very least be centrifugal rather than centripetal in its tendency.[208] The desire to save diversity proceeds from a wish to respect freedom. But it is important to be clear whether freedom of the Spirit is meant here, or freedom of the individual church to be itself. If it is the freedom of the Spirit to act in grace, it is hard to see why there should be any fear that the omnipotent can be constrained. If it is the freedom of the individual church, we need to be able to state what would be the value of a freedom which divides. That is what we must consider next.

What should churches do about it if they find themselves as a result of honest ecumenism now in conscience bound to rethink their positions? It has to be faced that to do something about it means being willing to change, to acknowledge the provisionality of what has gone before. Much hangs on the cohesiveness of a particular community as an entity. Without such cohesiveness there is no reason why the Christians who make it up should not join other churches. But it has rightly been thought ecumenically important that *churches* should unite, as little bodies of Christ in their various sorts of 'places'.

---

[207] Grotius, *Meletius or Letter on Those Things which are Agreed among Christians*, ed. G.H.M. Posthumus Meyjes (Leiden, 1988), p. 76, introduction, 3.

[208] This image is not intended to beg the question whether the Church has a centre on earth.

CHAPTER 3

Diversity

THE JUSTIFICATION OF DIVERSITY

'The universality of the Church involves, on the one hand, a most solid unity, and on the other, a plurality and diversification, which do not obstruct unity, but rather confer upon it the character of "communion".'[1] But 'balancing unity and diversity in the Church is a task never yet really accomplished'.[2] A doctrine of legitimate diversity in one Church is paradoxical. Nowhere has that paradox been held more creatively in balance than among the Orthodox.[3] Here, a body of autocephalous Churches deems itself to hold to the unalterable single ancient tradition enshrined by the Ecumenical Councils, while insisting in a number of respects upon the ecclesial completeness and independence of member churches and their consequent freedom to govern themselves and to be themselves. The legitimacy of that diversity consists in the mutual recognition of the Orthodoxy of the churches involved, and in adherence to a common tradition; and yet the common Orthodoxy does not reduce the diversity to uniformity.[4] On the contrary, it is seen as necessary to the Church that unity *should* manifest itself in a legitimate diversity. But the existence of diversity among Churches has been less clearly seen as a good elsewhere until comparatively recent years;[5] and the unavoidable paradox it implies is less easily resolved where the

---

[1] Pope John Paul II, Address, General Audience, 27 September 1989, no. 2, *Insegnamenti di Giovanni Paolo II*, 12(2) (1989), 679.

[2] Olivier Clément, response to Congregation on the Doctrine of the Faith on *The Church as Communion*, *Catholic International*, 3 (1992), 769.

[3] 'The Catholic Church tends to objectify unity, and the Orthodox Church, diversity.' Olivier Clément, response to Congregation on the Doctrine of the Faith on *The Church as Communion*, *Catholic International*, 3 (1992), 769.

[4] E. Lanne, 'Uniformité et pluralisme. Les ecclésiologies en présence', in *Christian Unity*, 353–74.

[5] See Lanne, *ibid.*, for an early attempt at the Council of Florence.

churches cannot point unequivocally to a continuing common tradition. Schillebeeckx argues that 'richly diverse unity-in-communion in no way calls for a formal, institutional and administrative unity, nor a super-church'.[6] 'Although there is a historical plurality as a system of exclusion, there is also a multiplicity which need not arouse opposition and can be experienced within communion and mutual recognition.'[7]

The principle which wins a wider enthusiasm for diversity today is not a new departure. Indeed, it is clearly Biblical. The gifts of the Spirit are many, and they are distributed differently in different places and to different individuals. In that way, the New Testament explains, the whole body of Christ is enriched and no member can fail to be aware of his or her need of the other members, for no one has every gift.[8] But for the first time, and this is something new in the climate of thought of the later twentieth century, this principle is seen as validating the natural desire of Christians in a variety of cultures and coming from many traditions, to preserve something precious and God-given in their own mode of Christian life.

A profoundly positive value can be given to the idea of diversity, especially as an aid to the Church in mission. 'It is not', suggested the Anglican Lambeth Conference Report of 1920, 'by the reducing of different groups to uniformity but by rightly using their diversity, that the Church can become all things to all men ... Diversity is essential to mission, as Christians commend the one Gospel in different cultures and languages, and among different races and human groupings.'[9] To quote a recent ecumenical Report, 'Variety of disciplines and ways of exercising authority ... variety of theological approaches ... even ... the variety of theological expressions of the same doctrine ... complement one another, showing that, as a result of communion with God in Christ, diversity does not lead to division; on the contrary, it serves to bring glory to God for the munificence of his gifts.'[10]

That is obviously right. But the sense in which it is obviously right can easily become confused with a number of senses in which it is less apparent that diversity is God's will for the Church. With the first of these we shall not be directly concerned: that is, with a church-

---

[6] E. Schillebeeckx, *Church: The Human Story of God* (London, 1989), p. 197.   [7] *Ibid.*
[8] 1 Corinthians 12:4ff.
[9] Over and above that pluriformity of rites which has always been accepted; and to which we shall come in a moment.
[10] ARCIC II, *Church as Communion*, 36.

manship founded partly on local or inter-tribal or inter-racial politics.[11] (Examples would be apartheid in South African churches, or
the incitements to mutual hatred of the opposing factions in
Northern Ireland.) Our concern is with ecclesiology, and in particular with the question whether diversity among Churches may
'legitimately' extend to differences in the fundamental conception of
what is 'Church', and even to separation of a sort which makes it
impossible to meet in a common Eucharist. 'The scandal is not that
there are differences but that these differences are used as an
obstacle to communion.'[12] Such phrases as 'unity in diversity' and
'reconciled diversity',[13] as they are sometimes used in modern ecumenism (and where they imply a *rapprochement* which stops short of
full organic union in one Church), may seem to express the confidence that even diversity which goes as far as this may not be at
war with the oneness of the Church.

At present, the acceptance of diversity, and still more the affirmation that diversity is valuable, presupposes a tolerance of the
persistence of differences from one's own 'form' or 'style' or 'structure' of church. That in its turn may assume that (at least some of)
those who call themselves Christians but live in a different sort of
church are members of truly ecclesial bodies. Or it may go the other
way and deny that. The most pressing of the difficulties this creates
in a divided Church concerns the existence of the diversity of forms
of 'self-definition' among churches which came into being, as local
worshipping congregations or groups of such congregations, in communities divided from one another. We saw in the last chapter how,
at first, it was often important to their survival to be able to state
how the community in question differs from others, and is itself right
where they are wrong, true Church where they are false. It has
become important to their continuance. There is, in other words,
what may have to be acknowledged ecumenically to be 'bad' diversity as well as 'good', a diversity which is of its nature divisive in the
Church, and which it is hard to argue can be a gift of the Spirit for
enriching the whole Church.

[11] The kind of thing touched on in Chapter I.
[12] Schillebeeckx, *Church*, p. 197.
[13] It is ironic here, in view of the enthusiasm of some later twentieth-century Lutherans for
these principles, that a leading nineteenth-century American Lutheran should have
written, 'Our Church desires uniformity not as if it were itself unity, or could be made a
substitute for it, but because it illustrates unity, and is one of its natural tendencies and its
safeguard', Krauth, p. 142.

It is important to be clear as we go on about the difference between diversities which reflect the variety of the human faces of the Church in different times and places and cultures, but which are non-divisive because they arise out of the diversity of gifts of the Spirit, and those diversities which come about in circumstances which break communion.

A second important and related test is whether the differences are seen by those who cling to them as absolute or provisional. In the self-definition of that in a given ecclesial body which makes it different from others, there may be present both elements of true and good 'diversity', and elements designed to differentiate divisively from others. Here we must not ignore the fact – and it is a psychologically important fact – of the suffering and deep, even passionate, conviction which caused people to die in past ages for beliefs which were then seen as being in opposition to those of other communities. That is a factor in itself, because the divisive 'differences' cannot all be traced back to 'misunderstandings', and mended by clearing them up.[14]

What I shall chiefly seek to show in this and the following two chapters is that diversity which divides can never be justified, and that the diversity which betokens the richness of the gifts of the Spirit is of its nature not intended to be static. That is to say, if it is truly to express the Spirit's spontaneity and capacity to meet local and specific needs, it must be provisional and therefore capable of development.

WHAT DOES CHURCH-DIVIDING MEAN?

No single visible ecclesial body can now claim to be complete, or claim itself to be 'the Church', in the expectation that other Christians must in time come to recognise that fact, and unite themselves with it on that basis.[15] The text of *Humani Generis* (1950) could still assert that the mystical body of Christ and the Roman Catholic Church are one and the same thing. Since the Second Vatican Council it is possible for the Roman Catholic Church to recognise that 'the Church . . . reaches out beyond the visible boundaries of the

---

[14] 'That cannot do justice either to . . . passionate struggle or to the weight of the realities at issue', Ratzinger, p. 104. Ratzinger, continuing the observations just quoted, suggests that we must try 'to transcend the positions adopted then and to attain a perception that overcomes that of the past'.

[15] Congar, *Diversités et communion*, pp. 235ff.

Roman Catholic Church and in some way embraces all the baptized who, both as individuals and as Churches, exist in a very real, if imperfect, communion with it'.[16]

So a first principle of ecumenical theology must be the recognition that we are dealing with a number of churches which something is keeping apart. 'Church-dividing' is not all of a piece. Churches may deem themselves to be divided in varying degrees.

(i) Christian communities in separation say to one another that one or more points at issue are so important that one side cannot consider the other to be a church at all if it does not hold them or act on them.[17] The division here is of the sort which requires the other to submit.

(ii) Or churches may be saying that they do consider one another to be churches but (for a variety of reasons) perhaps not fully, and for that reason or reasons union is not possible between them.

Recent examples make the same assumption that a community may be a true church but cannot be deemed to be fully the Church (to a degree which makes union possible), by those who are not in communion with it. Again, concession is required to bring the Church in question to ecclesial fullness.

(iii) A third position allows the other church in question to be seen as expressing a more or less legitimate 'particularity', but still one which is too 'diverse' for union to take place. Distinguished Roman Catholic theologians consider it possible for their Church to recognise the *Confessio Augustana* as a particular expression of the common Christian faith, but that has not made a single Communion of Lutherans and Roman Catholics possible yet.[18] An example of a slightly different sort is the Orthodox statement of Chambésy, 1973, that Orthodoxy 'regards the Christians belonging to the Evangelical Church, born of water and spirit, as members of the body of Christ . . . [but] they do not receive the grace which, in the fullness of the

---

[16] See the useful discussion in C. Hay, 'The ecclesiological significance of the Decree on Ecumenism', *Journal of Ecumenical Studies*, 3 (1966), 343–53, especially p. 344.

[17] Here refinements are possible. A Church cannot perhaps reasonably demand complete accord with dogmas defined by herself alone and which have no root in others' traditions. Congar, *Diversités et communion*, pp. 252–3. Nor would it be right to refuse unity if the other side or sides will accept everything but what has been defined after division by the Church seeking to set the terms. J.M.R. Tillard, 'L'expression de l'unitÉ de foi', *Proche-Orient chrétien*, 28 (1978), 193–201.

[18] *LWF VI*, p. 175 (18).

Orthodox Church, is bestowed on its members through the priesthood and which continually manifests itself as the bestowal of the gifts of the Holy Spirit preeminently in the sacraments.' In this case validity is distinguished from efficacy in rather the Augustinian way, and there is still deemed to be some crucial difference standing in the way.[19]

(iv) At a perhaps closer remove, it is possible for two churches to acknowledge the possibility of at least the appearance of fault on both sides, in other words to confess to one another that each can see that to the other it appears heretical, an imperfect realisation of the Church. This amounts to mutual recognition of the sincerity of the other's beliefs, coupled with respect, and a willingness to try to see the other's point of view. But it still does not make them one.

(v) Or two churches may take the convergent view that no reason for discord can be so great that it is not outweighed by a reason for concord. As Grotius says, all Christians follow one Teacher (*doctor*), and he acknowledges as his disciple only those who are peacemakers.[20] It is not at present clear that even this position will bring about union, though the *votum unitatis*, the 'will for unity' it embodies is certainly an indispensable beginning.

The real problem with all these degrees of division is that the other's otherness is seen as inseparable from defect. Respect for difference at the level of tolerance is not the same as accepting that difference is in some sense equivalence, that there really are many gifts of the Spirit to the Churches. There is always some counting-up of elements, especially of those elements which are especially believed to matter; and there is rarely an acknowledgement of the provisionality of the differentiating factors.

DIVERSITY AND DEVELOPMENT

It is easy to fall into the habit of thinking of diversity primarily in relation to pluriformity in the Church now, or at one given time. But the concept of 'diversity' over time, or 'development', must be of at least equal importance. The *Liber Ratisbonensis* of 1541[21] distin-

---

[19] (Chambésy 1973), p. 11.

[20] H. Grotius, *Meletius or Letter on those things which are agreed among Christians*, ed. G.H.M. Posthumus Meyjes (Leiden, 1988), p. 102 (91) and *ibid.*, p. 76 (Introduction, 3).

[21] See my *Problems of Authority in the Reformation Debates* (Cambridge, 1992).

guishes on these grounds between *dogmata* which are *plane necessaria*, and those which 'can be changed' because they are 'instituted to suit the circumstances of the time' (*pro ratione temporis instituta*).[22] The principle upon which the distinction is based here is that some matters have the *perpetuus consensus* of the universal Church, while others rest on the authority only of 'particular churches and synods' at a certain time.

During the period in the nineteenth century when the theology of 'development of doctrine' was itself being developed as a highly topical issue,[23] there was no notion of culturally inspired ecclesial 'development'. It was not equally fashionable to think it important to develop an ecclesial framework which would preserve the local cultural context in the mission-field. Although Christianity had of course from the beginning taken on local colour and adapted itself in some measure to the cultures in which it found itself, what is at present called 'inculturation' has not always by any means been identified as a good to be pursued in the way it is at present.[24] On the contrary, the old world's culture was taken to the new and superimposed upon the local culture, even replacing it. The twentieth-century consequences are still haunting the world in the form of resentment by Third World peoples of what is now seen as cultural oppression by the West.[25] The connection was not readily made at the time between the notions of development and reformulation of doctrine in different ages of the world as the needs and understanding of the faithful might change (diversity over time) on the one hand; and, on the other, the needs of the legitimate diversity of local Church life which might also require the acceptance of different formulations, but within a single period.

There is plentiful precedent in the decisions of councils of the early Church for the view that while some matters of order, if not of

---

[22] *CR* 4.211–12. This distinction is also of course relevant to the problem of 'essentials' discussed in Chapter 3.

[23] See Owen Chadwick, *From Bossuet to Newman: The Idea of Doctrinal Development* (Cambridge, 1957). See my *Authority in the Church: A Challenge for Anglicans* (Norwich, 1990), pp. 000–00 for a brief discussion and references. See recently J. Pereira, 'S.F. Wood and an early theory of development in the Oxford Movement', *Recusant History*, 20 (1991), 524–53. He suggests that it was a new idea of Wood's, and one about which Newman and Manning were dubious, that ' in common with other societies the Church has the inherent power of expanding or modifying her organisation, of bringing her ideas of Truth into more distinct consciousness, or of developing the Truth itself more fully'.

[24] On 'inculturation' see pp. 58–63 above.

[25] A dramatic case in point is the rise of 'liberation theology' in South America in reaction against what is perceived as the oppression and exploitation of Western capitalism.

faith, must be regarded as universally binding and necessary for salvation, others may legitimately vary locally. Less clear is the concomitant acceptance of variation over time, whether something once regarded as binding may cease to be so, or something once 'indifferent' become 'necessary to salvation'.

This was highly topical at the Reformation. The reformers of the sixteenth century made the accusation that the Church had been creating new 'necessities' for the faithful in the form of obligations which it had imposed upon them. The reverse possibility is canvassed in recent decades by Baum, who asks whether the teaching of the Church can change the other way, that is, from saying that something is binding to conceding that it is not. He gives 'as a typical example of an official position, binding at one time but later abandoned, ... the decisions of the Biblical Commission in the early years of this century'.[26] He identifies a series of problems which have to be solved in this connection:

 (i) The effect of historical context on the precise meaning of a defined teaching, in short, whether truths may in some way differ or have different values in different ages.

 (ii) The degree to which greater fidelity to the Gospel may come to qualify present teaching, that is, whether truths may be better understood as the Bible is more faithfully interpreted.

(iii) The degree to which the Church today is bound by the various ecclesiastical documents of the past.[27]

This series of difficulties about diversity over time creates a tendency to try to fix for good what was once seen by each church as important. The Roman Catholic Apostolic Constitution *Sapientia Christiana* of 1979 can only set 'substantial unity' over against the fact that 'the passage of time ... brings changes so rapidly that it seems impossible to lay down anything stable and permanent ... Diversity of places ... seems to call for a pluralism which would make it appear almost impossible to issue common norms, valid for all parts of the world.'[28] Other churches tackle the problem of

[26] G. Baum, 'The *magisterium* in a changing Church', *Concilium*, 1 (1967), 34–43, p. 34.
[27] *Ibid.*, pp. 38–9. See, too, H. Chadwick, *The Tablet*, 1 February 1992.
[28] John Paul II, *Apostolic Constitution 'Sapientia Christiana'*, Catholic Truth Society (London, 1979), *Norms of Application of the Sacred Congregation*, VI, pp. 13–15. The task in hand in this document concerns Ecclesiastical Universities and Faculties, and it is proposed that the best solution is to 'set down by law ... things which are necessary and are foreseen as being relatively stable' and to allow 'a proper freedom' in settling details of the Statutes of local Faculties.

diversity over time in their own ways. At one extreme stand the Orthodox, who would in principle allow no change or development over time, because that would involve a betrayal of tradition. But the autocephaly of the Orthodox churches has unavoidably led to inconsistencies, and to the need for the operation of 'economy' to reconcile them. Among the Protestant reformers of the sixteenth century and their heirs there is both a general insistence upon trusting 'Scripture alone' as the original and only standard, and, in a number of cases, a reliance upon a Confession of Faith drafted in the sixteenth century and embodying statements and formulations on points of controversy of the day. Nineteenth-century Anglicans explored notions of 'bindingness' and of 'standards' in their Lambeth Conferences.[29] The natural instinct is to look to the security of the fixed formula or statement, made at a time when the church in question had a strong sense of what made it itself.

Divisions in the Church can happen suddenly. Breaks take a very long time to mend. Division is in some respects historically a more stable state than unity. Each divided group is able in separation to give the prominence it wants to what it broke away to protect. That makes unity often not the highest priority in the thinking of a community which became itself by separation. That thinking has to be transformed by the realisation of what it is that has separated Christians and keeps them apart. And that means learning to think of one's church as provisional.

To sum up: diversity remains ambivalent. In practice the demand for it comes immediately from the churches. It arises only partly in response to the diversity of gifts of the Spirit, and much more strongly and controversially as an assertion of a distinctiveness which is not easily compromised for the sake of unity. In such contexts it tends to become set in time, and sometimes in past time. On the other hand, a case can certainly be made for the view that the Church is intended to be diverse in the sense that that increases its richness and its capacity to be what a variety of different believers need.

We may get a little farther by trying to separate the issues of diversity of faith or confession, and of order or rites (though they can often no more safely be prised apart than can Siamese twins). But we begin with the problem of diversity in matters of faith, since,

---

[29] *Episcopal Ministry*, paras. 121–5 and 169.

classically, this has been frowned on where diversity in at least those aspects of order which may be classified as 'rites' has not.

FAITH: THE PROBLEM OF CONTENT AND DESCRIPTION

There is a prior question to be answered before we can address all this. Even if it can be agreed that only 'in one faith' can there be 'one Church', there would remain the question what that 'one faith' consists of. It is a matter of trust and commitment. But it also has a content of specific 'beliefs'. Everyone might agree that Scripture contains the fundamental revelation of that faith. But it does not itself constitute a statement of the faith of manageable length to be used as a 'confession' in baptism. Some sort of summary is needed for practical purposes. Baptismal creeds and rules of faith appear in local use from an early date.[30] In the Church as a whole, it is possible to point to the Nicene Creed and to the decrees of other Ecumenical Councils as formulating agreed statements of the faith. But the non-Chalcedonian Orthodox Churches do not accept the ruling of Chalcedon;[31] the West has added a clause (the *Filioque*) to the Nicene Creed which the East cannot accept; even the Creeds most can accept do not cover every aspect of faith and order which churches have regarded as central – the Eucharist, for example; some churches reject all credal formulae;[32] and even where common adherence to the text at least of the Nicene Creed can be assumed, its translation into many languages with their own nuances makes it no longer in the strict sense a single agreed text.

Beyond even these partial agreements about texts lie further difficulties. Their clauses have been unpacked or elaborated, in terms appropriate for the times or for particular local needs. Thus 'the communion of saints' has a strong sense of the congregation of

---

[30] J.N.D. Kelly, *Early Christian Creeds* (London, 1950).

[31] Though one might now add the rider that 'on peut exprimer une authentique foi christologique sans emprunter la formule de Chalcédoine', Congar, *Diversités et communion*, p. 245.

[32] J.A. Nash, 'Political conditions for an ecumenical confession: a Protestant contribution to the emerging dialogue', *Journal of Ecumenical Studies*, 25 (1988), 241–61, written on the WCC project, 'Towards a common expression of the apostolic faith today', p. 245' cf. Franklin H. Littell, *The Anabaptist View of the Church* (Hartford, American Society of Christian History, 1952), p. 66. Such views are not confined to charismatics, Pietists and heirs of the Anabaptists. On Methodist thinking, see 'Doctrine and doctrinal statements and the General Rules', Part II, *The Book of Discipline of the United Methodist Church* (Nashville, 1984), pp. 40–85 and on the Baptists, E. Glenn Hinson, 'Creeds and Christian unity: a southern Baptist perspective', *Journal of Ecumenical Studies*, 23 (1986), 25–30.

gathered believers for some sixteenth-century reformers; for Roman Catholics it is likely to be most strongly evocative of their communion with the dead and a welcoming of the concern of those who are now with Christ for those still in the world. Then there is the problem of topics which are not directly covered in the Creeds at all, or barely hinted at, which have since become capable of dividing Churches, and on which a common statement has to be formulated, not returned to. The doctrine of justification by faith is again an important case in point. So, in one way and another, it has become very hard to say what common faith must consist of, even though the principle must still seem sound that such a 'one faith' would be shared by all Christians in a united Church.

Various lines of approach have been tried in the hope of finding a practical way round these partly theological and partly practical difficulties, by distinguishing between elements of the faith on which agreement is deemed to be essential and constitutive of the Church,[33] and elements which may legitimately be left to the discretion of individual churches, or even individual believers. If everyone agreed, there would be no need to ask questions about essentials at all. The ecumenically crucial question is, 'At what point can one say that the extent of agreement reaches so far that the points of disagreement in thought or divergence in practice come to look almost trivial and no real ground for the suspension of eucharistic communion?'[34] Or, to put it another way, is an agreement to differ itself an agreement which can restore communion, or an admission of defeat?

Substantial agreement[35]

Talk of a 'hierarchy of truths' has had a unitive thrust in recent decades of our own century; the notion was used eirenically by the Second Vatican Council. But there has also run, alongside discussion of the group of terms connected with hierarchy, another discuss-

---

[33] It can be argued that without certain points the Gospel kerygma would be radically compromised. See discussion in J.M.R. Tillard, 'Eglise catholique et dialogues bilatéraux', *Irénikon*, 56 (1983), 13, and p. 8 on the idea that some pluriformity of view is not only inevitable, but can be seen as enriching the Church.

[34] Henry Chadwick, '"Substantial agreement": a problem of ecumenism', *Louvain Studies*, 16 (1991), 207–19, p. 208.

[35] I have discussed these points in 'Rome's response to ARCIC and the problem of confessional identity', *One in Christ*, 28 (1992), 155–67.

ion concerned with the notion of 'substantial agreement',[36] of fundamentals, or essentials,[37] also having a unitive thrust. In both cases
the issue is whether Christians can agree that matters on which they
cannot be of one mind as ecclesial bodies can be deemed not
essential to salvation and thus not essential to the unity of their
churches with one another.

It has been suggested that these two sets of terms 'seek to answer
distinct questions. The hierarchy language is about the relatedness
of different elements in a totality of faith which belongs to and is
indeed constitutive of the Church ... Language about substantial or
fundamental agreement, is seeking common ground among Christians who are sure they share first principles but then find themselves
making deductions which are not identical.'[38] That is to say, here
the first principles also have to be expounded in common.

The debate about 'substantial agreement' or agreement in substance can take place point by point or piecemeal. That is convenient in the framing of agreed ecumenical statements. But it does
not automatically lead to a connected series of further agreements.
Nor, because such agreements in substance are not necessarily
explicitly located in the matrix of the whole, can it always be seen at
once what their implications are. The 'hierarchy of truths' is a
different matter. The discussion of Christian truths as interrelated
requires those involved to keep the wholeness of Christian faith
constantly before them. This is the preference where the Orthodox
have been involved in bilateral conversations. It is of course much
more difficult to arrive at any agreed statements of convenient
working size in that way. So, putting it at its broadest, the options
seem to be to look to a theory of truths of faith which concentrates
upon them as principles to be weighed severally against one another,
or to one which judges them as elements in a complex whole, which
are only truths of faith insofar as they are 'of the faith' in that
interconnected way. These are not mutually exclusive and they do

---

[36] A term used by ARCIC I. See below.

[37] Essentials and fundamentals were partly conflated by A. Aarflot in an address on the
Lutheran Church and the unity of the Church. He said that it is an 'ecumenical principle of
the Lutheran Reformation [that] there are some essential points in the faith that are
important for the unity of the Church, and likewise there are some points that are not
important. It is the principle of distinguishing between fundamental and non-fundamental
articles of faith.' *LWF VI*, p. 37(9).

[38] Henry Chadwick, '"Substantial agreement": A Problem of Ecumenism', *Louvain Studies*, 16
(1991), 207–19, p. 210. Congar agrees that the two groups of concepts are distinct. See 'On
the "hierarchia veritatum"', in *Diversités et communion*, p. 126.

not imply different views of the faith itself. But they are methodologically distinct.

'Substantial agreement' language also emphasises the problem of the relationship between being sure that we have agreement about the *thing*, and agreement at a verbal level, when words can be found in which the two sides can speak of it together. So there is a double agenda, about language and content. These two prove very hard to separate.

Perhaps the most important recent discussions to use the expression 'substantial agreement' or 'agreement in substance' have been in connection with the *Final Report* of the First Anglican–Roman Catholic International Commission, published in 1982. At the Lambeth Conference of 1988, the bishops of the Anglican Communion resolved almost unanimously that the sections on Eucharistic Doctrine and Ministry and Ordination were 'consonant in substance with the faith of Anglicans', and asserted 'that this agreement offers a sufficient basis for taking the next step forward towards the reconciliation of our churches grounded in agreement in faith'. There was more reservation about the section on Authority (which ARCIC itself regarded as less fully resolved). Here the text says only that a 'firm basis for the direction and agenda of the continuing dialogue on authority' has been achieved.[39] In the first case, substantial agreement is seen as a ground for the taking of actual steps towards unity; in the second, the failure to achieve quite that means that there must be further talk before any steps can be taken.

We also have to get clear the distinction between holding something in common and common ownership of the way it is put. The two Communions take different positions on authorising. 'For the Anglicans in ARCIC, the truth of an ecclesiastical definition primarily hangs on the content being consonant with Scripture and accepted sacred tradition and therefore more on the content than on the organs of authority through which the definition has been proclaimed or is now proposed'; for Roman Catholics it may depend 'more on the primate or the general council by whom the definition is given'.[40] 'There will not be the easiest of conversations between those who think the essentials are constitutive of the church and those who think that the essentials are those proposed for acceptance

---

[39] *The Truth Shall Make you Free: The Lambeth Conference, 1988, The Reports, Resolutions and Pastoral Letters from the Bishops* (London, 1988), Resolution 8.
[40] H. Chadwick, *The Tablet*, 1 February 1992, p. 137.

by the Church through its organs of definition.'[41] At the opening of the second Vatican Council John XXIII said that the substance of the ancient deposit of faith is one thing and the way it is presented is another. But we have not yet arrived at a common understanding of 'the relation between the sentences of a given religious tradition and the fundamental act of faith in God made by the individual believer within that tradition'.[42] Nor have we yet in common an understanding of the relation between 'the sentences of a given religious tradition' and the ecclesial being of the community of Christians who own them.

The Roman Catholic Church's official response to ARCIC I was delayed for nearly a decade. When it was published at the beginning of December in 1991 it contained a good deal of (at first reading) rather negative reflection[43] upon the character and implications of the 'substantial agreement' which the ARCIC Report believed it had achieved. In the course of its comments on details of the ARCIC text the *Response* gives a view of what substantial agreement on the topics of Eucharist, Ministry and Authority would comprise. It is instructive to take this here as exemplifying these difficulties. The first point to make itself felt is Rome's sense that not enough has been regarded as essential. A problem here is that ARCIC set out to deal only with points on which there had been divisive dispute in the past, and not to set out a full theology of Eucharist, Ministry or Authority. Rome would now like to see the treatment expanded, to cover 'the points of divergence remaining, as well as ... those other questions which must be taken into account if the unity willed by Christ for his disciples is to be restored'. There are 'areas which do not satisfy fully certain elements of Catholic doctrine and thereby prevent our speaking of the attainment of substantial agreement'. 'Thereby' is crucial. Agreement cannot be 'substantial', it is being argued, if it is incomplete (not sufficient) or insufficiently explicit (not unfolded).[44] This seems to move 'substantial agreement' talk into the arena of a hierarchy of interrelated truths.

The *Response* seeks to explain why this matters. What is not stated

---

[41] *Ibid.*

[42] M. Novak, 'The philosophical roots of religious unity', *Journal of Ecumenical Studies*, 3 (1966), 113–29, 113.

[43] Certainly seen so by J. Robert Wright in 'From lion to mouse: an opinion on the Vatican's recent document', *Episcopal Life* (February, 1992), 22.

[44] See again Chadwick, *The Tablet*, 1 February 1992, p. 136.

in agreement may have been left unconsidered (so that we do not know that we agree on it) or considered without success in reaching agreement (so that we know that we do not agree on it). 'There are still other areas that are essential to catholic doctrine on which complete agreement or even at times convergence has eluded the Anglican–Roman Catholic Commission.'

Even if we could say that substantial agreement implies the existence of enough common ground to walk on, but only in the areas where it has been achieved, we should still be left with the question whether it is firm ground. If its surface covers differences of subsoil, there will be risk of collapse later. 'Lack of clarity regarding baptismal regeneration', for example, may well point to a basic difference in soteriology and ecclesiology. It may well involve a significantly different understanding of grace.[45] That might mean that there remain 'base differences', which are huge.[46] These are real difficulties with the ecumenical method of seeking agreement piece by piece, and it is hard to see how they can ultimately be resolved except by trying the intrinsically much more difficult and lengthy Orthodox way of seeking also to set everything out in its relation to everything else.

Like the method of seeking substantial if piecemeal agreement, the notion that there are 'essential' articles of faith without which the Gospel would be radically compromised, has the advantage of reducing to manageable proportions the content of the faith on which churches must know themselves in agreement before they can be united. It does not solve the problems of stating those essentials in terms all can recognise; nor does it, in itself, provide a means of distinguishing essentials, not from inessentials, but from matters seemingly inextricably linked with them while not being in themselves clearly essential.

In its earlier phase, up to the late Middle Ages and the sixteenth century, this approach tended to speak of things 'necessary to salvation',[47] with particular reference to the notion that they must be set out, whether explicitly or implicitly, in Scripture.[48] This sense

---

[45] Vandervelde, p. 81.   [46] *Ibid.*, p. 83.

[47] See Henn, p. 171, and the concluding pages of Congar, *La Tradition et les traditions*, on 'necessary to salvation', also my *Language and Logic of the Bible*, (Cambridge, 1985), vol. II, pp. 39–41 on John of Ragusa's contribution.

[48] Peter Abelard, *Introduction to Theology* II.xiv, *PL* 178.1076, uses *aperte*. See, too, Congar, *Tradition et Traditions*, pp. 508–9.

of essentials being necessary to salvation remains a useful definitional touchstone.[49]

A nice point raised by Grotius is whether it is possible to be in error about fundamentals without departing from the fundamentals altogether. 'Junius' (François Dujon), one of the Leiden professors, used to say that the error of the Roman Catholic Church in fundamentals was forgivable as long as it did not depart from what was fundamental ('ita in fundamentis errare, ut a fundamentis non aberrarent'). Grotius likes the idea.[50]

On the other hand, it could be argued that it is possible so to *add* to fundamentals that the result is to distort them. That was the Calvinist Walaeus' view. He replied to Grotius that he could agree that Roman Catholic teaching might include the fundamentals of faith, yet they 'build up with one hand what they throw down with the other'.[51] Things are added to the fundamentals which entirely remove their force ('veri fundamenti vim omnino tollunt'). He thinks, for example, that it is not consistent for Roman Catholics to make the perfectly correct and fundamental assertion that Christ is the propitiation for our sins, and to teach at the same time that the merits of monks, confessors and martyrs can be dispensed to the faithful by pontifical authority in the form of indulgences. That seems to make Christ useless (*inutilis*) to them, not because they depart from the fundamentals by denying him, but because they try to add to his work a righteousness won by keeping the law.[52] They teach Christians to call on God through Christ who is their intercessor; yet at the same time they teach people to put their trust in the invocation of the saints and the cult of images. That is like giving people good food and also poison.[53] Although the good food is there, the result is their destruction.

The Anglican Joseph Hall thinks that 'there are three ranks of truths: ... the necessary truths are neither many nor obscure: the impertinent are many, and as litigious as useless: only the profitable are worthy of our studious and careful disquisition'.[54] Pastorally dangerous was the possibility that something unnecessary to sal-

---

[49] Is the idea of 'necessary' truths an implied constraint on divine freedom? Here we can get somewhere but not all the way, by distinguishing between what God necessarily is in himself and what he does for us freely in the incarnation and redemption. Henn, p. 168.

[50] *Ibid.*, p. 171. See Junius, *De Ecclesia*, in *Opera Theologica*, II.997, 1023.

[51] *Meletius*, p. 174.

[52] *Ibid.*   [53] *Ibid.*   [54] Joseph Hall, *The Peacemaker*, *Works*, VI, 628.

vation might be treated by the Church's authorities as though it were necessary, and the faithful misled as well as overburdened.[55]

Adiaphora

We are left with the question posed by Grotius, whether we ought to look for a minimum of agreement and regard the rest as points which simply need not be pressed. If we can show that the points on which we disagree are *adiaphora*, perhaps we can then unite? But another Church's insistence upon what we think are *adiaphora* may be a blockage, not only because there will then not be agreement on what constitutes the minimum, but also because that will indicate differences of valuation which may themselves be differences of faith.

In the sixteenth century there was much discussion of the notion that some things in a church's life might be 'indifferent'.[56] These were commonly identified as rites and ceremonies which a Church might or might not use, but which were not necessary for salvation; and they bring us to the borderline between matters of faith and matters of order. In the second century Irenaeus wrote to dissuade Pope Victor from excommunicating the Quartodecimans on the grounds of indifferent variation in rites – 'The very difference in our fasting establishes the unanimity in our faith', he says.[57] But details of the Church's life such as the day on which an ordination is to be held, or a baptism, did not seem unimportant to Leo the Great (440–61). He insisted that membership of the Church requires unity of faith *and* practice.[58]

It can certainly be argued that liturgy and life carry a theology within them, and that rites and ceremonies cannot be divorced from the faith.

Reformers of the sixteenth century argued that the Roman Catholic Church had been imposing upon the faithful the requirement that they hold these things 'indifferent' to be necessary for salvation. But there were shades of opinion about what this might imply. Jean Gerson had already said that for a human precept to qualify as belonging to divine law, it must be shown to have been

---

[55] Among numerous examples, Grotius, *Meletius* (90), p. 102, raises this difficulty.
[56] B.J. Verkamp, *The Indifferent Mean* (Ohio, 1977).
[57] *Ibid.*, p. 134.   [58] *Epistolae* 9; 16; 4; 138. *PL* 54.625–6, 698, 612, 101, 614, 625.

revealed and to be believed for the sake of obtaining heaven.[59] In a Supplication to King Henry VIII of England Robert Barnes says that '*res medie*, thynges that be indifferent . . . cannot be changed into thynges necessary'.[60] But Tyndale points out that some scriptural precepts, such as the Old Testament ceremonies connected with Circumcision or the Passover, are now indifferent. It cannot therefore be the case that a scriptural precept can never become a thing indifferent.[61] This would seem a strong argument for some doctrine of provisionality in connection with *adiaphora*, as elsewhere.

The positive argument that *adiaphora* might be helpful was put in the late eleventh and early twelfth century by Guibert of Nogent. He is clear that faith alone can be enough to save. Among the non-negotiable necessities of the Church's life, he places baptism and the Eucharist, 'which are so much common to Christians that our faith is vain without them' ('quia in tantum sunt Christianitati communia, ut sine eis subsistere non valeat fides nostra').[62] But he sees that there are other things which, even if they are not to be counted among the things supremely necessary to our salvation ('inter summe necessaria saluti nostrae'), and without which one cannot live rightly (*recte*), yet they are held, and preached in the churches, and they touch many lives for good. (Guibert has practices relating to relics in mind.) So he gives a strong colouring of desirability to what he regards as provisional.

In 1339, at the Synod of Constantinople, the Orthodox heard the argument from Barlaam of Calabria that many teachings are 'indifferent' and differences about them ought not to be a bar to unity. He claimed that this had been recognised by the Fathers. At Bonn in 1875 we meet in more explicit form the idea of the *theologoumenon*, a category of doctrinal statement which stands between mere theological opinion, and dogma as formulated in the Creeds and by the Ecumenical Councils. A Christian has a right but not an obligation to believe a *theologoumenon*.[63] It may follow that *theologoumena* too are 'indifferent', and again that difference about them ought not to be a bar to unity, provided their provisionality is accepted as something capable of being helpful, and also capable of adjustment.

[59] *De Vita Spirit. animae*, 21, *Oeuvres Complètes*, ed. P. Glorieaux (Paris, 1960), vol. iii, p. 16 and see Verkamp, *The Indifferent Mean*, p. 45.
[60] *Supplycatyon* (1534), Sig. Q., fol. iv (v), and see Verkamp, *The Indifferent Mean*, p. 41.
[61] *Expositions and Notes*, ed. H. Walter (Cambridge, 1849), p. 327.
[62] *PL* 156.613.   [63] Henn, p. 175. See, too, Congar, *Diversités et communion*, pp. 71–8.

In the sixteenth century, the negative side of the idea, that things inherently 'indifferent' for salvation may actually be a hindrance, already adumbrated by Augustine and a commonplace by the end of the Middle Ages,[64] is variously developed. This rested on the assumptions we have already met that such things will be of human making. It is argued that they may mislead the faithful into a superstitious belief that the mere performance of certain rites or ceremonies can save; that they may clutter the picture, so that the faithful cannot see which are the essentials; that they may create an intolerable burden for the faithful, although Jesus promised his disciples the lightest of burdens and the easiest of yokes. It may create in the faithful superstitious fear that they will be damned if they do not observe such and such a practice. It may encourage a concentration on externals, to the neglect of the *interior homo*.[65] To clear them out of the way would, on any of these views, be a rightful act of liberation for Christian souls. It is further argued by some that if a thing is not good (that is, if it is not demonstrably commanded by God), it ought to be seen, not as a matter of indifference but as a positive evil, and eliminated for that reason from the Church's life. There are salutary warnings here. A doctrine of provisional toleration of differences can not be extended so widely that it embraces with approval the giving of offence to others.

This is a two-way obligation, though. The potentially offended have a responsibility to try to accept, as those who wish to insist on certain points for their own community have a responsibility to consider the feelings of others. This is the rule of mutual charity, in which there is deferring to one another.

The hierarchy of truths

We must come back now to the hierarchy of truths. Grotius (1583–1645), the Dutch jurist and theologian posed the question: should a church (and *a fortiori* the Church) avoid framing, or stating formally as dogma, more doctrines than are necessary, because that would tend to be divisive? His is a 'minimalist' position. He assumes that 'essentials' will turn out to be few. It is not going to be possible for everyone to agree about everything, and once a point of doctrine has been stated and claimed by a party, it is very difficult for it to

---

[64] Letter 54.1; 55.19, 35, *PL* 33.200, 221, and see Verkamp, *The Indifferent Mean*, pp. 10ff.
[65] *Interior homo*, Verkamp *ibid.*, pp. 20ff.

yield, for self-image becomes bound up with it.[66] Grotius would argue that consensus must be highest authority in decision-making on matters of faith, and that that can be possible only on a relatively small number of essentials. So although it might be desirable, it is simply impossible to go beyond a minimum.

The sixteenth-century reformers and their Roman Catholic opponents continued a practice highly developed in the later Middle Ages, of framing 'theses', 'articles' or 'commonplaces' (*loci communes*).[67] These take the form of propositions which make truth-claims. Sometimes they are accompanied by syllogistic or other formally constructed arguments which support them. A statement which stands as a premiss in one argument may previously have formed the conclusion of another. So their actual relative truth-status does not vary,[68] only their dependence on one another to prove them true.

Joseph Hall would say, 'we all agree in fundamental truth, and ... those things wherein we differ are mere points of scholastical disquisition; such as may perhaps be fit for divines to argue in their academical disputations, not worthy to trouble the public peace, or to perplex the heads, much less the hearts of Christian people'.[69] On this view, secondary and 'lower-order' truths may be seen as proceeding from the higher-order 'fundamentals' by a process akin to that involved in a Boethian or Euclidean chain of axioms,[70] or, as Aquinas saw it, truths which form principles, from which conclusions may be drawn.[71] Lower-order truths might then have the demonstrative necessity and therefore the certainty of those of a higher order, but they would lack the flexibility of 'probability' which would make them, as it were, 'negotiable'. They would not differ in their 'truth-status' from 'inessentials' or matters low in the hierarchy of truths, except insofar as these latter are understood to

---

[66] Grotius, *Meletius*, (90), p. 102.

[67] See my *Problems of Authority in the Reformation Debates* (Cambridge, 1992).

[68] See Chadwick, 'Substantial Agreement', p. 210, and G. Vandervelde, 'BEM and the hierarchy of truths', *Journal of Ecumenical Studies*, 25 (1988), 79.

[69] Joseph Hall, *The Peacemaker, Works*, ed. P. Wynter, (Oxford, 1863), VI.608. Scholasticism can make some distinction between primary and secondary articles, but this has the disadvantage that it seems to neglect the unity and interconnectedness of all revealed truths. (See Henn, pp. 167ff., 172.) It can also be true as in Aquinas, *Summa Theologiae*, that the structural division into articles can give an appearance of their being all the same in importance.

[70] See my *Alan of Lille* (Cambridge, 1983), on the differences between the Boethian and the more complex Euclidean pattern.

[71] See Henn, pp. 168–9.

be things indifferent to salvation and able to be held or not held by
Christians as conscience dictates, without breaking communion.
This approach has the appeal to the Orthodox that it affirms the
organic character of the wholeness of the Church's teaching, but not
in that it can imply that truths may be in some way lesser or greater
in their power to compel assent.[72]

If this talk of a complex of relationships is right, a number of
ecumenical lessons seem clear. It is obviously important to keep
constantly in mind the relation of the truth at issue to 'the foundation of our faith'. In each case of disagreement, it is suggested that
'one must ask where the point at issue stands in the order of truth,
and how important it is in comparison with matters on which
partners in dialogue do agree'.[73] But it could be argued with equal
force that we should be looking not for 'importance' but for 'connection'. In other words, one might ask, if we do not hold this, what else
must we give up? Some things, though not essential or fundamental,
may *deserve* to be respected and (in the case of matters of order)
perhaps observed. That is to say, there may be worthwhileness,
value to the community, as well as truth, in a point at issue.

So far, I have been begging the question what the centre or
foundation may be, but the only answer to that is Christ himself. It is
both very simple and impossibly difficult to say how truths and
precepts may 'relate' to him. There is one Christ. Faith in Christ
saves. So there is at bottom one saving faith. But that is not the same
thing as saying that it is salvific to hold a particular set of truths. Nor
is it the same thing as saying that it is salvific to 'hold' a precept true
in such a way as to obey it. This is not the place to go into these
complex definitional issues. But they have to be signalled.

So there remains a set of questions about importance of the
authority which promulgates a truth in determining its place in any
hierarchy.[74] What is the place of the *magisterium* in relation to
fundamental articles? What place does the authoritative establishment of a set of fundamental articles leave for development of
doctrine? Who determines (or how is it to be determined) which are
the fundamental articles? Here it is customary to distinguish the *quo*,

---

[72] The Orthodox position is not easy to state unequivocally. Yet, in a list of theses of
L. Voronov we find two Orthodox assertions which are relevant here. A unity which
manifests itself in a legitimate diversity is necessary to the Church. That unity must be the
result of 'reciprocal recognition that [separated] Christians are Orthodox *quant au fond*'.
L. Voronov, 'Unité et diversité dans la tradition orthodoxe', *Istina*, 1 (1972), 21–6, p. 22.

[73] Vandervelde, pp. 79 and 80.   [74] See Chadwick, 'Substantial agreement'.

the authority by which a teaching gets its obligatory character, from the *quod*, the actual content of the teaching. The issue here is whether truth compels by simply being truth, or whether it can be made more compelling by some other warrant which attests to its truth. Here Congar argues for the 'restoration of the importance of the content of a doctrine in the face of the authority which promulgates it'.[75]

What we need ecumenically is a practical solution to the problem that Christians do not think exactly alike, the individual churches to which they belong do not speak of their faith in exactly the same terms, and it is tempting to take pride in the distinctiveness of one's special formulations. An approach about which less has been said than on substantial agreements, essentials, fundamentals and the hierarchy of truths, is the one we have already hinted at in discussing 'the justification of diversity'. There is a 'good' diversity which is a gift of the Spirit and which enriches the Church. There is a 'bad' diversity which reflects human resentments and which divides the Church. If we look at the points on which common faith is not readily identifiable in the divided churches they prove to fall on the whole into one category or the other. The test is whether the points distinctive to some churches are recognised by others, perhaps over time, to be valuable insights or needed correctives. The sixteenth-century reformers' stress on the centrality of the ministry of the Word has now been embraced by the Roman Catholic Church as of that sort. Other 'distinctives' prove not to be widely acceptable, and we may see these as likely (unless they are simply taking time to be recognised) to be misplaced. In other words, the ancient conviction that there should be unanimity remains fundamentally right. It may prove to be like Augustine's *perfectio currens*, a perfection not to be finally achieved in this world. But that does not make it any less the right goal.

That may be the case, without necessarily implying that all truths are equally *important* to salvation. It may also be the case without implying that all truths must be held equally firmly by all, whether or not they see them clearly.[76]

'We cannot be too stiff in the maintenance of the main truths',

---

[75] Y. Congar, 'Cinquant années de recherches de l'unité', in *Essais oecuméniques*, p. 89.

[76] Half a century ago Pope Pius XI warned against making a distinction between fundamental and non-fundamental articles, 'as if the former are to be accepted by all, while the latter may be left to the free assent of the faithful'. Encyclical *Mortalium animos* (1928), 9.

says Joseph Hall. 'Our life can never be better sacrificed than in so holy a quarrel ... but for other matters, that concern rather the ornament than the essence of religion, though they are fit to be known and resolved on; yet, with no other confidence than that we are ready to yield upon a stronger conviction.'[77] Does a theology of a 'hierarchy of truths' involve holding that although all truths are in fact equally truths some can be treated as matters of opinion because they are not equally obvious to everyone? Would that mean that private judgement alone could be the test? Would the alternative mean obedience against reason to any teaching of the Church, even though some have historically proved to be not quite right? Congar speaks in terms of perspectives and 'stratification within the totality of the truths of faith, which',[78] he argues, 'make up an organic and structured whole'. He thus in some measure succeeds in avoiding this difficulty by seeing all truths as tied together and entailing one another, in such a way that perhaps to hold one is indeed to hold them all. It remains a crucial question whether things low in a hierarchy of truths may be regarded as less important without in practice being regarded as less true, and if either, as dispensable or optional for Christians. The dilemma remains. Any doctrine of major or principal truths could imply that they may.

'Formally or legally considered', comments Congar, 'all dogmas, all "ecumenical" Councils, all sacraments are equal. But looking at things from the point of their content, their place in the saving structure of the Church, ... we must accept that there are major dogmas, major "ecumenical" Councils and major sacraments.'[79] These, he suggests, 'vary in their relation to the foundation of the Christian faith'.[80] For this variation a number of models or structures have been suggested. 'Essentials' can be seen as 'fundamental', and the relation of 'inessentials' to these fundamentals as one of hierarchical 'lessening of importance', rather than of 'unimportance'. Or the fundamental may be seen as central, with other matters ranged further and further out by degrees. Scripture endorses the use of the imagery of the centre which is also the foundation.[81] Or they may be related in some way which does not

---

[77] Hall, *The Peacemaker*, p. 626.   [78] Congar, *Tradition et traditions*, p. 519.

[79] Y. Congar, 'The idea of "major" or "principal" Sacraments', *Concilium*, 4 (1968), 16.

[80] Vatican II, *UR* 11.

[81] Colossians 1:26; 2:2; 4:3; Ephesians 3:4; 6:19; 1 Corinthians 3:11 (important for Luther); Hebrews 11:6. See, too, Congar, *Diversités et communion*, p. 214, note 12.

imply the ontological or moral inferiority of some to others, although that requires a special usage if the term 'hierarchy' is still to apply.

With a different emphasis, but the same sense of hierarchical subordination which is so hard to escape (although it implies other kinds of variation in the relationship of one idea to another), Congar writes of a progression. He describes how in the course of history, 'from God or Christ to the Church herself, and, in the Church, progressively downwards and more and more into her particular organisation ... from the idea of the grace of God, for instance, thinking passed to an extremely refined elaboration (useful and beautiful no doubt, but very remote), of the sacraments and the conditions and means of grace'.[82] There can be a danger, he thinks, as that happens, that the original deep truth will be partly lost sight of, and the more accessible domestic details of the Church's life come to seem the most important, because they touch life daily and directly.

But many modern vantage-points would see the touching of the domestic details of the Church's life as crucial. If fundamental articles are made a basis for only a limited and external unity, and do not bring about a shared life, their fundamental character is open to question. They certainly cannot be fundamental if they are separate from the life of the Church. In baptism itself there is a profession of faith in the form of a statement of fundamental articles.[83]

The relationship Congar would want to stress is that of all truths of faith to the 'centre'. 'We must leave the periphery and go to the centre', he says 'instead of cataloguing our different conceptions and noting the agreements or disagreements that result from them. We are being led to the very heart of the Christian faith; and the command we receive there is not to expound our own denominational points of view, but to be taught together by the Word of God. Then we shall verify the truth that it is by going to the centre that we find unity.'[84] He sees this process as a reversal of the trend he detects throughout history, since the fourth century, which, he argues, has been for the Church a movement out from the centre.

---

[82] Y. Congar, *Ecumenism and the Future of the Church*, pp. 108–9 and Henn, p. 154.

[83] Henn , p. 166. See Y.Congar, 'Unis dans le baptême désunis dans l'Eucharistie?', *Essais oecuméniques*, p. 249. On this point the Secretariat for Christian Unity has said that participation in the Eucharist expresses the full profession of faith and full insertion in the Church, for which baptism is only a beginning, *ibid.*, p. 252.

[84] Congar, *Ecumenism and the Future of the Church*, pp. 68–9.

The non-fundamentals or lower-order or inessential points may on this model be seen as 'externals', and contrasted with those 'inner' realities of the faith and of sacramental life which can never be matters of indifference to salvation. Such externals may in principle be indifferent or helpful or indeed (as many of the sixteenth-century reformers argued), a hindrance.

Any theory of the arrangement of essentials or fundamentals in a relationship to one another in a divided Church runs into the problem of points which are special or even peculiar to one community. Walaeus was not convinced by Grotius' argument that what could (he believed) be shown to be errors in the teaching of the Roman Catholic Church could be set aside, leaving a large part of their faith in common with that of other Christians.[85] He himself could neither consider such 'errors' as trivial enough to be set aside in this way, nor hold that sickness in one part of the body does not make the whole body sick.[86] 'I agree with you', said Grotius in answer, 'that there is in the Roman Church something in common with other Churches, and something which is peculiar to that Church. The one is Christian, the other for the most part antichristian.'

But he argues that not all matters of faith are equally weighty, that is, not all have the same *auctoritas*. He means by that that something which is held as a matter of consensus among all Christians, those things which are *communia*, these require a *notitia* which others do not. Matters necessary for salvation must be taught as being beyond question, others are *non necessaria*.[87] Something can certainly be done by way of distinguishing primary from secondary articles within a single system.[88] But that requires means of determining the weight to be given to each in the economy of salvation, the authority on which they are to be believed, their very truth; and all these are notoriously vexed questions ecumenically.[89]

However we are going to understand the relationships the truths in the 'hierarchy' bear to one another, clearly we must see the hierarchy of truths as forming a 'totality', an 'organic and structural

---

[85] *Ibid.*   [86] *Ibid.*, pp. 174–5.   [87] *Ibid.*, p. 177.
[88] See Henn, pp. 167ff., p. 172, on Congar's thought here.
[89] See H. Mühlen, 'Die Lehre des Vaticanum II über die "hierarchia veritatum" und ihre Bedeutung für der ökumenischen Dialog', *Theologie und Glaube*, 57 (1966), 303–5 on these points, and on 'value'. See, too, C.J. Dumont, 'Y a-t-il une hiérarchie de valeur entre les vérités de foi', *Les Voies de l'unité chrétienne, Unam Sanctam*, 26 (Paris, 1954), 151–61 and Vandervelde, pp. 74–84.

whole'. This would have the advantage of creating a set of checks and balances within which provisionality could work without its resulting in a liquefaction of all solid ground.

DIVERSITY OF RITES

In order to discuss the limits to the legitimate diversity of 'rites', we must settle on a working definition. A rite may be no more than a particular form of service or liturgical pattern.[90] Divisions have rarely been caused by differences over liturgy. It has always been relatively uncontroversial that rites in this liturgical sense may vary from place to place and from time to time (within limits which would, for example, make it unacceptable to include as part of the liturgy, say, the slaughter of a goat).

The principle that there may be legitimate local variation in the form of the liturgy is of considerable antiquity and has been widely reaffirmed century by century. When Augustine of Canterbury was sent on his mission to England, Gregory the Great encouraged him to construct a liturgy from the Gallican rite appropriate to the people's needs. Ralph Glaber, writing across the millennium, touched on various questions which have arisen about practices in some places known to him which are contrary to Roman use, such as singing the Te Deum on Sundays before Christmas and in Lent.[91] In 1006 Fulbert of Chartres writes that diversity of customs elsewhere is not a stumbling-block because it has always existed in the Church of Christ.[92] Jean of Fécamp writes, between 1018 and 1050, that the Church knows as her rules of existence Scripture, universal tradition and the local self-regulating community in its proper and particular form, where there is one faith in diverse customs.[93] Guibert of Nogent, nearly a century later, tried to clarify the rules. Those actions of the Church 'which are so communal to Christianity that our faith cannot subsist without them' cannot vary (baptism and the

---

[90] See Bernard of Clairvaux, *Letter* 174.1, *Opera Omnia*, ed. J. Leclercq (Rome, 1974), vol. VIII., pp. 388ff. to the Canons of Lyons who introduce a new *celebritas . . . quam ritus ecclesiae nescit*, and *PL* 183.333. Gerhoch of Reichersberg, *c.*1130, speaks of *baptismus, ritu ecclesiastico celebratus*, in *Opera inedita*, ed. D. and O. Van den Eynde, IIi (Rome, 1956), p. 10. Innocent IV (d.1254), *ritus seu consuetudo unguendi* (no. 2); *ritus secundum quem patriarcha . . . Chrisma conficit* (no. 5) of *Collectio Lacensis* II.445. Aquinas, for example, ST Ia IIae, q.102 a.6 ad.11. IIa IIae q.10.a.11. IV Sent. d.13.q.1.a.2.q.a.6. See, too, Congar, *Diversités et communion* (Paris, 1982), pp. 114ff. on this question.

[91] *Historiarum Libri Quinque*, ed. and tr. J. France (Oxford, 1989), Book III.iii, pp. 112–14.

[92] *PL* 141.192, letter 3.   [93] *Confessio Fidei* III.26, *PL* 101.1072.

Eucharist, for example).[94] He expresses the essential requirement
neatly, by contrasting 'difference in practice' with a departure from
'the [common] sense of the faith' ('etsi diversa sunt actu, nusquam
tamen discrepant a fidei sensu').[95] During the disputes between East
and West in the eleventh century some issues concerning differences
of rites were involved. Some, though not all, of the participants were
able to affirm with Theophylact, Archbishop of Bulgaria, that, as
long as dogma is not involved, differences of usage do not justify
schism.[96] Anselm of Canterbury argued in his letters on the sacraments that if unity of love in the catholic faith is preserved, a
difference of custom does not matter.[97]

It is in this historically well-founded confidence that in the twentieth century the Anglican–Orthodox Joint Doctrinal Committee
could make the statement that

> with regard to ecclesiastical customs or usages we distinguish two classes –
> those which according to St Photius are based on the authority of a general
> or catholic decree, and are thus obligatory for the whole Church; and those
> which have only a local character, and which every local Church is
> therefore free to accept or not. We agree with St Augustine that every
> Christian should accept the customs and usages of the Church to which he
> belongs.[98]

In the discussion of matters of faith we have met the idea that they
can be treated individually, and the view that they form an integra-
ted totality, so that no essential can be settled without reference to its
place in a hierarchy of truths. Similarly, 'rite' can mean a single
custom or liturgical sequence; it can also refer to a general 'way of
doing things'. Then 'rite' is seen as a complete pattern of ecclesial
life in a community, which may also be called a 'custom' or *consuetudo*.[99] Congar describes it in this sense as 'the multiple and coherent
expression of the faith as a Church has experienced it and continues
to experience it'.[100] When that is the case, the rite or custom is
regarded as having an integrity which means that it cannot be

---

94   *PL* 156.612–3, 'quia in tantum sunt Christianitati communia, ut sine eis subsistere non
     valeat fides nostra'.
95   *PL* 156.612.
96   Accusations against the Latins, 15, *PL* 126.245B. Others pointed out that the differences of
     rite might indeed involve theological differences.
97   *Opera Omnia*, ed. F.S. Schmitt (Rome/Edinburgh, 1938–68), 6 vols., vol. II p. 240.
98   G.K.A. Bell, *Documents on Christian Unity*, (London, 1924), vol. I, p. 41 and *Lambeth
     Occasional Reports*, 1931–8 (London, 1948), p. 54.
99   Anselm of Havelberg, *PL* 188.1140ff., for example.
100 See *Diversités et communion*, p. 124 and cf. *LG* 23 (4), *UR* 15–17.

mixed piecemeal with other rites. Celestine III (1191–8) laid down the rule that there should be no mingling of rites when East meets West.[101] Innocent III endorsed this principle, emphasising that a priest should be ordained and should celebrate the Eucharist according to his own rite.[102] The Council of Florence uses *consuetudo* in this way of the Eucharistic rites of Greeks and Latins (which it regards as of equal value).[103] The Greek rite had been recognised as legitimate for the Greeks since the sack of Constantinople in 1204; that was necessary to avoid open revolt among the Byzantines.[104] The Clementine Instruction of 1595 on mixed marriages somewhat gives the lie to this last confidence, when it makes the rule that a Latin husband or wife does not follow the rite of a Greek spouse, but a Greek wife does follow that of her Latin husband; children follow their father's rite, unless the mother is Latin.[105] Benedict XIV in 1742 in the Bull *Etsi pastoralis* established the principle that the Latin rite was in fact to be deemed superior. The position since is equivocal. Indeed, from the Orthodox point of view any such ruling is absurd, because Orthodoxy sees no need for the Eastern rites which belong to the Eastern churches to be guaranteed or protected externally to their exercise in the living community.

It is much harder to find examples of 'rite' in this sense of 'a complete pattern of life in an ecclesial community' used to refer to the rite of a local church (say the Gallican) within the Latin Communion. Its strongest early pattern of usage concerns the difference between Greek and Latin rites. Pius IV speaks of *ritus Germanicus*, but this seems to be a relatively uncommon use in pontifical documents.[106] At the same time, there is precedent for distinguishing within a given *cultus* (with approval or disapproval) between elements in the rite or custom which are peculiar to certain places; and those which are, or ought to be, universally observed in the Church because they have the authority of Scripture; or because they have the warrant of having been observed always and everywhere in the Church. Augustine distinguishes three categories of ecclesiastical customs: (i) those which have the authority of Scripture; (ii) unwritten customs inherited from the Fathers, which are

---

[101] *Decretals* I.ii.9, Friedburg, II. 120.
[102] *Acta Innocenti III, Pontificia Commissio ad redigendum Codicem iuris Canonici Orientali, Fontes,* Series III (Rome, 1944), see table for *ritus*.
[103] Bull *Laetentur Coeli,* 6 July 1439.   [104] Lanne, in *Christian Unity,* p. 368.
[105] Discussed by Congar, *Diversités et communion,* p. 121.
[106] *Ibid.,* p. 122.

observed worldwide and approved by the Apostles and by Councils of the whole Church; (iii) those used in some places but not others.[107] Innocent I in a letter of 416 to Decentius of Gubbio stresses that priests are not to allow any (local) diversity or variety in rites, nor to introduce any novelties, nor to do anything outside Roman practice. In an account of the trial of Arnulf, sent to Wilderode, Bishop of Strasbourg in December, 995, Gerbert of Aurillac cites Hincmar of Rheims. 'Certain ideas ... handed down by the apostolic men ... are preserved by the authority of ecumenical councils, and certain of these things have been changed in councils. But some of those which have been legislated on in regional councils, are adhered to unchanged by the authority of the ecumenical councils and henceforth must be kept inviolate.' What Hincmar calls 'half-truths ... resulting from no General Council nor even a regional one' are put forward by those who want to do what 'the ancient custom of the Church did not uphold' and which the Church has later 'excluded through its most powerful sanction'.[108] So although rites may legitimately vary locally they can traditionally do so only against a background of acceptance of a common way of life in the Church, which check excess or extravagance or error in local rites. In the sixteenth century, Nicholas Herborn comments in this vein on the German rite (*ritus theutonicus*) in his *Locorum Communium*. It is in a barbarous tongue, he says, and may lack due forms (*propriis characteribus careat*). As a result, it is not only foreign to the custom of the universal Church (*ab universalibus ecclesiae consuetudine alienum*), but also a mockery (*etiamne merum figmentum et caninum quoddam ludibrium*). Thus the framers of the rite both overturn the Church's custom (*ecclesiae morem invertere*) and have caused a shipwreck in the faith (*porro et naufragium in fide fecisse*).[109]

Rite and order

It is important, though far from easy, to distinguish in the historical story the matters of variation in 'order' which roughly belong to the realm of liturgy, and those which have to do not merely with 'rite' and 'ceremony' and 'custom', but with the deeper structures of the

---

[107] Cited by V.T. Istavridis, *Orthodoxy and Anglicanism*, tr. C. Davey (London, 1966), p. 141 from *Suggested Terms of Intercommunion* (1921), no. 9.

[108] *Opusculum Adversus Hincmarum Laudunensem, PL* 126.388–9, cf. Augustine, *De Baptismo*, iii.2, *PL* 43.139. See, too, *The Letters of Gerbert*, ed. H. Pratt Lattin (Colombia, 1956), no. 201.

[109] Nicholas Herborn, *Loci Communes*, ed. P. Schlager, *C.Cath.* 12 (1927), pp. 71–4.

Church's order and thus with its faith.[110] Variation in liturgy itself cannot be entirely without theological implications. The decision taken in some Reformation and post-Reformation communities in the West to do without a formal liturgical pattern altogether and worship with prayer, readings, preaching and hymns in a variable sequence, is a decision which seeks to state a theological position; as is the refusal to use any form at all (the Society of Friends) or to allow pure spontaneity to direct things as the Spirit wills (as in some charismatic Churches).[111] The external forms of a rite are inseparable from the ecclesial style they express.[112] Where a liturgy varies (for example in the order of the elements in the Eucharistic sequence), that, too, must have theological implications, and it should be recognised by the framers of the changes that there must be limits to what they may do.

The definitive early episode here was the debate about the proper date of Easter. The controversy proved to be an important test-case precisely because it was seen as Church-dividing. It began in the second century as the first serious test of the principle of 'one faith in many rites'. In 190–1 Victor, Bishop of Rome, threatened to excommunicate as heterodox the Quartodecimans who said that Easter must be celebrated on the fourteenth day of the moon even if it was not a Sunday. A party of bishops persuaded him the other way. Irenaeus, for example, argued that the difference in the fast confirms the unity in the faith.[113] The issue went beyond difference of rite because it made it appear that the Church was celebrating not one but two 'Easters', one of which must be false. (For this reason Cummianus explains in the seventh century that a Christian in the wrong on this point could properly be called a heretic because he is not celebrating the true Easter.)[114] 'What could be more beautiful and more desirable, than to see this festival, through which we receive the hope of immortality, celebrated by all with one accord

---

[110] Indeed, it is possible to define 'rite' itself in such a way as to blur the boundaries between faith and order. 'Qu'est-ce que le rite? Le rite, c'est la libre poésie des signes ou les paroles dont se sert l'Eglise, unité organique, pour exprimer, soit sa connaissance des verités divines, soit son amour sans borne pour son Créateur et son Sauveur, soit l'amour qui unit les chrétiens les uns aux autres sur la terre et dans le ciel.' A.S. Khomiakov, quoted as an example of an Orthodox view by Congar, *Diversités et communion*, p. 122.

[111] See chapter 2 on ecclesial identity.

[112] See E. Lanne, 'Eglises unies ou Eglises soeurs: un choix inéluctable', *Irénikon*, 48 (1975), 321–41, p. 323.

[113] Congar, *Diversités et communion*, p. 20 discusses the question as it looks in this period.

[114] *De Controversia Paschali*, PL 87.973. Also Bede *H.E.* IV.i.2, p. 321. See, too, Verkamp on the issues.

and in the same manner?', asked Constantine the Great.[115] 'Glorying in the private purity of their own way of life [they] detest our communion to such a great extent that they disdain equally to celebrate the divine offices in churches with us and to take courses of food at table for the sake of charity.'[116] Writing to King Geraint in the seventh century about the division brought about by the disagreement over the date of Easter, Aldhelm sees this difference on a point of order as profoundly divisive of communion. So, although it was always understood that rites might vary, it was also clear that it is by no means easy to say what constitutes one order in one Church when they do. Here, in short, is the best test of the notion of a provisionality in things which can allow churches to move together.

We find early concessions to the impossibility of achieving unanimity in all cases about matters of order. Nicaea's sixth Canon allows for a majority vote in the choosing of a new bishop where 'two or three bishops ... from natural love of contradiction, oppose the common suffrage of the rest'. Augustine deals with the diversity of usage and rites, and with the freedom which local churches have in this regard, in his letters to Januarius. These became the standard authority on the matter in the Middle Ages in the West and up to the Council of Trent. Augustine often recalls the answer Bishop Ambrose of Milan gave to his mother Monica when she asked why there was a fast on Saturday in Rome but not in Milan. 'Some things vary from place to place', Ambrose replied. Augustine argues on this basis that a Christian ought to do his best to conform with the practice of the Church where he finds himself. That which does not go against the faith, or against right behaviour, ought to be considered indifferent.[117] There is an important implicit respect for the local churches' ways here, which is very different from what seems to be in Augustine's mind about the requirement of unanimity of faith everywhere.

In the realm of order, two kinds of departure from a common rule were always to some degree acceptable. Special concessions could be

---

[115] Letter of the emperor to those not present at the Council of Nicaea, Eusebius, *Vita Constantini*, iii.18–20.

[116] Aldhelm to King Geraint about the Synod at Hereford in 672, Bede *H.E.* II.4, of *The Prose Works*, tr. M. Lapidge and M. Herren (Ipswich, 1979), p. 484.

[117] *Epistola* 54.ii.2 and 3, *PL* 33.200(201) in 400, cf. Gratian C.11 D.XII (Friedberg, 29–30). Cf. Letter 54.xviii.34 (*PL* 33.220–1) and Letter 36.ix.22 to Casulanus (*PL* 33.146) which is cited by Cervini at Trent during the debate on traditions of 23 February 1546, *CT* XII.511–24. See, too, Congar, *Diversités et communion*, p. 37.

made when circumstances made it difficult to keep the usual or common rule (the 'emergency' principle). Augustine of Canterbury consecrated his successor during his lifetime to ensure that there would be no gap, because the local Church was so young, and might not be able to manage the succession itself. In relating this, Bede, highly conscious that this must be seen as an emergency or extraordinary action, is careful to explain that St Peter himself set a precedent, for he is said to have consecrated Clement in his lifetime to be the next Bishop of Rome after him.[118] Bede also explains the procedure by which the Archbishop of Canterbury or York might consecrate a new archbishop for the other See, because Rome was so far away; the Pope would then send the pallium in confirmation of what had been done on his behalf.[119] Consecration by one bishop instead of a minimum of three was also allowed in the early English Church at a stage when it would have been impracticable to assemble three bishops for the task.[120]

Secondly, there was the understanding we have already noted, that certain matters of rite and ceremony could be regarded as locally variable even when there were no extraordinary circumstances – the principle on which Gregory the Great seems to have allowed Augustine of Canterbury liberty to do as he thought fit about the choice of liturgy.[121]

Both these kinds of concession can be seen as implying the existence of understood rules, from which they depart without challenging them; and thus of an underlying 'common order' which is normative but not indispensable. The authority for such a common order would seem to lie in some sense in its very 'commonness', that is, its universality. The authority for the departures appears to be local need, and its authorisation will normatively have to take place through the bishop, or through the bishops of the area acting collegially.

It is instructive to take a case in detail here, if we want to see the ecclesiological implications. Within a century of the formal separation of East from West in 1054, there were several attempts to mend the breach.[122] The first to see the difficulty about unity and diversity

[118] Bede, *H.E.* ii.4, p. 144.   [119] Bede, *H.E.* ii.18, p. 196.

[120] *Libellus Responsionum* and see Peter Hunter Blair, *The World of Bede* (London, 1970), pp. 61–5.

[121] *Ibid.*, p. 82.

[122] What follows is based on my article 'Unity and diversity: Anselm of Havelberg as ecumenist', *Analecta Praemonstratensia*, 67 (1991), 41–52.

at all clearly as having implications for the very concept of 'Church' was Anselm of Havelberg. Unable to fulfil his duties as bishop because his diocese was repeatedly laid waste by war, Anselm took refuge at the Imperial Court. There, his abilities as a scholar,[123] and perhaps already visible talents as a diplomat, made him Lothair's choice as ambassador to Constantinople in 1135. Anselm made use of his months among the Greeks to familiarise himself to some degree with the language and theological scholarship of the Orthodox tradition. The years 1136–42, spent partly in Italy with the emperor, also gave Anselm the opportunity to become an intimate of the papal court. After a gap of two years, during which he endeavoured to rebuild the ecclesiastical life of his diocese, he was invited to take part in talks with Greek theologians at Tusculum in 1144. This was not to be his last ecumenical encounter. Frederick Barbarossa was to send him as ambassador to Constantinople in 1152, and on the voyage there he had talks with Basil of Achrida at Thessalonika. But it was after the Tusculum discussions that he wrote, at the request of Pope Eugenius III,[124] perhaps the most remarkable mediaeval treatment of the complex of problems concerning the hierarchy of truths, essentials and inessentials, unity and pluriformity.

Anselm's *Dialogues* are fresh in their approach precisely because he was the first in his time to see the interrelatedness of the questions with which they are concerned. People often ask, says Anselm, why there are so many novelties in the Church of God (*tot novitates*).[125] They are prompted to wonder about this by the proliferation of new religious Orders (*tot ordines*). This multiplication of modes of living the religious life was evidently causing enough disquiet elsewhere for it to be necessary for apologists to take stock of it, and provide a rationale.[126] Anselm defends it. In the midst of diversity (*varietates*); altered by what is new (*adinventionibus immutata*); disturbed by new laws and new customs (*agitata*); tossed about almost yearly on the waves of change in rule and practice ('regulis et moribus fere annuatim innovatis fluctuans'),[127] the Church shows the living power of the Holy Spirit working within her.[128] This has always

123 On Anselm's studies at Laon, see Anselm of Havelberg, *Dialogus*, I, ed. G. Salet, *Sources chrétiennes*, 118 (Paris, 1966), introduction.
124 *Ibid.*   125 Book I.i, p. 34.
126 See *Libellus de Diversis Ordinibus et Professionibus qui sunt in Aecclesia*, ed. G. Constable and B. Smith (Oxford, 1972).
127 Anselm, *Dialogus*, Book I.i, p. 34.   128 Book I.ii, p. 44.

been so. He devotes most of his first book to a chronological account of the ages or *status* of the Church, to demonstrate the rule he seeks to lay down as the first principle in ecumenical problem-solving. There is and always has been only one faith, lived in many different ways ('semper unum una fide, sed multipliciter distinctum multiplici vivendi varietate').[129] Christians worship one God in one faith even when they do so in different modes of life ('diversis modis vivendi'), and with differences of rite in the sacraments. (Here he has the Eucharist particularly in mind: 'diverso sacrificiorum ritu'.)[130] If we study the history of the Church we see the *fides catholica* gradually being firmly established (*radicata*), and the canon in the form of precepts, prohibition, dispensations, forming *diversae regulae*, that is, rules on a variety of issues, amongst which some will not be uniform everywhere, or in every age.[131] Against those who think that flexibility is a recipe for decay ('omnem religionem tanto esse contemptibiliorem quantum mobiliorem'),[132] Anselm argues strongly that it is a sign of the richness of the diversity of the Spirit's gifts in the Church.[133]

The essential point in Anselm's view is that the faith must be one; when that is secure, pluriformity can confidently be seen as a positive sign of vitality in the realm of order. He was encouraging his readers to take a grand view of the unfolding of God's providential plan in the history of the Church, which would enable them to put the schism of East and West into perspective in the whole story of the history of salvation. (There is a useful lesson with modern reference here. The anxieties which get in the way of ecumenical *rapprochement* frequently tend to be of the sort which arise from concerns close to home and lack a sense of the perspective of the grand divine plan.)

In his prologue Anselm explains that it became plain at Tusculum that there were differences both of *doctrina* and of *ritus* between the Greeks and the Church of Rome. On both topics he himself has had discussions in Constantinople, in private as well as in public.[134]

Book II opens with a description of the circumstances of his talks with Nechites. Because his purpose is eirenic, he is careful to eliminate any suggestion of the adversarial in the debates as he reports them. He wants his readers to be persuaded not only that the Greeks

---

[129] Book I.ii, p. 44. [130] Book I.iii, p. 48. [131] Book I.ix, p. 82.
[132] Book I.i, p. 36.
[133] Book I.ii, p. 40. [134] Saltet, *Les Réordinations* (Paris, 1907), pp. 21–8.

are not monsters and heretics, but also that they are, in essentials, one in faith with the Latins and entirely open and reasonable in their willingness to be of one mind with the West in all matters of substance. He reports his own opening words to this effect. He has not come *ad contentiones*, but to discover with Nechites their common faith ('de fide vestra atque mea').[135] He wants to see them 'walk the way of charity together' ('simul gradiamur viam charitatis'), not contending arrogantly to score points in their reasoning ('non contendentes superba ratione'), but humbly seeking the truth together ('simul investigantes veritatem humili inquisitione').[136]

Anselm is sensitive to the difficulty over language, not only insofar as it concerns Greek and Latin, but also at the profounder level of the mutual misunderstanding which may arise from differences of style, approach and understanding in the very fabric of the lives of their respective Churches. 'It is not fitting for us to squabble over words', he tells Nechites. He wants to see such an *interpretatio* held between them *in medio* as they talk as may take and expound ('excipiat et exponat') the sense of each fully and exactly ('sermonem utrinque continuatim pleno et collecto verborum sensu'). In that way, he concludes, we shall be seen to be not sticklers for the words (*verborum observatores*), but enquirers into the meaning (*sententiarum investigatores*). Nechites accedes to the reasonableness of this, and so they begin.[137]

Anselm's initiative failed to unite East and West, as did other efforts in succeeding generations; but each attempt sharpened awareness of the problems raised by the apparently simple issue of differences of rite. At the Council of Florence matters were complicated by Western internal conflict over the 'plurality' of the Avignon schism and its aftermath. There was also a slow realisation that 'conciliarism' meant something rather different in West and East. In the East the bishops could not think that they would determine matters by their conciliar decision. It was understood to be necessary for the people to receive the decision to make it binding. Moreover, the multiplicity of the Churches of the East was a principle with them, as it could not be to Roman eyes.[138]

Alongside such enlarging understanding of the broad differences there continued the abrasion of the constant irritant of local conflict over differences of rites. At the end of the sixteenth century, after the

---

[135] *PL* 188.1163.   [136] *PL* 188.1164.   [137] *PL* 188.1164.
[138] Lanne, in *Christian Unity*.

Council of Trent when Roman Catholic preoccupation with rites sharpened,[139] the Greeks of Ancona were seen to be performing actions which troubled their Latin neighbours. Priests, not bishops, confirmed infants by signing them on the forehead (although with chrism consecrated by a bishop). It was the Greek practice to save the elements of the Eucharist from the Thursday of the Last Supper for the use of the sick for a whole year. When the laity communicated they dipped the bread into the wine.[140] It became important both to clarify what was going on and to insist upon a sharp separation of the rites of the two communities, lest in mixing them the ill-instructed created a monstrous hybrid lacking essential elements. Cardinal Santoro wrote in the 1590s on the ordination of Greek clergy, citing Innocent III and Celestine III, to instruct that Latins should not be ordained by Greek bishops or Greeks by Latin bishops, even using one rite or the other, let alone a mixture, or 'confusion' of the two.[141]

A new dimension of difficulty was added from the sixteenth century. The Protestant reformers were fond of arguing that matters of order and practice were thus being added to the list of those things which it had hitherto been necessary to salvation to believe. In the decade or two after the attempt to introduce the Interim of Augsburg (1548) some Lutherans came to hold that much if not all *ius ecclesiasticum* is liable to fall into that category. A driving force here, for the reforming churches sometimes faced hostile governments, was the need to make concessions to avoid persecution. Melanchthon insists, in the *Apologia* for the Augsburg Confession, that Lutherans want to maintain 'Church polity' and 'ecclesiastical hierarchy', even though they were created by human authority, because they have their purposes, and as things indifferent they put at risk nothing fundamental.[142]

'It is enough for the true unity of the Christian Church that the Gospel be preached in accordance with pure doctrine and the sacraments be administered in keeping with God's Word. It is not necessary that human tradition, or rites and ceremonies, instituted by men, should be alike everywhere', says the Augsburg Confession (Article VII), and many other Protestant confessional documents of

---

139 V. Peri, *Chiesa Romana e "rito" Greco: G.A.Santoro e la Congregazione dei Greci (1566–1596)* (Brescia, 1975), and cf. Congar, *Diversités et communion*, p. 121.
140 Peri, *Chiesa Romana*, pp. 221–5, cf. p. 241, Document XIII.   141 *Ibid.*, p. 217.
142 See *Papal Primacy and the Universal Church*, ed. P.C. Empie and T. Austin Murphy (Minneapolis, 1974), p. 123.

the sixteenth century and later echo its ideas. When the Confutation of the Augsburg Confession of the Lutherans was framed in 1530, it was possible to say, from a Roman Catholic vantage-point, that the Lutherans were to be 'praised in that they think that variety in rites does not fragment the unity of the faith'. Jerome is cited, as attesting that 'unaquaeque provincia in suo sensu abundat'. There are, however, deemed to be some universal rites which all Christians must observe.[143]

The ecumenical implications of retaining in a united Church practices 'neither commanded nor forgiven', for the sake of pleasing one or other of the partners, were much in the minds of the framers of the Lutheran Formula of Concord later in the century. Article X of both the Epitome and the Solid Declaration discuss at length what should be done about such things. Melanchthon, John Bugenhagen, George Major, Caspar Cruciger, tended to the view that where there was disagreement in doctrine, indifferent rites and ceremonies might be reintroduced for the sake of unity. Matthias Flacius, John Wigand, Nicholas Gallus and Anthony Corvinus thought not. The difficulty was that adiaphora would cease to be matters of indifference when these ceremonies are intended to create the illusion (or are demanded or agreed to with that intention) that two opposing religions have been brought into agreement and become one body.[144] A crux here is coercion. Liberty ought to allow a Church to use such ceremonies as well as to choose not to use them.[145] 'Any coercion or commandment darkens and perverts.'

It seems likely that in a future united Church there need be no real difficulty about the continuance of diversity in liturgy, at least where that could not be seen as divisive in implying substantive differences of faith. In trying to settle on forms of worship in the 'mixed polity' of united churches of the kind which have already come into existence locally in the Indian sub-continent, embracing churches formerly of the episcopal, Presbyterian and Congregational traditions, the United Church of North India produced a volume of *United Church Worship*, which addressed itself to this difficulty. Its approach was to respect existing traditions in the uniting Churches. Worship need not involve written orders of

---

[143] *Confutation of the Augsburg Confession*, ed. H. Immenkötter, *C. Cath.*, 33 (1979), p. 97, Jerome *Epistola* 71.6, *CSEL*, 55.7.6ff.

[144] G. Tappert, *The Book of Concord* (Philadelphia, 1981), p. 611.

[145] *Ibid.*, p. 494 and p. 612.

service, it insists, although they may be helpful. No book now in use should be displaced, unless the local Church Council or Synod chooses to replace it. 'No minister and no congregation will be compelled to use this book.' It is envisaged as a book of 'guidance' for 'ministers and congregations', not a preceptive manual; it is to 'help them so to frame the form of service for any particular occasion that it will be orderly and will contain all that it ought to contain'. It is also eclectic, made up of 'elements' from many 'traditions'.[146] It is too soon to say whether these will prove the right guidelines in the larger arena.

In the case for and against diversity, Scripture speaks on both sides. Diversity of gifts is as clearly a mark of the Spirit as unanimity. If we may provisionally identify 'being of one mind' with a unity in faith which we are still seeking to achieve, there is no difficulty historically in showing that – both in principle and in practice – unity in faith has always gone with some diversity of life. This is perhaps the fundamental and inalienable character of the dualism of unity and diversity in the Church's history. Yet Eucharists must be deemed to be one in their expression of faith in one Christ. This brings us to questions of restoring order, for that provides machinery through which provisional structures may move together and bring unity and diversity into a right relation.

[146] (Mysore, 1962), pp. 1–2.

CHAPTER 4

Restoring to order

THE SECURITY OF THE SACRAMENTS

If we have been arguing that rites and ceremonies are in part things indifferent, or at least variable, where matters of faith are not, can we go further and say that consensus in the faith is really all that is needed to unite the churches,[1] and that the institutional and structural differences are merely man-made externals?[2] Should we hold that diversity in the deeper matters of order is another and profoundly serious issue, because in certain respects the systems of order in today's separated churches are anomalous with respect to one another? (That is to say, the criteria of what Anselm of Canterbury would have called *rectus ordo* in one Church are not satisfied in others.)

In earlier centuries, the problem could not have been stated in that way because it implies that churches out of order with one another can still both be churches. In terms of an ecclesiology which insisted that one existing visible Church alone is the true and mother church, and others must come into conformity with it, the act of rectification which is needed looked rather different; it then required an act of God in or by the mother church to make good the anomaly. On the present-day view that the separated churches are in some sense all truly churches, it cannot so readily be held that some have anomalies of order and others not. They may be seen as simply differing in their provisions for order. Or they may be seen

---

[1] Cf. K. Rahner and H. Fries, *Unity of the Church: An Actual Possibility* (Philadelphia, 1985).

[2] This possibility was discussed in the Reformation period. See R. Norris, 'Episcopacy', in *The Study of Anglicanism*, ed. S. Sykes and J. Booty (London, 1988), pp. 296ff. Over against this would stand the pronouncement of Vatican II that to be 'fully incorporated' into Christ's Church means to 'accept all the means of salvation given to the Church together with her entire organisation'. *LG* 14, and see too, E. Yarnold, *In Search of Unity* (Slough, 1989), especially pp. 17–29.

perhaps as all or many in some measure deficient. Both these latter views require an element of provisionality in the self-understanding of the churches, and take it as a starting-point that the task is to mend whatever it is that makes differences of order divisive. They can also proceed on the assumption that order is not intrinsically repressive. That is important, and difficult to do, in the face of centuries of evidence in the Church's life that institutionalised order always has a tendency to get too big for itself.

There is a major problem about talk of provisionality in the realm of order. It can seem to leave the faithful uncertain what to trust in the Church's life. If we do not know where we are on the subject of ministry in the Church, argues Bartholomew Latomus, writing against Martin Bucer in 1543–5, the *communio fidelium* is left in uncertainty. Who are the faithful to trust in matters of doctrine? How are they to be sure that the sacraments are duly administered?[3] Moreover, if one baptism or Eucharist is thought better than another, because of the worthiness or superior orders of the minister, the Church is again left in a state of profound insecurity.[4] Latomus is making assumptions here about the powers of the ministry to 'carry' the authenticity of the sacraments and right teaching, which we might now want to qualify by stressing that the minister acts only in and with the community he serves. But he is pointing to a perennial difficulty in a divided Church, and one of central ecumenical importance. There must be confidence that the faith is being maintained and the sacraments validly and efficaciously administered. There can be no room for uncertainty. If it is to be an ordinary (that is regular and trustworthy) means of grace, a sacrament must be beyond question a sacrament.

Baptist and Reformed Christians have tended to see the Church in its visible form as an 'event', a 'happening', breaking through into the world in the life of the local churches as a manifestation of the invisible reality of the one Church. On this view the assurance that there is a true Eucharist is purely spiritual, and lies in its fruits, its recognition and acceptance by those who participate, and the evidence of the effectiveness of its witness and service.[5] Orthodox, Roman Catholics, Anglicans and other traditions which have a

---

[3] B. Latomus, *Zwei Stretschriften gegen M. Bucer*, ed. L. Keil, *C.Cath.* 8 (1924), p. 118.
[4] *Ibid.*, p. 142.
[5] *Baptist–Reformed Conversations* (1977), p. 36, *Growth*, p. 149.

more extensive and continuous visible structure would stress the importance of the Eucharist's taking place within the framework of that structure or order. That is to say, except possibly in an emergency situation (such as in prison or on a desert island), where an ordained minister is not available, they would insist that the Eucharist ought only to be celebrated by a group of people led by a president who has been ordained as a 'minister in the church of God'.[6]

That is an expression which implies that ordained ministry is a more than local and more than temporary ministry; it is a ministry answerable not only to the Holy Spirit and to the community it serves, but to the whole Church throughout the ages. On this understanding the Eucharist is certainly an 'event', and certainly it is to be recognised and accepted by those who participate, and to issue in the witness and service of the Church's mission. But it is also consciously an act at one with the single offering of himself which Christ made once and for all, and so with the great Eucharist of the whole Church always and everywhere, celebrated together. Here the visible linking together of the ordained ministry everywhere and age by age is an important sign that that is what is happening.

When Peter found to his amazement that the Holy Spirit was working among the gentiles, he insisted that they should be baptised, that is, made members of the Christian community in Christ (Acts 10: 44–8). Sometimes the call of the Spirit clearly came through the settled community. At Antioch the Spirit told the leaders of the community to send out Barnabas and Saul to travel as missionaries (Acts 13: 1–5). The Church has found that it needs both charismatic spontaneity and order if it is to be responsive to human needs and at the same time protected from the fanaticism or delusions of those whose 'call' is in their own minds and not really from the Spirit. Where common order has broken down, this balance of the freedom of the Spirit and the discipline of order is put under a stress which makes the natural tension of the two a negative instead of a positive factor in the Church's life, and creates a sense of insecurity about the sacraments which is inimical to a confident and outgoing ecclesial life.

---

[6] The Disciples of Christ see the Lord's Supper as so much an act of the total congregation that it does not always require an ordained minister 'for its observance', see A.T. DeGroot in *Intercommunion*, p. 156.

REPEATING THE UNREPEATABLE?

In practice, confidence that the sacraments are true sacraments in the divided Church has come, as a rule, to involve different difficulties in the case of baptism and the Eucharist. These sacraments differ in two respects which are significant here. Baptism is once and for all for each person, while the Eucharist is repeated. And the Eucharist is held by most Christians to require a duly commissioned minister for its administration, while that is not an absolute requirement for baptism. Baptism in emergency even by lay men and women has always been accepted. So the problem of confidence in baptism does not turn on confidence in the authenticity of ministry. In the case of baptism confidence depends on the principle articulated by Augustine that God is the minister of baptism. Provided the intention to baptise is clear, and baptism is done in the name of the Trinity and with water, it has been accepted as true baptism and therefore unrepeatable (with some Orthodox reservations), by all but those communities which hold that the believer's saving faith is an essential element and that therefore infants cannot be baptised because they cannot make a confession of faith for themselves.

Important here is the 'community' character of the sacraments. Baptism is concerned not only with the purging of sin and the reconciliation with God of the individual baptised, but also with his or her admission to membership of the body of Christ, the community of the Church. It is at this point that common baptism breaks down ecumenically, because the acceptance of the validity and efficaciousness of one another's baptisms, which is almost universal, does not prove to entail full acceptance of one another's communities as Church.

The baptismal controversies of the first Christian centuries turned on the difficulty that if baptism is deemed to be an unrepeatable act which purges the sinner once and for all of the stain of original sin, with its consequences, there must be no question of rebaptism in any act of the Church to restore a heretic or schismatic to communion. Therefore if such a candidate wishes to enter the catholic Church he cannot simply be baptised afresh. Indeed it is a matter of crucial importance that it should be established whether he has already been baptised. Augustine's argument that although baptism may be valid outside the church it cannot become efficacious until the baptised person becomes a member of the catholic community

allows that by the same token, the existing baptism then becomes efficacious. The Greek Fathers consistently say not only that there can be no efficacious sacrament outside the Church, but also that outside the Church no sacrament can be even validly performed. Yet the Greek churches did sometimes accept those who wished to be admitted to them without giving them baptism. There was therefore some possibility of contradiction between theory and practice in the East as in the West.[7]

The precedent set by not behaving consistently may in itself constitute a useful principle of provisionality. It will be a sign of the need to adjust practice, to move closer to other churches where there is division because it has not proved possible for one or both sides to keep all the rules. The problem of unrepeatability arises again in the case of ordinations, at least in any ecclesiology which takes ordination to confer a permanent character.[8] Ordination, it was widely held in early and mediaeval centuries, cannot be valid unless the person ordained has been baptised. The *Penitential* of Theodore (690–740), Archbishop of Canterbury, says that if someone ordained proves not to have been baptised, he must not only be baptised, but ordained afresh, for he had not previously been ordained at all. This became a key text (though not necessarily with correct attribution), for Ivo of Chartres, Gratian and others in the study of canon law in the mediaeval West.[9] What seems to be at issue here is not only the status of the individual as a forgiven sinner, but also the relationship in which ordination places the ordained person, and the bishop in particular, to the ecclesial community. His commissioning must certainly first involve membership.

There are various ways in which a minister may be deemed to be not truly a minister or to have become unfitted for his ministry. He may be personally unworthy in some way, a sinner. Or he may stand in some impaired relationship to the Church. (He may be a heretic, a schismatic, excommunicated.) In the first instance the defect is clearly in his person, and the personal unworthiness of the minister was, as we have seen, held by Augustine and most of the West after him not to invalidate the sacraments he administers, for their validity depends on God as their author. But if there is a defect in the

---

[7] Cf. Y. Congar, 'Propos en vue d'une théologie de "l'Economie" dans la tradition latine', *Irénikon*, 45 (1972), 160. Congar suggests that Cyprian in the West, and with him the Orthodox tradition, would say that the Church itself is the true sacrament, and that the episcopate is the generating and regulating element. *Ibid.*, p. 159.

[8] See pp. 234ff. [9] Congar, 'Propos', p. 168.

community which commissioned him, or he has become separated from the Church, the position would appear to be rather different. In the first centuries of the Church the general line on ordinations made in schism or heresy seems clear. Heretics who are in schism 'from the Church of God ... can have no power or grace, for baptising, laying on of hands and ordaining'.[10]

A line is being drawn here between what is at issue when an individual wants to return to the Church (or to enter it from a separated community), and what is at stake if a person representing a whole community as one of its ministers wants to be deemed not only a member of the catholic Church but a holder of ministerial office in it. It was always a strong concern of Rome to make it possible for those outside to return to the Church.[11] If what was lacking was grace given in and by the Holy Spirit, that could, arguably, be made good by the imposition of hands (with that limited intention) upon those who had been baptised outside the Church, but still in the name of the Trinity.[12] There were difficulties here, not least that it implied the 'acceptance' of heretical baptism in separated communities, but not of confirmation.[13] Whatever could be done for individuals, however, there could be no possibility of considering ministers ordained outside the Church to have authority to forgive sins, for example. It was essential to be sure that they truly had the gift of the Holy Spirit for the purpose. 'Eos solos posse peccata dimitti qui habent Spiritum Sanctum', says Cyprian. Moreover, sacraments administered by schismatics are administered without the Church's law or licence (*nullo sibi iure concessa*).[14] The

---

[10] See Saltet, *Les Reordinations* (Paris, 1907), chapters 1, 2.   [11] *Ibid.*, pp. 2–4 and p. 18.

[12] *Ibid.*, pp. 22–5 Imposition of hands may have various intentions, among them confirmation as well as ordination.

[13] The practice continued in the Roman Church and in churches of the Gallican rite in the West. Saltet, *Les Reordinations*, pp. 22–3

[14] *Ibid.*, pp. 22–3, 28, 30. It is of some importance for the modern ecumenical implications of all this that distinctions should be made between different groups of those in separation, as was, for example, attempted by the Council in Trullo (692). There was a general division of heretics into two categories: Arians, Macedonians, Novatians, Quartodecimans, Apollinarists, whose baptism was accepted but whose confirmation and ordinations were to be repeated, and Eunomians, Montanists, Sabellians and all others, for whom baptism too must be deemed not to have taken place and therefore repeated. Saltet, *ibid.*, pp. 39ff. The ninth century saw a debate about the episcopal acts of *chorepiscopoi*. These reappeared in the West in the eighth century, because the mission in Germany was creating an urgent need for more bishops. The Council of Meaux of 845 said that *chorepiscopoi* should not be ordaining above the level of the subdiaconate, and then only with the consent of the diocesan. But Rabanus Maurus about 842–7 says that *chorepiscopoi* can ordain priests and deacons with the consent of the bishop. The issue was whether these country-bishops were

scene is different today because we are speaking not of heretical or schismatic communities but of true ecclesial bodies which are divided.

The Eucharist is the context in which the reasons for continuing anxiety become plain. Visible communion in its fullness is to be able to join in a common celebration of the Eucharist, not as two or more groups or parties in an 'ecumenical service', but as one body in a single act of worship.[15] We are dealing not with individuals but with communities wishing to return to communion.[16] Although we can in many cases recognise one another's communities to be truly 'ecclesial', acknowledge a common baptism and speak of a common faith, we are obliged to talk still in terms of 'degrees' of visible communion while we cannot meet in one Eucharist. That is a profoundly serious matter. Unless Christians are together in their celebration, says Paul, and in harmony, it is not the Lord's Supper that they eat (1 Corinthians 11: 20).

To put it bluntly, an important (though not the only) reason why Christians cannot go freely to one another's Eucharists is that not all Christians are sure that what others are doing is truly the sacrament. There are a number of reasons for uncertainties about the Eucharist, some of them falling into the category of differences of understanding of the nature and meaning of the Eucharist itself (for example over its sacrificial character). But, most importantly, the common celebration of the Lord's Supper can take place only within the Church and therefore only when we can agree what is Church and what is not. For most communions it is understood that the Eucha-

truly bishops and therefore had in fact authority to ordain. See P. Hinschius, *System des Katholischen Kirchenrechts mit besonderer Rücksicht auf Deutschland*, vol. II, p. 161 (Berlin, 1878).

[15] A breach of communion in the Eucharist is constitutive of a separated ecclesial body or bodies. Canon V of the Council of Antioch of 341 deals in this light with the case of a cleric who separates himself from the Church by gathering a congregation about him and setting up an altar. Those who refuse to be drawn into secession of this sort are not separated. It is required in a letter of Cyril of Alexandria to Nestorius, at the time of the Council of Constantinople in 381, that the Catholics remain in communion with all those laymen and clergy whom Nestorius has cast out or deposed for their faith. In the period of the Easter controversy in Anglo-Saxon England, too, we find a strong association between shared Eucharistic communion and common order held together with common faith. In Bede's account of the bishops of Demetia they are accused of 'glorying in the private purity of their own way of life', so that they 'detest our communion to such a great extent that they disdain ... to celebrate the divine offices in church with us' (*H.E.*, II.4). Cummianus, Abbot of Iona (d. ?669) claims that, as Jerome puts it, all 'conventicula dogmatum perversorum' are to be identified by the fact that they 'do not eat the Lamb in the one Church' ('agnum in una Ecclesia non comedunt'), *PL* 87.972.

[16] Cf. G. Canellopoulos, 'Christian reunion from the point of view of the Eastern Orthodox Church', *Church Quarterly Review*, 96 (1923), 247–305, p. 270.

rist is taking place in the Church where someone is recognised by the community as commissioned to lead the act of worship by saying Christ's words of consecration of the bread and wine. That is not to say that the minister's proper or 'regular' commissioning is what makes the Eucharist possible, or that it is necessarily constitutive for the presence of 'Church'. But it is a token that all is well and that order is being preserved.

It would seem that, ecumenically speaking, baptism does not present great problems in relation to provisionality. Only those communities which practise a strict believers' baptism and those which have no sacraments at all, would have real difficulty in accepting one another's baptism.[17] So the move to unity would not involve repeating the unrepeatable. The Eucharist, however, depends on the ministry to a still massively problematic extent, in the sense that we lack devices by which churches can deem their ministries to be provisional and changeable in form, or form of commissioning, without losing all security in their own sacraments. Some devices for rationalising the realities of the provisional have been tried, however, within the relatively strict confines of the traditional episcopal structure. It may be helpful to look at these next.

ECONOMY AND DISPENSATION

There has long existed machinery within the Roman Catholic and Orthodox communities for putting things back into 'order' in cases where individuals or communities want to be restored to a communion out of which they have in some way been deemed to have fallen. We need to look now at that machinery, as a setting for what can be said about the modern ecumenical task of uniting communities which may never have been in communion and have therefore not fallen out of communion; and bringing together separated bodies which are all nevertheless deemed to be Church. That is almost without precedent in early or mediaeval Christianity.[18] Cyprian took it that 'the canonical and charismatic limits of the Church invariably coincide', that is, that the sacraments can be validly administered only within the Church and under her laws. To

---

[17] That is clear in the Lima text on Baptism, Eucharist and Ministry.

[18] Although it is not true to say that Roman Catholic and Orthodox systems have no experience of it.

recognise the validity of baptism or order administered outside the Church is to allow that the Holy Spirit may act outside the unity of God's people, and thus division. Some were prepared to accept that a 'valid hierarchy' might exist even in division, and that that might make it possible for orders to be given in apostolic succession outside the Church,[19] which the Church could then, in principle, recognise.

To clear the decks, it is important to see where precedent ends. There is certainly precedent in both Eastern and Western Churches for using devices which deem an act performed in violation of normal order (or more narrowly of canon law), to have been in fact performed in conformity with these. Acts of 'economy' (*oikonomia*) (the East) have sometimes been regarded as acts of God's mercy in a fallen Church; sometimes as acts of the universal Church itself; sometimes as acts of the Church locally. Acts of dispensation (the West) have been regarded as allowing an exception to a law made by the Church. The notion that either might be reciprocal actions of two churches seeking to mend communion, where those churches are divided denominationally, is something relatively new to the second half of the twentieth century.

What are the options in putting things together again? The first is to do nothing. An error of faith can be put right by repentance and coming round to the consensus view. So it can be asked why anything should need to be done officially or formally to 'restore to order' persons or actions which have not conformed with ecclesial normality in matters of order but which now wish to be 'restored to order'? Is the desire not enough?

One option here would seem to be to require no more than repentance and amendment of practice in future. (Though the nature and direction of such 'amendment' would itself have to be agreed.) As we shall see when we come to the reconciliation of ministry, something of the sort is suggested in a number of ecumenical proposals where the underlying concern is to avoid imputing to either party any lack or incompleteness[20] in their pre-existing order.[21]

But there has always been a sense that something needs to be *done*, and seen to be done, for the good of the Church (that is, for *utilitas*),

---

[19] Florovsky, 'Limits', p. 119. Kotsonis, p. 384. Florovsky, 'Limits', p. 125.

[20] *Lutheran-Episcopal Dialogue* III.

[21] There is early precedent for something like this. A Council of Carthage allows Donatist clergy to be received without reordination in cases where that will sustain peace among Christians. Kotsonis, p. 62 and Saltet, *Les Reordinations*.

or for necessity's sake, if not out of respect for 'right order' at least so as to meet the pastoral need of reassuring the faithful. This is in its essence the 'decently and in order' principle of 1 Corinthians 14: 40.

One of the root meanings of *oikonomia* is 'stewardship'.[22] This right use of the gifts entrusted by God is a responsibility of all Christians, but it is also necessary for there to be provision for pastoral exercise of stewardship[23] on behalf of the whole community. In Orthodox, Roman Catholic and Anglican tradition, the bishop is the chief officer who has pastoral responsibility (acting alone or with his fellow-bishops) to dispense, or exercise economy. The classic purpose of acts of 'economy' in the Eastern churches has been to 'accomplish' what has not been accomplished in the former 'disorderly' act. Thus the law is not abrogated but fulfilled, the individual soul is saved and the Kingdom is forwarded. In this way any dilemma as to whether to put first the due keeping of the law or the saving of the individual is resolved by doing both.[24] The act of economy sets no precedent, and does not alter the law.[25]

Law's inherent weakness is that it must always be cast in general terms, and circumstances may not always fit those terms. To waive it in special circumstances may be deemed a mere refinement of its terms to fit the particular case. So the overriding factor in making the decision to act in economy is to do what will be agreeable to God and for the good of the Church as a whole, about something which has happened because of fallible human action in some particular quarter.[26] So the broad lines of the purpose of *oeconomia* in the Orthodox churches are clear. It is an act of mercy, the counterpart of strictness in the application of the Church's laws, an indulgence. It is inexact where law is exact.[27] It seeks to do what is agreeable to God, in the interests of the Church as a whole, putting salvation and the forwarding of the Kingdom, and peace before strict adherence to canon law.[28] It is the essence of provisionality.

But the concept and the practice of 'economy' embody certain paradoxical elements. 'The Church is an authoritative body which

---

[22] *Constitutional Practice and Discipline of the Methodist Church* in Britain (1964).
[23] English Methodism for example has seen ordained ministers as 'stewards in the household of God and shepherds of his flock'.
[24] Kotsonis, pp. 53–6.
[25] 'Economie et théologie sacramentaire', *Istina* 3/4 (1972), 17. *Dispensation,* Report by a Commission of the Church of England (London, 1944), p. 65.
[26] Kotsonis, p. 62.   [27] 'Economie et théologie sacramentaire', p. 17.
[28] For the Church of Christ 'is not subject to a legalistic system', *ibid.*, p. 17.

can freely regulate her policy towards her means of grace and interpret them, not of course contrary to the Word of God expressly commanded in the New Testament, but independently of any particular view which may prevail at any time, in such a way as to meet the needs of the time.'[29] That might be taken to imply that the only criteria for the use of economy are local and temporary and provisional, but the evidence is strongly that economy is a matter of grand vision, and has always at heart the preservation of overall orderliness in the Church.[30]

In the Western church (Anglican and Roman Catholic sharing a common canon law until the sixteenth century), similar grand criteria apply to the granting of dispensations (although these became more a matter of regulation and less spontaneous acts of mercy). To justify the exception a greater good must be secured and a greater evil avoided. The dispensing authority must look to grounds for mercy which have a higher moral force than those which argue for strictness. There must be an attempt to fulfil the deeper intention of the law as being in accordance with the will of God; as Christ did when he broke the law of the Sabbath to heal on the Sabbath day.

A dispensation was always strictly a legal procedure, but a theology lay behind it. At the same time, and as paradoxically as in the case of economy, dispensations could be made only from laws in the making of which the dispensing bishop or one of his predecessors had participated, and so there was a strict limit to the scope of the power of dispensation beyond the local. A further limitation, taking matters out of the realm of the eternal, was the confining of dispensations to temporary allowances dictated by circumstances and not intended to bring about any permanent alteration in the law itself. As in the case of economy, no dispensation could be made from divine law, but only from the Church's own laws.[31] The powers of bishops to dispense were seen to derive from the right of binding and loosing given by Christ to the Apostles, and to be inherent in their orders and of divine origin; although the details of the penalties fell under the heading of the variable and human. To take a recent example: the Ecumenical Patriarch replied to an enquiry by an

---

[29] Canellopoulos, 'Christian reunion', *Church Quarterly Review*, 96 (1923), p. xcvi. See too D. Genakopoulos, 'A new reading of the Acta', in *Christian Unity*, p. 344.
[30] Canellopoulos, 'Christian reunion'.
[31] Begging, for the moment, the question which is which.

Anglican–Orthodox Commission of 1932 that the Church does not have the power to recognise ordinations conferred by churches whose apostolic succession has been interrupted, because that is deemed a breach of God's ordering.[32] These principles all speak of aspects of the dispensation's locality, or particularity, or temporality of application, its relevance strictly to the human and variable and provisional in the churches' lives.

The early grants of dispensations were chiefly in modification of the penalties which would have been prescribed by the bishop for the penitent to perform when a heretic, schismatic or serious sinner was received back into the Church after excommunication.[33] Although no early text sets out a theory of dispensation it seems to have been understood that synods had greater powers of dispensation than bishops acting singly, but a provincial synod, for example, could not alter the law made by a higher synod, although it could dispense from it for particular occasions. The underlying principles here are both territorial and hierarchical. The interdependence of the vertical axis of hierarchy and subordination and the horizontal axis of the distribution of Christendom into territorial dioceses under their bishops and provinces under their metropolitans is fundamental.[34]

It was of some importance to be clear which laws could be dispensed from and which not. The early Decretists placed certain laws in the category of 'natural law', which could not be changed: the decrees of the first four General Councils and the Canons of the Apostles, for example. A first requirement of any scheme of reunion requiring the changing of legal requirements by dispensation would be to identify laws which could not be so treated. That would mean agreeing a basis on which they could be distinguished as perennially or universally or locally applicable.[35]

---

[32] Report of the Joint Doctrinal Commission appointed by the Ecumenical Patriarch and the Archbishop of Canterbury for consultation on the points of agreement and difference between the Anglican and Eastern Orthodox Churches (1932), p. 19.

[33] Report on *Dispensation*, London, 1933, p. 2.

[34] In practice, in Roman Catholic canon law at present dispensations are made in relation to marriage, vows and oath and certain impediments to ordination. There is no provision for putting right what is deemed an imperfect conferring of orders outside the Communion.

[35] There is the question of validity here. An action carried out in violation of the law will be irregular. It may also be invalid, unless a dispensation is granted. Three basic principles are set out in present Roman Catholic canon law. If there is 'doubt as to whether the law' is law at all (*dubium iuris*) the purported law can have no binding force. If there is doubt as to the facts, dispensation may be made by ordinaries. Some dispensations may be reserved to particular authorities, and in such cases ordinaries may grant dispensations in instances

There is precedent for retrospective dispensation, made on the grounds that the law was not binding in the circumstances then obtaining. That would give us a provisionality about time. In such a case there would strictly be no need for dispensation, but it might be pastorally valuable to clarify the situation. Or it might be argued that the law was binding at the time, but is dispensed from now with reference to the past event.[36]

Also of some potential ecumenical usefulness is another principle which can be seen to derive from the rule of provisionality. This is the understanding that a dispensation may become 'customary', that is, normally granted without too much difficulty, although still without setting a precedent; as is that which allows condoning or forbearance. In such a case, a dispensation is not granted, but the offence is passed over, in trust that it will not be committed in the future.

The accepted *purposes* of dispensation are also potentially helpful ecumenically, and again in the light of some notion of the provisionality of the existing individual churches. Sometimes strict enforcement of the law may, paradoxically, frustrate the intention of the law itself. The law against pluralities is designed to ensure sound pastoral provision for local congregations. Yet it may be that combining several parishes in the charge of one priest will best secure that provision in present-day circumstances where there is a shortage of priests. So the general criterion of securing a greater good or avoiding a greater evil by granting a dispensation is of importance here.

Proportion is important. There must be just and reasonable cause for a dispensation, consideration of the circumstances and also of the gravity of the law from which dispensation is to be given. Otherwise, the dispensation is illicit.[37]

Between Roman Catholic and Orthodox common order is only partly in mutual disarray. There is a disjunction in two main areas: with regard to the jurisdictional powers of the Bishop of Rome as Universal Primate (which the Orthodox cannot accept) and in connection with Holy Orders. Here Roman Catholics accept Ortho-

where dispensation would usually be granted by those authorities (Canon 14). A dispensation may be defined as the relaxing of a merely ecclesiastical law (*legis mere ecclesiasticae*) (85) for the sake of the spiritual good of the faithful.

[36] This is a device of obvious ecumenical relevance, where it is necessary to remove an anomaly arising out of past action.

[37] It will also be invalid unless it is made by the legislator himself or his superior (90i).

dox Orders, because there has been no break in apostolic succession. But Orthodox do not accept Roman Catholic sacraments, including Orders, because they are deemed to be the actions of heretics. Within their own systems Latins and Orthodox Christians have developed detailed devices for rectifying disruptions of order on a comparatively small scale, but not for addressing the issues which stand between them. The Council of Florence admitted some possibility of pluralism on the *Filioque* and on Papal primacy.[38] Here there was an attempt to legitimise a diversity of formulation which the two parties recognised to be founded on a difference of theological perspective.[39] Nevertheless, it did not prove possible for them to restore order between them to their mutual satisfaction.

The limits

The crux of all questions of restoring to order lies in the limits of what a church or churches may do. The issue here is not so much what it may be legitimate to do, if by that we mean what a church may try to legislate for within the scope of its own legislative rules;[40] it is what it is actually in the power of a church or churches to do,[41] by way of modifying or dispensing from that law. Such power must often claim a higher authority than the legislative. Whether the Church or individual churches are seen as the instigators, instruments or vehicles of an act of mutual restoring to order, the question of authority arises. Divine mercy is either to be taken as acting directly, or as mediated through the organs of the Church or churches. Or else the Church or the churches may themselves be seen as the authorities, but that may imply that the action they take concerns a matter of rite or ceremony which is of human origin.

A useful distinction which can help in the implementation of principles of provisionality can be made here, though not easily. Some organisations and administrations in the Church's life may be

---

[38] E. Lanne, 'Les différences compatibles avec l'Unité dans la tradition de l'Eglise ancienne jusqu'au xiie siècle', *Istina*, 8 (1961–2), 227–53.

[39] E. Lanne, 'Uniformité et pluralisme', in *Christian Unity*, p. 359. It could be argued that the Greeks explicitly demanded only two things: that the Pope should not be able to convoke an ecumenical Council without the agreement of the emperor and the patriarchs, and that the Pope should not call a patriarch to his tribunal to judge him, but, if the need should arise, send his emissaries into the province in question, and see justice done by the local authorities in the emissaries' presence. *Acta Concilii Florentini, Acta Graeca*, p. 451.

[40] See chapter 5 on decision-making.

[41] J. Thomson, 'Economy', *Journal of Theological Studies*, 16 (1965), 368.

seen as 'purely functional' and of human institution. These can be changed, but will need to be replaced by something similar to get the job done. 'All churches also possess forms in which they express some of the essentials of their faith and theology. These forms are derived by the churches from the Bible – for example, the ministry, the synod, the congregation.'[42] These will be non-negotiable because of divine institution. The difficulty remains to agree which is which and that is harder in the case of 'polities' outside the episcopal pattern.

The provincial Council of Toledo in 1355 argues that provincial constitutions can bind the faithful to certain penalties but that it does not have the authority to make them guilty.[43] This partly reflects the distinction between divine and human ruling. But at issue here is not only the question of the territorial limitation of jurisdiction, but of the limitation that a provincial or local authority in the Church cannot legislate for matters affecting the whole body of the faithful. If, for example, Toledo could create sins by determining that guilt should accrue to certain actions, such sins would either be peculiar to the faithful in that one region (which is absurd), or the Council of Toledo would have legislated for the whole people of God. The problem here is clear enough, but it has been less obvious how far a local decision-making body can determine the sacramental validity of actions within its own sphere of jurisdiction, for sacramental validity may be deemed a 'universal'.[44] If we extend that concern to embrace the particular or 'local' in the extended or metaphorical sense in which it is loosely deemed to include denominations, we have arrived at one of the principal remaining ecumenical problems.

A first ecumenical consideration must be the relationship between local and universally conceived acts of restoring to order. It is a principle of great antiquity in the undivided Church that each bishop will respect the jurisdiction of other bishops.[45] But in a divided Church the separated churches are autonomous in ways which may mean that the habit of thinking of other local needs, or for the whole Church, may be lost.

---

[42] Ehrenstrom and Muelder, p. 106.
[43] See M. Herron, *The Binding Force of Civil Laws* (Paterson, 1958), p. 35.
[44] Cf. Kotsonis, p. 407.
[45] Even in the absence of division, there is good and early precedent for careful consideration of local needs. When Pope Vitalian appointed the Greek Theodore Archbishop of Canterbury in 668 he sent the Latin monk Hadrian with him to ensure that he brought no Greek customs into England which might not be acceptable in the Latin tradition.

Emergency

Two theses were discussed by George A. Lindbeck in the period of the Second Vatican Council. 'The first asserts that a Catholic church, such as the Roman, has an ecclesiological character which makes it in important respects a fuller manifestation of the Church than are Protestant Churches.' The second argues that even if that were so, it could be 'more unfaithful to the gospel than are reforming movements which it has expelled'.[46] In order to be able to say that, he suggests, the Protestant reformers of the sixteenth century had to make a significant shift from the position that Rome is the homeland and the aim was to return to it (when 'Papal tyranny' and current errors are removed), to thinking of the Protestant communities as the 'Promised Land' of the true Church. The issue might then become whether, 'when there is a break in the regular order because of a dire emergency', God bridges the gap and legitimises the new order.[47]

The principle has often been proposed that 'the need of the time', in other words, conditions of emergency, may make tolerable what would otherwise not be accepted. Urban II invoked it in 1088, in connection with the Daibert affair, saying 'multa pro temporum necessitate patienter tolerant'.[48] (He had been ordained deacon by Wezelo, who had himself been consecrated by heretics.) Luther used it in making his own ministers, as did Wesley. In conceding that what has been done has been done in emergency, there would seem to be a concession, too, that some restoring to order is appropriate.

Do we then postulate that God may 'allow an emergency to arise which is serious enough to justify a break such as occurred at the Reformation'? If that could be so, was the Reformation in fact like that?[49] It is on the assumption that some such legitimation occurred that the plans for 'mixed polity' we now turn to have been possible. Again the concept of provisionality fits.

MIXED POLITY

Why can churches which recognise true ecclesiality to be present in

---

[46] George Lindbeck, 'A Protestant View of the ecclesiological status of the Roman Catholic church', *Journal of Ecumenical Studies*, 1 (1964), 243–7, p. 243.
[47] *Ibid.*, p. 245.   [48] Saltet, *Les Réordinations*, p. 240.   [49] 'A Protestant view', p. 245.

one another not in practice yet go on from there to build and then to share a common order?[50]

The first question to be answered here is whether a given structure can be said to be so integral to the being of a Church that it cannot continue as 'Church' without it.

Three main systems have been in use, the episcopal (normatively with a personal episcopate in historic succession); the 'Presbyterian', in which a college of presbyters governs; and the 'Congregational', with self-regulating individual worshipping congregations. So the issue is whether a 'reconciled diversity' of all three should be aimed at (in which all these polities are simply agreed to be all right as they are), rather than some form of synthesis; whether all can somehow make an equal contribution to the eventual structure; whether, even if all are agreed to be valid polities, it may still be best for everyone to settle on one of them, on the grounds that a federal structure within a united Church would imply the continued existence within it of churches founded on partly incompatible ecclesiologies and thus not sharing a common understanding of what it is to be 'Church'.

There are historical lessons to be learnt. The modern ecumenical movement began in the late nineteenth century largely as a result of the pressures felt in the mission-field. There Christians who had gone out as 'Methodists', 'Anglicans', 'Baptists', 'Roman Catholics' and so on found their converts puzzled by the divisions between these followers of the one Christ; and they were unable to engage with differences which largely had their origins in the preoccupations of a Western intellectual climate of thought. The result was a drive towards union and the framing of a common polity. As early as the 1850s there were moves toward cooperation and schemes for mixed-polity federations. In this situation, it might reasonably seem that discussion of differences of implicit ecclesiology between the different systems was unnecessary, and that, 'the way to unity is to unite', as J.S. Chandler briskly put it in an article of 1920.[51]

---

[50] J. Wolmuth raises the point that it would be possible to have free arrival at unanimity with the consequence that the Greeks would have to give themselves up to the Latins, 'Kircheneinigung durch Konsense?', in *Christian Unity*, pp. 187ff.

[51] *United Church Herald* (March, 1920), p. 597. There were also some dangers, not least the risk that there would be a tendency to regard it as unimportant to clarify what was being done, theologically speaking. 'They won't know the difference' is an attitude which ties in with a tendency to patronise well illustrated by a Methodist missionary writing in the *Methodist Recorder* in 1931, 'Most of our Indian Christians know little or nothing about [the Scheme of Union]; and, drawn as they are chiefly from the depressed classes, only just emerging

In practice, some blurring of categories occurred. 'Pastors have become missionary superintendents, presbyters have become bishops, and the bishop of a single congregation has had in time a diocese added unto him.'[52] 'There somehow seems to be a universalizing tendency in the missionary situation itself.'[53]

Nevertheless, when it came to more thoroughgoing attempts to set up common structures which would create a single United Church for the whole of South India, it proved necessary to try to identify the distinctive elements in each system so as to see more clearly how they were to be brought together. The Tranquebar Manifesto of 1919 attempted this, with two leading ideas in mind. The first was that all three systems should have a place, on the understanding that they are complementary and none is sufficient without the others. That notion depended upon being able to point to certain distinguishing features of each in particular. The experiments in doing so were not wholly successful. The 'Congregational' element is seen as giving every member immediate access to God; the Presbyterian as 'delegated, organised', so that 'the Church could unite in a General Assembly, Synods or Councils in organised unity'; the episcopal as 'representative' and 'executive'.[54] This is not only a highly schematised and not entirely accurate picture, but it places all the emphasis upon authority structures and cannot take account of the infinite subtlety of the differences of style and atmosphere of life.

The second leading idea of the Manifesto was that some means must be sought to 'permit' ministers of the uniting churches to celebrate the Eucharist in churches other than their own churches of origin. Here, it was thought essential to provide for a service of commissioning for the purpose, for it could be argued that a new kind of church was coming into being in which not every, or perhaps any, existing minister was duly commissioned. This was to be a matter of free choice for the ministers concerned, but in the expectation that all who desired 'authority to officiate at the Communion throughout the whole Church' would 'present themselves to receive at the hands of all the bishops of the united Churches a commission for such celebration of the Communion'.[55]

These key principles were now debated, and their limitations

from darkness and ignorance into the light of the Gospel of Christ, there is no reason why they should be troubled with the technicalities of a discussion which could only confuse them.' Quoted in Ehrenstrom and Muelder, p. 224.

[52] N. Smyth and W. Walker, *Approaches towards Church Unity* (New Haven, 1919), pp. 52ff.
[53] Sundkler, p. 14.   [54] Cf. Sundkler, p. 101.   [55] *Ibid.*, p. 103.

began to become apparent. The idea that a single polity might be set up even if it took the best from each of the existing systems was attacked on the grounds that it went against the Holy Spirit's manifest intention that there should be diversity in the Church; and that it would entail a narrow uniformity.[56]

The same objection would, *a fortiori*, stand against choosing one of the three polities in preference to others. The solutions arrived at by the local united churches so far have varied. Local united churches are most readily feasible among churches which have a 'Congregational' or 'Presbyteral' ecclesiology. A set of pastoral circumstances helped to bring about the union of Methodists, Presbyterians and Congregationalists in the United Church of Canada in 1925. The driving force here was the need to provide a ministry to thin and widely scattered populations, especially in the western provinces. There had already been unions in Methodist and Presbyterian Churches during the nineteenth century, and from the late 1860s the Protestant denominations began to send delegates on a 'fraternal' basis to the annual meetings of one another's churches. This contact made it apparent how large a basis of agreement there was between them, and they were able to move forward.[57] But even if all the churches in a given area were involved ('all in each place'),[58] that would have the limitation, as long as the wider ecclesial entities of each were not all committed in the same way, that such a local united church could not be unequivocally 'the Church of God' in that place. And it would not ultimately be enough to do together all that could be done. The Lund principle (of 'doing together all that we can')[59] while still not united, is an interim principle. The role of a local united church such as those of the Indian sub-continent and Canada in the ecclesiology of one future wholly united Church is problematic. A local United Church is not 'the' Church of God, even if all the churches represented in the area are united in it.[60]

A gulf remains between personal episcopal systems on one hand

---

[56] Bishop Whitehead wanted to see the broadest possible basis even of doctrine. 'We have now learned', he argued, 'that the path to unity lies not through uniformity, but through a frank recognition of the manifold variety of the work of God's Holy Spirit and a wise toleration of differences of belief and practice within the one body of Christ.' Message to the General Assembly of South India United Council of Churches, 9 September, 1919, Sundkler, p. 105.

[57] Ehrenstrom and Muelder, pp. 176–7.   [58] WCC, 1981.

[59] Framed by the Lund Faith and Order Conference of the WCC, 1952.

[60] J. Tillard, 'Eglise catholique romaine et Eglises unies', *Irénikon*, 55 (1982), 19–23, p. 20.

and collective or presbyteral systems of *episcope* on the other. Presbyterian and some Lutheran traditions, among others, insist that there
is no differentiation of orders between priest and bishop, and therefore no essential difference in their relation to the community. So
even where Lutheran communities have bishops they speak of their
'installation' rather than their 'consecration' or 'ordination', on the
understanding that the bishop holds no orders higher than those of
other ministers. Among Baptists the emphasis upon the autonomy of
the individual worshipping communities, the priority of the local
church, remains strong. 'Each Church has liberty, under the guidance of the Holy Spirit, to interpret and administer His laws', says
the Declaration of Principle, which forms the basis of the Baptist
Union in Great Britain. In unions of Baptist churches self-governing
congregations may delegate certain responsibilities to a central
association and its instruments and authorise them to carry out
certain actions on their behalf. But decisions taken at that level will
normally have to be ratified in the local congregation, which will
decide for itself whether they are of the Holy Spirit.[61] That does not
mean that a duly constituted Assembly, Association or Union of
Baptist Churches is without ecclesial significance; merely that it does
not have authority to override the decisions of the local Church.[62]

In recent unions among churches of the 'Presbyterian' Reformed
tradition two streams of thought have begun to merge. Presbyterians
have tended to take the provisions of the 'General Council' at
Jerusalem described in Acts 15 as establishing the definitive scriptural model for a system of Church-government by a meeting of elders.
A corporate oversight clearly understood as episcopal in character
could be exercised in that way, without appointing individuals as
bishops. Calvin stressed in the ecclesiastical ordinances for Geneva
(1541) the ecclesial importance of such grouping of congregations.
In many 'Presbyterian' polities, a governing body has emerged,
made up of equal numbers of pastors of congregations and elders,
and exercising collective oversight over the congregations in a territorial area; it acts as an appeal court if any congregation is unable to
resolve its difficulties internally. Where there are higher authorities,
for example at national level, that governing body acts on behalf of
the local congregation there.

In Britain and in some other parts of the world, a merging of the

---

[61] *Episcopal Ministry*, paras. 135–6, pp. 60–1.   [62] *Ibid.*, p. 61.

'Independent' or Congregational and the 'Presbyterian' polities has been achieved, by creating some form of 'District Council' which has a measure of authority in relation to the local congregations and which has something of the form of a Presbyterian presbytery.[63]

Lutheran arrangements vary, because Lutheranism has historically embraced (in different geographical areas) both a personal episcopal and other, collectively episcopal structures.[64] The Scandinavian Lutheran churches retain a variety of *episcope*, in Sweden without interruption to the historic succession, in Norway and Denmark through presbyteral succession and without their being consecrated to a separate order. In some German states and cities, secular rulers might have the title *summus episcopus*, while leaving the ecclesiastical and spiritual government of the Church in the hands of a synod. The tendency in Lutheranism since the mid-twentieth century has been to return to some form of personal episcopal government,[65] and to subordinate the autonomy of the local congregation to a higher personal episcopal oversight. (This is of course the reverse of the process by which in the ancient episcopal Churches the parishes developed by enlargement of the diocese.)

In all these systems of collective *episcope*, as in the episcopal systems which appoint individuals to the episcopate, 'place' is of central importance. Local churches are grouped, where they are grouped at all, on a local and regional basis. In Methodism, too, the Circuit and District are fundamental to the organisation of the Church as a whole, most strikingly in England where there are no Methodist bishops.

So systems of collective *episcope*, and those in which personal episcopacy has been reintroduced as the pattern of oversight has evolved and changed, have in common a relationship of the local worshipping congregation to the wider Church in which the smallest local communities tend to be related by freely joining together in some way rather than to be derived from a larger whole such as a diocese (in a way which gives them a natural family relationship). In order to work together, they have had to give up some of their autonomy to the governing body in which they unite, although that may, as in the case of some of the Baptists, be done with the proviso

---

[63] *Ibid.*, para. 142, p. 66.
[64] On reasons for local variation in Lutheranism, see I. Asheim and V.R. Gold, *Episcopacy in the Lutheran Church* (Philadelphia, 1970). See, now, *The Porvoo Common Statement* (London, 1993).
[65] *Episcopal Ministry*, paras. 143ff., pp. 67–8.

that the local congregation retains the right to act autonomously in accepting or rejecting the decision of their governing body.

Luther did not think he was founding a Lutheran church. He and many of the other reformers saw the focus of the concept of the visible 'church' as lying in the gathered congregation. So, for example, Anglican–Lutheran union would not be the forming of one church out of what were previously two but one church out of many. Equally, we cannot envisage the ultimate union of the Church in terms of the aggregation of a number of ecclesial blocks. This profoundly important difficulty is easily obscured by the habit of talking of 'Baptist–Reformed' Conversations, 'Orthodox–Roman Catholic' Conversations, 'Lutheran–Roman Catholic' Conversations, and so on. In bilateral and multilateral conversations the participants rightly treat one another as equals, as deserving of mutual respect, with the result that it can become hard to remember that they are not necessarily the same *kinds* of ecclesial body. Nor do they form ecclesial units which can be united in the same way.

There is of course no guarantee that all will be well in the realm of order even within a single polity. Sisterhood of churches among the Orthodox has its internal problems, as does the primacy-in-conciliarity of the Roman Catholic Church and the working of provincial autonomy within the Anglican Communion. Internal repair work is needed in the restoring of order, as well as the mending of anomalies of order between churches. *A fortiori*, higher structures are never going to be easy to set up or to maintain in a future united Church. Unfamiliarity is unattractive; vested interest (historically as strong a factor in Church as in State) resists change; there is likely to be fear of being 'taken over' (especially by the Papacy); even the lack of an absolutely clear understanding of existing ecclesiologies stands in the way of the union of polities.[66]

What then should be aimed at as a preliminary by way of resolution of the discrepancies and anomalies in order in the Church? We can realistically hope for the gradual removal of

[66] These points are well expressed by J.P. Warwick, 'Organisational Politics and Ecumenism', *Journal of Ecumenical Studies*, 11 (1974), 293–308: 'While individual believers may rationally assent to principles of unity, they will not give up accustomed authority structures and patterns of association without pain and struggle. Fears of ancient enemies, such as the papacy ... may be temporarily submerged in an atmosphere of good will only to surface at critical points of action ... The larger the organisational apparatus in a church the greater the resistance to change from incumbents of official positions ... The greater the extent of internal conflict, tension or friction within a denomination the more remote the prospects of organisational unification with other churches', pp. 294–6.

resentments. For example, it may usefully be asked whether, if the
reasons for the reformers abandoning the 'personal' episcopal system
in the sixteenth-century West can be clearly understood by all their
present-day heirs and those reasons tested against the different
circumstances of other ages so as to get a fair sense of its value to the
Church, Protestant churches which do not have a personal *episcope*
might be able to accept such an episcopal system in a future united
Church. At the same time, those churches which have placed a high
emphasis upon the diocese as the fundamental unit of the Church's
organisation may learn to value the congregation as the 'local'
church in a way which gives its distinctiveness respect within the
diocesan 'local church'. There certainly needs to be recognition of
the provisional character of all structures between the local and the
universal, that is the metropolitan or provincial, in which autonomy
or autocephaly is vested in some present systems. Such patient
adjustments to assumptions and prejudices built, as we have been
seeing, out of historical stresses and partly distorting the natural
balance of local and universal may, in time – and it will be a long
time – help to remove stumbling-blocks.

Mutual recognition and reconciliation of ministry

Not all Christian communities share a common understanding of
the meaning of the ordaining or commissioning of ministers, or of the
nature of ministry; there is also, and accordingly, considerable
variation in the means of making ministers. And yet, as the World
Council of Churches puts it, in a future united Church, 'it must be
possible ... that ministers be able to fulfil their ministry, upon
invitation, in any Church'.[67] So mutual recognition of ministry
remains the single greatest need to be met on the way to full visible
and Eucharistic unity. A relationship of ministry, as it is at present
established by ordination in separated communities, needs to be set
up with the community of the united Church.

In any attempt to create a shared ministerial commissioning in
one Church the first question which has to be answered is what in
the Church's ministry is directly of God and therefore perpetual,
and what is at the disposal of human ordering to fit the needs of
particular times and places. A ministry with special responsibility in

[67] ARCIC I, M 17.

the Church has variously been seen as of divine or human institution, or as involving both.

All shades of Christian opinion would identify the calling of the Holy Spirit as essential, but some see that calling as common to all believers (with perhaps some extraordinary exceptions whom God calls to a prophetic or reforming ministry in an age of crisis in the Church).[68] The commissioning of those who are to lead the community is then seen as an act of the Church in which there may be local variation. For instance, it may be for a limited time or able to be withdrawn by the people who gave it. Thus it has, though under the Holy Spirit, in some respects a merely human authority.

This theme was stressed by sixteenth-century reformers who wanted to argue that the existing ecclesiastical hierarchy was not of Christ's ordaining, but a human arrangement.[69] Nevertheless, it was accepted almost universally that the calling of the Holy Spirit in and through the Church, with recognition by the Church, remained non-negotiable essentials in the making of ministers with special responsibilities in the congregation. There was, in other words, a divine ordinance that such a ministry should exist, even though it might, as some held, be for human deciding what form it should take.[70]

The sixteenth-century Reformed communities held that Christ instituted a ministry which the Church should receive, celebrate and transmit as a gift of grace. 'God has always used ministers for the gathering or establishing of a Church for himself, and for the governing and preservation of the same; and he still does, and always will, use them so long as the Church remains on earth.'[71] The Second Helvetic Confession distinguishes between the ministries of elders and deacons, which are, it holds, at the free disposal of the Church to provide for, and the 'essential ministry' of 'the episcopal,

---

[68] French Reformed Confession of Faith, 1559, Article 31, in A.C. Cochrane, *Reformed Confessions of the Sixteenth Century* (London, 1966), p. 155.

[69] Melanchthon, for example, in his apology for the *Augsburg Confession* (XIV.Iff.) says that it has been Lutheran policy to maintain the Church polity and various ranks of the ecclesiastical hierarchy, but strictly on the understanding that 'they were created by human authority'.

[70] That is the principle expressed by Article XX of the Anglican Thirty-Nine Articles, which says that the Church has power to decide 'rites and ceremonies' but which is intended to be taken alongside Articles which maintain that the ministry must be 'called and sent' (XXIII) and specifies three orders of bishop, priest and deacon (XXXVI). That is not to imply that the three Orders are in fact necessarily of divine origin.

[71] Second Helvetic Confession, and see J.J. Von Allmen, 'Ministry and ordination according to Reformed Theology', *Scottish Journal of Theology*, 25 (1972), 75–88, p. 75.

presbyteral, pastoral or doctoral' sort. The Saxon-American Lutheran C.F.W. Walther (1811–87) took the same classically Lutheran view that a ministry with pastoral responsibility was not optional but essential to the Church, and thus not of human but of divine ordering. On the other hand, he would say that the imposition of hands 'is not of divine appointment', but merely 'an apostolic church ordinance', and therefore only 'a public and solemn confirmation of the call'.[72] The divine elements are non-negotiable in mutual recognition of ministry; the human must be negotiable. But it is not universally agreed which are which.

These very general principles: that it is God's intention that there shall be a ministry with a special relationship to the community; and that it is for the community to determine its character and who shall exercise it, were variously stated and applied among sixteenth-century reforming bodies. At one extreme was the view that the local congregation was the body with authority to accept or reject a given ministry. Some declared themselves free to substitute ministers of their own for those placed among them by the Church of Rome, or to receive as their ministers those whom the Roman Catholic Church had 'discharged' by episcopal authority from their ministry.[73] But such straightforward independent exchange of ministries on a congregational basis was not acceptable to all. The Lutheran Augsburg Confession insists upon 'regular call' (Article V). The Anglican Articles say 'it is not lawful for any man to take upon him the office of publick preaching, or ministering the sacraments in the Congregation, before he be lawfully called, and sent to execute the same' (Article XXIII). There grew up, in fact, in most Protestant churches, a settled system for the commissioning of ministers.

Among the Reformed, ordination is seen to signify the presentation of a man to the Spirit, so that he may be filled with the *charismata* to exercise his ministry (so ordination involves an *epiklesis*); the presentation of a man to God as a dedicated offering (a notion strong in Calvin); the authorisation or bestowal of public mission; and the ingrafting of a man into the sequence of his predecessors in the apostolic ministry which was instituted by Christ and is therefore one of the constitutive elements of the Church's permanent character.[74]

---

[72] T.C. Tappert, *Lutheran Confessional Theology in America* (New York, 1972), pp. 233–4.
[73] Cochrane, *Reformed Confessions*, p. 71.
[74] Von Allmen, 'Ministry and ordination', p. 80.

The Savoy declaration of Faith and Order (1658) argues that each 'gathered' church is given by God 'all that power and authority which is in any way needful for their carrying on that order and discipline which he hath instituted for them to observe'.[75] Officers elected by such Churches must themselves accept the call, and they must be set apart by fasting and prayer in preparation, but although they will normally be appointed by the imposition of hands that is not deemed to be essential. And if they move to another Church they must be elected afresh. They do not take their office or any 'order' with them.[76] But these ideals did not hold everywhere in Reformed circles.

For Orthodox, Roman Catholics and Anglicans there has remained no disagreement that an ordained minister must be called by God in and through the Church. In such episcopal systems there is a built-in universality. For Roman Catholics, Orthodox and Anglicans the bishop, unlike the priest, is the link through whom his own community and other communities with their bishops may act as one Church. This linking extends through time too, so that all Christians in every age are united in their local churches by means of the links their bishops provide. It is because of his authority within the wider Church that in episcopal churches the bishop is the minister of ordination. Thus he is able to be the instrument by which priests and bishops are made ministers in 'the Church of God',[77] and authorised to serve wherever the local bishop consents to their doing so, either on special occasions or by becoming pastors of worshipping communities.

So in these churches ordination is deemed to be for life and unrepeatable and to have taken place in the universal Church and not merely locally. A newly ordained minister must have an 'office' to take up, that is a 'title' or pastoral charge. He must be ordained specifically to serve a local worshipping community. But when he moves from one charge to another he takes his 'orders' with him, still under episcopal authority. Exchange of ministers within such an

---

[75] J.W. Beardslee, *Reformed Dogmatics* (New York, 1965), p. 144. Wollebius (1586–1621) lists the elements necessary in his view to the making of ministers in the Reformed way. God must call the candidate, and it is he who bestows the gifts for ministry. The church chooses those who are suitable and inducts them into their office, with all the *coetus*, or 'gathering' of the faithful participating in the rite. Legitimate calling requires examination of the faith and morals of the candidate, his formal 'choosing' and the confirmation of the choice by the laying on of hands. There was some variation in the accepted list of elements.

[76] *The Savoy Declaration of Faith and Order*, ed. A.G. Matthews (London, 1959), pp. 122–4.

[77] As the Anglican *Ordinal* puts it.

episcopal system assumes the collegiality of bishops in the wider Communion and requires only letters testimonial from one bishop to another witnessing to the good standing of the minister who is moving from one diocese to another.

The bishop in such a system is the minister with special responsibility for overseeing the examination and preparation of candidates and also for presiding at their ordination, himself laying on hands 'in the face of the Church; that is, before the congregation and with their consent'.[78] Yet the bishop's act is not itself alone enough to make a minister. He acts on behalf of the Church and as the proper authority; and as the instrument of the Holy Spirit's calling in the Church which is associated with the laying on of hands itself. The 'human' and 'divine' elements in the making of ministers are thus seen to work together in this office, and the bishop's person is their common channel.

A sticking-point in the matter of the making of ministers has been the imposition of hands. It is clearly in most systems more than a blessing.[79] There has, as a rule, been no difficulty if it is understood simply as 'expressive of the Church's recognition of the minister's call', as English Methodists put it. It may be seen as having 'utility' without being essential, in the words of Matthias Loy, a Lutheran of nineteenth-century Pennsylvania (1828–1915).[80] But in the Orthodox, Anglican and Roman Catholic churches it is understood that the imposition of hands has two different functions, both important to the nature of ordination. First, it seals the gift of the Spirit for that specific purpose. (It has not been disputed that the imposition of hands can have different intentions: in confirmation and ordination, for example); secondly, it links the new minister to all those who are ordained as the Church's pastors. That is important, because of the difficulties which otherwise arise about the transferability of ministers and the duration of their commission.

Between the 'Congregationalists', the Reformed or 'Presbyterian' and the 'episcopalian' Roman Catholic, Orthodox and Anglicans in the patterns of their 'regular calling' stand Lutherans, Methodists and others who have, or have evolved, provision for systems of

---

[78] Anglican *Ordinal*, 1662, Preface.
[79] E. Ferguson, 'Attitudes to schism at the Council of Nicaea', *Studies in Church History*, 9 (1972), 62, argues the other way.
[80] G. Tappert, *Lutheran Confessional Theology in America* (New York, 1972), pp. 254ff., and see M. Loy, 'The Lutheran doctrine of Ordination', *Evangelical Quarterly Review*, 16 (1865), 303–28.

oversight to enable ministers to be *recognised* as already ministers, by congregations other than those to which they were first appointed. Both Lutheran and Methodist communities have bishops in some parts of the world and not in others, and thus a variety of means of achieving this mutual recognition of ministry.

In eighteenth-century America Swedish and German Lutherans found themselves in difficulties over precisely this point of supracongregational leadership when they sought union. In 1744 it was proposed that there should be 'yearly meetings' of ministers with 'a few of the elders of the congregations 'at which they should 'consult together in regard to the best establishment of each congregation'. But to go further and seek to make 'a Church regulation, which should forever unite the Swedish Ministers with the German' was to run into the difficulty that the Swedes 'stood under their archbishop and the Consistory, without whose approbation they could not enter into such a union' (Manual 46), and that in any case the proposed Regulation was not in keeping with existing Swedish church-laws or the Swedish Manual for church ceremonies (Manual 16). There was no existing machinery of competent authority which could resolve these problems for both communities and make it possible for them to exchange ministers.

An acrimonious and lasting controversy was generated by the proposals for the reconciliation of ministry in the South Indian Churches, which underlined how limited are these rough equivalences and attempts to find likeness between polities. The tendency at this time was to seek to avoid too clear a doctrine of the character and function of the historic personal episcopacy, and to insist upon it merely as a 'fact', without implying an ecclesiology which might prove unacceptable to the non-episcopal churches.[81]

The underlying problem was whether an episcopate could be made central to the new United Church, while at the same time the absolute equality of the ministry and membership of the existing uniting churches was recognised.[82] This seemed at the time an honest attempt to return to patterns of order in the early Church, in which it could be argued that there had been something like an

---

[81] This 'fact not theory' approach was widespread in Faith and Order debates in the 1920s outside India as well as within it. This line of thought was derived at an early stage from the work of patristic scholars such as Headlam and Streeter, see Sundkler, p. 102 and p. 174. There were contemporary discussions among Anglicans about the advisability of seeing the 'historic episcopate' of the Lambeth Quadrilateral as a 'fact' not a 'doctrine'.

[82] Sundkler, p. 12.

'episcopate of congregationalism'.[83] But it was also an approach which was open to the accusation that some sort of camouflage was being proposed. Free Churchmen did not think they needed episcopal ordination, so that the proposed service of commission would supply nothing they could recognise as necessary; the inclusion of episcopal ordination would be there merely to satisfy the Anglicans.[84]

It was thought that something might be achieved at one level simply by 'a general recognition of all that is good and true in other Churches'.[85] At another, it might be managed by saying, as Palmer suggested in his three-point account, that a plan for union exists in the mind of God; that it must involve 'dying and rising again' (in other words, the acceptance that there were existing deficiencies); that although there is a due order in the Church, there may be exceptions to it.[86]

What was less easy to make acceptable was implied criticism of existing ministries.[87] At the episcopalian end of the spectrum there was concern that there should be no confusion, for example, about the role of presbyters in ordination. It might be possible to allow their participation in the consecration of bishops as 'a legitimate symbolism' in the inaugural service of consecration, but subsequently it should be avoided, because that would confuse. It could be retained only if it was explained that the presbyters were not taking part as consecrators, said the Lambeth Conference of 1930. At the other end of the scale, the Congregationalists could feel that they were making all the concessions, and that, whatever was being said, equal validity of existing ministries was unlikely to be affirmed.[88]

A number of theological principles was put forward on which these difficulties might be resolved. It was argued that devices which would usually be unacceptable might be permitted in circumstances of emergency or 'the stress of necessity'. That had precedent. It

[83] V. Bartlett, *Church Union News and Views* (November, 1932), p. 92.

[84] Bernard Lucas, protagonist of Liberal Congregationalism, cited in Sundkler, p. 108.

[85] Sundkler, p. 14, quoting from the assembly about the proposed union of the Anglican and Mar thoma churches.

[86] Sundkler, p. 117.

[87] The Anglican General Council of India, Burma and Ceylon responded to a revised scheme of 1929 by saying that union must be achieved, 'without passing judgement upon any particular form of ministry or view of ministry'; but that it could not admit an 'equally certain validity of all ministries'. Sundkler, p. 215.

[88] A Report of the Joint Commission of January 1931 said that Congregationalists in England wanted to see 'equal validity of ministries' accepted, 'symbolised by the participation of presbyters in episcopal consecration'. Sundkler, p. 223.

would also make it possible to leave the situation open to rectification at some later date 'in case the whole Church should adopt terms of union different from those at present adopted in South India'.[89] This approach admits the unsatisfactoriness and theological untidiness of going ahead with mutual recognition and reconciliation of ministries without resolving the underlying ecclesiological differences. But it puts pastoral need first.

A second approach, which also avoids obliging any of the participating churches to admit any 'inferiority' of its present ministry to that of any other (particularly the episcopal), is to affirm the imperfection of all ministries in the Church. For example, it could be said that the ministries of all separated Communions are by the fact of separation imperfect and limited in authority. Forms of what could be considered 'supplemental ordination'[90] could then be used without any necessary implication that the candidate's previous commissioning had been in some way defective or invalid. One such formula, suggested for South India in 1943, says, 'Receive the Holy Ghost for the work of a presbyter in the Church of God, both for the continuance of that work which thou hast done hitherto, and for the performance of that work which is now committed unto thee by the laying on of our hands.'[91] The objection to this is that, although it implies a fresh commissioning for new work, and therefore casts no doubt upon the earlier commissioning of the individual, it is hard to see how a minister already commissioned in 'the Church of God' as the Anglicans understood themselves to be, could need additional commissioning in order to be a minister in a newly united church; and again, in the case of this suggestion, the underlying ecclesiological differences between Congregationalist, Presbyterian and episcopalian conceptions of the relationship of minister to community are not addressed. (That is not to say that their existence was ignored in these debates. The Presbyterians in particular were pressing on the subject of parity of ministry between bishops and presbyters.)[92]

Relationship to the community

Where there is no formal authority structure 'it is the minister with the dramatic personality who often gains a higher prestige than that

[89] Suggestion from Palmer, Sundkler, p. 246.   [90] See Sundkler, p. 308.
[91] Letter of Palmer and Western to V.S. Azariah, November 1943, Sundkler, p. 308.
[92] Sundkler, pp. 250–4.

which is accorded the official priests of other religious movements'.[93] On the opposite side it can be argued that 'in any hierarchical system the possibilities of a meaningful practice of mutual criticism are attenuated'.[94]

The elements of ministerial commissioning express a theology of the relationship of the minister to the community. A key principle is that the presence of a pastor makes it possible for the community to behave as one body. That is why he can act as their representative and in focussing their common life. That is of particular importance in connection with the debate about 'priesthood'. It was usual for reforming communities of the sixteenth century to insist upon 'the priesthood of all believers' and to look askance at the notion of a 'priesthood of the ordained ministry',[95] if by that was meant a priesthood different in kind from that which all believers share, and held by the ordained minister as a power exclusively his own. Methodist tradition also rejects the concept of 'priestly virtue inherent in the office'. The main thesis that ministry must be distinguished from priesthood 'failed to persuade all of Christendom'.[96] The notion of 'priesthood' in connection with a collective exercise of 'the priesthood of all believers' was never controversial in the same way.[97]

In practice that collective exercise of the priesthood of all believers normally involved, even in reforming communities especially suspicious of 'personal priesthood', a leadership by a minister specially commissioned in a 'regular' way, to make it possible for the community to act as one in its celebration of the sacraments. Leadership involving power to exercise discipline and authority to govern in the Church was also acceptable, indeed mandatory, in most reforming churches.[98]

---

[93] P.M. Harrison, *Authority and Power in the Free Church Tradition* (Princeton, 1959), p. 217.

[94] *Ibid.*, p. 219.

[95] *The Priesthood of the Ordained Ministry*, Faith and Order Advisory Group of the Church of England General Synod (1985).

[96] *Ibid.*, p. 83. Von Allmen suggests that it may be helpful to stress the idea of the apostolate.

[97] *The Priesthood of the Ordained Ministry*.

[98] The Reformed Belgic Confession (1561) speaks of the minister as 'governor'of the Church with responsibility for 'discipline' (Article 30). The nineteenth-century Lutheran Walther sees the minister as having an authority which distinguishes his ministry from the priesthood of all believers. This is authority to preach the Gospel and administer the sacraments, together with 'the power of a spiritual tribunal'. Tappert, *Lutheran Confessional Theology*, pp. 233–4.

There are strict limits, however. This is not, says the Lutheran Walther, a 'lordship' in the Church and the minister has no power to make new laws, or to impose excommunication 'without the previous knowledge of the entire congregation'; nor can he 'arbitrarily ... introduce ceremonies and matters of indifference in the church' as obligations upon his people. Methodist practice gives the minister 'a principal and directing part' in the life of the Church. So there is a consistent and generalised tendency to regard pastoral leadership as an essential means by which the community is held together in unity by disciplinary authority, both where occasional special action is needed to preserve harmony; and as a regular thing, maintaining unity and harmony where it already exists.

In the view of the episcopal churches the disciplinary responsibility of the minister inheres in him personally because of the pastoral charge entrusted to him and no other in the community; and also because his commissioning empowers him to act in 'binding and loosing'. This picture of things, familiar to Roman Catholics, Anglicans and Orthodox, is partly echoed in the 'Brief Order for Confession and Forgiveness' in the Lutheran book of Worship of the United States of America. 'As a called and ordained minister of the Church of Christ, and by his authority', says the minister, 'I therefore declare to you the entire forgiveness of all your sins, in the name of the Father, and of the Son and of the Holy Spirit.'

Once we talk, in whatever terms, of authority 'inhering in' or even more simply as 'belonging to' the office of minister because of the special relationship in which he is placed both to Christ and to the community he serves, we are coming close to the question of the duration of ministerial office. Lutherans have generally understood ordained ministry to be a lifelong commitment, but not to be 'indelible' as Roman Catholics, Orthodox and Anglicans would think it. It is possible but anomalous for a minister to leave the ordained ministry, and were he to do so, he could not be reordained. In practice, those once commissioned in a regular way as Lutheran ministers tend to constitute the pool of ministers from which the office of ordained minister is filled in local communities as needed. There is, in other words, a *de facto* distinction of office and order.[99]

---

[99] Although it is not the Lutheran way to speak of 'orders', as a rule.

The distinction between lifelong and irrevocable ministry and indelibility would thus seem to be a fine one.[100]

SOLUTIONS

Any two or more Communions may arrive at an agreement which will result in mutual recognition and reconciliation of one another's ministries. But what is required to achieve that end will vary in each case. If the aim is to achieve one ministry in one Church, the problem is mathematically vastly more complex. There is the further difficulty that a bilateral or local *rapprochement* may produce a mutually recognised ministry but on a basis which will not prove to be acceptable in its turn to other ecclesial bodies. A 'local' case in point is the experiment in the United Churches of the Indian subcontinent which opened it to question whether the bishops of the new churches could go to the Lambeth Conference. To take a 'bilateral' example, the recent *Niagara Report* on *Episcope*, framed by representatives of Anglicans and Lutherans, suggests that both stand in a similar position in that 'the succession in the presiding ministry of their respective churches no longer incontestably links those churches to the *koinonia* of the wider Church' (58). On that basis proposals are made for steps to be taken which will result in mutual recognition of ministry between Anglicans and Lutherans without explicit reference to the question of the universality of the resulting common ministry in a future united Church.[101]

So there has to be both detailed attention to the particulars of the relationship between two ecclesial communities and a clear sense of where the mutual resolution of their differences would place the resulting united church in relation to the future universal united Church.

Several possible approaches to solving these problems have been proposed. At one end of the spectrum it can be taken that the

---

[100] Although reforming communities of the sixteenth century and their heirs have continued to dislike the term 'indelible'. Zwingli, for example, denied in his Sixty-seven articles of 1523 (LXI) that ministerial 'character' could exist or be indelible. In Methodist ministry the Full Work is to be the 'sole occupation' of the minister. But here, too, there is a reluctance to talk of 'indelibility'. If ministry was seen as for a term only, and as always answerable to the community which gave authority, the minister could not be able to claim powers peculiarly and independently its own.

[101] That is not of course to suggest that that issue was not in the minds of the framers of the *Report*, but only that an achievement which seems within reach has got in front of the picture and proved so attractive as to make this larger consideration seem less urgent.

uniting churches are both fully churches, with no defect on either side and their ministries therefore duly ordained by a 'regular calling'. All that is required to achieve a common ministry is simple recognition. Then 'a Church can officially declare the ministry of another Church to be valid, even without special guarantees that formal apostolicity has been preserved'.[102] 'There need be no suggestion of reordination, mutual recommissioning of ministries, crypto-validation, or any other ambiguity.'[103] This was the mode used in the forming of the Church of South India in 1948. It has been seen from the standpoint of some Roman Catholic theologians as possibly or partly justified on the following grounds:

(i) that the Second Vatican Council speaks of *ecclesiae*, so it need not be held by Roman Catholics that the Protestant churches are not churches;[104]

(ii) that these churches have preserved the 'charismatic structure';

(iii) that their ministries had their origin in emergency situations which make them 'extraordinary ministers', and therefore a form of ministry for which there is sound precedent.[105] Congar thinks, writing from the same tradition, that Protestant ministries could be accepted by the Roman Catholic Church 'as what they consider themselves to be',[106] but that of course would not create a single ministry in one Church because it would leave in play a multitude of partly incompatible conceptions of ministry.

Between Anglicans and Lutherans the method proposed by the *Niagara Report* has already been referred to. Its proposals rest upon the belief that there has in fact been no break in continuity in either community, for continuity is simply communion over time, and that has been preserved in each tradition.[107] In both accounts, conti-

---

[102] See G. Tavard's useful article, 'The recognition of ministry', *Journal of Ecumenical Studies*, 11 (1974) 65–83, p. 70.

[103] *Niagara Report*, 115.

[104] See Kilian McDonnell, 'Ways of validating ministry', *Journal of Ecumenical Studies*, 7 (1970), 209–65.

[105] Tavard, 'The recognition of ministry', p. 71.

[106] See 'Quelques problèmes touchant les ministères', *Nouvelle revue théologique* (October, 1971), 785–800, especially pp. 797–9.

[107] 'Succession in the presiding ministry of a Church ... stands in the continuity of apostolic faith', *Niagara Report*, 94, p. 44, quoting *The Ministry in the Church*, 62. The Church needs 'God's continuity in order to continue in God's Word and to abide in *koinonia* or communion with Christ and with each other', *Niagara Report*, 28, p. 18. The Lutheran churches are said to have 'received the focus for God's faithfulness to them' in the Creeds, in their sixteenth-century Confessions and in 'the continuity of the ordained ministry

nuity of ministry is being seen as inseparably conjoined with the maintenance of the community in the faith and with the secure administration of the true sacraments. The *Niagara Report* says that the presiding ministry which has oversight in the Church 'is never to be viewed apart from the continuity of apostolic faith'.[108] The question is whether, as this text suggests, continuity in the faith is in itself enough to guarantee the authenticity of the sacraments and to unite ecclesial bodies in a single visible universal Church to the extent that we can say there are really no breaks to be mended at all.

If so straightforward a solution seems doubtful of general acceptance (for there is a lack of reassuring precedent for it), a second possibility, further along the axis, is conditional recognition. Here something is deemed to be defective in the orders of one or both Communions, but the objection that there is a defect may be waived by an act of 'economy' (*oikonomia*) or by dispensation or their equivalent on one or both sides. Something along these lines was proposed in the 1920s between the Orthodox and the Anglicans, on the basis that the Orthodox, as the only true Church, could nevertheless recognise in Anglicanism a tradition of faith and life which approximated to their own. It was suggested that if the whole Anglican episcopate in synod declared the faith of the Anglican churches to be the same as that of the Orthodox, union might become possible, and then by an exercise of 'economy', Anglican baptism and orders might be recognised by the Orthodox.[109] Anthony Khrapovitksy, Metropolitan of Kiev, suggested that

through which the Word of God has been preached and the sacraments and rites of the Church had been administered.' The Anglicans, correspondingly, are said to have 'as the focus for God's faithfulness to them', the Creeds, the Book of Common Prayer, and 'the continuity of the episcopal office through which clergy have been ordained for the preaching of the Word of God and the administration of the sacraments and rites of the Church'. *Niagara Report*, 85, p. 41.

[108] *Niagara Report*, 54, p. 31.

[109] Orthodox theologians were especially concerned here to get round the objections which had made Anglican Orders null and void in the view of *Apostolicae Curae* in 1896. Faith and Order volume, *The Priesthood*, pp. 129ff., and J. Thompson, 'Economy', *Journal of Theological Studies*, 16 (1965), 368–420. See, too, I. Kotsonis, *The Validity of Anglican Orders* (Massachussets, 1958). This of course makes Anglican Orders a special case for Roman Catholics. Tavard suggests that it might be looked at as having been a disciplinary decision, and therefore not infallible, 'Recognition', p. 77. See, too, J.J. Hughes, *Absolutely Null and Utterly Void: An Account of the 1896 Papal Condemnation of Anglican Orders* (Washington, 1968). The English Roman Catholic hierarchy had sent the text to the Russian hierarchy. A.I. Bulgakov argued that if it could be shown that the Anglican Church had retained a correct faith about the priesthood she could also have kept 'a glimmering of the light of grace, sufficient to enable her orders to be acknowledged as valid'. A.I. Bulgakov, *The Question of Anglican Orders* (Church Historical Society, 1899), p. 45.

recognition would not depend upon the degree of heresy but upon the attitude of the holders of the heresy towards the Orthodox Church; and also that if the outward and visible part of a sacrament had been performed in the heresy, then the inward and spiritual part would be conveyed by reconciliation with the Orthodox Church, and the former part need not be repeated.[110] Here economy would be understood to work 'as a result of the presence and action of the Spirit', so that 'the Church would be able to authenticate sacraments which do not fulfil all the normal conditions of authenticity. The Spirit thus supplies what is wanting in the historical embodiment and continuity of the order of salvation.' This comes close to Western canonical notions of *ecclesia supplet*.[111]

Other Orthodox theologians have been less sure that autogeneration of the apostolic succession in a heterodox hierarchy could be possible. G. Florovsky rejects the notion that the Orthodox Church might have 'the power and right, as it were, to convert the has-not-been into the has-been'.[112] G. Tavard, looking especially at the case of the problem as it stands between Rome and the Protestant West, likes the idea that if it is agreed that the faith of the differing churches is, beyond divergences in formulation, 'identical as concerns the eucharist and the ministry ... one may think that as soon as the essential structures of faith and doctrine are established in a Church, the remaining deficiencies of its spiritual structure are supplied by the Lord'.[113] This is not a case of *ecclesia supplet*, of the Church supplying, but of God's supplying what is needed 'through' the Church.

Further along the axis again, we come to solutions involving formal liturgical acts. At its simplest, such an act might take the form of a restoration of communion, where it is understood that nothing is added to anyone's orders.[114] The reconciling churches meet as equals.

There might, further along still, be a liturgical act in which the churches did not meet in full confidence on both sides that they were

---

[110] 'Why Anglican clergy could be received in their Orders', *The Christian East*, 8, 2 (1925).
[111] Tavard, 'Recognition', p. 73; M. Villain, 'Can there be apostolic succession outside the chain of imposition of hands?', *Concilium*, 34 (1991), 87–104. On *ecclesia supplet*, see Y. Congar, 'Propos en vue d'une théologie de l'Economie dans la tradition latine', *Irénikon*, 45 (1972), 194 and 200, and A.M. Landgraf, 'Beiträge der Frühscholastik zur Terminologie der allgenmeinen Sacramentlehre', in *Dogmengeschichte der Frühscholastik*, vol. III.1, pp. 109–68.
[112] Florovsky, 'Limits', p. 123.   [113] Tavard, 'Recognition', p. 74.   [114] *Ibid.*, p. 69.

equals. This would involve a mutual imposition of hands intended 'to endorse' a previous acknowledgement of one another's orders, which would of course allow the possibility that something remained to be done beyond straightforward recognition, which this act would supply. This is not quite conditional reordination, but it is close to it. An additional ceremony is being provided, which may be understood to supply a want, or be an act of penitence and reconciliation, or of invocation of the Spirit, or of commissioning for a fuller and broader ministerial stewardship, or more than one of these things.[115]

In conditional reordination (properly speaking), the intention of the ordainer or ordainers is restricted (either mentally, or by outwardly visible modification of the normal form of ordination),[116] so that there can be no confusion of what is happening with reordination.[117] The act places in God's hands the question whether ordination has already taken place or not, and leaves it to him to do what may need to be done. It is of course only in a system which takes ordination to be unrepeatable that it is important to see things this way.

Plain reordination may, however, be appropriate in such a system where ordination has simply not taken place, or where there is a problem of 'contamination' of orders.[118]

On a basis which seems quite new in the history of ecclesiology, it

[115] McDonnell, 'Ways of voidating ministry' and Tavard, 'Recognition', p. 69. The Les Dombes Group envisaged such a process as being particularly helpful in a situation where a local act of mutual recognition of ministry might precede the final full worldwide reconciliation of the churches involved – as has happened variously in the united churches of the Indian subcontinent. *Pour une Réconciliation des Ministères* (Taizé, 1973).

[116] Tavard, 'Recognition', p. 68.

[117] This is not used in the Roman Catholic Church to recognise the ministries of persons ordained in other churches, but it has sometimes been used for Roman Catholic ordinations about which there is some reason to be doubtful. J.J. Hughes however was ordained conditionally after being ordained in another church.

[118] Saltet, *Les Réordinations*, pp. 30–1, Cyprian, Letter 67.c.3. This problem arises for some in the Anglican Communion in the case of those who have taken part in the consecration of a woman bishop. See E. Ferguson, 'Attitudes to schism at the Council of Nicaea', *Studies in Church History*, 9 (1972), 57–63. In the tenth and eleventh centuries, simoniacal purchases of bishoprics were not uncommon. Such bishops would themselves be validly consecrated, but their ministry would not be licit. Therefore any ordinations they might perform would not be valid, and they would have to be repeated. Aquinas put this principle in the form of a distinction of the *character* of the sacrament (which is conferred by simoniacal ordination), the grace (which is not), and the right to exercise ministry (which is also not thus conferred). *Summa Theologiae* IIii q.100 a.6 ad 1. Between the period of the controversy about simony and the sixteenth century a new notion developed, of a jurisdiction inherent in and intrinsic to the powers conferred by ordination. It could then be seen that the reason why the simoniac bishop could not ordain was because he had no real subjects. In the 1590s, in the course of the debates about problems arising in areas of

is now possible for uniting churches to think not in terms of one returning to the other's fold, but of each coming to the others as an ecclesial body in which there has been a mixture of wheat and tares at the human level and consequently perhaps defect and certainly need for repentance. The churches admit that they may not have been open to the guidance of the Spirit, that we do not know what may be acceptable to God, that it cannot be certain that the ministry of either church is agreeable to him exactly as it is.[119] Uniting communions can then agree in humility that there may have been defects on all sides in the theology and practice of making ministers. Working on this basis, there should indeed be no need to avoid any suggestion of reordination, mutual recommissioning of ministries, crypto-validation or any other ambiguity.[120] That is to say, there would be no presumption in any of the participating churches that it alone has a ministry commissioned by the Holy Spirit and pleasing to God in its ecclesial setting. Where there is humility, there must, on the contrary, be the presumption that only God can know for certain who are truly his ministers in his Church.

But that is not to say that it is a matter of indifference what elements individual churches have included in the making of their ministers, and with what understanding of the ministerial office they have done so. As Wollebius puts it, 'The form of the Church is a two-fold Communion' first of the Church with Christ as its head, and secondly of the members of the Church with one another.[121] God has always called his ministers in and through the Church, and certain elements have from the beginning normally formed part of that process: at least recognition by the community; preparation and setting apart for service; a rite of formal commissioning. It is of

Italy and elsewhere, where Greek and Latin rites overlapped geographically, Cardinal Santoro gave his opinion on the ordination of Greek clergy. If anyone is ordained by a heretical or schismatic bishop, Santoro believes that he receives the *character* but not the power to use the orders which he has been given. The same will apply generation by generation to all those in the line of succession from such a person. The ordainers cannot give what they themselves lack. Peri, *Chiesa Romana e 'rito' Greco*, pp. 218–19. The sixteenth century saw cases of men ordained under the protestant régimes of Henry VIII and Edward VI in England, who wanted to be reconciled with the Roman Catholic Church in Roman Catholic Mary's reign. These were deemed not to have received orders at all, on the grounds that those who made them ministers lacked this inherent authority. Y. Congar, *L'Eglise, de Saint Augustine à l'époque moderne* (Paris, 1970), p. 277.

[119] J. Kotsonis, p. 62 suggests that this is the key point.
[120] If by that is meant any suggestion that any one participating body secretly regards the ministry of the other as defective and wishes to repair the defect, and the others rightly resent any such imputation.
[121] Beardslee, *Reformed Dogmatics* (New York, 1965), p. 137.

great significance that when the reforming churches of the sixteenth
century and later varied or modified the rules they did so with an eye
directly upon traditions into which, as they saw it, abuses had crept.
So the elimination of episcopal ordination or the declaration that the
imposition of hands is not essential in fact, constitutes a comment
upon an existing system, and thus the revised *schema* of ordination
in these churches was a conscious variant of the older pattern.

Now if churches seek to come together instead of to distinguish
their practices from one another, the communion of 'the members of
the churches with one another' becomes important in determining
what ought to be the constitutive elements. It can then be argued
that mutual charity requires not a minimalist but a maximalist
approach to the question what each needs to do, with the acceptance that all must be prepared to do whatever has not been done in
the making of their own ministers, but which is done in other
communions. On that principle, every safeguard is given and it
ought to be possible for ministers 'to fulfil their ministry, upon
invitation, in any church'.[122]

It is instructive to end with a comment on the dangers which may
follow from too robust a view that order in the Church can be
repressive – the fear which shaped so much Reformation revolt.
'The American Churches', notes Stephen Neill, 'have developed
enormous headquarters in which of necessity everyone is an administrator in one capacity or another. The chief administrators tend to
run these institutions exactly as though they were a large business
corporation or a bank – the distinction between colleagues and
employees is quite rigid.'[123] This image jars with much that has been
said in this chapter about ancient patterns and classic points of
order, because it brings us sharply into a modern world. That is
salutary. But it reminds us that mending the old divides, without
which it is really very doubtful whether the Church can again enjoy
a common order, takes us only part of the way to the creation of an
order which can be flexible enough to hold its shapeliness and
pastoral appropriateness in a world where pressures of quite another
sort will inevitably assault it.

---

[122] *One Baptism, One Eucharist, and a Mutually Recognised Ministry*, WCC (1975).
[123] Stephen Neill, *God's Apprentice*, ed. E.M. Jackson (London, 1991), p. 239. This was written
polemically by an author who believes that the WCC became like this at a time when
those 'who valued their originality and independence simply had to get out in order to
save their own souls'. The danger to which he points is for our purposes here best regarded
as a general one.

CHAPTER 5

Decision-making

DECISION-MAKING IN ONE CHURCH

A future united Church will have to be able to make up its mind. It is currently strongly argued that three elements must be present in the visible, organic, structural unity of a future united Church. The first two, common faith and mutual recognition of sacraments and ministry, we have been considering. The third is the bringing into being of common structures for making decisions.

This raises all sorts of issues about the way a common decision-making process could work and what would be the source of its authority.[1] It also makes it necessary to think further about the character of consensus,[2] and about the handling of a larger quantity of material for decision than has ever been presented before.

Two interacting decision-making processes have gone on throughout the history of the Church. One is formal, involves meetings of the churches' representatives or pronouncements by leaders, and results in statements (decrees, resolutions). The other is informal, involves the whole people of God, and consists in their active reception (and sometimes their call for the modification or development) of such decisions. The relationship between the two has always operated *ad hoc* and *de facto*. We are not yet in a position to agree which makes a matter of faith or order binding on the faithful, though it is hard to see how the answer can be other than

---

[1] 'The value of any consensus ... will to a large extent depend on the authority of the body which eventually endorses it'. Rome's *Response* to the *Final Report* of ARCIC I, 5 December 1991. See, too, on the process by which the Roman Catholic Church makes statements, Yarnold, *In Search of Unity*, pp. 25–7.

[2] One author suggests, if 'its purpose is to unite rather than divide ... an ecumenical creed is not the place for ... party polemics, or sectarian specificity. It is not a Reformation-style confession with the intention of defending a distinctive identity.' James A. Nash, 'Political conditions for an Ecumenical Confession: a Protestant contribution to the emerging dialogue', *Journal of Ecumenical Studies*, 25 (1988), 241–61.

'both together'.[3] For reasons of space, and also because it is important to see the way forward in these two areas before we can get any
further, I shall confine myself mainly to them in this chapter.

Reception[4] as an instrument of communion

'Quod omnes tangit, ab omnibus tractari et approbari debet.' 'What
touches everyone should be discussed and approved by everyone.'[5]
Justinian's first formulation of this principle (in 531) was designed to
fit the case where several individuals in late Roman society held a
tutela (guardianship). Their common administration could not be
ended without the consent of all. The notion became current in a
different context in the thirteenth century, partly under the influence of Innocent III (1198–1216), himself once a student of law at
Bologna and always conscious of the usefulness of legal principles.[6]
From his time it was used not only in cases where specific procedures
had to be determined, but also as enunciating a general rule of the
life of the Church: that is, that the members of the community
should join actively in approving what affects them all. Indeed it
could be taken so far as to lodge the ultimate authority in the
Church in the community as a whole. In practice, this was rarely
what happened in ecclesiastical decision-making in the Middle
Ages, or in political decision-making either. But there was, nevertheless, a growing theoreticians' interest in the idea of community,

---

[3] The *Final Report* of the First Anglican–Roman Catholic International Commission said that
'at certain moments the Church can in a matter of essential doctrine make a decisive
judgement which becomes part of its permanent witness' (ARCIC I, *Final Report*, Authority
II.24–7). Responding to the text, Rome comments that ARCIC holds that reception of a
defined truth by the People of God, 'does not create truth nor legitimise decision' (Elucidation 3 to Authority text), but also sees the 'assent of the faithful [as] required for the
recognition that a doctrinal decision of the pope or of an ecumenical council is immune from
error' (Rome's *Response* and ARCIC Authority II.27 and 31). 'For the Catholic Church, the
certain knowledge of any defined truth is not guaranteed by the reception of the faithful that
such is in conformity with Scripture and tradition, but by the authoritative definition itself
on the part of the authentic teachers' (Rome's *Response*). ARCIC defines doctrinal definitions of the sort which would fulfil conditions of bindingness by councils, as being concerned
with 'fundamental doctrines' or 'eternal truths of salvation'. 'The Catholic Church believes
that the councils or the Pope, even acting alone, are able to teach, if necessary in a definitive
way, within the range of all truth revealed by God' (Rome's *Response*).

[4] J.M.R. Tillard, 'Eglise catholique et dialogues bilatéraux', *Irénikon*, 56 (1983), 6. A key text
comes at the end of Augustine's *De Trinitate*.

[5] The tag originates in a law of Justinian of 531, inserted into the second edition of the Code
(c.7.x.1.23, Friedberg, II.152).

[6] For a study of the principle, see Y. Congar, 'Quod omnes tangit ab omnibus tractari et
approbari debet', *Revue historique de droit français et étranger*, 36 (1958), 210–59.

which provided a strong background on the secular side. Though it continued to be a largely clerical responsibility to make decisions in the Church, there, too, there was talk of the people's part in the corporate decision-making.[7]

All this amounted to a crucially important clarification of the idea of the *consensus fidelium*, the consent of the faithful, which underlies Vincent of Lérins' dictum of the first half of the fifth century. If the Church is to keep to what is agreed at all periods, everywhere, by everyone, it must necessarily use as a test the general assent of the faithful. But that need not equally necessarily imply the active consideration and agreement for which both Biblical and modern ideas of the shared responsibility of all members of the community would press.[8]

Despite these late mediaeval stirrings, there was still a lack of a developed theology in sixteenth-century writers in the area of 'reception'. The Anglican Calfhill in 1565 mentions the notion of retrospective ratification when there is subsequent assent by the faithful.[9] But he does not explore the question whether the *consensus fidelium* can do, or ought to try to do, more than recognise and embrace, as in harmony with the apostolic faith, a truth which is presented to it already formulated. Nevertheless, the notion of an active 'embracing' is clearly present.[10] Melanchthon is able to define the Church as people embracing the Gospel, *homines amplectentes Evangelium*.[11] The essence of this 'active welcoming' is that it is not an individual but a collective act of the people of God. It shifts the emphasis of the word consensus towards the idea of a shared understanding, *con-sensus*.

It would not perhaps now be disputed by many Christians that the consent of the faithful involves an active embracing of the Church's faith and life in mind and heart,[12] not a simple 'realisation', but a consent of the judgement; nor perhaps that no Christian can legitimately be excluded. It is less clear how in

---

[7] B. Tierney, *Foundations of the Conciliar Theory* (Cambridge, 1955).

[8] But reception is perhaps in principle not a jurisdictional act. Reception seems to stand in a relation to law of 'confirming', giving *firmitas*.

[9] He asks 'what moved the faithful to refuse the second of Ephesus and willingly embrace the Council of Chalcedon', and answers in terms of their 'examining their decrees by Scripture'. Calfhill, PS, pp. 10 and 151.

[10] Rogers, PS, pp. 210, 210–11; Nowell, PS, p. 117.   [11] *CR* 24.401, cf. 406 and 409.

[12] See R. Greenacre, 'Two aspects of reception', in *Christian Authority: Essays in Honour of Henry Chadwick*, ed. G.R. Evans (Oxford, 1988), pp. 40–58.

practice such processes of active general reception are to work in the forming of a united Church or in the sustaining of its common life.

Many varying procedures have been in evidence worldwide as the Reports and Agreed Statements of the ecumenical conversations of recent decades have begun to circulate. Sometimes a professional body of theologians has been appointed to consider the document; sometimes it has been conscientiously discussed first at the minutest local level, in parish study-groups and then brought (in the Anglican pattern, for instance) to deanery and then diocesan and then provincial synods; sometimes it has been held over for consideration by a body deemed competent to speak 'officially' for the Church in question;[13] sometimes it has been virtually ignored.

In the case of some churches whose decision-making structures are very different or even mutually incompatible at present, it can even be argued, for example, that 'it is unclear if there is any process possible' by which the two Communions 'can commit themselves to an agreement on faith of any sort'.[14] Commonly there have been expressions of confusion and uncertainty from lay people to whom the theological problems and categories of thought involved may be unfamiliar. All this experience raises important questions about the time-scale for collective decision-making through 'reception' by all; it may be that we must think in terms of centuries, not decades. Certainly the experience of the early Church in the reception of points in the Creeds would bear that out. Yet it was achieved.

But this body of preliminary experience also requires us to give some thought to the workings of the machinery. Y. Congar speaks of 'the process by which an ecclesial body makes truly its own a determination which it has not itself given, recognising in the measure which it promulgated a rule which is consonant with its life'.[15] An ecclesial body must be a community legally capable of making its consent corporately.[16] Although individual Christians may vote with their feet and move from one church to another, that does not unite the Church. Churches cannot unite with one another unless they consent as ecclesial entities to that union. But the

---

[13] See Rome's *Response* to ARCIC and Christopher Hill, 'The fundamental question of Ecumenical Method', *Catholic International* 3.3 (February, 1992) 134–40.

[14] Edward Yarnold, *In Search of Unity* (Slough, 1989), referring to the Anglican Communion and the Roman Catholic Church.

[15] Y. Congar, 'La "reception" comme réalité ecclésiologique', *Revue des sciences philosophiques et théologiques*, 56 (Paris, 1972), 369–403, p. 370.

[16] Cf. Canon 26 of Roman Catholic Code of 1917, 'communitas legis recipiendi capax'.

provisional character of all individual churches means that we have to think in terms of an interim mutual tolerance where some ecclesial communities have been able to receive fully, what others cannot accept wholly into their own ecclesial life. There would also have to be mutual recognition of the provisional ecclesial communities in their provisionality, from which that imperative of mutual tolerance would proceed and upon which it would rest.[17] That would look not only to reception of one another's faith as the true faith, as each community's own as well as the other's; but also of one another's order and ecclesial life. Reception has an effect. Churches wishing to remain in unity do so by mutual reception and recognition; churches reaching for the reconstruction of unity may achieve it in that way.[18] The will for unity is itself a powerful drive in reception.[19]

Complementary to mutual reception is common reception of what are perceived to be the absolutes of faith. Congar defines 'to receive'[20] as finding to be in harmony with apostolic truth. In principle that which is in harmony with apostolic truth ought to be able to be recognised as such by all individual ecclesial communities and thus received by them as also their own. There ought ultimately to be unanimity of this sort in reception. Only then can it be truly *con-sensus*.

But that will not necessarily always have exactly the same application for each community in the shaping of its common life. So we must also try to distinguish between what may, arguably, have to be received only by a local community and what may require reception by the whole Church. The most obvious example of something which must be universally received is Scripture.[21] An instance of something which it might be inappropriate to 'receive' generally is a particular pattern of liturgical practice – although each church in a united Church would surely have to approve the others' rites in principle as being in keeping with common order. This raises the difficulties in connection with the place of diversity among Christian

---

[17] H. Meyer, 'Les Présupposés de la réception ecclésiale ou le problème de la "recevabilité"', *Irénikon*, 59 (1986), 5–19.

[18] See Tillard, *The Bishop of Rome*, p. 4, on the difference between reception in a context of reconstruction of unity and reception when remaining in unity.

[19] J.M.R. Tillard, '"Le Votum eucharistiae", L'Eucharistie dans le recontre des chrétiens', *Miscellanea liturgica in honore di Sua Eminenza il cardinale G. Lercaro*, 2 (Paris, 1967), 143–94.

[20] Congar, *Tradition et traditions* (London, 1966), p. 253 (English translation), and 'La réception comme réalité ecclésiologique', p. 37, definition cited.

[21] Although there remains disagreement about the status of the apocryphal books.

communities which we have been looking at, as well as being in practice very hard to achieve. But it seems, nevertheless, to be a non-negotiable requirement of a satisfactory doctrine of reception, at least in the long term.

COUNCILS

The Church's characteristic answer to conflict or schism has been to call a council.[22] The first recorded occasion on which this happened is described in Acts 15. Paul and Barnabas were in difficulties in Antioch over the teaching of missionaries from Judaea who were insisting that believers in Christ must be circumcised. Paul and Barnabas were 'sent' to Jerusalem to consult the Apostles and elders there. This 'council' decided after discussion that the gentiles need not be bound by this obligation, and the representatives from Antioch went home with a letter giving the decision of their meeting, so that the Christians in Antioch might understand the reason for the ruling and accept it by their own free consent (Acts 15:1–35).

There is a paradigm here for much of the subsequent development of conciliar theory. The leaders of the communities, or others chosen by their communities for the task, act as its representatives. Decisions are taken under the guidance of the Holy Spirit and in an effort to conform with the teaching of Jesus; they have in mind the good of the community and the welfare of individual Christians within it. They are put before the people for them to receive and accept, but also with some sense of their having an authority derived from the decision of the meeting (Acts 15:28).

Indeed, councils can succeed in their purpose only if everyone involved can accept at least their interim authoritativeness to settle whatever is at issue. For that reason, the calling, constitution, conduct and decisions of councils have all, from time to time, become the subject of dispute. That was part of the difficulty during the period in the sixteenth century when it was hoped that a General Council might be summoned, which would resolve the differences which were dividing the Church in the West. On one side, it could confidently be asserted that, 'as obedient sons of the German and Roman Church, ... we submit ourselves and our cause to a General

[22] The word 'synod' is used here as synonymous with 'council'.

Council. Whatever has been defined by a Council, we believe fervently and firmly to have been defined by the Holy Spirit, and we embrace it obediently and with joy.' On the other, there was good hope at first. If the Augsburg Confession did not prove a basis for the settlement of outstanding differences, the preface offers 'in full obedience, even beyond what is required, to participate in such a general, free and Christian council as the Electors, Princes and estates have with the highest and best motives requested'. As we shall see, such hopes were stopped in their tracks by the loudly voiced conviction that a council summoned by the Pope would be no true council at all, but the work of Antichrist.[23]

The underlying lack of consensus about what makes a council and what it can do remains a problem ecumenically today. But the resolution of the divisions which are bound to threaten even in a future united Church will certainly continue to create the need for such meetings. The question is whether they should or can be conciliar in any traditional sense; and if not, what alternative structures and purposes they might have. Before we can consider that, we need to look at the old patterns and the difficulties they raised.

The sources of conciliar authority

Comments through the ages on the grounds and sources of the authority of conciliar decisions repeat certain well-defined themes, and we should perhaps review them at the outset. The first concern is that a body which is to make decisions with any degree of authoritativeness in the Church should act under God and thus, in some sense at least, with divine sanction. Revelation by miracle is commonly pointed to as authoritative at an early stage, in both East and West, because it carries divine attestation.[24] The Holy Spirit is present in the synods of the Church, says Pope Celestine in a letter to

---

[23] J. Cochlaeus, *Aequitatis Discussio super consilio delectorum Cardinalium (1538)*, C.Cath., 17 (Münster, 1931), p. 8 and see G.R. Evans, 'The attack on the Fourth Lateran Council', *Annuarium Historiae Conciliorum* (1991) 241–66. See, too, J.T. McNeill, *Unitive Protestantism* (London, 1964), pp. 109ff.

[24] John Moschus (550–619), for example, tells the story of a monk who argued that since all those who presented him with their conflicting opinions threatened with hell any who disagreed with them, he had no means of knowing which was the truth unless he was shown by a miracle. *Le Pré spirituel*, Sources chrétiens (Paris, 1946), no. 26, pp. 65–7 and Introduction, p. 30 and see H. Chadwick, 'John Moschus and his friend Sophronius the Sophist', *Journal of Theological Studies*, 25 (1974), 41–74.

the Synod of Ephesus in 431. 'A synod of priests gives witness to the presence of the Holy Spirit . . . and since this is so, if the Holy Spirit is not absent from so small a number, how much more may we believe he is present when so great a multitude of saints is assembled together?'[25] Emphasis is also placed on the presence of Christ (cf. Matthew 18:20). The Anglo-Saxon scholar, Aldhelm, writing to King Geraint about the 'episcopal council' held at Hertford in 672 speaks of 'Christ offering his protection' to the meeting.[26]

The authority of Scripture is universally acknowledged. To take an instance: the twenty-first of the Anglican Thirty-Nine Articles says that 'things ordained by [General Councils] as necessary to salvation have neither strength[27] nor authority, unless it may be declared that they be taken out of Holy Scripture'. This was a response to the fear in many sixteenth-century reforming minds that a council was likely to behave as an institution having human authority, and as though its decrees could add to Scripture or even outweigh or contradict its teaching.

There is, however, a further and ecclesiologically important factor. The authority of councils derives, suggests Pope Celestine in the same letter to the Synod of Ephesus in 431, not only from the presence of the Holy Spirit but also from the reverence which is due to the original 'council of the Apostles'; there would seem to be a sense in which all subsequent councils are 'in' that council and derive the authoritativeness of their decrees from it. There is a further sense in which all conciliar authority can be seen to proceed from that of earlier councils and so on backwards, to this first apostolic conciliar gathering. Councils have made consistent reference to the work of earlier meetings. Bede describes Anglo-Saxon conciliar receiving (*suscipimus*) of the five Ecumenical Councils (325, 381, 431, 451, 553) and the Council held at Rome in 649.[28] At Basle on 15 February 1432 the council insists that it is in every way duly assembled ('debite legitimeque ac rite initiata et congregata'); and so that there may be no doubt in anyone's mind about its power (*potestas*) it ordains and decrees afresh two declarations from the Council of Constance two decades earlier. The idea that a given

---

[25] Labbe and C. *Concilia*, III.613.

[26] Aldhelm in, *The Prose Works*, tr. M. Lapidge and M. Herren (Ipswich, 1979), pp. 155, 481ff. In keeping with this emphasis upon divine authorising is the insistence which we find not only in the sixteenth-century debates, but as early as Ceolfrith's eighth-century *De Legitima Observatione Paschae*, that nothing can be changed by human authority alone.

[27] *Vis* having the sense of 'force'.   [28] Bede, *H.E.* IV.17, p. 386.

council must be 'in' the first and all subsequent councils rests on the principle that, even though it can in fact assemble only a limited number of leaders of the Church at a given place and time, each council is a meeting of the whole Church in every age. So it cannot operate without reference to all other councils.

Representativeness

The concept of 'representation' is important here, because it is traditionally by 'representation' that the whole Church is able to be 'present' when only a small number of individuals actually meets. The concept of 'representation' can have a number of shadings and weightings, however. In an episcopally led church, the question arises whether a bishop can speak bindingly for his people as their representative. There are questions about the role of theologians when they give 'expert' advice.[29] They do not then necessarily speak as bishops even if, in some cases, they happen also to be bishops. The recent 'Cologne declaration' shows Roman Catholic theologians confronting the hierarchy.[30] In short, all sorts of problems arise about who may speak for a given church or churches (as a whole or in a particular place), in such a way that believers recognise that they are being spoken for.

The notion of representativeness came in for a good deal of discussion from the later Middle Ages. In Innocent III's time the composition of a General Council was modified so that it became 'representative' in being an 'assembly of estates' to which all the constituent elements of the Church are summoned either in person or through representatives.[31] But there was no definitive contemporary theoretical analysis of the concept of representation or satisfactory attempt to define the precise relation between a General Council and the universal Church.

[29] Aquinas already saw some of the difficulties. He poses the question whether anyone can ask on his own behalf for a licence to teach theology. He argues that the *doctores sacrae Scripturae* are ministers of the Word of God, just as prelates are. But he makes three differences between the *cathedra magistralis* and the *cathedra pontificalis*. The seat of a teacher has no eminence (*eminentia*), but gives only the 'opportunity to communicate knowledge'. It requires a lesser perfection and only 'sufficient knowledge'. (*Quodlibet*, III.q.4.a.1.) It is nevertheless the case that the teacher has a serious responsibility not to lead the faithful astray, for it can be asked whether it is culpable to hold false opinions if one is merely following one's master. (Aquinas thinks ignorance is no excuse.) (*Quodlibet* III.q.4.a.2.).

[30] Metz, Salamanca, pp.369–401, on the Cologne Declaration.

[31] Tierney, *Foundations of the Conciliar Theory* p. 47 and see Hauck, Tierney note 1 to p. 47, for further references.

The Council of Basle in its first session of 14 December 1431, is deemed to be *repraesentans universalem ecclesiam*,[32] in an age of conciliarist theory, when it is especially important to be able to get the balance right between saying that the bishops represent the Church and saying that the Pope represents the Church.[33] In the eyes of Johannes Eck a century later,

The Church is the congregation of all the faithful who are of the body of Christ. Thus, when the primates and senior clergy (*potiores*) of any province decide something, the whole province is said to have decided; so the prelates of the Church are called the Church, for they represent her and those subject to them. Otherwise the Church could never be assembled (*congregari*).[34]

The question of the existence of an inherent authoritativeness of any body, person or persons in the Church has arisen in several connections. The first and most obvious instance is the bishop, in whom there is understood to be an inherent authority which includes teaching authority. In the Roman Catholic Church a *magisterium* exists, deemed to be capable of determining issues for as well as on behalf of the faithful.[35]

The membership of councils was also widely discussed in the sixteenth century. Three points commonly arose here: whether it is important that the council should consist of 'good men';[36] whether a larger number carries more weight than a smaller number; whether a council must be 'representative' of the whole Church. These two last points are interrelated. The English Latimer says that larger numbers are not necessarily better; it is not a matter of majority decision.[37] There was some awareness here of a patristic sense that a council should have the widest possible base, but apparently no strong feeling in favour of the universality for which Cyprian and Celestine had pressed. 'Representativeness' is a complex matter in sixteenth-century eyes. If Ignatius had argued at the turn of the first century that the whole Church entrusted to a bishop is present in his

---

[32] *Conciliorum Oecumenicorum Decreta*, ed. G. Alberigo (Bologna, 1973), p. 455.

[33] Tierney, *Foundations*.

[34] *Enchiridion locorum communium*, ed. P. Fraenkel, *C.Cath.* 34 (1979), pp. 22–32, Chapter I, Proposition 3.

[35] See Rome's *Response* to ARCIC.

[36] Latimer, PS, I.288. (But Cranmer says that error is still possible, PS 2.53.)

[37] Latimer, PS 1.288, cf. S.L. Greenslade, 'The English reformers and the Councils of the Church', *Oecumenica* (1967), p. 101 In practice, synods and conferences often resort to the majority vote, and that can be said in a sense to have an authority of this working kind, at least where consensus is not yet to be had.

person,[38] this sense seems less strong in the sixteenth-century debates. Indeed Luther can revile the whole idea of representativeness.[39]

The question which has more recently come to be important is whether a council can be representative of the whole Church unless it consists of bishops, clergy and laity.[40] On the question of representativeness, Field comments that those with 'authority to teach, define, prescribe and to direct' have the 'deciding and defining voices', but that laymen may be present too, 'to hear, set forward, and consent unto that which is there to be done'.[41] In many churches clergy and lay people now expect not only to be present but to vote. That expectation can coexist, as it does for example in the General Synod of the Church of England, with a recognition that bishops represent their people in a way unique to their office, while lay members of the synod may be made 'representatives' only by election, and therefore on a different model and understanding of what it is 'to represent'.

A development of this is the idea of a church's meeting by parts, or 'houses'.[42] In such a structure not all those present stand in the same relationship to their communities. In any case, if some churches continue not to have bishops in a future united Church, they will send representatives to its conciliar gatherings who cannot stand in the same relationship to their communities as bishops do. The sisterhood and implied equality of the churches which come together in a council will function equitably only if those who represent them there stand in at least equivalent relationships to their respective churches. Within the traditional episcopal system this presents no difficulty in the sense that all bishops may be deemed to stand in the same relationship to their people. So we have to ask whether an ecumenical 'council' in a future united Church could do its work of decision-making in circumstances where there was incommensurability of the principles about representation of his community on which each was present.

---

[38] Henry Chadwick, 'The status of ecumenical Councils in Anglican thought', *Orientalia Christiana Analecta*, 195 (1973), 393, citing Ignatius *Ad Ephesianos* 1; *Ad Magnesianos* 2; *Ad Trallianos* 1.

[39] E.g. WA 39.192–3.

[40] E.g. Whitaker, PS 22 and 415; Fulke, PS 1.253; Jewel, PS 3.205.

[41] Richard Field, *Of the Church*, Book V, 48, vol. IV.3.

[42] As in the House of Bishops, House of Clergy and House of Laity in the Church of England's General Synod.

Each and all

The notions of 'representativeness' and of an 'inherent authority' (although these are not the only foundations of conciliar authority) underlie in the thought of many commentators from the late Middle Ages, the principle that councils can make decisions which are in intention or fact decisions of the whole Church and expressions of its common mind. Certain themes run through the great Councils of the fourth and fifth centuries, and their own self-image of their authoritativeness. These councils repeatedly had to deal with threats to faith and order. They seek to make rulings consonant with the earliest belief and practice, and with the continuing tradition of the church since then, and to do it as of one mind. There is a strong sense of the danger that 'separate assemblies' with 'different doctrines' will tend to 'isolation' (where there is no 'common judgement among all of them'), and also to a sense of exclusiveness and superiority among those who so separate themselves.[43] The Synodal Letter of Antioch (341) speaks of 'joining together in unity of mind and concord and the spirit of peace'. Its Canons regard the 'setting up of an altar' by the leader of a 'private assembly' as an act of ecclesial divisiveness, for he thus institutes a separated eucharistic fellowship (V); to counter such acts and to settle all sorts of lesser, disciplinary, disputes, the same council urges regular meetings of synods in each province (XX).

The Council of Constantinople (381) wrote a Letter to the Emperor Theodosius in which it asserts that 'first of all we renewed our unity of heart with each other';[44] the Synodical letter from Constantinople's assembled bishops to those met at Rome takes the same line. 'Our disposition is all for peace, with unity as its sole object ... with common consent'.[45] This theme of agreement in unity is repeated in Canon I, which reasserts 'the faith of the 318 Fathers assembled at Nicaea';[46] in 451 there is an affirmation of the duty to keep 'in common the faith which has come down to us today through the apostolic succession'.[47] Thus the 'common mind' is seen

---

[43] Synodical Letter of the Council of Gangra c.345.　　　[44] Labbe and C., *Concilia* II.945.

[45] Theodoret, *Historia Ecclesiastica*, ed. L. Parmentier and F. Scheidweiler (Berlin, 1954), vol.V, p. 9.

[46] Also Council of Ephesus 431, Letter of Pope Celestine to the Synod, Labbe and C., *Concilia*, III.613.

[47] *Definition of Faith* of Chalcedon 451, Tanner I.83.

to be not merely shared by those present and their contemporaries, but by Christians of earlier ages.

It is of some importance to the understanding of the relationship of the local to the universal Church that a principle of agreement by 'each and all' makes its appearance in these councils. When the letters of Cyril of Alexandria to Nestorius, and of Nestorius himself, were read out to the Council of Constantinople, each bishop in turn gave his opinion and then all the bishops cried aloud together to confirm the unanimity of their condemnation of Nestorius.[48] The same acclaim by 'each and all' happened twice at Ephesus (431) and Chalcedon (451).[49]

Unanimity in the faith, and unity in one communion, are strongly felt from an early date to belong together. After Constantinople in 381 Cyril wrote to Nestorius to send him the council's twelve anathemas, stressing that the bishops declare themselves in communion with those, both laity and clergy, whom Nestorius has excommunicated or deposed for their failure to conform with his beliefs.[50]

The authority of these Councils is understood to lie ultimately in the guidance of the Holy Spirit in their deliberations not in the consensus itself. The consensus is an indication that the council has heard and been guided by him. It is thought to follow that if two or three may gather in Christ's name a greater number will carry a greater authority than a smaller as witnesses to the Spirit's teaching. But at the same time, the authority of councils is also deemed to lie in their continuity in the faith of the Apostles in which they are owed the reverence which is due to the first council of the Apostles at Jerusalem. These axes, of authorisation by the Holy Spirit, and of authority continuous with that of the Apostles, intersect and remain inseparable from the agreement of those meeting in each council. It is in this way that 'each and all' extends beyond the particular meeting. As the first Canon of Chalcedon of 451 says, 'the canons of the Holy Fathers made in every synod until now, should remain in force'.

The ecclesiological concerns which Bede reads back into the English Synod of Whitby debate of 664 about the date of Easter are also visible in his accounts of the Councils of Hertford (672) and Hatfield (679). He describes how Theodore, then Archbishop of Canterbury, summoned a council of bishops together with 'those

---

[48] Labbe and C., *Concilia*, III.462. [49] Labbe and C., *Concilia*, III.503 and 617, IV.562.
[50] Labbe and C., *Concilia*, III.462 ff. .

who loved and knew the canons of the Fathers (*canonica patrum statuta*)', whom he describes as 'many masters of the Church (*magistris ecclesiae pluribus*)'. These 'academic theologians' Bede sees as assembling *pariter*, on an equal footing with the bishops, but it is the bishops who give the agreement which constitutes the *actio synodica*. There is only the barest record in Bede of discussion at the meeting. Theodore was a dominant president. He 'taught' (*coepit docere*) that those present were to observe what conduced to the unity and peace of the Church. The text Bede gives of the synod's decrees takes the form almost of a charter in the name of Theodore, in which Theodore describes what he said, in the first person. He presented the bishops and scholars with an outline of their task, which is to deliberate together (*commune ... tractemus*) so as to preserve (*ut ... serventur*) incorrupt (*incorrupte*) what has been decreed and defined (*decreta ac definita*) by Fathers whose soundness is well proved (*probabilibus patribus*). These are not loosely expressed considerations, but a tight package of principles required for the proper enactment of conciliar decrees. Theodore next asked the assembled bishops each in turn if they were willing to keep the 'canonical decrees' of the ancient Fathers ('ea quae a patribus canonice sunt antiquitus decreta custodire'); and they all said yes. Then, and here a comparison with Innocent's procedure at the Fourth Lateran Council is irresistible,[51] Theodore produced a book of what he claimed to be such canons,[52] and pointed out to the assembly ten to which he wished them to give special attention.

Theodore's next general synod was at Hatfield in 679. Bede rather puzzlingly suggests that Theodore had recently heard (*his temporibus audiens*) that the faith of the Church at Constantinople had been greatly disturbed by Eutyches' heresy. It seems much more likely that what had come to his attention was the first Lateran Council of 649, held at Rome, which is mentioned in the record of the Hertford synod reproduced in Bede's text, and which was followed by the exiling of the Pope by the Emperor Constans II. The heresy at issue, and of keen contemporary interest, was that of the Monothelites.[53] Theodore, says Bede, assembled many bishops and learned men,

---

51 See Evans, 'The attack'.
52 The canons are given by Bede. Their origin is puzzling. Not one of the canons of Hertford is identical with the wording of any canon in the Latin tradition. On the other hand, the *sententiae* are familiar enough, and some can be identified as conflations of other canons. *H.E.* IV.5, pp. 348–50. I am indebted to Martin Brett for this observation.
53 Bede, *H.E.* IV.17, p. 386.

and made a thorough enquiry of each so as to establish the orthodoxy of his beliefs. He discovered nothing to disturb him. All were of
one mind in the catholic faith ('unanimem in fide catholica ...
consensum'). Theodore thought it advisable, however, to have this
consensus recorded in 'synodal letters' (*synodalibus litteris*) so that
those who came after should have guidance and a point of reference.

The text of the synodical letter gives date and place and says that
Theodore presided as archbishop of the island of Britain and of the
city of Canterbury; that the other bishops of Britain sat with him,
and they had the Gospels before them. Acting collegially (*pariter
tractantes*), they expounded (*exposuimus*) the true and orthodox faith,
as it was delivered by Christ to his disciples face to face, and as those
eye-witnesses handed it down through the Creed and as all the holy
and universal Councils and the whole chorus of those learned and
respected in the Church through the ages, have transmitted it. The
confession of faith the bishops make is of an orthodox doctrine of the
Trinity. Bede gives no more than the points about consubstantiality
in unity and equality in glory and honour.[54] He does, however,
include the passage in which the Council receives (*suscipimus*) the
five Ecumenical Councils (325, 381, 431, 451, and that of Constantinople in 553); and the council held in Rome in 649. In
aligning themselves with the fathers of these councils, the bishops (or
at least Theodore, who was presumably the draftsman), use the
Filioque clause in their doxology.

The events of these meetings demonstrate the subtlety of the
practical working-out of the 'each and all' principle even in a
remote corner of the Christian world at this comparatively early
date.

Equality and leadership

Bishops who meet in council meet as brothers, on a basis of equality,
as a *collegium*.[55] There is therefore historically a duality of authority
in the running of councils, with a *primus inter pares* among the bishops
(or, on a different basis which we shall come to in a moment, a
secular authority such as an emperor, a prince or a magistrate)

---

[54] The same 'collegiality' of equality is present in presbyterian systems in the college of
presbyters.
[55] The advent of women bishops in the Anglican Communion makes this perhaps a less
uncontroversial term.

taking the role of overall leader. This question of the interrelationship of equality and leadership is still germane to any attempt to resolve differences between churches by means of meetings. Sisterhood of churches and brotherhood[56] of bishops has always been of the essence of conciliarity. But equally there has always been personal leadership.

Severus of Antioch couples the decision of the Apostolic See and of the 'whole synod' and says that their combined decisions cannot be 'reversed' by any authority.[57] In the West the relationship of the Apostolic See to the decision of the Church through a council, and in the East that of an autocephalous Church's patriarch and that of a council of bishops, remains a vexed question; but in the West it could be said with some confidence even in the seventh century that the decree of the Apostolic See is the decree of the universal Church. 'Audita decreta sedis apostolicae immo universalis ecclesia'; once the decree of the Apostolic See, which is that of the universal Church, has been heard, it cannot legitimately be gainsaid, argued the Roman party at the Synod of Whitby.

Someone, not necessarily the same person, must call a council together, preside at it, declare it ended and (perhaps) in some way 'ratify' its decrees so as to give them legal (as distinct from theological) standing. The authority of kings or other secular rulers falls into a separate category, because the ruler is a layman and he cannot 'speak for the Church' as its bishops arguably can. He is not placed in the same relationship to the community by his coronation as they are by their ordination. Yet councils have been convened by secular rulers since the first centuries. The Synodal Letter of Nicaea in 325 notes that it was 'our most religious sovereign Constantine who brought us together from our several provinces and cities'. The emperor's Letter, read to those assembled at Constantinople in 553, looks back over the consistent achievement of a series of emperors in calling synods to settle controversies: Constantine at Nicaea; Theodosius at Constantinople in 381; Theodosius the Younger, at Ephesus in 431; Marcion at Chalcedon in 451; since Chalcedon, he says, there have continued to be controversies, and now it seems that the only way to resolve them is to call another council.[58] The emperor summoned the sixth Ecumenical Council at Constantinople in 680–1; the Emperors Constantine and Irene that at Nicaea

[56] *Select Letters*, Book VI, I.40.   [57] Labbe and C., *Concilia*, V.568.
[58] Labbe and C., *Concilia*, VII.49.

(787).[59] We find secular authority even apparently determining controversies, as the king did at the Synod of Whitby.

The collapse of the old imperial patterns, and the later division of the Church from 1054, resulted in a substantial gap before any further council could meet with a claim to be universal. The best candidates were the series of Lateran Councils held in the West in the twelfth and early thirteenth centuries. These were of papal summoning, and because of the schism, they could not include the Greeks. That was tried at Lyons in 1274 and at the Council of Florence (1438–45). But in essence the framework had undergone a lasting change, and it was no longer possible for any secular world leader to be looked to as the natural convener of a council of the whole Church.

Nevertheless, in the anti-papalist mood of the sixteenth-century reforms in the West, some form of secular summoning was wanted. In Germany the princes were enlisted as leaders in certain aspects of church affairs. As the preface to the Lutheran *Book of Concord* explains, the Augsburg Confession was presented to the Emperor Charles V at Augsburg in 1530; the preface itself ends with the names of over fifty princes, nobles and city authorities who have subscribed to the Book of Concord.[60] 'General Councils may not be gathered together without the commandment and will of princes', says Article 21 of the Church of England's Thirty-Nine Articles.

The role of the Bishops of Rome was always marked out to some degree from that of other patriarchs, at first because the early Ecumenical Councils were predominantly affairs of Eastern Christendom. There does not seem to have been any consultation with the Pope in the case of the calling of the Council of Nicaea in 325. Pope Celestine had already condemned Nestorius as a heretic and excommunicated him before the Council of Nicaea was called in 431. The council made up its own mind. Although it concurred with Rome's sentence in the event, it acted before the arrival of the delegates from Rome. The Roman party approved its action at a second session held after their arrival. Similarly, at Chalcedon, the meeting did not accept the Tome of Pope Leo without making its own decision as to its orthodoxy. The fifth Ecumenical Council did not accept written material on points of doctrine from the then

---

[59] Tappert, *Book of Concord*, p. 3. The preface was written between 1578 and 1580.
[60] Though it was said at the sixth Council that Nicaea 325 was called by Constantine and Sylvester.

Pope, and in fact took his name from the diptychs. The third Council of Constantinople excommunicated the dead Pope Honorius for Monothelitism,[61] and the seventh Ecumenical Council was certainly called without involving the Pope.

Papal summoning thus became the norm only after the schism of 1054 with the undisputed primacy of the bishop of Rome in the West. Papal authority has long been held by some to be capable of overriding consensus. Huguccio[62] says that the Pope's authority is greater even than that of the Apostles, *ratione prelationis*, because of the jurisdiction he exercises. Vatican I's *ex sese, non autem ex consensu ecclesiae* with its assertion that the Pope has an authority which does not derive from the consensus of a council is a modern development of this principle.

BINDINGNESS

Can a council have the authority to make binding decisions? Should it seek to do so? In what circumstances? Binding upon whom? Binding in perpetuity? Early councils certainly saw their task as one of making decisions in matters of faith and order which would settle disputes. This bindingness seems to have been seen as proceeding from the consensus of the churches assembled in their representatives. These 'representatives' met as the 'persons in whom' their communities are united and thus it can be argued that their authority depended on their speaking the mind of the Church. Such a council could also pronounce an anathema, in this case on the authority of the power to bind and loose entrusted to its member bishops as successors of the Apostles.[63] But these assumptions came under stress. In the late Middle Ages in the West the balance of power between Pope as monarch and assembled bishops in council became the subject of controversy, so that it was more difficult to see decisions as representing consensus. The reformers of the sixteenth century would not countenance the possibility of a council's making decisions which would add to Scripture by binding the faithful to rules and beliefs not set out there. No one's faith can be 'bound' by a

---

[61] See K. Riessner, *Die Magnae derivationes des Uguccione da Pisa* (Rome, 1965), and H. Heitmeyer, *Sakramentenspendung bei Häretikern und Simonisten nach Huguccio* (Rome, 1984).

[62] Cited in Congar, 'Quod omnes tangit', p. 269.

[63] From the sixth century it became possible to distinguish anathema from excommunication, with anathema separating completely from the body of Christ while excommunication only excluded its subject from the sacraments. Gratian, *Decretum*, II, canon 106.

council unless what it says can be confirmed out of Scripture; councils cannot make a rule of faith, says the Anglican Tyndale.[64]

A more recent model, seeking to avoid talk of finality in conciliar decrees, has been one of simply 'meeting for mutual counsel and support'. That was the ideal which the Lambeth Conferences of Anglican Churches set before themselves from 1867, but not without anxious preliminary discussion. It was an ideal framed in order to rationalise an already inherently painful situation of tension between unity and autonomy among the provinces of the enlarging Anglican Communion. There was great anxiety to prevent interference by the mother church in England (which it was feared would be possible through the medium of a council with power to bind); and also to avoid any risk of a majority view being imposed by such a council everywhere in the Anglican Communion. So when the Lambeth Conference called itself 'conference' not 'council', that reflected a conscious concern to stop the making of decrees or decisions which would be binding locally everywhere. This particular structure was set up at a time (in the mid-nineteenth century), and within a polity (the episcopal), where the representatives of local churches who would meet were naturally bishops. And it was also, within such a system, relatively easy to see how each province under its metropolitan or primate might remain autonomous in certain matters within a single communion.

More recent models still look different again. The World Council of Churches calls itself a 'council' but does not seek to mimic the ancient councils of the Church. Nor can it, because it embraces many different polities, and those who represent their local churches in it do so on many different understandings of the manner in which they 'represent'. Again, no binding decisions can be made by such a 'council'.

Degrees of bindingness

Bindingness might be thought to vary in degree, depending on whether it fell into the sphere of faith, order or discipline. Formal expressions of faith such as the Niceno-Constantinopolitan Creed have been authorised from time to time, with the intention that they

---

[64] Tyndale, Cranmer, Whitaker and a host of others in the Anglican community in the sixteenth century agree that Scripture is the guide and judge of all that councils do, and that they can have no authority to go against it.

should be binding on all Christians, and with provisos against their being altered. We have seen that rules about order in the Church, and certainly about liturgy, may vary to some degree locally, and be binding in one place but not another. In the case of morals or discipline, sanctions may change. (Attempted suicide may be always a sin, but at some times and in some places it has been punishable by law, in others not.) There may even be tensions or seeming conflicts between councils in their intention to bind. Eck in the sixteenth century comments that *concilia plenaria* can determine *varie*, according to the 'quality and condition of times, persons, etc.', so long as it is without prejudice to the faith.[65] There can also in principle be variation in the appropriate sanctions accompanying a binding decision. It might be deemed a condemnation to damnation to disobey; it might be deemed no more than a misbehaviour deserving a minor discipline.

The question of degrees of bindingness, and that of variation in conciliar decrees, is linked to the possibility that a council may err. Because of the nature of their conciliar ecclesiologies, Orthodox and Roman Catholic thinking on this issue has been, of necessity, generally hard-line. If a true council acts under the guidance of the Holy Spirit, it cannot be conceded that the Holy Spirit would allow the Church to go wrong, sometimes for many generations. Moreover, chaos would ensue if no one could be sure which conciliar decisions were to be relied upon. Eck in the sixteenth century says, 'Take away the authority of councils, and everything in the Church is ambiguous, doubtful, *pendentia*, uncertain.'[66] The Orthodox have taken the view that the early Ecumenical Councils laid foundations which cannot be changed. Where difficulties have arisen later they have, as we have seen, sought solutions by 'economy'.

By contrast, the sixteenth-century Protestant reformers stressed that councils are made up of men and men make mistakes.[67] The Anglican argument, from the period of the formulation of the Thirty-Nine Articles, has also been that councils may err (Article 21); for there are visible contradictions in their decrees. There was much early Anglican underlining of the importance of consonance with Scripture as providing the test of all conciliar decrees in case they contained errors, as well as in case they contained additions.

Another, more recent and potentially ecumenically helpful way of

---

[65] *Enchiridion*, ed. P. Fraenkel, *C.Cath.* 34 (1979), p. 41.   [66] *Ibid.*, p. 38.   [67] *Ibid.*

looking at bindingness, is in terms of the notion that a council's deliberations are themselves in 'process'. G. Baum, writing on Vatican II's constitution of the Church, points to 'the doctrinal development that has taken place in the Council' while the documents it produced 'were being discussed and composed'.[68] This can be seen as an important recognition that conciliar decrees form a stage in the process of reception and their bindingness has to be weighted in that light.

Legislation

Although Vatican II teaching on collegiality concerns *magisterium* as much as legislative power, the making of laws by councils presents special problems of bindingness. The Second Vatican Council came to the conclusion that there are two ways in which the college of bishops of the Roman Catholic Church may act as a source of law. The first is in an Ecumenical Council; the second is in their united action as bishops dispersed all over the world.[69] It was important to the theology of the Second Vatican Council that these ways of acting should be seen not as something which may change from age to age, but as arising from the nature of the college of bishops itself, and therefore perpetual. It can be argued that this makes it impossible for the college to delegate its legislative powers, and that that in turn means that in practice the Pope will be the personal legal source, with the college of bishops acting through him as a united whole. In other episcopal systems the synod itself may be seen as the source of law, with the complication (which makes itself strongly felt in Anglican provinces) that ecclesiastical legislation may have to be ratified by a secular legislature, since matters of property and other issues overlapping with secular concerns will be covered by it.

Laws thus made are legally binding (on various understandings of their enforceability) in the geographical area which the council represents. They can also be changed and thus they are recognised *de facto* to be essentially human rather than divine. So neither in the making of laws in the Church, nor in their temporary variation or long-term alteration, is it perhaps possible to be sure that anything more than a 'human' obligation is involved. 'The legislator has the

[68] G. Baum, 'The constitution of the Church', *Journal of Ecumenical Studies*, 2 (1965), 1–30, p. 3.
[69] Ratzinger, p. 51, *LG* 22.

prerogative of making the law, but how far it does or does not oblige must be left up to God.'[70] Erasmus here puts his finger on a central difficulty of any theory that the Church or churches have power to vary the provisions of laws enacted in due order within their own body or bodies in such a way that those laws are also varied in the sight of God. One solution is to see the legislative process itself as extending beyond the making of law.[71] After the law is made, there must be a promulgation, so that the law is known to the people. Finally, there must be approbation and acceptance of the law by those who are to be affected by it – in short, its reception.[72] ('Leges, instituuntur cum promulgantur, firmantur cum moribus utentium approbantur.')[73] In modern ecclesiastical legislating in many churches, this approbation and acceptance may come into play before the actual making of the law, in discussions of the way it should be framed.[74]

Questions arise here about the status of laws which have been made by due process in one communion or ecclesial body or church, in another – in cases where their subject is not merely of local relevance but concerns a matter of faith or universal order or morals. The locally framed legislation does not create by its own authority a new necessity for the whole Church, or indeed for its own (since it can be changed). But the wider Church may come to recognise and accept that necessity.

Paradoxes can arise from the fact that the Church 'is juridically ordered, and yet its true bond of unity is communion in charity'.[75] Law by due process has its place, but its place is within the community's willing acceptance and its force is ultimately given to it by the community and not by coercion by a higher ecclesiastical authority.[76]

---

[70] Erasmus, *Ichthyophagia, Opera* VI.1055, i.796,663, Verkamp, p. 39.
[71] By due process which may vary from place to place and time to time and circumstance to circumstance.
[72] See W. Ullman, *Origins of the Great Schism* (London, 1948, repr. 1967), pp. 191–213; Tierney, *Foundations of the Conciliar Theory* (Cambridge, 1955), pp. 220–37; Zabarella, *Lectura super Clementinis* (Venice, 1487).
[73] Gratian, *Decretum.* IV.c.3.
[74] A recent case in point is the debate about the legislation concerning the ordination of women in the Church of England in 1991–2.
[75] L. de Echevarría, 'The theology of Canon Law', *Concilium*, 8 (1967), 5–8.
[76] 'The canonist ... although he knows that there is a theology at the heart of Canon Law also knows that any social ordering has its own autonomy, its own rules, concepts and expression, and that its various canons, articles and laws form their own system, orientated

A more extreme manifestation of the recognition of the human limitations of the making of law in the life of a church is the strong Orthodox sense that legislation cannot be adequate to express the full divine mystery of the Church. That has resulted in the absence of any strong drive, comparable with that in the Roman Catholic Church, to bring together systematically a comprehensive body of canon law; Orthodox canons have mostly been framed to meet specific needs as they have arisen.[77] Another and different lesson is being learned by Anglicans as they struggle with the question of legislating province by province for the ordination of women, where there is not yet even local consensus as to whether the authority to change the law to make it possible is in fact vested in the churches.

It is possible to take the view that autocephalous churches may make their own rulings, provided that they do not violate truths of faith and that they take into consideration previous canon law. In Orthodox teaching and practice, that has led to a good deal of the inconsistency already noted, because it rests upon an ecclesiology which is not wholly clear. That is to say autocephalous churches are in fact acting both as provinces competent to vary but not to change canon law; and as distinct ecclesial bodies competent to take a view of the ecclesial standing of other bodies calling themselves churches.

EXISTING CONCILIAR STRUCTURES IN THE DIVIDED CHURCHES

The Roman Catholic system

In present-day Roman Catholic canon law the regular conciliar functions of the episcopate[78] are discharged in meetings of bishops chosen by the episcopal conferences throughout the world to represent them (Canon 346.1). Such a synod is called by the Bishop of Rome, who ratifies the election of its members, settles topics for discussion in advance of the meeting, determines the agenda, presiding in person (or through others), concludes, transfers, suspends and dissolves it (Canon 344). The synod has responsibility only as long as

---

to the implementation of particular matters.' T.J. Urresti, 'Canon Law and theology: two different sciences', *Concilium*, 8 (1967), 12.

[77] J. Meyendorff, *Orthodoxie et catholicité* (Paris, 1965), pp. 99–100.

[78] As distinct from any extraordinary council which may be called from time to time, such as Vatican II.

it is in existence. Once it is concluded by the Bishop of Rome, that responsibility ceases (Canon 347).

This series of Canons falls within the section on the hierarchy of the Church, which in its turn forms the second part of the section on the people of God. The Pope and the other bishops are understood to be agents of the Church, and the crucial questions concern the relationship of the authority of one to the other, that is, the way in which 'this undeniable duality is represented as the one authority in the one Church'.[79] This has been the classic tension in the Roman Catholic Church since the last mediaeval centuries, when papal claims to plenitude of power enlarged and a 'conciliarist' reaction set in. The present solution is to regard the representatives of the college of bishops who serve in the synod as the Pope's advisers as helping him discharge his office of leadership in the universal Church.

There is still a good way to go in making the balance of episcopal and primatial authority clear and workable. The Second Vatican Council considered the history of the holding of councils 'in order to settle conjointly, in a decision rendered balanced and equitable by the advice of many, all questions of major importance'. It discussed the relationship of St Peter's successor and the bishops, 'the successors of the apostles', in terms of their communion with one another and the bond of unity, charity and peace which unites them. But it also insists that 'the college or body of bishops has for all that no authority unless united with the Roman Pontiff, Peter's successor, as its head, whose primatial authority ... over all, whether pastors or faithful, remains in its integrity'. The Roman pontiff is seen as retaining to himself personally a 'full, supreme and universal power over the whole Church ... which he can always exercise unhindered'. The college of bishops, on the other hand, has 'supreme authority over the universal Church' only 'together with their head, the Supreme Pontiff, and never apart from him'.[80] So in the present Roman Catholic system the decrees and decisions of the synod of bishops are deemed to be made by the delegation of papal powers, rather than to derive from the college of bishops itself.[81]

Primatial authority in decision-making stands in at least three

---

[79] Cf. Ratzinger, pp. 47ff.   [80] *LG* 22.

[81] Ratzinger, p. 50. Cf. Tillard, *The Bishop of Rome*, p. 13, who suggests that 'Catholic theology' on 'the status of episcopal conferences' since Vatican II 'has been quite incoherent', p. 13.

(though overlapping), main relationships: to that of the primate's brother-bishops in whom their own churches meet; to that of councils themselves; and also to that of the whole people of God. It could be asked at the opening of Vatican II whether an ecumenical council was still needed after the establishment of the dogma of the Pope's infallibility.[82] But Vatican II itself brought about the 'shift in emphasis by which one now understands the Pope's function by looking at the bishops and not the other way round'; this 'ties in with ... the movement from an ecclesiology starting with the idea of the universal Church divided into portions called dioceses, to an ecclesiology which understands the Church as the communion of all the local churches'.[83] At the same time there came into being a clearer understanding that the local churches are above all portions of 'the people of God'.

A council cannot be anything other than a periodic event. Indeed, it can be argued that it should be 'something rare and exceptional in the life of the Church' which 'can thus justify for this special case a bishop's lengthy absence from his see'.[84] On the other hand, as the Church of England has discovered, it is difficult for a General Synod meeting regularly for only a few days at a time to frame satisfactory legislation in its actual discussions. The most that can be hoped for is some cursory debate on texts placed before it, and the taking of a majority vote. In a worldwide communion or a future united Church these problems must be exacerbated by distance and the time it takes to travel.

The Roman Catholic Church's response to all these calls for adjustment and balancing of roles and contributions is still under consideration. It has been suggested that individual bishops' conferences might discuss the proposed agenda of the united synod and make their own local conciliar decisions, so that their delegates would go to the synod itself with their mandate. That might, in effect, make each synod an ecumenical council, because it would be as though the whole college of bishops had been present. The drawback would be that there would be no means of reconciling

---

[82] Tillard, *The Bishop of Rome*, p. 32.   [83] *Ibid.*, p. 37.

[84] Ratzinger, p. 53. Were a regularly held synod regularly to extend throughout a substantial period of time it would have the effect of taking a bishop away from his diocese so much that he could easily not carry out the primary local pastoral task upon which his function as minister of unity in the wider Church depends. The Council of Trent restored the bishop's duty to reside in his diocese, *CT* Session VI, 13 January, 1547, *Conciliorum Oecumenicorum Decreta*, p. 682.

differences at the synod itself, since none of the delegates would be allowed to change his position as a result of discussion there. There could be no coming to a common mind. So there remain at present intractable tensions here between the claims of local and universal.

The Orthodox

The Orthodox churches test their theology of councils against the principles evident in the period of the early Ecumenical Councils. Synodical gatherings have remained important since. The ecclesial focus resides in the local community with its bishop. This is the one Church in each place, present universally in each locality. Within this order, which is seen as a mystery as well as a structure, is also held the institutional structure in which local churches are grouped geographically with their metropolitan. The local churches can meet in synods, so that they can make common decisions. That is in principle possible above all in ecumenical synods, 'which are the supreme authority in the Church, and the voice through which the catholic Church speaks, in which there is a constant effort to preserve and strengthen its unity in love'.[85]

At the Council of Florence, there was discussion as to where authority to decide to unite with Rome might lie. 'However much the Roman Church counts (*valeat*)', it was argued by the Greeks, 'it counts less than an ecumenical synod of the universal Church.'[86] At the same time, the Greeks assembled at the Council could not make a decision binding on their churches without reference; 'that is not for us to answer, but the whole Eastern Synod'.[87] So Greeks and Latins came to the council on different understandings. The Greek delegates did not, and could not, have the 'ample faculty to act' which Eugenius IV was empowered by his office to grant to the individuals he sent as pontifical legates.[88] On the other hand, although Eugenius could give his delegates authority to make decisions, the Roman side had to concede that union could not be effected by direct or vicarious Papal *fiat*. Only a council could bring it about. It is *maxima necessaria* that there should be a council, and anyway the Greeks require it, explains a letter of Eugenius' delegates.[89]

---

[85] *Old-Catholic Orthodox Conversations.* III/2, 26.   [86] *CF* Vi., p. 159.
[87] See J. Gill, *The Council of Florence* (Cambridge, 1959), p. 267.
[88] *CF* Ii., p. 36.   [89] *CF* Ii.48.

The chief bone of contention on the Western side was whether a Universal Synod or General Council has power directly from Christ (*immediate a Christo*) to make decisions, or whether papal authority must be exercised as standing between Christ and the council. John of Torquemada argued that if a synod makes a decision when the Pope is not personally present, it does so, not on any authority which it receives directly from Christ, but on the authority of the Roman Pontiff. He cites Aquinas on the point.[90] In a sense, this was a domestic issue, currently controversial in the West and carrying no force for the Greeks themselves. But it compounded for both sides the question of the authority the Council of Florence could have to decide for union. In essence the Greeks could accept only the decision of a universal council, representing the universal Church, but it must first be clear to them that the meeting at Florence was such a council. The Latins in general could accept only a decision which, although conciliar, had its ultimate ecclesial authority on earth in the decision of the Bishop of Rome, for as Andrew of Escobar forcefully puts it, 'it belongs to him alone to decide'.[91]

A dimension of the question 'who has authority to decide?' which was, if anything, even more important to Greeks than to Latins, was that of the universality of the Church through time.[92] The question of authority to decide, then, remained fundamentally unresolved between the two sides, because they were assuming different ecclesiologies and lodged the focus of ecclesial identity in different places. For the Greeks it was a universality stretching back in the tradition and embodied in the present in the common mind of a Church which must always be obedient to that tradition; which could make no changes; which must, as a matter of principle, resist development; and which profoundly believed itself to enshrine catholicity already. For the Latins it was a universality of the 'mother church' whose ecclesial focus was the Bishop of Rome. He is able to make binding decisions and definitive pronouncements, to delegate authority which is nevertheless always his, to say, 'where I am, there is the Council of all Christians', even if he says it with the provisos,

---

[90] *Contra impugnantes Dei cultum et religionem*, 4 and *CF* IVi.9.   [91] *CF* IVi, no.46.

[92] It came as something of a shock to Martin Luther when, early in his career as reformer, he approached the Orthodox in the belief that they would be sympathetic to the reformers' case against Rome, only to find himself smartly criticised for extolling the value of 'private interpretation', and told that there could be no 'correction' of tradition. See Colin Davey, *Pioneer for Unity: Metrophanes Kritopoulos and Relations between the Orthodox, Roman Catholic and Reformed Churches* (London, 1987), pp. 51 and 57–8.

'with the Emperor and the Patriarch and especially when all the patriarchs and cardinals are there'.[93]

An agreed statement on *Conciliarity and Primacy* framed by the Orthodox–Roman Catholic Consultation in the United States in 1990 contains a useful definition of the *status quo* in terms acceptable today to both East and West. 'It is the synod which, together with the primate, gives voice and definition to the apostolic tradition' (6). 'The fullest synodal expression of the Church's universal reality is the gathering of bishops from various parts of the world in "ecumenical council", to deal with questions of urgent and universal importance by clarifying and defining the "ecumenical" faith and practice of the apostolic tradition.'[94]

Councils in early Protestantism

The place of councils was important in early Protestant discussion for two reasons. There was a hope at first that a General Council might be called to reform the Church. Secondly, there was a series of attempts within the Protestant movements to resolve differences amongst themselves by holding meetings for mutual consultation.

Luther's discussion of the first possibility was conducted with growing reservations. There was also Anglican concern in the sixteenth century, among the reformers, that councils called by a Pope could not be free.[95] The bishops who came to it would be all the Pope's men and must vote as he directs.[96] There were attempts to show that, apart from the earliest councils, a secular sovereign has normally conferred validity upon the proceedings by his summoning of the council and by his ratification of its decrees.[97] Luther argued that councils are human, and therefore inevitably imperfect and prone to error; that the Holy Spirit cannot be constrained by any such human institution as a council must be; that experience shows that the saintliness of the participants in a council need be no guarantee of its freedom from error; that truth is not necessarily arrived at by majority vote; that the 'unanimity' test of Vincent of Lérins is itself not infallible, for the only true test is conformity with

---

[93] *CF* Vi.26.   [94] *Greek Orthodox Theological Review*, 35 (1990), 217–20.
[95] See Greenslade, 'The English Reformers', pp. 101, 104.
[96] Jewel, PS 3.205.   [97] Rogers PS 3.205.

the Word of God. God's action in a council is of a prophetic sort, and may turn out unexpectedly.[98]

Alongside this assault upon the powers of councils to settle disputes reliably (that is, upon the truth-claims which may be made for their decrees), runs a series of attacks upon their ecclesiality. Luther thought a council was not the Church in any substantial sense, but only *per accidens*. (Though it has the attribute of 'representing' the Church as she speaks through it: *representans ... per se loquendo*.)[99] Moreover, he is convinced that if a council were to be held, it would not be ecclesial at all if it were presided over by the Pope, for that would mean that it would be in the Devil's hands.[100] Calvin could take in some respects a more sanguine view but he did not think councils could represent the Church. Like Luther he held that the conclusions of a council could have authority only in so far as they were scriptural, that is, they could have no authority in their own right. And like Luther, he denied that the Holy Spirit could be bound by councils.[101]

The second area of conservative Protestant thought on the subject of councils concerned formal and informal meetings among Protestants to try to resolve differences between parties. As early as 1520, in his *Address to the Nobility*, Luther was arguing for an attempt to unite his own reformers with the Bohemians.[102] In 1525 a Colloquy was held at Marburg with the purpose of resolving differences between Swiss reformers, those of Strasburg and the Lutherans. This first formal conference for unity in the history of the Reformation foundered partly over the Eucharist, as others were to do. But it was also difficult to go forward because it was as yet unclear whether all participants were willing to remain out of communion with the Roman Catholic Church. It was, in other words, hard to say whether the meeting was between parties or churches.[103]

During the 1530s and 1540s Bucer and Melanchthon worked energetically for union, but with differing *foci*. Bucer wanted especially to see Protestants unite. Melanchthon wanted above all to reunite the Lutherans with the Catholic Church, but with a Church which had acknowledged her errors and joined the reformers in

---

[98] So as to keep the Church humble and make her recognise her dependence upon him. D. Fischer, 'Ministères et instruments d'unité de l'Eglise dans la pensée de Luther et de Calvin', *Istina*, 30 (1985), 25ff.
[99] WA 39i, 187.   [100] Fischer, 'Ministères', p. 27.   [101] *Ibid.*, pp. 27–9.
[102] WA VI.454–5.
[103] On all this, see McNeill, *Unitive Protestantism*, especially p. 143.

reform.[104] Neither was happy in principle with disunion in the *regnum Christi*. Bucer thought it the most serious wrongdoing possible to fight against the union of the Church (*sic oppugnare ecclesiae unionem*).[105] And he clearly conceived that union as consisting not in the reconciliation of a number of Churches, but in the oneness of a single Church. It thus remained very difficult for reformers to conceive of 'Church' in its universality without reference to Rome, even if Rome was thought of in highly negative terms. Calvin can admit that some Roman congregations are true churches of Christ. He argues that it is the Roman Church as a whole which is in error.[106]

Calvin was drawn, partly by Bucer, into an interest in union activities among Protestants, and he was relatively active in this connection during his Strasbourg years, and increasingly after the opening of the Council of Trent.[107] Thomas Cranmer launched a project to bring a conference together (1547–50), during the minority of Edward VI, when he had good freedom of action. Melanchthon would not be drawn and the scheme collapsed. The most obvious failures were to arrive at any constitutional basis on which the churches might meet, and to mend the continuing separation of Lutherans from Reformed.

The Anglican Lambeth Conference

William Laud's *Conference* with Fisher the Jesuit in 1622 represents a new departure in Anglican thought because Laud gave serious thought to the question of the powers of independent action of provincial or national synods representing only part of the universal Church. The problem of *partes* of the Church finding themselves in particular difficulties had been sharply at issue in the sixteenth century. Georgius Cassander (1513–66), for example, wrote a *Consultatio* at the Emperor's request in 1564, to try to bring peace between his Roman Catholic and Protestant subjects, in which he refers to the *ecclesiae partes*.[108] It was at exactly the period of Laud's

---

[104] *Ibid.*, pp. 144, 149.
[105] *Briefwechsel der Brüder Ambrosius und Thomas Blaurer*, ed. T. Schiess, 3 vols., vol.I.203.
[106] To Sadoleto, *CR* 33.403.
[107] See, for example, a letter of 1450 to Bullinger, *CR* 39.28ff. on the importance of cultivating *societas* and *amicitia* among Christian ministers, so that their churches may 'faithfully agree together'. See, too, McNeill, *Unitive Protestantism*, p. 195.
[108] *Opera* (Paris, 1616), p. 1013.

debate with Fisher that the Sacred Congregation for the Propagation of the Faith was founded by Gregory XV (1621–3) to be
responsible for coordinating the Church's missionary work
throughout the world *per partes*; in Protestant Europe; in the new
mission-fields of America, Asia, Africa; in relations with the Orthodox Churches.[109] There was recognition here that these geographically distinct and spiritually various areas were going to
present local difficulties which would need carefully coordinated
oversight if unity was to be held together. Laud was confronting the
problem which the Congregation was set up to prevent in the new
mission-fields and to try to solve elsewhere: of actual division. 'The
making of canons, which must bind all particular Christians and
Churches, cannot be concluded and established', he said, except in a
General Council.

He considers two possibilities: that a General Council, once
called, might not be able to make up its mind; and that a General
Council 'by reason of manifold impediments' could not be called. In
the first case, 'if being called, they will not be of one mind', he
suggests that 'that very not agreeing is a shrewd sign that the other
spirit hath a party there against the Holy Ghost'. He is optimistic
that in all fundamental matters Scripture is 'able to settle unity and
certainty of belief', and he argues that *in non necessariis*, in and about
things not necessary, there ought not to be a contention to a
separation.

In the second case, when a situation arises – as it had done in the
sixteenth century – when there is an emergency with which only a
General Council can deal, but it is not possible to hold one, the
Church must pray for such a council and either wait for it, 'or else
reform itself *per partes*, by national or provincial synods'. He con-
tends that that ought not to be a startling idea.[110] It is 'as lawful for a
particular Church ... to reform what is amiss in doctrine or
manners' as it is for it to 'publish or promulgate' the catholic
faith.[111] It is surely better to do that than wait?[112] He cites Jean
Gerson as his authority for saying that a Church may be reformed
per partes.[113] Laud sees this as an emergency measure only and not as

[109] *Sacrae Congregationis de Propaganda Fide Memoria Rerum*, ed. J. Metzler (Rome, 1971), I.79ff.
[110] William Laud, *Works* (Oxford, 1849), 2.235 (XXVI.14), cf. *The Acts and Monuments of John Foxe*, ed. J. Pratt (London, 1877), 5.138–42, on Henry VIII's grounds for rejecting the papal invitation to a Council at Mantua in 1537.
[111] Laud, *Works*, 2.167 (XXIV.1–2).   [112] *Ibid.*, p. 169 (XXIV.2).
[113] Jean Gerson, *De Concilio Generali*, 1.

a warrant for independent provincial action at large. And his *partes ecclesiae* are conceived of rather like Cassander's, as geographically 'local' churches within one Body, rather than as the miscellaneous *partes* of a broken body.

Herbert Thorndike (1598–1672) took up the question of the independent action of 'parts' of the Church, again without entering seriously into the question whether such 'parts' may by their action constitute themselves distinct 'churches' in the sense of separate ecclesial bodies. He discusses a 'provincial' structure in terms of the question of the seniority of metropolitans in ancient tradition, derived from the practice of giving special honour to those churches which were founded by the Apostles.[114] But the main thrust of his argument is an insistence that no 'part' of the Church can be right to act independently in a way which sets unity at risk:

> The unity of the Church being of God's law, and so enabling to limit the terms upon which the power of the Church is held and exercised by canonical right; it cannot be in the power of any part to cast off those laws, by which it is bounded within the compass of God's law, at pleasure: because they are the conditions, upon which the unity of the whole stands; which no part can say they will renounce.[115]

'Divine institution', he believes, 'ordereth all Churches to be fit to constitute one Church, which is the whole.'[116] He wrote in the heat of the contemporary English debate between Presbyterians and those who thought bishops essential, but he puts his finger on a problem of wider importance. In his own view a body which does not act as a 'part' of a single Church but wants to call itself a 'church' independently 'is founded merely upon human usurpation, which is schism'.[117] That is to say, it is not a church at all. It places itself still further in breach of unity than a 'part' which seeks to act independently 'at pleasure', and Thorndike would want to deny it any ecclesial status. 'Which is the true Church remains invisible, so long as it remains in dispute', he adds.[118]

Like Thorndike, Henry Hammond thinks that independent

---

[114] H. Thorndike, 'The laws of the Church', in *An Epilogue to the Tragedy of the Church of England, Works* (1952), vol. 4, p. 431 (III.20), cf. William Beveridge, *Codex Canonum Ecclesiae Primitivae, Works* (Oxford, 1848), Book II, Chapter 5.

[115] Thorndike, 'Laws of the Church', p. 464, III.20.   [116] Thorndike, *ibid.*

[117] *Ibid.*, p. 918 (III.49), cf. F.R. Bolton, *The Caroline Tradition of the Church of Ireland* (London, 1958), p. 65, on Ussher's scheme of synodical government to meet the Presbyterian challenge.

[118] *Ibid.*, p. 893, III Conclusion.

decision-making *per partes* without a catholic intention is schismatic, and may threaten the claim of a community to be a true church at all.[119] Butler (1692–1752), in his Sermon to the Society for the Propagation of the Gospel, emphasises the duty of all Christians and all 'particular' churches to act for unity. Christians, he says, ought to 'take advantage of an occasion of union, to add mutual force to each other's endeavours in furthering their common end'.[120]

In 1863 John Colenso, Bishop of Natal, appealed to the British Privy Council against a judgement of his own archbishop deposing him for his opinions.[121] The case raised a principle of provincial jurisdiction which prompted the Canadian bishops to declare themselves 'disturbed by recent declarations in high places in our Mother-land', in reference to the Colonial branches of the mother church.[122] They proposed as a means of ensuring that the decisions affecting provinces or the whole Communion were not made in the English Convocation without the participation of those they would subsequently touch, that there should be a 'National Synod of the Bishops of the Anglican Church at home and abroad'.[123] This they saw as a 'means ... by which the members of our Anglican Communion in all quarters of the world should have a share in the deliberations for her welfare, and be permitted to have a representation in one General Council of her members gathered from every land'.[124] The enterprise was conceived by the Canadians at this stage as essentially conciliar, indeed as the next best thing to 'the assembling of a General Council of the whole Catholic Church' which they recognised to be 'at present impractical'.[125]

The proposal was taken seriously and discussed in both the Lower and the Upper House of the English Convocations. There strong prejudices emerged on the subject of councils, and both clergy and bishops expressed views much coloured by sixteenth-century and subsequent Anglican theology.[126] Canon Seymour was concerned

119 Henry Hammond, *Of Schism*, ed. J. Fell (Oxford, 1849), p. 213.
120 Joseph Butler, *Sermons on Public Occasions, Works*, ed. J.H. Bernard (London, 1900), vol.I, p. 214.
121 See *Historical Records of the Church of the Province of South Africa*, ed. C. Lewis and G.E. Edwards (1934), pp. 310–56.
122 They regarded recent events as 'tending to shake the conviction, always so dear to us, that we in the Colonies were, in all respects, one with the Church of our parent country'. Printed in R.T. Davidson, *Origin and History of the Lambeth Conferences, 1867 and 1878* (London, 1888), p. 32.
123 *Ibid.*, pp. 34–5.   124 *Ibid.*, p. 33.   125 *Ibid.*, p. 34.
126 Dr Jebb saw Councils as an 'emergency provision', for 'a temporary consultation between the different branches of Christ's Church'. They make, he thought, 'an appeal to the law

over the question of 'bindingness'. 'I understood', he said, that 'it was a received axiom in the Catholic church that ... articles of faith were not binding upon the whole Church until the Church had received them ... laymen giving their assent in the ancient Church.'[127] One speaker had a vision of the ecumenical possibilities of the beginning which might be made as a 'result of all the bishops in communion with us'. It 'may be that we shall unite, first with the Greek Church, and afterwards with other Churches'.[128]

The Dean of Westminster drew attention to the question[129] who had the authority to call together a General Council, and the order of proceeding it should follow, who ought to be 'judges' in it and 'what doctrines are to be allowed or defended'.[130] In the debates of the Upper House the question of bindingness was a preoccupation. 'That which is not a council of the Church, cannot pretend to do that which it belongs to a council to do – i.e., to lay down any declarations of faith', said the Bishop of Oxford. 'Such declarations are binding when laid down by a properly constituted Council or Synod', he thinks, 'because such bodies have a right to claim the inspiration and ruling presence of him who guides his Church to a right decision. I do not believe that any body but a council, claiming to act as a council, can look for the fulfilment of those promises which are made to the Church.'[131] Archbishop Longley reassured

of God, to the universal belief of the Christian Church'. They enable those who hold 'the divine authority of the Church' to 'say what is the faith of the church from the beginning'. He sees the bishops as acting not as representatives of the people of God but as those having the responsibility of guardianship. *The Chronicle of Convocation*, 13 February 1867, p. 724. Canon Hawkins thought bishops should meet in Council 'to bring them to a better understanding of the common wants of the Church'. *Ibid.*, p. 729. The Dean of Westminster argued that councils had had a place in the early centuries, but their history since had not been encouraging. 'The general course of their steps has been marked by crime and sin'. *Ibid.*, pp. 731–2 and cf. Chadwick, *Orientalia*, p. 397 on this point.

[127] *Ibid.*, p. 778, 14 February.
[128] J.W. Joyce, *ibid.*, pp. 768–9, 14 February. Some anxiety was focussed on the question of the role of the laity. 'I am perfectly sure,' said Canon Blakesley in the debate of February 13th, that 'the English laity would not think themselves sufficiently represented by the Bishops of this Church'. *Ibid.*, p. 719. He also suspects that councils may make 'a wrong authoritative decision' which it then becomes necessary to 'explain by some fresh theory, which in its turn requires new glosses of authority to explain it'. *Ibid.*, pp. 720, 715. He himself saw no need for a council. He thought all necessary questions could be settled by 'a few intelligent, sincere and pious men, having the confidence of their several Churches, with the ocean penny postage and a little correspondence'. *Ibid.*, p. 720.
[129] Richard Field had insisted upon the importance of openness. There must be no 'secret' meeting, a point with which the Dean of Westminster agreed in 1867, and which he criticised in the conduct of the first Lambeth Conference. Richard Field, *Of the Church*, IV.3, V.49, p. 15.
[130] *The Chronicle of Convocation*, 1867, p. 789.   [131] *Ibid.*, p. 804.

the Upper House that at the meeting to be summoned in response to the Canadian bishops' request 'no declaration of faith shall be made, and no decision come to that shall affect generally the interests of the Church'. The meeting should be for 'brotherly counsel and encouragement'.[132] Thus the question of lay participation and 'representativeness' of the laity and clergy need not arise, nor issues of bindingness or of the calling and constitution of councils. What was attempted was something new. 'We have no distinct precedent to direct us'.[133]

But major problems about provincial autonomy have made themselves felt. The 1920 Committee Report on the Development of Provinces took it that 'each national or Regional Church or Province would necessarily determine its own constitutional and canonical enactments'.[134] The 1930 Conference argued that the Anglican Communion belonged, with the Orthodox Churches, to a type of ecclesiastical organisation which stressed regional autonomy rather than 'centralised government'. An ideal picture was drawn of the first four centuries of the 'common life, resting upon a common faith, common sacraments, and a common allegiance to an unseen Head'. On this view, 'every Church in our Communion is free to build up its life and development upon the provisions of its own constitution', with the strict proviso that 'local Churches have no power to change the Creeds of the universal Church or its early organisation'.[135] If there were to be divergence to the point of disruption, 'formal action ... would belong to the several Churches of the Anglican Communion individually', with the advice of the Lambeth Conference 'sought before action is taken by the constituent Churches' carrying 'very great moral weight'.[136]

The Lambeth Conferences have, however, now set a precedent, for a meeting of representatives of autonomous churches in communion with one another, which has the intention of fostering common action and maintaining common faith and order, but neither legislative power to enforce anything agreed in it nor the intention that its Resolutions shall be 'binding' upon all provinces. Such a pattern is certainly one possibility in a future united Church, and indeed meetings of the World Council of Churches are to some degree cast in that mould.

[132] *Ibid.*, p. 807, Davidson, *Origin and History*, p. 7.   [133] *Ibid.*, p. 10.
[134] Lambeth, 1920, Committee Report on the development of Provinces, p. 78.
[135] Lambeth, 1930, Committee Report on the Anglican Communion, I.7.   [136] *Ibid.*, I.8

THE FUTURE

It may be objected that even if there is good precedent for the holding of councils in the churches of the past, the purposes they served may not be appropriate in the united Church to come. There are plentiful declarations of purpose in the literature about councils. The *intentio* of the Council of Basle, as stated in its opening session, was to put all heresy to flight and lighten the darkness with Christ's true light; to bring an end to current strife; to purge vice and corruption. In 1606, the Anglican Richard Field reflected at some length on the matter. General Councils, he thought, were called for three reasons, 'the suppressing of new heresies, formerly not condemned'; 'a general and uniform reformation of abuses crept into the Church'; and 'the taking away of schisms grown into patriarchal Churches, about the election of their pastors'. Today, a Roman Catholic apologist can speak of informing, correcting, and encouraging.[137] One could multiply examples, but the pattern is plain. There is always a peacemaking function in conciliar meeting, a purpose of restoring order and discipline where something has gone wrong; and of clarifying points of faith where those have come into dispute. Such needs are certainly going to continue to make themselves felt in a future united Church, with exactly the same broad division between decisions which must have universal reference (those on points of faith, which can never properly be local); and decisions on points of discipline and order, which may sometimes apply only locally.

The Roman Catholic Church has given more systematic detailed thought to the ecumenical uses of councils in the present stage of the ecumenical process than any other single church has yet done. It reports that existing 'Ecumenical Councils of Churches' and 'Christian Councils' vary a good deal in their activities and in their self-understanding. Commonly, they are 'fellowships of Churches and other Christian bodies which seek to work together, to engage in dialogue and to overcome the divisions and misunderstandings existing among them'. They differ crucially from one another in that Christian Councils (unlike Councils of Churches) may include 'as voting members bodies and agencies other than Churches'. 'Councils [of Churches] are autonomous bodies and no one Council of

---

[137] Ratzinger, p. 61.

Churches is a sub-unit of another.' It may be possible to join a local council without being obliged to join a national one. 'The sole formal authority of Councils is that which is accorded them by constituent members.'[138] These are, in short, 'councils' in only a limited and interim sense, by definition.

Moreover, councils of churches are not themselves churches. And they cannot usurp the position of the churches which comprise their membership. Because they are composed of separated churches they will face issues on which they will not be able to reach consensus. The best that can be done is to safeguard consciences.

A profound respect for the integrity and individuality of its member churches will lead a Council to develop procedures for ensuring that a minority dissent will be adequately expressed for the mutual benefit of the Council, its members and all to whom the Council speaks. It would seem desirable that Councils be constituted in such a way that the various members can all accept the full measure of involvement possible for them.[139]

The World Council of Churches has also given the matter a great deal of thought.[140] At present ecumenism is perhaps at a 'pre-conciliar' stage.[141] Nevertheless, a series of earlier steps can be identified which suggest that there is progress towards ecumenical conciliarity. The New Delhi meeting of the World Council of Churches (1961) stressed the importance of visible unity's local character. The Church is 'made visible as all in each place who are baptised into Jesus Christ and confess him as Lord and Saviour are brought together by the Holy Spirit, into one fully committed fellowship, holding the one apostolic faith, preaching the one Gospel, breaking the one bread, joining in common prayer, and having a corporate life reaching out in witness and service to all'. 'At the same time [Christians] are united with the whole Christian fellowship in all places and all ages in such wise that ministry and members are accepted by all, and that all can act and speak together as occasion requires for the tasks to which God calls his people.'[142]

---

[138] Secretariat for the Promotion of the Unity of Christians, *Réunis à Rome*, 22 February 1975, 4.A.d.v, *More Postconciliar Documents*, ed. A. Flannery (Dublin, 1982), p. 170.

[139] *Ibid.*, pp. 173–7.

[140] 'Reconciled diversity' has been a popular theme among Lutherans; it comes close to the notion of 'conciliar fellowship', with its stress on the preservation of distinct church fellowships as custodians of the divided traditions. *LWF VI*, p. 175, para. 17.

[141] J. Deschner, 'L'Unité visible, communauté conciliare', *Irénikon*, 48 (1975), 468–78, p. 475.

[142] *Report*, p. 116.

The Uppsala meeting (1968) pressed for diversified unity with 'common life and witness, a conciliar fellowship of local churches which are themselves truly united', while recognising that this may be a sign of the future unity of humanity in a conciliar community. Here universal unity is looked to as an ideal, but for the future.

It is not likely to be disputed that any conciliar meeting in a future united Church should, first and foremost, take place as far as it can know under the guidance of the Holy Spirit and in the presence of Christ; that it should be in accordance with Scripture; that it should seek unanimity among its human participants, with each and all freely giving their full consent. Each local church, that is to say, should give its agreement for itself, and all local Churches act together as the one Church. But these are very general principles, as perhaps they must be to be unexceptionable.

The New Testament examples of Acts 15 and Galatians 2 show councils called not routinely but to meet a specific local need, and set a pattern for welcoming representatives in all their diversity as representing the whole Church. There is pooling of experience in discussion. Different viewpoints are raised (Paul advocates diversity, Peter unity, James that it is God's will for both liberty and unity to be preserved). There is a natural sequence in which frank controversy is followed by an open invitation to everyone to contribute to the debate, a listening to the Word of God in relation to everyone's experiences, a considering of Scripture and tradition, and a collective decision of the whole assembly, seeking not just consensus but the will of Christ.[143]

The ancient and traditional conciliar model could be adopted in a future united Church only if it were to meet in and through its representatives speaking for and on behalf of 'local' churches which recognised one another's equality. Protestant churches without a tradition of councils nevertheless almost all find meetings to make decisions together a practical necessity. Such meetings are crucial to the ecclesiology of Presbyterian and Methodist systems. But even Congregationalist and Baptist churches have increasingly tended to form higher unions than the strictly local, within which it is possible to meet in their representatives. Yet as things stand at present, the representatives would come with different understandings of the relationship in which they stood to their churches. There would be

---

[143] Deschner, 'L'Unité visible', pp. 471 ff.

bishops; elected delegates; those holding an office of oversight for a limited period only; some even perhaps (by the standards of others), self-appointed. There would almost certainly be bodies whose ecclesiology prevented them from sending anyone at all. Those present would come with a variety of degrees of authority to speak for their churches, or to enact or take part in decisions which would bind them. The flaw, in short, would be that the meeting remained a gathering not of one Church in its local churches but of many churches seeking agreement. The 'each and all' motif of early conciliar decisions would tend to become 'one church one vote' and democratic decision-making replace consensus as the end in view.

If the churches were to meet in their representatives in this multifarious way, it would remain unclear whether councils are an act of local churches in relationship or an act of the catholic Church, as the early Ecumenical Councils were understood to be. Ecumenism at the local level is not secondary nor merely derivative. It is an attempt to live the life of the Church in each place. 'It has an initiative of its own, and its task is a wider one than merely implementing world-wide ecumenical directives on a small scale.'[144] It is also in practice often the case that 'within these regions the other Christian churches and ecclesial communities often have the highest level of their churchly authority whereby they make those decisions which direct their life and shape their future',[145] so that unity is most readily understood in local life. Nevertheless, local unity expressed in local decision-making cannot be enough, because it cannot act with a fully universal intention.[146]

So we are a long way from seeing our way even to the pattern of conciliar decision-making which will be possible in a future united Church, and still less to the modes of its practical implementation. But we are beginning to see the difficulties more clearly. Above all we are beginning to understand, in the period after a good deal of agreement has been reached and there is confidence about sharing a

---

[144] Secretariat for the Promotion of the Unity of Christians, *Réunis à Rome*, 22 February 1975, I.2. *Vatican II: More Postconciliar Documents*, Ecumenical Collaboration, 22 February 1975, p. 157.

[145] Secretariat for the Promotion of the Unity of Christians, *Réunis à Rome*, 22 February 1975, I.2. *More Postconciliar Documents*, p. 158.

[146] 'With the awareness that in a given place it is the vehicle of the presence and action of the catholic church, which is fundamentally one, the local church will be ready to take care that its free initiatives do not go beyond its competence and are always undertaken within the limits of the doctrine and discipline of the whole Catholic Church, particularly as this touches the sacraments.' *More Postconciliar Documents*, p. 158, para. 2.

common faith, that that alone is not enough to unite divided communities. Here things have not really changed since the period after the Reformation. 'Nor has it been apparent that even the acknowledgement of underlying unity of faith can bring about unity,' Joseph Hall puts it gloomily. Nothing will happen without the will to succeed. 'If, by the universal consent of all, it should appear that both word and sense are entire, that both principles and necessary conclusions thence deduced are undeniably sound, "yet", saith Bellarmine, "there can be no peace with Lutherans".'[147]

---

[147] Joseph Hall, *Roma Irreconciliabilis, Works*, p. 354.

CHAPTER 6

Communion

Most of the issues with which this book has been concerned have a long history of debate within the history of the Church, to which we can look to get bearings. 'Communion' is a relatively recent addition to the technical vocabulary[1] of at least the ecclesiological areas of systematic theology. It does not appear in Roman Catholic usage in the decrees of councils until as late as the Second Vatican Council.[2] Nevertheless it is now central to ecumenical thinking,[3] and we must place it squarely at the end of this enquiry.

That is not easy to do with absolute clarity. 'Communion' is not a univocal term.[4] And its various meanings are not always fully shown even in the most recent work to be related to one another in ways which are themselves unequivocal.[5] There have, however, been some substantial achievements of coordinated definition. The Statement of the Second Anglican–Roman Catholic International Commission, *Church as Communion* (London, 1991) points out that in the New Testament the term 'Communion' (12),

ties together a number of basic concepts such as unity, life together, sharing and partaking. The basic verbal form means 'to share', 'to participate', 'to have part in', 'to have something in common' or 'to act together'. The

---

[1] Apart from the phrase 'the communion of saints' and the well-established range of usages connected with Eucharistic 'communion'. There was some late-mediaeval movement of the idea of the 'communion of saints' (*communio sanctorum*) with which Augustine is most comfortable, towards talk of the *universitas fidelium praedestinatorum*, the brotherhood, gild or community of the predestined, which is Wyclif's preferred framework of reference in the late fourteenth century. See J.T. McNeill, *Unitive Protestantism*, (London, 1964), pp. 25–6.

[2] With the exception of *communio cum Christo* at the Council of Florence. *Conciliorum Oecumenicorum Decreta*, p. 547.

[3] It was a major theme of the Fifth World Council of Churches Conference on Faith and Order in 1993, whose documents are in process of publication.

[4] Congregation for the Doctrine of the Faith of the Roman Catholic Church, *The Church as Communion*, vol. 3, printed in *Catholic International* (September 1992).

[5] There is, for example, a need to integrate 'the concept of communion with the concepts of people of God and Body of Christ'. *Ibid.*, 1. See, too, the list of aspects in the WCC Dublin statement referred to below.

noun can signify fellowship or community. It usually signifies a relationship based on participation in a shared reality (e.g. 1 Corinthians 10:16). This usage is most explicit in the Johannine writings: 'We proclaim to you what we have seen and heard, so that you also may have fellowship with us. And our fellowship is with the Father and with his Son Jesus Christ' (1 John 1:3; cf. 1 John 1:7).[13] In the New Testament the idea of communion is conveyed in many ways. A variety of words, expressions and images points to its reality: the people of God (1 Peter 2:9–10); flock (John 10:14; Acts 20.:8–9; 1 Peter 5:2–4); vine (John 15:5); temple (1 Corinthians 3:16–17); bride (Revelation 21:1); body of Christ (1 Corinthians 12:27; 1 Corinthians 10:17; Romans 12:4–5; Ephesians 1:22–3). All these express a relationship with God and also imply a relationship among the members of the community. The reality to which this variety of images refers is communion, a shared life in Christ (1 Corinthians 10:16–17; cf. John 17) which no one image exhaustively describes. This communion is participation in the life of God through Christ in the Holy Spirit, making Christians one with each other.

The text adds (14) that, it is characteristic of the Apostle Paul to speak of the relationship of believers to their Lord as being 'in Christ' (2 Corinthians 5:17; Colossians 1:27–8; Galatians 2:20; cf. also John 15:1–11) and of Christ being in the believer through the indwelling of the Holy Spirit (Romans 8:1–11).

This relationship Paul also affirms in his description of the Church as the one body of Christ. This description is integrally linked with the presence of Christ in the Eucharist. Those who share in the supper of the Lord are one body in Christ because they all partake of the one bread (1 Corinthians 10:16–17). The dimension of 'abiding in love' together is also strongly in evidence in the New Testament [15].

From this proceeds a

necessary expression in a visible human community ... which suffers with Christ in anticipation of the revelation of his glory (Philippians 3:10; Colossians 1:24; 1 Peter 4:13; Romans 8:17). Those who are in communion participate in one another's joys and sorrows (Hebrews 10:33; 2 Corinthians 1:6–7). There is mutual giving and receiving of spiritual and material gifts, not only between individuals but also between communities, on the basis of a fellowship that already exists in Christ (Romans 15:26–7; 2 Corinthians 8:1–15).[6]

---

[6] The Dublin draft of a working document for the World Council of Churches Conference on Faith and Order held in Santiago de Compostella in August, 1993, presses in addition the implication of all this for sharing in the Church. Printed in *Ecumenical Trends*, 21 (1992), 97ff.

The question at the heart of all this must be whether we are looking to communion of individual persons or communion of churches in a future united Church. If a case can be made, as I believe it can, for the view that churches with a small 'c' are always provisional, and exist only as a specific or local expression of the relationship of individual persons in Christ which is the Church, then the primary communion must ultimately be that of persons. It can be convincingly argued that there is no conflict here: 'the universal communion of the faithful and the communion of the Churches are not consequences of one another but constitute the same reality seen from different viewpoints'.[7]

In the Trinity[8] the relationships between the Persons have three characteristics significant for our purposes, which are uncontroversial for all Christians. First, the Holy Spirit and the Son take their origin from the Father. Secondly, each Person of the Trinity has a relation to the others. Thirdly, each of the Persons is very God and they are coequal.[9] In the Church, too, all individual or local churches must have their origin from the one Church Christ himself founded and thus from Christ. They must all be related to one another. And in a future united Church they will be all equally churches, indeed each will *be* the Church in its place. In all these respects communion is fundamentally a matter of relationships, and of relationships which must be understood in terms of what we glimpse of the divine model of all right relationship.

In another respect an ecclesiology of communion must be Trinitarian. Christ is the founder and Head of the Church and communion in the Church is always with him. And the Holy Spirit moves in the Church, informing its actions and decisions. He is 'the Spirit of Communion'. The CDF document says that the 'mystery of the personal union of each human being with the divine Trinity and with the rest of mankind ... having begun as a reality in the Church on earth, is directed towards its eschatological fulfillment in the

---

[7] Congregation for the Doctrine of the Faith of the Roman Catholic Church, *The Church as Communion*, 10, printed in *Catholic International* (September 1992).

[8] *Church as Communion*, 15.

[9] Outlined in this way by Mark Santer, in reply to a request from Sam Van Culin on behalf of the Anglican Consultative Council, 12 January 1990, that he should write 'on matters of appropriate "restraints in matters of faith and order" which need to be exercised by autonomous Provinces if they are to maintain their life in communion with each other'. Church of England General Synod, Faith and Order Advisory Group paper 91/27, 30 March 1990.

heavenly Church',[10] and thus draws out the implication which must always be central to a 'Trinitarian' view of the Church. The Church's fullness of being, and that of all the persons who make up the Church, is that of the Kingdom to which it looks and for which it now works.

Further: the New Testament is clear that communion with God and fraternal communion among Christians are the inseparable faces of communion in the human and divine ecclesial community.[11] These two axes, the vertical and the horizontal, are complementary.[12] The Bible speaks of a communion in the Church in which there is mutual acceptance (Romans 15:7), a 'making room for' one another (2 Corinthians 7:2), a willingness to defer to one another ('Be subject to one another', Ephesians 5:21). Paul stresses that 'None of us lives, and equally none of us dies, for himself alone' (Romans 14:7). Here the parallels with what we understand of relationship in the Trinity cannot be closely sustained because while all these might be seen to reflect what we understand of the relationships of the Persons of the Trinity, there is a creaturely interdependence in the relationships of the churches in a way there cannot be thought to be in the omnipotence of the Godhead.

And we are pointed to another crucial difference. Churches are not themselves persons.[13] We have been arguing that one of the most important distinctions to make in talking of communion is between the communion of individuals as persons with one another and the communion of ecclesial bodies. There is a great difference which is important here between welcoming or permitting the individual from one church (at least in certain circumstances) to participate fully in another church's Eucharist and two communities celebrating a single Eucharist together.[14] There are plentiful examples of the first, although the details of the rules vary from case to case. In 1717 Archbishop William Wake authorised inter-communion between members of the Church of England and individual

---

[10] Congregation for the Doctrine of the Faith of the Roman Catholic Church, *The Church as Communion*, vol. III, printed in *Catholic International* (September 1992).

[11] J.M.R. Tillard, 'L'Eglise de Dieu est une communion', *Irénikon*, 53 (1980), 451–68. See, *ibid.*, p. 451 on the notion that Vatican II is marked by two ecclesiologies, one hierarchical and the other of 'communion', which proves the dominant one. Tillard sets these out in terms of vertical and horizontal axes.

[12] Congregation for the Doctrine of the Faith of the Roman Catholic Church, *The Church as Communion*, vols. III and V, printed in *Catholic International* (September 1992).

[13] But see Appendix to *Episcopal Ministry* on the corporate person.

[14] 'A Church may by unilateral action welcome members of other churches to share as guests in its Communion services', *ibid.*, p. 18.

members of the Reformed Church of Zurich.[15] In a similar spirit a Methodist minister will welcome to the Eucharist any individual communicating member of another church who is willing to come, and 'any Methodist would willingly take Communion from the priest' of the Roman Catholic, Orthodox or Anglican churches, 'if he knew that the priest were willing that he should'.[16] The second is a different matter. It is much harder to be sure that all Christians mean the same thing by 'being in communion', if that is seen to involve the moving together of the separated churches themselves into a new relationship.[17]

If the goal is to form a single Communion from the many which now exist, so as to recreate the 'communion of communions' of the first undivided churches, that would place the individual Christian of today in a complex interim double relationship to his own and to the potential wider Communion.[18] For example, the individual in an existing Communion might be deemed to be in 'some, though imperfect, communion with another church', even though his own Communion remained still separated from it by 'obstacles . . . to full ecclesiastical communion'.[19] Such talk of 'imperfect' and 'full ecclesiastical' communion in the documents of Vatican II and after[20] and of 'degrees of communion' in other connections, provides an opening for new approaches to the problem of achieving a single worldwide Communion in which the now-separated churches recognise their total interdependence in the one. These have about them an air of compromise and of making the best of a bad job; they are of the interim at best. But they are positive and hopeful.

Less than communion or 'coexisting in division'

In his *Cur Deus Homo* at the end of the eleventh century, Anselm of

---

[15] N. Sykes, *Theology* (May, 1948), p. 176. In the seventeenth and to the nineteenth centuries intercommunion was often needed only in the case of persons living abroad and wanting to receive the sacrament. But that has ceased to be the most common situation.

[16] *Intercommunion*, p. 155, paper by Rupert Davies.

[17] See, on a common participation in the same realities, A. Housiau, 'Incarnation et communion selon les Pères grecs', *Irénikon*, 47 (1974), 457–8.

[18] 'Persons committed to ecumenism are still readily suspected of disloyalty to their own Churches.' Paul Richardson, 'Ecumenism at rest', *Living Stones*, 4 (1) (1992) quoting Walbert Buhlmann, *The Coming of the Third Church* (Slough,1976), p. 219.

[19] Here the Roman Catholic Church. *UR*, 5.

[20] Kilian McDonnell, 'Vatican II (1962–4), Pueblo (1979), Synod (1985): Koinonia/Communio as an integral ecclesiology', *Journal of Ecumenical Studies*, 25 (1988), 399–427, p. 399.

Canterbury approached the question why God became man by suggesting that if we postulate that Christ did not become man and try to explain events without him (*remoto Christo*), we shall find that no other account of things will fit the facts, and we shall have to put the Incarnation back in its place in the economy of salvation. Here we can do something similar by looking at the anomalies which arise if we postulate that anything 'less than communion' can be satisfactory among Christians.

Christians belong to Christ. Christ can have only one Body, and it is his declared will that his people should be one.[21] From that starting-point it has been argued that even when on the surface Churches are divided, an invisible communion or *koinonia* remains, because those who do indeed truly belong to Christ in their own communities must also truly belong to one another even outside those communities. 'Real but incomplete unity' is sometimes spoken of as perhaps inevitable in our fallen human condition, sometimes as a stage on the way to a communion which ought to be more fully realised in this life, and towards which Christians must work. It is thought of as like Augustine's *perfectio currens*, the only perfection which is attainable in this life, and incomplete; but nonetheless a real perfection. Its 'reality' can be thought to consist in the actual visible evidence of cooperation in joint service, in acts of witness, in meeting for worship and prayer. Or it may be seen as real in a deeper sense, of which mutual recognition of a common baptism is an important sign.[22] But in either case, it is incomplete where it stops short of bringing a community of Christians 'into communion' with one another, wherever they are unable to share fully in a common celebration of the Eucharist in one Church. There cannot be the profound commitment to one another which 'communion' implies between churches which agree to remain independent.

The last few decades have seen attempts to speak positively and hopefully of this communion which is not yet complete communion in one Church.[23] In a letter of Cardinal Willebrands on discussions held during his visit to the Orthodox Patriarch, written in January 1969, there is talk of profound communion which, although not yet

[21] John 17:22.
[22] 'All who are baptised in the one Spirit into the one body are united in the Eucharist by this sacramental participation in this same one body.' ARCIC II, *Church as Communion*, 15, citing 1 Corinthians 10:16–7; 12:13.
[23] See McDonnell, 'Vatican II', on degrees of communion and degrees of belonging.

complete, exists here and now between the two sister Churches of Rome and the Orthodox.[24] A letter of Pope Paul VI to the Patriarch Athenagoras speaks of 'communion ... almost complete', though 'still short of perfection'.[25] In ARCIC II's *Church as Communion*, of 1991, we meet the expressions 'real though imperfect communion', 'degree of communion', 'communion ... impoverished'.[26]

In the Anglican–Orthodox Dublin Agreed Statement of 1984 it was realised that Anglicans were able to speak of stages of mutual *rapprochement* by Churches in which full communion could be approached progressively, and authoritative rulings could control the degree of eucharistic sharing which was deemed appropriate at each stage (19). This kind of talk had no meaning for the Orthodox participants, for whom '"communion" involves a mystical and sanctifying unity created by the Body and Blood of Christ', and for whom there 'can be "communion" only between local churches which have a unity of faith, ministry and sacraments' (20). No ecclesial ruling can govern or partition such communion or make it a matter of 'degree'.[27]

Often a form of compromise is made by putting an adjective or some other qualifying term before 'communion'. Thus 'full communion' might be said to exist even when 'each communion recognises the catholicity and independence of the other and maintains its own, and each believes the other to hold the essentials of the Christian faith'. That creates a situation where, 'subject to ... such ... safeguards as local discipline may properly require, members of the one ecclesial body may receive the sacraments of the other'. But the two bodies 'remain autonomous and fraternal, without elevation of the one to be judge of the other'. 'Inter-communion' is still less close, although it may involve some eucharistic sharing. But 'apart from serious intention to seek either organic union or full communion, and in an explicit or implicit disregard of doctrinal differences which exist or are widely believed to exist between the ecclesial bodies concerned [inter-communion] ... runs the major risk of implying that the Lord's intention for his Church is to have a large number of diverse ecclesial bodies, all of which are equally valid or invalid expressions of his will for his people, with the consequence

---

[24] Stormon, p. 207.   [25] Stormon, p. 232.   [26] Paragraphs 2, 30.
[27] The same point arose in the course of the old Catholic–Orthodox Conversations at Chambésy, Bonn and Zagorsk (1977–81).

that the painful realities of division and group rivalry are ignored or condoned'.[28] So at issue here is the question whether any adjective which diminishes communion can be acceptable.

There are various ways in which this falling short of the ideal seems to be understood. It may be argued that it consists in the lack of will for organic unity, if that is understood in terms of a merging of ecclesial entities into one Church structure. Or the 'incompleteness' of imperfect communion may consist in the absence of one or more of the obvious dimensions or marks of unity; agreement in common faith; common sacraments (the administration of which is inseparable from the sharing of a common ministry); common instruments of decision-making.[29]

One way of getting over the difficulty that however we look at it it does not seem satisfactory but only an interim arrangement, is to put the emphasis not on the inadequacy of the incomplete communion but on the provisionality of the churches which make it up. Then it is the churches which need to move together to be a single communion which will need no qualifying adjective.

Sacramental communion and communion of faith

The sacramental nature of the Church itself is inseparable from its character as 'communion'.[30] The defining mark of a single Communion has always been the sharing of one Eucharist. Eucharistic communion rests upon a prior baptismal communion.[31] That already exists as a mark of communion, and much more universally than eucharistic communion in the divided Church. It is widely accepted that 'the same things happen ... wherever and to whomever [baptism] is administered'.[32] So it can be argued that in this respect at least, all who share in the 'holy things' of the sacramental life are made holy through them; because they share in

---

[28] H. Chadwick, 'Full communion with other episcopal churches', *The Churchman*, 3 (1981), 218–28.

[29] These are compatible with the Lambeth Quadrilateral.

[30] The CDF text speals of the universal Church as the 'body' of the churches, and the connection with the Body of Christ is clear.

[31] J. Erickson, Salamanca, pp. 653–77.

[32] H. Fries, 'The ecclesiological status of the Protestant Churches from a catholic Viewpoint', *Journal of Ecumenical Studies*, 1 (1964), 205–6. The exceptions are chiefly churches which hold that only adult believers' baptism can be true baptism, and therefore do not recognise the existing baptism of some of those who come to them.

them together, they are in communion with one another.[33] This is central. If it can be held that the mystery of the sacramental presence of Christ operates in each local Church in its 'life of grace', communion certainly exists in that way between the Churches. But common eucharistic *communio* does not follow a common baptism,[34] for the reasons we have been examining in the chapter on restoring order. Communion remains imperfect so long as the Eucharist in each Church is not recognised by everyone as constituting one Eucharist with all others in such a way that all can celebrate it together.[35]

The Last Supper was the foundation act of the Church, and the Church therefore lives on in eucharistic communities. The Orthodox have taken a significant lead in developing a eucharistic ecclesiology with this strong emphasis.[36] But for the Orthodox a key element in this view is a stress upon the local eucharistic community as already complete, as the Church in each place, possessing Christ fully. That can make external unity seem to be of secondary importance, and not constitutive for the Church because the 'sharing' is mutual.[37] No word in Greek or any of the Slavonic languages corresponds to the word 'inter-communion'. The idea can be expressed only periphrastically.[38] That is because it 'presupposes different Churches ... which are not simply the local congregations of one Church, but denominations'.[39] That is a healthy warning that other churches ought not to be using the word 'inter-communion' (or 'communion' with any other qualification either),

---

[33] ARCIC II, *Church as Communion*, 14. On centrality, see N. Afanasieff, 'La Plénitude de l'Eglise se trouve là ou se célèbre l'eucharistie', in J. Meyendorff, *The Primacy of Peter* (London, 1963), The Church which Presides in Love, 76.

[34] Fries, 'Ecclesiological statur'.

[35] See J. Meyendorff, 'L'Eglises-soeurs. Implications ecclésiologiques du Tomos Agapis', *Istina*, 20 (1975), 35–46, p. 42 on *Anno Ineunte* (1967) sent by the Pope to the patriarch.

[36] J.D. Zizioulas, 'Verité et communion dans la perspective de la pensée patristique grecque', *Irénikon*, 50 (1977), 451–60. H. de Lubac in the Roman Catholic Church has also been important, in developing a Eucharistic ecclesiology with the emphasis on linking the idea of the Church as the body of Christ with the idea of the Eucharist in which the Lord is bodily present and gives us his body as food. See on this Ratzinger, p. 7, and *LG* 26.

[37] The point is conveniently discussed in Ratzinger, p. 9, and see chapter 1' pp. 18ff on what is constitutive for the Church. See, too, the CDF document, 8, which suggests that it is wrong to say that 'every particular Church is a subject complete in itself, and ... the universal Church is the result of a reciprocal recognition on the part of the particular Churches'.

[38] *Intercommunion: The Report of the Theological Commission appointed by the Continuation Committee of the World Conference on Faith and Order together with a selection from the material presented to the Commission*, ed. D. Baillie and J. Marsh (London, 1952), p. 19.

[39] *Ibid.*, p. 18.

because the need to use it is a clear sign that the full sharing is not yet possible.

There is the additional complication that there remain not only the barriers set up by such differences about order, which we have already considered, but also radical differences of sacramental doctrine. If all churches are not celebrating the same thing in the Eucharist, they cannot make Eucharist together.[40] Where such differences do not present stumbling-blocks the lack of unified order may become (in itself) no insuperable problem. 'The whole history of the first ten centuries of Christianity has been precisely a history of schisms and their healing, and the healing was never complete.' Yet it was possible to hold Ecumenical Councils.[41] It has also until recently been true that the various churches which make up the Anglican Communion have been in full eucharistic communion with one another, although they are entirely autonomous and without any unity of government or jurisdiction.[42] That has been possible because they have a shared heritage of sacramental theology. But where these differences are stumbling-blocks, even the existence of an otherwise common faith is sometimes proving not to be enough to found eucharistic communion on.

We have discussed in chapter 3 the problems of maintaining community of faith in the one Church. We looked there at the reasons why it remains one of the greatest difficulties ecumenically to agree what the essentials of that common faith should be, and what may be regarded as legitimately variable locally or in individual conscience. We need now to ask why, while 'communion in the faith is the condition for the full manifestation of charity expressing itself in concelebration', such communion in the faith is a necessary but not in itself a sufficient condition for eucharistic union.[43]

We find the phrase 'communion of profession' (*communio professionis*) in the *Liber Ratisbonensis*, produced in connection with the meeting at Ratisbon in 1541 which came so close to mending the differences which were dividing the reformers and Rome. It is envisaged there not only as a communion of true faith, but also as a communion of lively faith working through love (*vivae fidei per caritatem efficacis*).[44] To this communion belong only those who are

[40] Especially relevant here are differences about the real presence and sacrifice, *ibid.*, p. 27.
[41] Florovsky in a paper presented to the above Commission, *ibid.*, p. 47.   [42] *Ibid.*, p. 24.
[43] Address by Paul VI, July 1967, Stormon.   [44] *CR* 4.201–2.

joined in the 'unity' of this faith, under one Head who is Christ, in the Holy Spirit, and who communicate in spirit in the sacraments. A closely similar notion is found in Latomus, as he seeks to define the Church for Martin Bucer in a text of 1543–5: 'It seems to me that the Church is the communion of the faithful.' He insists on the obedience of such a communion to the Word of God and upon its sharing common sacraments. To secede from that communion of the faithful, which is in every age a communion of common profession with the Fathers, is to be a heretic and to be cut off (*segregatus*) from communion.[45] The position in practice seems to be parallel to that of the relation of baptismal to eucharistic communion. Eucharistic communion presupposes baptismal communion, but baptismal communion does not in itself necessarily make eucharistic communion possible. Analogously, eucharistic communion is an expression of 'communion of profession' or 'common faith', and therefore presupposes it, but common faith does not seem necessarily to make eucharistic communion possible where common order and a common sacramentology are lacking.

Always paramount is the concern to be sure that it is within a church that the celebration is taking place. The World Council of Churches is not itself a church, and so it cannot hold its own Eucharist. A great anxiety which keeps churches apart in the Eucharist is the concern to ensure that it is not compromised in any way by uncertainty about the ecclesial validity of the corporate act of celebrating it. They want to be sure that when they take part in a celebration of Holy Communion they are truly in possession of the Lord's promise that he will live in them and they in him.[46] So, paradoxically, it can be the very seriousness with which it is taken which prevents for the present that eucharistic communion of all Christians in which Christ is present in his one body. When Christians hold off from one another's Eucharists or feel that they cannot admit those from other Churches to full participation they do so out of a deep conviction of the sacredness of the act and of its implications. It is never a decision taken lightly. It cannot be stressed too often that it is no good seeking quick and easy ways to reunion because that security will be missing.[47] The lesson for now must be that there ought to be no rushing of fences; but at the same time no

---

[45] B. Latomus, *Zwei Streitschriften gegen Martin Bucer (1543–5)*, C.Cath., 8, ed. L. Keil (Munster, 1924).
[46] John 6:56. [47] *Intercommunion*, p. 22.

resting satisfied with the glaring anomaly of a common baptism which does not lead to a single Eucharist.

The relationship of unity to communion

Perhaps we may get further by thinking in terms of the community of salvation. The Council of Florence endorsed the view that no one could be saved who did not remain within the bosom of the one Church.[48] 'Outside the *unity* of the Church noone shall be saved from hell', argues Cochlaeus.[49] He thus adds an ecumenically crucial amendment to the principle that there is no salvation outside the Church. His chief concern is to point out to Lutherans the danger of the proliferation of sects, which he thinks will increase out of all control after the death of Luther himself. He pleads that the sectarian spirit is a recipe for damnation; in schism souls are in danger, but to seek peace is profoundly salvific (*saluberrimum*). It seems to him to follow that salvation lies in unity. A similar idea is expressed by Latomus, writing polemically to Martin Bucer. He, too, stresses the damage done to the *communio ecclesiastica*, and the way 'unity is violated', by the secession of its members.[50] He makes the point that no one who divides the Church can be 'in the Church'.[51] 'Nothing in the Church is more necessary to salvation than unity.'[52]

Nicholas Herborn goes a step further still and says that no one who is outside the unity of the Church can participate in the *communis sensus*. To hold common views with those who do so participate is not enough. The *sensus* must derive through the Church universal, its councils, its received custom. On such a view saving faith itself seems to be restricted to those who do not break the unity of the Church.[53] The *Liber Ratisbonensis* (1541) endorses the opinion that the non-divisive are themselves the very foundation-stone of the Church; and the unity of doctrine they preserve sustains the Church 'at least in those things which are necessary to religion and salvation (*pietas et salus*)'.[54] Calvinist teaching comes close to making the same claim. The Belgic Confession of 1561 says that there is no salvation

[48] H. Denzinger, *Enchiridion Symbolorum*, 24th edn (Barcelona, 1946), p. 714.
[49] *Aequitatis Discussio*, C.Cath., 17 (1931), 10–11. 'Extra ecclesiae unitatem nemo a gehenna salvabitur.'
[50] Ed. L.Keil, *C.Cath.*, 8 (1924), 143.   [51] *Ibid.*, p. 15.
[52] *Ibid.*, p. 143. 'Nihil magis necessarium esse ecclesiae ad salutem quam unitatem.'
[53] Ed. Schlagl, p. 51.   [54] *CR* 4.204–5.

outside the one catholic Church, which is a holy congregation or assembly of believing Christians, dispersed over the whole world.[55] Calvin laid heavy emphasis upon the importance of unity in the Church. He clearly saw that it must be one body united to one Head. 'All should unite (*coalescere*) in one body, so that the Church may be one diffused throughout the world, not many.'[56] He argued that Christians have a solemn obligation to maintain communion in one body, for if we break up into different bodies, 'we depart from him also'.[57] He held that this single communion must be maintained even though the Church may have many faults.[58]

We have, then, something more than lip-service being paid on all sides, even in circumstances of painful division, to the principle that the Church as the community of salvation must be one, and constitute a single communion. In what relationship does an imperfect or incomplete communion stand to the unity outside which there can be no salvation? We have seen that Augustine's answer, in dealing with Donatist baptism, was to speak in terms of a validity which is not efficacious until it is brought within the single communion. That again would imply that the Church cannot be truly the community of salvation until it is one.[59] But it cannot so simply be proposed as the solution where we cannot point to one church among those at present existing, reunion with which would resolve the difficulty. If we are working with a model of many true but divided churches, we have to find another way.[60]

Communion and the problem of the weeds

'To be a member of the Catholic Church is to be implicated with some very disreputable people. It is not a community of the pure and worthy, but of the good, the bad and the ugly.' 'To someone who is not a Catholic and who wishes to communicate we should have to put the question: do you really wish to find yourself bound

---

[55] Articles 27–9. J.T. McNeill, *Unitive Protestantism* (London, 1964), p. 80, and Schaff, *Creeds of Christendom*, vol. III, pp. 416–21.

[56] *CR* 34.39.   [57] Commentary on 1 Corinthians 1:13, *CR* 77.316.

[58] Calvin is of course arguing that the Church of Rome, not that of the reformers, is the schismatic. Cf. T. Maruyama, *The Ecclesiology of Theodore Beza* (Geneva, 1978).

[59] Cf. G. Wainwright, 'La confession et les confessions: vers l'unité confessionnelle et confessante des chrétiens', *Irénikon*, 57 (1984), 5–25, p. 8.

[60] Here we come to the possibility that 'application of the term communion to the particular churches taken as a whole' is 'analogical'. CDF document, 9.

up with all these people?'[61] We meet again and again a contrast between two pictures of the Church. On the one side stands the conviction just expressed that the visible communion of the Church on earth fully includes the wheat and the tares (for some of the tares will turn out to be wheat). On the other side stands the conviction 'that there is on earth a little holy flock or community of pure saints under one Head, Christ. It is called together by the Holy Spirit in one faith, mind and understanding. It possesses a variety of gifts yet is united in love without sect or schism.'[62] This communion stands unblemished. It may lie for all practical purposes (and the mainstream reformers of the sixteenth century accepted that) within an 'outward association' of the Church, whose members include 'hypocrites and evil men'.[63] So the visible Church will look as it does to Roman Catholics. But its mixed membership will not be its real membership. Calvin saw the invisibility of the true Church as its shame and humiliation. It ought to be visible. God has withdrawn it from human sight as a punishment for sin.[64] But like all the reformers, he believed that the invisible Church has been revealed and made visible by God in the true preaching and hearing of the Word and in the administration of the sacraments according to the Word.[65] It is therefore possible to point to a Church which is both pure and visible.

For Luther and Calvin, 'communion' had a vigorously social and practical slant, which we ought to set alongside the more mystical notion of the 'communion of saints'. The first places the emphasis on the way relationships among Christians transcend time and unite the living and the dead; the second especially perhaps upon the separation between those who are Christ's and those who are not. (That was important for Augustine, too.) We can speak of 'the communion of saints' and place the emphasis variously on the great whole of the body of the faithful, alive and dead; in Lutheran terms, on the assembly of the saints who share the association of the same Gospel and the teaching of the same Spirit;[66] in Calvinist terms, on the holy congregation or assembly of believing Christians dispersed

---

[61] T. Radcliffe, 'The Demands of the Mass', *The Tablet* (1 December 1990), pp. 1544–6.
[62] Luther's *Large Catechism on the Creed*, Tappert, *The Book of Concord*, p. 417.
[63] *Apologia for the Augsburg Confession*, Articles VII and VIII.
[64] *Institutes* IV.ii.3; cf. *CR* 30.770, where Calvin quotes Augustine, *Ad Vincentium*, Letter 48. See, too, McNeill, *Unitive Protestantism*, pp. 43–4.
[65] Cf. *Augsburg Confession*, VII.
[66] *Apologia for the Augsburg Confession*, Articles VII–VIII,

throughout the world;[67] also in the thought of the sixteenth century, on the communion of the faithful, set apart by and in and for the Word of God (*vacans verbo Dei*) and using the sacraments of the new law;[68] or on the source of unity which expresses itself in the Eucharist and whose agent is the Holy Spirit working through the Gospel.[69] (The concept of communion in the Gospel is strong in contemporary Roman Catholic apologists, too. Bartholomew Latomus says that nothing is more necessary to salvation than the unity in which Christians are joined in one 'like the body of a Gospel society (*quasi corpus societatis evangelicae*)'.[70]

Communio among Lutherans seems to have two predominant senses, one of 'gathering (*congregatio*)', as in the Augsburg Confession;[71] the other of 'making common (*communicatio*)'.[72] It is also divided by Luther into 'internal and spiritual' and 'external and bodily'. Spiritual communion lies in the faith, hope and love Christians have in God and which they direct towards God. Bodily communion consists in the participation in the sacraments which are signs of communion in faith, hope and charity, and it extends from there to include the 'social' or 'sharing' communion in practice (*usus*), converse (*colloquium*), and common life (*habitatio*).[73] For Luther, communion involves active fellowship, personal relationship of members of the body, a *societas* and *communitas*.[74] Calvin, too, is strong on 'social' aspects of communion. He stresses the importance of discipline to protect the sacraments from the possibility of their being touched by scandal, and to establish a righteousness within the local Christian society. Christians express communion by living a disciplined and industrious life.[75]

Calvin thought the discipline exercised by the visible Church important here. The Christian, while holding that only God sees the Church and knows it to be his, must be obedient to it as its face appears to him, that is, in its administration of Word and Sacrament.[76] The Christian's obedience is, for Calvin, part of the disci-

---

67 The Calvinist *Belgic Confession* of 1561 speaks in these terms, Articles 27–9, and see McNeill, *Unitive Protestantism*, p. 80.

68 Latomus, *Zwei Streitschriften gegen Martin Bucer*, p. 14.

69 D. Fischer, 'Ministères et instruments d'unité de l'Eglise dans la pensée de Luther et de Calvin', *Istina*, 30 (1985), 34–7, speaking of Luther.

70 Latomus, *Zwei Streitschriften*, p. 143.   71 *Augsburg Confession*.

72 On these two senses, see Fischer, 'Ministères', p. 12.

73 *Werke*, I.639 (1518).   74 McNeill, *Unitive Protestantism*, pp. 30–2.

75 *Ibid.*, pp. 46ff.

76 *CR* 30.754.

pline which protects the sacraments from scandal and is the bedrock of social righteousness. Luther also sees the vocation of the faithful as including the living of a disciplined and hard-working life.[77] Thus visible communion comes to have both a strong social emphasis and a requirement of visible good living in those who form part of it.[78] It is essentially a communion of those who appear to be demonstrably already wheat, although there can be no guarantee that there are no weeds in it.

The Roman Catholic concept deals in a rather different way with the paradox that in the society of the Church on earth there is less than the perfect communion of the saints. There is not only the embracing within it of the sinner who proves to be a recidivist, and to need forgiveness again and again; and who behaves like a weed much of the time. There is also a picture of the visible Church as a body hierarchically constituted and canonically defined.[79] This exists as a single reality with the mystical body of Christ, but in some relationship with it which is never itself fully definable.[80] 'The Church as society and the mystical body of Christ' are two 'aspects' of the reality of the Church which 'can never be the same in the existential and historical order ... in fact, conflicts between them arise and will continue to arise until the very end of human history'.[81] Nevertheless, the visible society exists as 'a social body, as body hierarchically constituted and canonically defined', and on that basis the Encyclical *Mystici Corporis Christi* of Pius XII of 29 June 1943 'proceeds to show that this body has Christ as Founder, Head and Redeemer constantly present to it in the power of the Spirit'.[82] Orthodox ecclesiology would accept the hierarchical picture and would stress perhaps even more strongly the mystical dimension.

We have, then, a broad contrast between the mystical and 'hierarchical' emphasis of the Orthodox and Roman Catholic systems and the 'gathered' and 'social' concepts of many of the Protestant Churches. In Pius XII's Encyclical *Mystici Corporis Christi*, three

---

[77] McNeill, *Unitive Protestantism*, pp. 46ff.

[78] Not of course as itself justifying, but as a sign or fruit of justification.

[79] Pius XIIs Encyclical *Mystici Corporis Christi* begins with this point. On the implication that there is an identity between this body and the Church of Rome, see G. Baum, 'The ecclesial reality of other Churches', *Concilium*, 4 (1965), 34–46. As Baum stresses, at the Second Vatican Council there was anxiety about asserting this identity without qualification, p. 36.

[80] See Vatican II's *Constitution on the Church, LG* 8.

[81] Cardinal Lercaro, Archbishop of Bologna, quoted in Baum, 'The ecclesial reality', p. 37.

[82] *Ibid.*, pp. 34–46.

requirements are stressed: baptism, orthodoxy of faith, and belonging to the Church's legal unity. Non-Catholics could not be members of the body if it was defined in that way. But this image of the body has its limitation. It 'can only offer the idea of member in the sense of limb', comments Ratzinger, while the notion of the 'people of God' is more flexible, with its concomitant notions of being joined in many ways, or related. So the theme of 'the people of God 'is presented in the Second Vatican Council's texts as an ecumenical bridge because it does not disqualify in the same way.[83] Nevertheless, there remains a significant amount of bridging to be done between these two conceptual frameworks before they can offer a joint solution.

The Congregation for the Doctrine of the Faith stresses that

ecclesial communion is at the same time both invisible and visible ... As an invisible reality, it is the communion of each human being with the Father through Christ in the Holy Spirit, and with the others who are fellow sharers in the divine nature. ... In the Church on earth, there is an intimate relationship between this invisible communion and the visible communion in the teaching of the apostles, in the sacraments and in the hierarchical order ... the common visible sharing in the goods of salvation (the holy things), especially in the eucharist, is the source of the invisible communion among the sharers (4.6).

Models of ecclesial communion

Despite the significant ecclesiological breakthrough of the recognition of the true ecclesiality of other churches, it is of course clear in the Vatican II and subsequent Roman Catholic documents that the consummation looked to is still union with Rome. But the basis on which this may be possible has altered from an insistence upon the swallowing up of all other Churches in such a union, to some framework of mutual respect in which sisters may come to be at one with their mother, or join together, preserving their own ecclesial being. It should be stressed that the model of unity with which Rome had been operating was not without its parallels elsewhere. Other Churches have themselves had to make (or have yet to make) the same shift from a concept of union in which their own position as

---

[83] The problem it poses is that the concept can become the 'vehicle of an anti-hierarchical and anti-sacral idea of the Church', Ratzinger, p. 15. It has thus been viewed with suspicion in some Roman Catholic quarters. While that remains the case it cannot resolve the difficulty.

the one true Church is recognised, to the notion of a union on a basis of mutual recognition between Churches. In the late nineteenth century, C.P. Krauth, writing as an American Lutheran, set out the alternatives. A continuing 'intermingling and division, ... internal separation and warfare', with 'the territory of Christendom forever ... divided between antagonistic communions, or occupied by them conjointly', is set against the vision that 'one of these specific forms [will] lift itself above the tangled mass and impose order on chaos ... [a] world-dominating type of Christianity'. That is the role he envisages for Lutheranism.[84] He sees no third possibility, no glimpse of a unity by coming together of churches which are all equals.

A further development, whose fuller implications are only just beginning to be seen, shows up new difficulties which may arise, as it were, on the other side of an achieved communion. We have to ask how far communion and autonomy or autocephaly, as at present understood, are compatible. The Anglican Communion of provinces, each autonomous in its legislative authority, has lost its previous full mutual recognition of ministry since some provinces began to ordain women to the priesthood and more recently to the episcopate, while others cannot recognise their ordination (or that of a male priest ordained by a woman bishop).[85] As a result, the Eames Commission, set up by the Archbishop of Canterbury, according to Resolution I of the 1988 Lambeth Conference, has explored a theology of incomplete and imperfect communion in an attempt to define the character of the communion which can be salvaged at present for Anglicans. There is plenty of goodwill here but no machinery, and it is proving unrealistic to hope that communion can be maintained by goodwill alone. Schism is a fact of the Anglican situation, and it has been breeding something close to hatred in the United States of America.

A number of models and images of a single communion are in play in discussion at present. Two broad divisions need to be made at the outset and these instances exemplify them clearly. On one hand stand models of uniting ecclesially distinct identities in which something of their original ecclesial identity remains separate within the union.[86] On the other stand conceptions of a union which will result

---

[84] Krauth, p. vii.   [85] See the first Resolution of the 1988 Lambeth Conference.

[86] G. Wainwright, 'La confession et les confessions: vers l'unité confessionnelle et confessante des chrétiens', *Irénikon*, 57 (1984), 5–25, p. 8.

in the forming of a single organism in which there will still be diversity but not separative ecclesial identity.[87] Here it is once more of the first importance to distinguish between the 'local churches' (congregations, dioceses, provinces) which, as 'the Church in each place' in the Orthodox, Roman Catholic and Anglican systems potentially retain their completeness as churches within the universal Church; and 'churches' conceived denominationally, which would be transformed by union and could not survive it as distinct in any sense which is separative[88] or over against other churches.

The contrast between these first and second goals of union is strikingly apparent in texts produced in ecumenical conversation. One speaks of 'full communion between our Churches'; and adds the gloss 'by full communion we here understand a relationship between two distinct Churches or communions. Each maintains its own autonomy and recognises the catholicity and apostolicity of the other, and each believes the other to hold the essentials of the Christian faith.' 'To be in full communion means that churches become interdependent while remaining autonomous.'[89] Another holds up 'the union of all Christians in the one Church'.[90] Important to such a model may be the understanding that it is not the creation but a 're-establishment' of communion which is envisaged, 'according to the common experience and tradition of the ancient Church', which 'will find its expression in the common celebration of the Eucharist'.[91] We said at the outset that there are problems with that, that we cannot simply go back to the beginning. Nevertheless 'restoration' is likely to be a theme hard to separate from the conception of one Church because that one Church must be one in inclusion of the whole Church through time, as well as in its inclusion of all churches now.

---

[87] Gerald Moede, 'Methodist participation in Church union negotiations and united Churches', *Journal of Ecumenical Studies*, 12 (1975), 367–88, p. 368, cites 'the readiness to give up separate identity' from 'Notes from the Limuru Discussion'. *Mid-Stream* (1970), 22.

[88] As distinct from separate.

[89] See ALERC, para. 62 and ALERC, Joint Working Group 25, 27.

[90] AQ (1977), *Mystery of the Church*.

[91] Common Document, 1978, of the ORC Joint Coordination Group. See Colin Davey, 'Orthodox–Roman Catholic Dialogue', *One in Christ* (1984), 350. Cf. J.M.R. Tillard, 'Eglise catholique et dialogues bilatéraux', *Irénikon*, 56 (1983), 9–10. Tillard stresses that we should be testing against the tradition of the undivided Church, which would give secure norms.

A communion of communions

Let us take next solutions which retain ecclesial identity or distinctness of the uniting communions. The notion that we should be
aiming at a 'communion of communions' raises questions similar to
those we looked at in chapter 1 in connection with the relation of
local to universal church. Is such a communion in any way (temporally, ontologically or logically) prior to or possessed of a primacy
over the pre-existing communions?[92] Is the higher communion to be
thought of as a communion of the same kind, or is it in some way
different in kind? Is the communion of communions the same thing
as the catholic or universal Church?

J.M.R. Tillard addresses this complex of difficulties with the
suggestion that communion must in fact always involve a network
of communions. God is himself the communion of the Trinity;
mankind is made to be in communion with him but cannot
ultimately participate in Trinitarian communion as the Persons
themselves do in the Godhead; Christians have communion in the
salvation won by Christ, within the fraternal bond of the baptised;
these modes of communion are themselves made possible by the
once and for all and irreversible act of communion which is the
'Christ-event'; that in its turn guarantees the communion of apostolic witness down the ages; and it is in Christ that the Eucharist, the
sacrament of communion, is celebrated.[93] On this understanding it
can be argued that the Church of God is the Church of churches,
that is, a communion of what are already full communions of life
and structure, made up of individuals. Christ brings together the
people of God who meet in the Eucharist; there they become a
single ministerial body having one of their number as a minister of
union.[94] But that does not tell us whether such communions may
themselves constitute local churches (although they may certainly
contain local churches), either of gathered congregations or of a
diocese or even of a nation; that is, whether they may continue

---

[92] Relevant here is the CDF document on Communion discussed earlier, which makes the
assertion that the universal Church is ontologically and temporally prior to the local
Church. See p. 294.

[93] See Tillard, *Eglise d'Eglises*, pp. 399–400 and pp. 323–4. See, too, Wainwright, 'La confession et les confessions', *Irénikon*, 57 (1984), 5–25 and J. Robert Wright (ed.), *A Communion of
Communions: One Eucharistic Fellowship* (New York, 1979).

[94] See Wainwright, 'La confession et les confessions', pp. 5–25.

to be of different sorts, as in the divided churches of today's Christendom.[95]

The chief difficulty with this solution is that it does not differentiate ecclesially between churches which have a universal intention, that is, which see themselves as microcosms of the universal Church, or as its parts; and those which have traditionally seen themselves as the sole 'true Church' over against other claimants. Nor does it in itself resolve the issue of the *locus* of the true Church, that is, whether the Church lies primarily or essentially in the communion of communions or in the constituent communions, or whether that is even an appropriate question to ask.[96]

The communion of equals and hierarchical communion

Contrasting emphases mark the two axes of possible union between ecclesial bodies which are to remain distinct in their identity. The new communion thus formed may be hierarchical, in which the bond ties daughter churches to a mother; or sisterly, in which sister churches unite as equals. The thrust of Vatican II's *Lumen Gentium* is hierarchical. Communion in the one Church of Christ is communion with the See of Rome, in which the Church of Christ subsists (*subsistit in*). That is not seen as incompatible with the existence of a variety of *coetus* or particular Churches, which may have their own traditions and rites, adapted to place and circumstance. A 'wonderful communion (*mirabilis communio*)' flourishes between them, where variety does not diminish unity.[97] But it remains essentially different from the conception of a sisterhood of churches which remains the most congenial to Orthodox Christians.[98] The model which sees the one Church as made up of local sister-churches has the great strength of its antiquity and the continuity of the precedent for it. Its weakness is the difficulty of making it work in places where the Churches to be reconciled do not form distinct geographical units, but share a territorial area.

---

[95] *Eglise d'Eglises*, p. 400.   [96] ARCIC prefers 'a communion of Churches'.
[97] *Orientalium Ecclesiarum*, 2.
[98] A. de Halleux, '*Fraterna Communio*', *Irénikon*, 58 (1985), 291–310, stresses that only in the Western structure is it strictly possible to have hierarchical communion.

Reconciled diversity

The concept of 'reconciled diversity' has been developed especially vigorously among Lutherans.[99] A text on 'The Ecumenical Role of the World Confessional Families in the one Ecumenical Movement' proposed the phrase in December 1974. A statement on 'Models of Unity' during the Proceedings of the Sixth Assembly of the Lutheran World Federation in 1977 spoke of 'the abiding value of the confessional forms of Christian faith in all their variety' and suggested that 'this diversity, when related to the central message of salvation and Christian faith, far from endangering' unity brings about a situation where 'this centre actually loses its divisive character and can be reconciled into a binding ecumenical fellowship in which even the confessional elements have an essential role to play'. Such diversity is seen as preserving and integrating confessional traditions 'within itself in all their distinctiveness'. It is, however, not seen as amounting to 'a detailed and final description of the goal of our striving for the unity of the Church'.[100]

Nevertheless, the notion of a communion of 'reconciled diversity' not only accepts that a fully organic union in one Church is likely to prove unattainable at least in the foreseeable future, but argues that there are reasons why it may in fact be more desirable to seek to achieve mutual acceptance among Churches which will preserve their character and special gifts in a reconciliation with one another. Harding Meyer puts this model forward as a proper middle way between organic union and a mere federation of separated Churches (to enable them to work together in service and in social and political arenas). He takes the view that this is the right way to go on the grounds that attempts at organic union in different parts of the world have frequently failed; that history shows that the Church must adapt to differences of context locally and over time; that it is becoming clear especially in the Third World that theologies must grow in response to indigenous conditions and respect the context in which they find themselves, such adaptation being not only legitimate but necessary. The essence of this view is that it is right and

---

[99] H. Meyer has been important in establishing the concept. See below.
[100] *LWF VI*, pp. 173-4.

proper that some differences will remain, but that they can cease to be divisive.[101]

Communion of ecclesial types or families

A concept of 'types' of ecclesial life, corresponding more or less to the confessional 'families' of Lutherans, Reformed, Orthodox and so on, would seem especially important here. A number of churches of Eastern Christendom are in communion with the See of Rome but retain (according to the terms drawn up in forming the union) rites and language and canon law of their own. The principle here is, however, that that which is retained as peculiar to the uniate Church is non-divisive, and falls into the category of 'rites'.[102] It has often proved to be the case that even when agreement seems to have been reached over matters of faith, and proposals for the setting up of structures of common life promise agreement too, a scheme for union fails, even at the last moment, and the reason appears to lie in a sense on either or both sides, that something of the very quality of ecclesial life will be compromised.[103] Cases in point are the Covenant scheme in England and the proposals for union between Methodists and Anglicans. This brings us back to the deep differences of style and approach we looked at in chapter 2, and the stubborn persistence of those differences which seem to reflect profound and persistent differences at the level of the very making of human beings.

A humble acceptance of existing provisionality seems the only way forward here. In any case, it would seem naive to imagine that present diversity would remain unchanged.

All parties in a truly Christian reunion would undergo tremendous changes in their comprehension of both the center and the fullness of the gospel, and in their concrete practice, organisation and psychology. There would, of course, be great diversity within the reunited Church, but the originally Roman and Orthodox parts might come to differ as much from their

---

[101] H. Meyer, 'La notion d'unité dans la diversité réconciliée', *Irénikon*, 57 (1984), 27–51. See, too Wainwright, 'La confession et les confessions'.

[102] See D. Attwater, *The Christian Churches of the East* (Milwaukee, 1937).

[103] See E. Lanne, 'Pluralisme et unité: possibilité d'une diversité de typologies dans une même adhesion ecclésiale', *Istina*, 14 (1969), 171–90, and J. Willebrands, 'Moving towards a typology of Churches', *Catholic Mind* (April 1970), 35–42.

present shape as they now differ from the Churches of the early, pre-Constantinian era, and the originally protestant segment would become as different from contemporary Protestantism as this is from the sixteenth century Reformation.[104]

If that is right, it is a hopeful reflection.

Communion cannot mean absorption or domination of one church by another; it cannot impose uniformity as a condition of unity but it will not insist upon rights which are divisive. It is not about models but about belonging to Christ. The primary communion is with him. All else follows from that.[105] 'As Christ has received you, receive you one another' (Romans 15:7). Paul's agenda is still with us. To believe it is impossible for the Church to be one is to offend against faith, hope and charity. It is to let anger and resentments stand in the way and to resist divine love.

---

[104] George A. Lindbeck, 'A Protestant View of the Ecclesiological Status of the Roman Catholic Church', *Journal of Ecumenical Studies*, 1 (1964), 243–70.
[105] J.M.R. Tillard, 'Does the Ecumenical Movement need a viable Ecclesiology?', paper given at St Louis, September 1991.

Conclusion

The stages of dividing the Church are not the same as those of mending it. Not least among the differences is the shifting of priorities which makes unity an overriding consideration, where some other leading idea had previously seemed more important, even if that meant division. At present we are in an era where there is more *rapprochement* than separation. The truth must surely be that all right priorities are reconcilable, and we ought not to seek to choose between them but to find them harmonious with apostolic faith and order. That requires a synthesis.

The achievement of communion by successive approximation is, in practice, proving to be the method both of local ecumenism; and of those engaged in international bilateral and multilateral dialogues, as they begin to turn their minds towards practical steps which can make the one visible Church a reality. This is in accord with the Lund principle of 'doing together all that we can', with the 'all' enlarging as churches grow closer. But it carries dangers.

The first is that an incomplete union may seem satisfactory; with the result that the process may halt somewhere along the way. There is a risk of diminishing the great vision of one communion in one Church, so that it is lost sight of in the immediate pleasure of growing mutual warmth, and the great hope sacrificed for the present achievement. A second danger is of a certain mechanicalness, almost of trading (for example, the implication that 'a limited doctrinal agreement can lead to a limited intercommunion').[1] A third is that it is not always easy to see where to go next after a given point has been satisfactorily reached. Local united churches such as those in the Indian subcontinent cannot go forward

---

[1] H.R. McAdoo, 'Stages in the process of growing together', *Anglican–Roman Catholic Dialogue: The work of the Preparatory Commission*, ed. A. Clark and C. Davey (London, 1974), p. 86, and E. Hamerle, 'Old Catholic–Orthodox Dialogue', *One in Christ* (1990), 158–9.

together at present by any foreseeable mechanism into a single united Church.

In an attempt to avoid at least the second of these dangers, lists of appropriate stages have been drawn up. Some of these lie on the easily accessible side of the point at which commitment begins. One list, for example, begins with prayer for one another, which becomes prayer *with* one another; inner renewal; the identification of the unity already shared; getting to know one another; each church's studying of its own past history; joint study of the history; persever- ance across the 'discouragement barrier' familiar to ecumenists.[2] The key elements in making progress beyond that point normally require the essential preliminary acceptance of doctrinal agreement and its declaration by the churches involved. Here a line along which a solution may be found to the problem of difference about what is essential suggests itself. In the discussions between the Church of England and the Church of Finland in 1933–4 it was pointed out that all that separated the two in confession was that there was 'a difference of emphasis'.[3] Each thought different things more important but both could accept the same things taken as a body. It is not quite as simple as that, but there is room for progress here.

Secondly, and here again comes a crucial stage of commitment, there must be a stage of recognising one another as possessing catholicity and apostolicity, mutual recognition and reconciliation of ministries and the celebration of the Eucharist together. These are inseparable. We have seen that without the first the second is impossible. Equally the third cannot be reached without the second, although there may be eucharistic hospitality to members of one church by the other, or even some form of joint celebration, with an ordained minister of each participating church consecrating bread and wine.

Thirdly, the common life of the uniting churches must be expressed both in pastoral sharing and in common mission. Here several practical questions arise in any stage short of full union. Bishops, priests, deacons or other ministers of one Church may exercise liturgical functions and pastoral care in the other if invited to do so, but the authority to invite and the limits of what may be done by the invited minister will depend upon the rules of the

[2] R. McAfee Brown, 'Nine steps to unity', in J.A. O'Brien, *Steps to Christian Unity* (London, 1965), pp. 57–71.
[3] *Lambeth Occasional Papers, 1931–8* (London, 1948).

inviting Church, and will not necessarily be fully reciprocal. We have been considering the evidence that these barriers to interchangeability of ministry can ultimately be fully overcome only by creating a single ministry in one Church.[4]

The fourth stage on the way to communion requires the setting up of some means of making decisions together, so as to prevent the united Church dividing again in future. Such organs of consultation and communication will, if they operate at times of crisis, help in emergencies; if they become a regular thing, they can express the growing fellowship and make common witness, life and service possible. They will prevent unilateral decisions being taken on matters of doctrine or order or morality without prior consultation and agreement; they will discourage one church from embarking on a course of action which hurts or embarrasses another. The essence of such structures must be the equality of those who participate in the consultation.[5] No body becomes the judge of the others. The counsel is brotherly. The crucial difference between the conciliarity of the ancient churches and the structures which might be set up on the way to unity today, is that in the system of the early and mediaeval centuries, and in Orthodox, Roman Catholic and Anglican churches today, there has been a common understanding of the role of episcopal ministry in conciliar fellowship. The non-episcopal churches could not, *ipso facto*, meet in their bishops, and each would thus send representatives whose relation to their churches and whose authority to speak for them would vary.

There are no easy answers to all this, and certainly none to be found quickly. I have been suggesting throughout this book that a key to the ultimate solution of these besetting problems of the divided Church may lie in the acceptance that some of what we have ecclesially, and cling to most passionately in our separation, is provisional. Churches and existing communions[6] have sometimes been able to see themselves in that light. I have chiefly been concerned to set out the issues and their interrelationship, because in many areas that is as far as we can go as yet; and because I hope that the endeavour to do so will itself prove a step on the way to discovering solutions.

But there is a negative as well as a positive side to this argument. It is potentially dangerous to suggest that elements in the churches'

---

[4] See Chapter 4.   [5] A. Joos, *Irénikon*, 44 (1971), 23–8.
[6] Notably perhaps the Anglican.

life ought to be open to alteration if we are not yet able to agree together which these may be. It is also dangerous to suggest it where there is no real recognition of equality and mutuality, for there are historically well-founded fears of attempts by powerful ecclesial interests to get the others to do all the changing. So the presumption must be that things are mainly as they should be. The Holy Spirit has always preserved the Church in the churches. It follows that changes needed to unite the Church cannot be of a sort which requires real loss of its essential and unique ecclesial being for any community. It would seem to follow, too, that every church which sees for itself (even if after a period of painful realisation) that it may need to change, will be able in time to make any alteration freely and gladly, under what it comes to understand is the guidance of the Holy Spirit.

Above all, the test of all changes ecumenically speaking must be that they are in the direction of convergence. If the recognition of provisionality means the acceptance of a capacity for change, ecumenical change must always be with a view to coming together in faith and life. That is not inimical to the preservation of diversity, where diversity means richness and variety. It is inimical to a diversity conceived and sustained as a function of division. It has to be possible for each of us to say, in his or her own church,

My denomination must grow less in my eyes if I am to grow more towards Christ. I am willing that my denomination shall be forgotten if thereby may be hastened the unity of the Church of our Lord. That denomination is most prophetic that is willing to disappear for Christ's sake – to go to its disappearance as deliberately as Christ went to his crucifixion.[7]

---

[7] Peter Ainslie (Disciples of Christ), *Faith and Order, Proceedings of the World Conference, Lausanne, August 3–21, 1927* (London, 1927), p. 343.

Select bibliography

Agreed Statement on Conciliarity and Primacy in the Church, Orthodox–Roman Catholic Consultation in the United States, *Greek Orthodox Theological Review*, 35 (1990), 217–20

Alberigo, G., ed. *Christian Unity: The Council of Ferrara-Florence, 1438/1–1989*, Alberigo (Louvain, 1991)

Allmen, J.J. Von, 'The continuity of the Church according to Reformed teaching', *Journal of Ecumenical Studies*, 1 (1964), 424–44

Asheim, I. and V.R. Gold, *Episcopacy in the Lutheran Church* (Philadelphia, 1970)

Baillie, D. and J. Marsh, eds., *Intercommunion: The Report of the Theological Commission appointed by the Continuation Committee of the World Conference on Faith and Order together with a Selection from the Material Presented to the Commission* (London, 1952), p. 19

Bandera, A., 'Yglesia particular y Iglesia universal', *Ciencia Tomista*, 105 (1978), 80–7

Batiffol, P., *Le Catholicisme de s. Augustin* (2nd edn, Paris, 1920), 2 vols.

Baum, G., 'The constitution of the Church', *Journal of Ecumenical Studies*, 2 (1965), 1–30

Bea, A. and Visser't Hooft, W.A., *Peace among Christians*, tr. J. Moses (New York, 1967)

Beardslee, J.W., *Reformed Dogmatics* (New York, 1965)

Beinert, W., 'Dogmenhistorische Anmerkungen zum Begriff "Partikularkirche"', *Theologie und Philosophie*, 50 (1975)

Bell, G.K.A., *Documents on Christian Unity*, vol. I (London, 1924)

Benz, E., *The Eastern Orthodox Church. Its Thought and Life* (New York, 1963), p. 84, first published as *Geist und Leben der Ostkirche* (Hamburg, 1957)

Bertrams, W., 'L'"ufficio dell'unità della" Chiesa e la moltitudine delle Chiese', *Vita e pensiero*, 54 (1971)

Boff, L., *Ecclesiogenesis: The Base Communities Reinvent the Church* (Maryknoll, 1986)

Bouyer, L., *L'Eglise de Dieu* (Paris, 1970)

Bowmer, J.C., *Pastor And People: A Study of Church and Ministry in Wesleyan Methodism from the Death of John Wesley 1791 to the Death of Jabez Bunting, 1858* (London, 1975)

Bradburn, Samuel, *The Question, 'Are the Methodists Dissenters?' Fairly Examined* (1792)

Braithwaite, W.C., *The Beginnings of Quakerism* (London, 1912)

Brent, Allen, 'Ecumenical reconciliation and cultural episcopates', *Anglican Theological Review*, 72 (1990), 255–79

Canellopoulos, G., 'Christian Reunion from the point of view of the Eastern Orthodox Church', *Church Quarterly Review*, 96 (1923), 247–305

Chadwick, H., *The Circle and the Ellipse* (Oxford, 1959)

'Full Communion with other Episcopal Churches', *The Churchman*, 3 (1981), 218–18

Church as Communion, an Agreed Statement by the Second Anglican–Roman Catholic International Commission (London, 1991)

Church as Communion, The, Letter to the Bishops of the Catholic Church from the Congregation for the Doctrine of the Faith, *Catholic International*, 3 (1992), 761–5

Cochrane, A.C., *Reformed Confessions of the Sixteenth Century* (London, 1966)

Codex Iuris Canonici (Rome, 1983)

Colombo, G., 'La teologia della Chiesa locale', in *La Chiesa Locale* (Bologna, 1969), 17–38

'La teologia della chiesa locale', *Vita e pensiero*, 54 (1971), 261–5

Conciliorum Oecumenicorum Decreta, ed. J. Alberigo (Bologna, 1973)

Congar, Y., 'Quod omnes tangit ab omnibus tractari et approbari debet', *Revue historique de droit français et étranger*, 36 (1958), 210–59

Tradition et traditions (London, 1966)

L'Eglise, de Saint Augustine à l'époque moderne (Paris, 1970)

'Propos en vue d'une théologie de l'Economie dans la tradition latine', *Irénikon*, 45 (1972)

Diversités et communion (Paris, 1982)

Essais oecuméniques: le mouvement, les hommes, les problèmes (Paris, 1984)

'La "reception" comme réalité ecclésiologique', *Revue des sciences philosophiques et théologiques*, 56 (Paris, 1972), 369–403

Corridan, James, 'Authority and freedom in the coming ecumenical church', *Journal of Ecumenical Studies*, 12 (1975), 315–47

Crowther, Jonathan, *The Methodist Manual* (Halifax, 1810)

Davey, Colin, 'Orthodox–Roman Catholic Dialogue', *One in Christ* (1984), p. 350

Pioneer for Unity: Metrophanes Kritopoulos and Relations between the Orthodox, Roman Catholic and Reformed Churches (London, 1987)

Davidson, R.T., ed., *The Five Lambeth Conferences* (London, 1920)

Dianach, S., *La Chiesa misterio di communione* (Turin, 1977)

Draper, J., ed., *Communion and Episcopacy* (Cuddesdon, 1988), p. 42

Duane Beals, J., 'John Wesley's concept of the Church', *Wesleyan Theological Journal*, 9 (1974), 28–35

Dulles, A., *The Catholicity of the Church* (Oxford, 1985)

Duquoc, C., *Provisional Churches: An Essay in Ecumenical Ecclesiology*, tr. J. Bowden (London, 1986)

Dvornik, F., *Byzantium and the Roman Primacy* (New York, 1966)

Ehrenstrom, N. and W.G. Muelder, *Institutionalism and Church Unity* (London, 1963)

Empie, P.C. and T. Austin Murphy, eds., *Papal Primacy and the Universal Church*, (Minneapolis, 1974), p. 123

Episcopal Ministry: The Report of the Archbishops' Group on the Episcopate (Church of England) (London, 1990)

Evans, G.R., 'Unity and diversity: Anselm of Havelberg as ecumenist', *Analecta Praemonstratensia*, 67 (1991), 42–52

Problems of Authority in the Reformation Debates (Cambridge, 1992)

Fahey, Michael A., 'Ecclesiae sorores ac fratres: sibling communion in the pre-Nicene Christian era', *Catholic Theological Society of America, Proceedings*, 36 (1981), 15–38

Fairchild, H.P., *The Melting Pot Mistake* (Boston, 1926)

Faith and Order, Proceedings of the World Conference, Lausanne, August 3–21, 1927 (London, 1927), p. 343

Faris, J.D., *The Communion of Catholic Churches: Terminology and Ecclesiology* (New York, 1985)

Ferguson, E., 'Attitudes to schism at the Council of Nicaea', *Studies in Church History*, 9 (1972), 57–63

Field, Richard, *Of the Church* (Cambridge, 1847–52), 5 vols.

The Final Report of the First Anglican–Roman Catholic International Commission (London, 1982)

Fischer, D., 'Ministères et instruments d'unité de l'Eglise dans la pensée de Luther et de Calvin', *Istina*, 30 (1985), 24–7

Florovsky, G., 'The limits of the Church', *Church Quarterly Review*, 117 (1933–4), 117–31

Forte, B., *La chiesa icona della Trinità: Breve ecclesiologia* (Brescia, 1984)

Fox, George, *Journal (1647)*, ed. J.L. Nickalls (Cambridge, 1952)

Friedberg, E., *Corpus Iuris Canonici* (Leipzig, 1879–81), 2 vols.

Fries, H., 'The ecclesiological status of the Protestant Churches from a Catholic viewpoint', *Journal of Ecumenical Studies*, 1 (1964)

Gerson, Jean, Tractate on the *Unity of the Church*, 1409, ed. E. du Pin, *Gersoni Opera Omnia* (Antwerp, 1706), II 113–18

Gill, J., 'The Church Union of the Council of Lyons (1274) portrayed in the Greek Documents', *Orientalia Christiana Periodica*, 11 (Rome, 1974)

Greenacre, R., 'Two aspects of reception', in *Christian Authority: Essays in Honour of Henry Chadwick*, ed. G.R. Evans (Oxford, 1988), pp. 40–58

Gui, Bernard, *Manuel de l'Inquisiteur*, ed. C. Douais, *Practica Inquisitionis heretice pravitatis* (Paris, 1886), and abridged G. Mollat (Paris, 1926)

Hall, Joseph, *Works*, ed. P. Wynter (Oxford, 1963), 10 vols.

Halleux, A. de, '*Fraterna Communio*', *Irénikon*, 58 (1985), 291–310

Hamerle, E., 'Old Catholic–Orthodox Dialogue', *One in Christ* (1990), 158–9

Harekes, P. Stanley, 'The Local Church; an Eastern Orthodox perspective', *Ecumenical Review*, 29 (1977)

Harrington, T.J., 'The local church at Rome in the second century: a common cemetery emerges amid developments in this "laboratory of Christian policy"', *Studia Canonica*, 23 (1989), 167–88

Harrison, P.M., *Authority and Power in the Free Church Tradition: A Social Case Study of the American Baptist Tradition* (Princeton, 1959)

Hay, C., 'The ecclesiological significance of the Decree on Ecumenism', *Journal of Ecumenical Studies*, 3 (1966), 343–53

Henn, W., *The Hierarchy of Truths according to Y. Congar* (Rome, 1987)

Hill, Christopher, 'The fundamental question of ecumenical method', *Catholic International*, 3.3 (February, 1992), 134–40

Hudson, A., *The Premature Reformation* (Oxford, 1988)

Hughes, J.J., *Absolutely Null and Utterly Void: An Account of the 1896 Papal Condemnation of Anglican Orders* (Washington, 1968)

Hutnik, N., *Ethnic Minority Identity* (Oxford, 1991)

In Christ – A New Community, Lutheran World Federation, VI (Dar-es-Salaam, 1977)

Istavridis, V.T., *Orthodoxy and Anglicanism*, tr. C. Davey (London, 1966)

Johansen, A., 'The writings of theologians of the Moscow Patriarchate on ecumenical themes', *Journal of Ecumenical Studies*, 12 (1975)

Jones, A.H.M., 'Were ancient heresies national or social movements in disguise?' *Journal of Theological Studies*, 10 (1959), 280–98

Kerr, D.A., ed., *Religion, State and Ethnic Groups*, (New York, 1992)

Knox, R., *Enthusiasm* (Oxford, 1950)

Kotsonis, I., *The Validity of Anglican Orders* (Massachussetts, 1958)

Kotsonis, J., *Problémes de l'Economie ecclésiastique* (Gembloux, 1971)

Krauth, C.P., *The Conservative Reformation and its Theology* (Minneapolis, 1871, reprinted Philadelphia, 1963)

Kress, Robert, 'The Church as *Communio*: Trinity and Incarnation as the foundation of ecclesiology', *The Jurist*, 36 (1976)

Küng, H., *Theology for the Third Millennium*, (NewYork/London 1988)

Lambeth Occasional Papers, 1931–8 (London, 1948)

Lanne, E., 'Eglises locales et Patriarcats', *Irénikon*, 34 (1961)

'Les différences compatibles avec l'Unité dans la tradition de l'Eglise ancienne jusqu'au xiie siècle', *Istina*, 8 (1961–2), 227–53

'Pluralisme et unité: possibilité d'une diversité de typologies dans une même adhésion ecclésiale', *Istina*, 14 (1969), 171–90

'L'Eglise locale: sa catholicité et son apostolicité', *Istina*, 14 (1969), 46–66

'L'Eglise locale et l'Eglise universelle: Actualité et portée du thème', *Irénikon*, 43 (1970), 497–506

'Jusqu'à quel point une primauté romaine est-elle inacceptable pour les églises orientales?', *Concilium*, 64 (1973)

'Eglises unies ou Eglises soeurs: un choix inéluctable', *Irénikon*, 48 (1975)

Leff, G., *Heresy in the Later Middle Ages* (Manchester, 1967), 2 vols.

Legrand, H., 'Nature de l'Eglise particulière', *Unam Sanctam*, 71 (Paris, 1969), 113–15

Lindbeck, G.A., 'A Protestant view of the ecclesiological status of the Roman Catholic Church', *Journal of Ecumenical Studies*, 1 (1964), 243–79

Loy, M., 'The Lutheran doctrine of ordination', *Evangelical Quarterly Review*, 16 (1865), 303–28

Lubac, H. de, *Les Eglises particulières dans l'Eglise universelle* (Paris, 1971)

McAdoo, H.R., '*Stages in the process of growing together*', *Anglican–Roman Catholic Dialogue: The work of the Preparatory Commission*, ed. A. Clark and C. Davey (London, 1974)

McDonnell, Kilian, 'Vatican II (1962–4), Pueblo (1979), Synod (1985): Koinonia/Communio as an integral ecclesiology', *Journal of Ecumenical Studies*, 25 (1988), 399–427

McKendrick, K., *The Promise Fulfilled: A History of the Modern Pentecostal Movement* (Springfield, Missouri, 1961)

McNeill, J.T., *Unitive Protestantism* (London, 1964)

McNutt, William R., *Polity and Practice in the Baptist Churches* (Philadelphia, 1935)

Mansi J., *Sacrorum Conciliorum Nova et Amplissima Collectio* (Florence, 1759–Leipzig, 1902), 34 vols.

Marot, H., 'Note sur la Pentarchie', *Irénikon*, 32 (1959), 436–42

Martin, D., *Tongues of Fire: The Explosion of Protestantism in Latin America* (Oxford, 1990)

Meyendorff, J., *Orthodoxie et catholicité* (Paris, 1965)
  'Eglises-soeures. Implications ecclésiologiques du *Tomos Agapis*,' *Istina*, 20 (1975), 35–46

Meyer, H., 'La notion d'unité dans la diversité reconciliée', *Irénikon*, 57 (1984), 27–51
  'Les présupposés de la réception ecclésiale ou le problème de la "recevabilité"', *Irénikon*, 59 (1986), 5–19

Moede, Gerald, 'Methodist participation in Church Union negotiations and United Churches', *Journal of Ecumenical Studies*, 12 (1975), 367–88

Montgomery, J.W., *Ecumenicity, Evangelicals and Rome* (Michigan, 1969)

Neill, Stephen, *God's Apprentice*, ed. E.M. Jackson (London, 1991)

The Niagara Report, Report of the Anglican–Lutheran Consultation on Episcope, 1987 (London, 1988)

The Niagara Report of the Anglican–Lutheran International Commission (London, 1989)

Nichol, J.T., *Pentecostalism* (New York, 1966)

O'Brien, J.A., *Steps to Christian Unity* (London, 1965)

d'Ors, A., 'Iglesia universel et iglesia particular', *Ius Canonicum*, 28 (1988), 295–303

Packer, J.I., ed., *All in Each Place* (Abingdon, 1981)

Papers of Conference on the Local and Universal Church held at Salamanca, 1991

Peri, V., *Chiesa Romana e "rito" Greco: G.A. Santoro e la Congregazione dei Greci (1566–1596)* (Brescia, 1975)

Piepkorn, A.C., *Profiles in Belief: The Religious Bodies of the United States and Canada* (New York, 1977–9), 3 vols.

Rahner, K., 'On bishops' conferences', in *Theological Investigations*, tr. C. Ernst (Baltimore, 1961 ff.), vol.VI 377–9

Rahner, K. and H. Fries, *Unity of the Church: An Actual Possibility* (Philadelphia, 1985)

Rahner, K. and J. Ratzinger, *The Episcopate and the Primacy* (New York, 1962)

Ratzinger, J., 'The ministerial office and the unity of the Church', *Journal of Ecumenical Studies*, 1 (1964), 42–57
  Church, Ecumenism and Politics (Slough, 1988), tr. R. Nowell, first published as *Kirche, Ökumene und Politik* (Cinisello Balsamo, 1987)

Read, W.R., V.M. Monterroso, and H.A. Johnson, *Latin American Church Growth* (Grand Rapids, Michigan, 1969)

Official *Response* of the Roman Catholic Church to *The Final Report* of the First Anglican–Roman Catholic International Commission, printed in *The Tablet* (December, 1991)

Roburg, B., 'Einige Quellenstücke zur Geschichte des II Konzils von Lyon', *Annuarium Historiae Conciliorum*, 21 (1989), 108–9

Saltet, L., *Les Réordinations* (Paris, 1907)

Sartory, T., 'Reunion of Christians despite Catholic dogmas', *Journal of Ecumenical Studies*, 1 (1964), 82–98

Savoy Declaration of Faith and Order, The, ed. A.G. Matthews, (London, 1959)

Schillebeeckx, E., *Church: The Human Story of God* (London, 1989)

Schmüte, H., *The Role of the Augsburg Confession* (Philadelphia, 1977)

Smyth, N. and W. Walker, *Approaches towards Church Unity* (New Haven, 1919)

Spinka, M., *John Hus at the Council of Constance* (New York/London, 1965)

Stormon, E.J., ed. and tr., *Towards the Healing of Schism*, (New York, 1987)

Sundkler, B., *The Church of South India: The Movement towards Union, 1900–47* (London, 1954)

Sykes, S. and J. Booty, eds., *The Study of Anglicanism*, (London, 1988)

Tappert, T.C., *Lutheran Confessional Theology in America* (New York, 1972)

Tavard, G., 'The recognition of ministry', *Journal of Ecumenical Studies*, 11 (1974), 65–83

Thompson, J., 'Economy', *Journal of Theological Studies*, 16 (1965), 368–420

Tierney, B., *Foundations of the Conciliar Theory* (Cambridge, 1955)

Tillard, J.M.R., 'Anglican–Roman Catholic dialogue', *One in Christ*, 8 (1972), 242–63
  'L'Eglise de Dieu est une communion', *Irénikon*, 53 (1980), 451–68

'Eglise catholique romaine et Eglises unies', *Irénikon*, 55 (1982), 19–23
L'Evêque de Rome (Paris, 1982), *The Bishop of Rome*, tr. J.Satgé (London, 1983)
'Eglise catholique et dialogues bilatéraux', *Irénikon*, 56 (1983), 9–10
'L'Universel et le Local: Réflexion sur Eglise universelle et Eglises locales', *Irénikon*, 60 (1987), 483–532
Eglise d'Eglises: l'ecclésiologie de communion (Paris, 1987)
Vandervelde, G., 'BEM and the hierarchy of truths: a Vatican contribution to the reception process', *Journal of Ecumenical Studies*, 25 (1988), 74–84
Van Dusen, H.P., *One Great Ground of Hope: Christian Missions and Christian Unity* (London, 1961)
Valentini, D., *Il nuovo Popoli di Dio in cammino: Punti nodali per una ecclesiologia attuale* (Rome, 1984), p. 56
Vatican Council II: The Conciliar and Post Consiliar Documents, ed. A. Flannery (Rome, 1988)
Verkamp, B.J., *The Indifferent Mean* (Ohio, 1977)
Vogel, C., 'Unité et pluralité des formes historiques d'organisation ecclésiastique du IIIe au Ve siècle', in *L'Episcopat et l'Eglise universelle*, ed. Y. Congar and B.P. Dupuy (Paris, 1962), 591–636
Voronov, L., 'Unité et diversité dans la tradition orthodoxe', *Istina*, 1 (1972), 21–6
Wainwright, G., 'La confession et les confessions', *Irénikon*, 57 (1984), 5–25
Ware, K., 'Catholicity and nationalism: a recent debate at Athens', *Eastern Churches Review*, 10 (1978), 10–16
Warwick, J.P., 'Organisational politics and ecumenism', *Journal of Ecumenical Studies* 11 (1974), 293–308
Welch, C., *The Reality of the Church* (New York, 1958)
Wesley, John, *Journal*, in *Works*, ed. F. Baker (Oxford, 1975), vols. I–
Wright, J. Robert, ed., *A Communion of Communions: One Eucharistic Fellowship* (New York, 1979)
Yarnold, Edward, *In Search of Unity* (Slough, 1989)
Zizioulas, J.D., 'Verité et communion dans la perspective de la pensée patristique grecque', *Irénikon*, 50 (1977), 451–10
Being as Communion (St Vladimir's Press, 1985)

Index

Adiaphora 190–2, 212
Africa 32f., 47, 75, 281
Alexandria 61, 81, 96, 98
Ambrose of Milan 204
Anabaptists 39, 64
analogy 114
Anglicanism 16, 26, 32, 46, 49, 51, 53, 58,
    59, 78, 81, 86, 98–102, 104, 150, 151–3,
    165, 200, 213, 221–2, 228, 237–8, 241,
    243, 244, 246, 253, 269, 295, 297, 308
Anselm of Canterbury 212, 295–6
Anselm of Havelberg 206ff
Antioch 61, 69, 81, 131, 214, 256, 266
Antichrist 131ff
anticlericalism 138
Apostles 22, 222, 268
apostolic succession 212–50
apostolicity 19, 133–5
Aquinas, Thomas 96, 193
articles 150, 193–4
Augsburg Confession 55, 133, 150, 158, 178,
    210, 257
Augustine of Canterbury 57, 88, 199, 205
Augustine of Hippo 5, 30–42, 44, 74, 92,
    128, 158, 192, 204, 215, 296, 303
authority 198 and *passim*
autocephaly 163–4, 174
autonomy 163–6, 283–5

baptism 29, 30, 31, 55, 70, 110, 215, 298
Baptists 77, 127, 139–40, 141, 167, 213, 228,
    231, 232
Basle, Council of (1431) 260, 286
Bede 43, 60, 258, 263, 264
Bible 3, 25, 42, 167, 170, 175, 211, 253, 258,
    294 and *passim*
bilateral conversations, agreements,
    statements 1, 16, 233, 244, 254
bindingness 268–73
bishops 78–106, 238
Boethius 193
Bucer, Martin 137, 279

Bullinger, Heinrich 38, 134
Byzantium 69, 74

Calvin, Calvinism 39, 147, 304–5
Canada 167
canon law 54, 219–225, 273–6, and see
    legislation
Canterbury 55, 61, 80, 100, 101, 216, 264–5
catholicity 19, 25, 42–6
Chalcedon, Council of (451) 266–7
charism 46, 137–9
Christ 4, 6, 20–1, 29, 43, 50, 102, 109, 148,
    149, 169, 194, 215, 228, 293, 297, 314
Church-dividing 177–9
Colenso, John 283
communion 107, 291–314
conciliarity 78ff, 273–285
conditional reordination 248
confessional
    identity 58, 125
    traditions 20, 55
Congar, Y. 196
Congregationalism 210, 288
consensus fidelium 180
Constantinople 61, 69, 95, 191, 201, 262
Constantinople, Council of (381) 92, 262,
    263, 264
continuity 24, 50
corruption 39
creeds 25, 183
culture, cultural identity 4, 27, 74–7, 116,
    171
Cyprian 39, 108, 217
Cyril of Alexandria 263

decision-making 251–89
development of doctrine 125, 179–83
diaspora 70–4
Disciples of Christ 167
dispensation 219–225
dissidents 127
diversity 47, 174–211, 312–3

326

Donatists 23, 30, 33ff., 127, 145, 303
Duquoc, C. 11, 12

each and all 199–120, 262
ecclesial communion ix
ecclesial entities ix, 41, 176
ecclesiogenesis 122
ecclesiology 3–12, and passim
economy 219–225
Ecumenical Councils 43, 175, 191, 223, 300
Ecumenical Councils of Churches 2, 286–90
elements of Church 20ff., 46
emergency 30, 36, 227
episcopacy 76–106, 212–249
episcope 212–249
error 131–2, 221, 270
eschatology 17
eschaton 5
essentials 184–99
ethnicity 58, 62
Eucharist 14, 21, 48, 50, 133, 183, 209, 211,
    218–9, 279, 298
Eugenius III, Pope 206
Eugenius IV , Pope 88, 276
Eusebius 162
Evangelicals 144, 170
extra ecclesiam 29

faith and order 174–211
Faith and Order Conference
    Lausanne 1927 2
Fathers 126, 264
faultiness 39
felix culpa 3
Field, Richard 26, 38, 261
filioque 155, 225
Florence, Council of (1438-45) 2, 57, 71, 87,
    97, 114, 201, 267, 276, 277, 302
Fox, George 147ff.
Franciscans 64, 136
freedom 137–46
fundamentals 29
future United Church 2, 3

gathered churches 48–51, 54
Gerbert off Aurillac 161, 203
Gerson, Jean 132, 133
gifts 172
Gnostics 128
Gospel 14, 47, 167, 209
grace 1
Greeks 37, 126, 156, 201, 206ff, 216, 267,
    276
Gregory the Great 25, 60, 94, 199, 205
Grotius 179, 189, 192, 198
Gui, Bernard 128, 135

Hall, Joseph 39, 88, 89, 123, 124, 143, 189,
    193, 196, 290
Hammond, Henry 282–3
heresy 127, 215, 223
hierarchy of truths 184–5, 192–9
history 4
holiness 19, 143, 145
Holy Spirit 13, 29, 30, 43, 122, 126, 137–9,
    155, 158, 173, 175–6, 214, 231, 257,
    263, 279, 293
human and divine 28–9
Hussites 172

identity ix, 120–173
Ignatius of Antioch 44
image 114
indefectibility 19
Innocent III, Pope 87, 252, 259
intention 24
interdependence 25
invisibility 19, 20
Irenaeus 91, 190

Jerome 92
Jerusalem 61, 69, 112, 263
Jewel, John 98
Joachim of Fiore 136
jurisdiction 101, 103ff., 224
justification by faith 155

Kingdom 17, 21
koinoina, see communion
Küng, Hans, 127

Lambeth Conferences 100ff., 162, 175, 182,
    186, 240, 244, 269, 280–5
Lambeth Quadrilateral 26, 27
language 15, 185, 208
Lateran Council, Fourth (1215) 264, 267
Laud, William 280ff.
legislation 219–225, 252, 271–3, 273–6 and
    see canon law
legitimate diversity 176
limits 103, 219, 225–6
local church 19–119
Lollard 172
Luther 227, 233, 278
Lutheran World Federation 58, 89
Lutherans 58, 62, 77, 86, 102, 131, 141,
    146, 157–60, 166, 169, 210, 231, 232,
    236, 238, 239, 242, 244, 304, 305, 308,
    313
Lyons, Council of (1274) 156, 267

magisterium 271
Manichees 128, 129

Melanchthon 279
Methodism 18, 19, 65, 77, 86, 141, 144, 145, 168, 228, 230, 232, 238, 239
microcosm 114
ministry 214–50
miracle 22
mission 63–70, 75
mixed polity 227–244
Moltmann, J. 6
Moscow 61, 68, 72
mother church 74, 83, 87–91, 212
multilateral conversations, agreements, statements 233, 254
mutual recognition 234–41
mutuality 115, 116, 117
mystical Church 54

Newman, John Henry 125
neoplatonism 126
new churches 121–30
Nicaea, Council of (325) 59, 204

Old Catholics 16
order 22, 137–9, 212–50
ordination 238
Orthodox 2, 13, 40, 43, 46, 49, 51, 52, 55, 69, 70, 72, 80, 86, 88, 91, 95–8, 102, 105, 113, 126, 143, 153–61, 162–6, 171, 174, 178, 182, 201, 213, 221, 224, 237, 238, 246–7, 273, 276, 278, 285, 297, 299, 313

Papacy 24, 47, 57, 132, 268, 273, 277, 279 and see primacy
partialness 28–42, 280–3
particular church 116
parts of the Church 114–5
Patriarchs, patriarchates 61, 91ff.
Paul, St. 18, 29, 33, 91, 256
Pentarchy 93
Pentecostalists 140–2
perfection 142–3
Peter, St. 91–106, 214
pilgrimage 73
place, Church in each 124
Plato Platonism 5
pluriformity 179
plurality 175
politics 76
poverty 135–7
presbyters 49
Presbyterians 141, 210, 228, 230, 231, 238
prepositions 117
priesthood 242ff.
primacy 91–106, 224–5
priority 106–20

proselytism 70
Protestantism 169
providence 7
provinces 78–86, 226
provisionality x, 11, 12, 73, 133, 145, 213, 221, 224, 225 and passim
purity 23, 32

Quakers 141, 147

Rahner, K. 6
Rastafarians 145
Ratzinger, J. 33
reception 252
reconciled diversity 228, 312–3
Reformation 7, 39, 44, 59, 85, 121, 129, 172, 181, 203, 227, 290
Reformed, the 166, 213, 235, 236, 238, 313
reformers of the sixteenth century 1, 25, 157ff.
religious orders 24, 133
representation 119, 259–61
rites 199–212
Roman Catholicism 12, 18, 40, 44, 45, 46, 49, 51, 53, 65, 69, 82, 86, 95, 105, 131, 153–66, 169, 171, 177, 178, 181, 193, 198, 213, 221, 222, 224, 228, 237, 238, 275, 286, 306
Rome 81, 87–106
Russia 67

sacraments 28, 29, 30, 31, 49, 214–60, 298–302
Satan 131, 281
Schillebeeckx, E. 6, 7
schism 30, 35, 132
sects 128ff.
sisterhood of churches 87–91, 311
society 76–7
soteriology 43
style 176
substantial agreement 184–90
syncretism 75

territory 51–5
Tertullian 91, 134, 143
testimonial letters 52
Third World 4, 23, 49
Thirty-Nine Articles (Church of England) 150, 270
Thorndike, Herbert 282
Tillard, J.M.R. 310
Tomas Agapis 160
triadic structure 77–91
Trinity 217, 293

United Churches (Indian subcontinent)
210, 229ff., 239
universal intention 161–6
universality, see catholicity
Urban II, Pope 227

Vatican Council, First 268
Vatican Council, Second 1, 7, 40, 49, 83,
90, 106, 153, 177, 245, 271, 274–5, 291,
295, 311
Villanova, Arnold of 135
Vincent of Lérins 42, 253, 278
visible unity 20
votum unitatis 14, 115

Waldensians 128, 129
Wesley, John 67, 147
William of Tyre 37
witness xi
Wittenberg 33
Word and Sacrament, ministry of 25–6
World Council of Churches 6, 18, 234, 269,
287, 301
Wyclif 131, 172

Zwingli 39